THE NEW BOOK OF KNOWLEDGE

THE
NEW BOOK
OF
KNOWLEDGE

Scholastic Library Publishing, Inc.
Danbury, Connecticut

VOLUME 14

O

ISBN 0-7172-0540-1 (set)

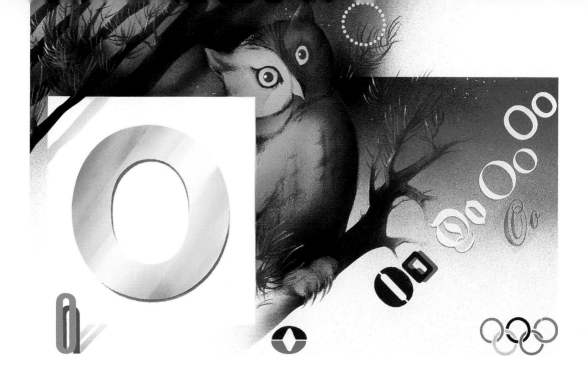

O, the 15th letter in the English alphabet, was the 16th letter in the ancient Hebrew and Phoenician alphabets and the 15th letter in the classical Greek alphabet. The Hebrews and Phoenicians called it *ayin* (pronounced ahyin). The Greek O is called *omicron*.

Some language scholars believe that the Phoenician symbol *ayin* represented an eye and that the word meant "eye." The letter *ayin* looked like this: ◯

The Greeks based their alphabet on that of the Phoenicians. They named the letter *omicron,* or "little O." In Greek, as in many other languages, the letter O had many variations of sound. At first *omicron* was used for all the O sounds. Later, the letter *omega,* or "great O," was added to the Greek alphabet. *Omega* was used mainly for the long O sound, as in *ode.*

The form of the Greek alphabet learned by the Romans did not include the letter *omega.* The Romans, therefore, used just one O for all the sounds of the letter. It was this O with its many variations that England and the nations of western Europe inherited when the Romans conquered them.

In English the letter O, like all the vowels, is pronounced in many different ways. The words *note, not, book, boot,* and *bought* contain the main sounds of the letter. When there are no silent letters in the word, a single O usually refers to the sound in the word *not.* A double O always indicates either the sound in *book* or the sound in *boot.* A silent A, as in *toad,* or a silent E at the end of a word, as in *rode,* gives what is called the long O sound.

In chemistry, O stands for the element oxygen, and in physics it stands for ohm, a measure of electrical resistance. In modern numbers, O stands for zero. Frequently the letter O is used as an abbreviation for old, as in O.T. for the Old Testament of the Bible. O can also stand for organization, as in OAS for Organization of American States. On maps O usually stands for ocean.

Reviewed by MARIO PEI
Author, *The Story of Language*

See also ALPHABET.

SOME WAYS TO REPRESENT O:

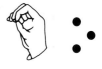

The **manuscript** or printed forms of the letter (left) are highly readable. The **cursive** letters (right) are formed from slanted flowing strokes joining one letter to the next.

The **Manual Alphabet** (left) enables a deaf person to communicate by forming letters with the fingers of one hand. **Braille** (right) is a system by which a blind person can use fingertips to "read" raised dots that stand for letters.

The **International Code of Signals** is a special group of flags used to send and receive messages at sea. Each letter is represented by a different flag.

International Morse Code is used to send messages by radio signals. Each letter is expressed as a combination of dots (.) and dashes (––).

OAKLEY, ANNIE (1860–1926)

Expert sharpshooter Phoebe Anne Oakley Mozee was born in Darke County, Ohio, on August 13, 1860. Her remarkable skill with a rifle brought her fame, and eventually she was known worldwide as Annie Oakley.

Oakley's father died when she was 4 years old. But from the age of 9, Oakley's keen eye and steady hand enabled her to kill birds in flight and animals on the run. For many years the family lived on the money she made by selling quail and rabbit meat to local merchants. In five years she was able to pay off the mortgage on the family farm.

Some of the quail Oakley sold were bought by a hotel in Cincinnati. The manager noticed that of all the birds he bought, those shot most skillfully were supplied by Oakley. He was so impressed by her accuracy that he proposed a contest. He made a bet with a famous marksman, Frank E. Butler, that Oakley could beat Butler in a shooting match. On the arranged date, each contestant shot at 25 birds. Butler brought down almost all, but Oakley had a perfect score and walked off with the prize.

Frank Butler wrote to his opponent and visited her, and eventually the two were married. In 1885 they joined Buffalo Bill's Wild West Show, of which Oakley was the star for 17 years. As part of her act, she would shoot a cigarette from her husband's mouth, or a playing card thrown into the air.

Oakley's fame spread. She performed before Crown Prince Wilhelm of Germany and Queen Victoria of England. In 1901 she was injured in a train accident; but until the end of her life, she kept her reputation as the greatest markswoman of her day. Oakley died on November 3, 1926, in Greenville, Ohio. Her life story was the basis for the popular musical *Annie Get Your Gun* (1946).

Reviewed by TOM MORRISON
Buffalo Bill State Historical Park

OASES

A fertile area with green plants or crops is a welcome sight to the desert traveler. Only the presence of water can change parts of a desert into these garden spots. Desert land that receives enough water to allow plants and crops to grow is called an oasis. All of the world's major deserts contain oases.

Oases vary in size. They may be small patches of land shaded by date palms. They may be large areas with enough water to support a settlement or even a city. Smaller oases are places for rest where desert travelers and their animals find food and water. Larger oases are busy marketplaces. Whether large or small, oases contrast greatly with the emptiness of the surrounding desert.

Oases are very fragile. In times of drought, the vegetation of an oasis can be destroyed if too many people and animals move there in search of food. Cutting down trees on an oasis is especially damaging because trees help the oasis hold soil and absorb water.

Natural oases are found along rivers and streams that flow into deserts and where underground springs are close to the surface. Brief periods of rain also help to nourish plants and grasses in a natural oasis.

In the western Sahara, rain from the Atlas Mountains collects in valleys (wadis) and forms small streams. These streams provide water for the bustling oases of Laghouat and In-Salah. The Loa River in northern Chile flows across the Atacama Desert and irrigates the oasis town of Calama. In the Libyan Desert, where few visible streams flow, oases like Kufra are fed by underground water.

In parts of the Sahara, machinery has been used to dig deep wells that provide enough water to support whole communities. Modern technology has allowed governments to create new oases there, and to settle people on them.

Irrigation projects have brought water to other desert lands, too. Because of large irrigation works near the Kara Kum desert in southern Central Asia, the Khiva oasis has become an important region for growing cotton. Canals that were built from the Colorado River across the Colorado Desert irrigate the once dry Imperial Valley in southern California. This valley is really a vast oasis and has become one of the world's most productive desert lands.

Dates are the basic food in many of the world's hot desert oases. They have become an important export crop. Fruits, vegetables, cereal grains, and cotton are also grown in well-watered oases. No land is wasted, and the oasis farmer gets a large crop yield. Oases provide places for trade. Herdsmen of the desert exchange animal products (hides, meat, and milk) for crops grown in the oasis. Caravans transport much of the goods traded in oases of the Middle East and Asia.

Oases provide places for settlement. Although desert lands have few permanent

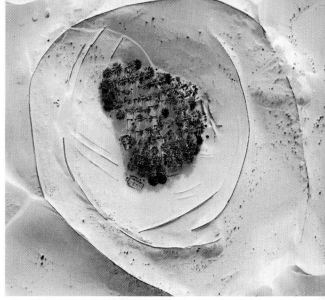

An aerial view of an artificial oasis in the Sahara. The palm trees provide shade for hot and weary travelers.

residents, oases are usually densely populated. Tashkent, Bukhara, and Khiva in Uzbekistan have grown into cities. Cairo, the largest city in Africa, began as an oasis. Phoenix, Arizona, and Salt Lake City, Utah, are examples of other oasis cities.

Reviewed by HOWARD J. CRITCHFIELD
Western Washington State College

OATS

Oats are the seeds of a plant belonging to the grass family. When you think of oats, you probably think of the breakfast cereal called oatmeal or of oatmeal cookies. These are the only forms in which many people eat oats. What happens to the rest of the huge crop of oats? Most of it is used for animal food.

▶THE HISTORY OF OATS

The first oats probably originated in the cool, moist areas of eastern Europe. For centuries people considered oats to be a weed. Some authorities think that oats were cultivated for animal food by the early Greeks and Romans. It was not until the 1200's that people began to depend on oats as one of their important foods.

Oats were brought to some small islands off New England in 1602 and spread rapidly in North America during the next 50 years.

Although oatmeal is a traditional food of the Scottish people, Scotland is not the leading oat-producing country. Russia is the biggest producer, with the United States, Canada, and countries of northern Europe also producing great quantities of oats.

▶THE OAT PLANT

Oat plants grow from about 2 to 5 feet (0.5 to 1.5 meters) tall. The leaves are long and slender. Each stem has a head with many small, delicate branches. The branches end with little spikes on which the flowers blossom and, later, the grains form. The plants can grow in cool, moist climates. Oats do not need special soils. As long as the land is not too wet, oats will often grow well in places where other crops cannot be grown.

In cool climates oats may be planted in the spring. In warmer climates they may be planted in the fall. Once the land has been prepared, oats may be planted with a drill or sown broadcast (scattered over the surface of the soil). The grain ripens in three months.

The edible seeds of the oat plant are tucked inside spiky flower heads (*inset*). When the plants are dry and yellow (*left*), it is harvesttime.

▶ DISEASES OF OATS

Oats can be injured by diseases and pests. However, the damage to oats from insects is not as great as the damage from diseases. Rusts and smuts (fungus diseases) can cause extensive loss to an oat crop. The Victoria blight killed many plants in 1946. New varieties were grown that were resistant to this blight. Then, in 1951, another serious disease attacked oat crops. Other new varieties of oats were developed. These varieties, now in use, are resistant to present diseases and are also highly productive.

Most diseases will not develop unless there is a particular set of weather conditions. Some losses may be avoided or reduced by good soil management or proper crop rotation. Danger from some diseases can also be decreased by eliminating plants that carry the diseases.

▶ USES OF OATS

Oats have many varied uses. They are a valuable food for animals and people. Oats are also good for cleaning—they are used in beauty soaps and skin medications. In recent years many industrial uses have been developed not only for the oat itself but also for its hull (hard outer covering).

Stock Feed. More than other cereal crops, oats are used as a general-purpose feed for animals. Harvested oats, mixed with other cereal grains, are used for all livestock and poultry. Young oat plants are sometimes used for pasturage. Sometimes the green plants are made into pellets to be sold for animal feed.

Since their food value is so high, oats are considered especially valuable for horses. When Samuel Johnson was writing his dictionary in England, he said in it that oats were "a grain which in England is generally given to horses but in Scotland supports the people." A Scotsman replied, "Yes, and that is why in England you have such fine horses and in Scotland we have such fine men."

Food for People. When oats are milled for people to eat, the hull and its parts are removed, but the germ and other parts that are very rich in vitamins and minerals are left in. Breakfast cereals made of oats are inexpensive, high in energy value, and a good source of protein. Oatmeal is richer in certain vitamins than whole-wheat flour, especially in vitamin B_1, a vitamin very important to the nervous system. It is also a rich source of the minerals iron and phosphorus.

Other Uses. Oat flour, because of its natural antioxidant properties, has the unusual ability of slowing down the rate at which some foods spoil. For this reason it is mixed into foods such as peanut butter, margarine, and butter candies. It is dusted over nuts and potato chips. Oat flour is being used more and more to help preserve foods, especially since some stronger antioxidants have been found to be poisonous.

The most important use for oat hulls is in the manufacture of furfural, a colorless, oily liquid. Furfural is used in the manufacture of lubricating oils, nylon, plastics, and many industrial and medical products.

Reviewed by GRANT M. CARMAN
Agriculture Canada

See also GRAIN AND GRAIN PRODUCTS.

OBELISKS

An obelisk is a slender stone shaft with a pyramid-shaped top. The first and most famous of these monuments were made in ancient Egypt. Usually an Egyptian obelisk was carved from a single stone. Some famous memorials in the United States—such as the Bunker Hill and Washington monuments—are obelisks that are made of many small pieces of stone.

To the ancient Egyptians, the obelisk was a symbol for the sun god. Obelisks were usually made in pairs and placed on each side of the gates to temples and tombs. The tops were often covered with bright metals, such as gold, to reflect the sun's rays. Inscriptions in hieroglyphics (picture writing) on the four sides named the pharaohs or private individuals who had ordered the obelisks.

Many Egyptian obelisks came from a granite quarry near Aswan. No one knows exactly how the Egyptians were able to move these tremendous shafts, many of them over 24 meters (80 feet) tall. It has been estimated that more than 20,000 workers would be needed to pull one. From the quarry the obelisks were dragged to the Nile River. There they were loaded onto barges and shipped to different cities.

Throughout history, Egyptian obelisks have been sent all over the world. The ancient Romans were very impressed by them. After the Romans conquered Egypt in 30 B.C., they moved about 15 obelisks to Italy, of which 13 stand in Rome today. No one knows how they did this.

The moving of an obelisk was first fully described by the Italian architect Domenico Fontana. In 1585, Fontana was asked by the pope to move an obelisk that had been brought to Rome 15 centuries earlier. He only had to move the obelisk from behind St. Peter's to the square in front of the cathedral. Although the distance was small, the operation was carefully planned and took nearly a year. A legend says that a sailor saw that the ropes holding the obelisk were getting hot and were about to snap. He called for water and saved the monument. As a reward his family supposedly was given the right to sell palms in St. Peter's Square.

In the 19th century three obelisks were moved from Egypt. The first was taken from

An obelisk made for the Pharaoh Thutmose I stands at the Karnak Temple in Luxor, Egypt. It dates from the 16th century B.C.

the Temple of Luxor to the Place de la Concorde in Paris in 1836. An obelisk from Alexandria was set up on the banks of the Thames in London in 1880. The mate to the London obelisk was given to the United States. In 1881 it was placed in Central Park in New York City. From its inscriptions, we know that it was made for the Pharaoh Thutmose III about 1454 B.C. The New York and London obelisks are each called Cleopatra's Needle. It is not known how these obelisks received their popular name. Medieval Arab writers called them pharaoh's great needles. Cleopatra was perhaps the best known of the pharaohs who ruled in Alexandria, but it apparently was not realized that she reigned nearly 1,500 years after the obelisks were made.

Reviewed by BETSY M. BRYAN
The Brooklyn Museum

OBESITY

Obesity—excessive body fat—is a fast-growing epidemic and one of the largest public health problems in the industrialized world. It increases the risk of many diseases, as well as of early death, and may lead to social and emotional problems.

In the United States, two out of three adults are overweight. Within this group, one in three is obese. An adult is considered overweight when a measurement called the Body Mass Index (BMI) is 25 or more. Obesity is defined as a BMI of 30 or more. (For more information about the BMI, see the feature accompanying this article.)

Although many children have excess body fat, the medical community does not term them obese. Instead, they are said to be "at risk" of being overweight or simply "overweight," based on the BMI. Recent figures indicate that nearly one in three American children is at risk and one in six is overweight. Studies show that those who remain overweight throughout their school years are more likely to be obese adults.

Obesity is sometimes linked to certain medical disorders, such as diabetes, and to genetic (inherited) traits, such as a greater tendency to store excess calories as body fat. In most cases, however, lifestyle plays a major role. In the United States and elsewhere, people are snacking more often, eating larger portions, and consuming more fattening foods, such as fast foods and sugary soft drinks. And they are less active than in the past, spending more of their leisure time watching television or sitting at the computer. When the food energy, or calories, taken in each day exceeds the energy spent in physical activity, body fat rises.

Obesity is considered a significant public health issue because overweight and obese people have many more health problems than people of normal weight. They are at much greater risk for cardiovascular disease, type II diabetes, high blood pressure, certain types of cancer, and lung and bone problems. Many overweight children suffer from adjustment problems and depression, which can be severe and may not disappear with age. Because of the health problems associated with it, obesity is expensive. In the United States, health care costs related to obesity are estimated to exceed $120 billion each year. For all these reasons, the risk of obesity should be identified early in life and controlled.

A doctor or other health professional is the best person to determine whether a person's weight is healthy. For an adult, this is done by calculating the BMI. For a child, it is done by calculating the BMI during each checkup and plotting it on a graph, then observing how it changes as the child grows. A child is considered at risk when the BMI reaches the graph's 85th percentile and overweight when the BMI reaches the 95th percentile.

If a weight problem is identified, a doctor will first rule out any medical condition as the cause, then may recommend a weight-control program of diet and exercise. As part of this program, people are taught how to select the right foods and portion sizes. They are advised to limit sugary drinks and fruit juices, to eat meals at home whenever possible (for more control over food choices), and to be more physically active.

For adults with health problems caused by excess weight, other treatments may include drugs that suppress the appetite and surgery to reduce the size of the stomach so that less food is needed to feel full. These treatments are not used for overweight children except in extreme cases. Instead, doctors prefer to control the rate of weight gain and allow a child to grow into the weight gradually.

To contain the obesity epidemic, many experts say prevention is also necessary, including large-scale public health measures. For example, school systems can help fight obesity by providing healthy lunch programs, physical education classes, and after-school activity programs. Communities can also play a role by creating more places for physical activities, such as parks and playgrounds.

ROBERT MURRAY, M.D.
Columbus Children's Hospital
The Ohio State University

Did you know that...

an individual's weight and height can be used to estimate the health risk of being overweight? Divide weight in kilograms by height in meters, then divide by height again. This gives the Body Mass Index (BMI). The higher the BMI, the greater the risk. To calculate BMI using pounds and inches, use the same formula, then multiply the final figure by 703.

This striking nighttime photograph of the Mount Palomar Observatory (*above*) in California also reveals the optical telescope behind its dome-shaped top. An astronomer sits in the telescope's prime focus cage (*left*), which is used for wide-angle viewing of the sky.

Astronomers learn about most objects in space by studying the light and other forms of radiation the objects emit. So, most of the research done with observatories concentrates on collecting and analyzing the various forms of radiation: gamma rays, X rays, ultraviolet light, visible light, infrared radiation, microwaves, and radio waves. By carefully studying the types of radiation coming from objects such as planets, stars, galaxies, and quasars, astronomers can learn much about them and about the history and evolution of the universe.

OBSERVATORIES

Observatories used by astronomers to study the universe are called astronomical observatories. They usually contain different kinds of telescopes, computers, cameras, and other types of special equipment astronomers need to make observations of objects in space.

Observatories have been built for use on the Earth or in space, and they are usually owned and operated by governments, research institutions, or colleges and universities. While most observatories are used by professional astronomers to do original research, some also help train future astronomers. Astronomers who use observatories usually specialize in a specific area of research such as planets, stars or galaxies, or the origin and evolution of the universe.

▶ TYPES OF OBSERVATORIES

There are many types of astronomical observatories. Each one may be built and equipped to do specific types of research and to detect and analyze specific forms of radiation. For this reason, astronomers sometimes need to use different types of observatories for their work.

Optical Observatories

The type of observatory that is familiar to most people is the optical observatory, which houses an optical telescope and other special instruments. Optical observatories are used to detect and analyze the visible light that comes from objects in space. These observatories are usually located in high, remote places where the sky is often clear and where there is very little dust, mist, or chemical pollution in the atmosphere. Such locations also

The Electromagnetic Spectrum

Electromagnetic radiation travels through space in the form of waves. Visible light is the only form we can see with our eyes. Special instruments are used to observe and study the other forms.

have a darker night sky than places near the bright lights of cities. Among the major optical observatories in the United States are Mount Palomar Observatory in California, the Kitt Peak National Observatory in Arizona, and international observatories on the extinct Mauna Kea volcano in Hawaii. Other important optical observatories are located in such places as the Andes mountains of Chile and the Canary Islands off the west coast of Africa. The high plateau of Antarctica, one of the driest and least polluted places on Earth, is rapidly becoming another major observation site.

Most optical observatories are easy to recognize because of their dome-shaped tops. These domes protect the telescopes, which are very delicate instruments, from wind and weather. Each observatory building usually houses a single large optical telescope. The tube of this telescope, which contains its lenses and mirrors, is connected to a special stand, or mounting, driven by computer-assisted motors. One set of motors moves the telescope from object to object. Once pointed at an object, the telescope is moved slowly by another set of motors so that it turns at the same rate as the Earth is rotating on its axis but in the opposite direction. This keeps it pointed at the object.

The domes of optical observatories have a large slit that is opened when the telescope is in use. There is no glass in this slit because imperfections in the glass or dust on its surface could distort any image seen through the telescope. The dome can be rotated so that the telescope can follow a particular object as it moves across the sky.

To get good images or data, a telescope usually must have a clear view through steady air, so there is no heating system in an observatory dome. If the dome were heated, the hot air would rise and float out through the open slit. This would make the air around the observatory unsteady, and any objects seen through the telescope would appear to ripple and distort. At the Mount Palomar Observatory, each of the domes and the buildings underneath them have double walls with cool air between them. As a result, the astronomers do not have to wait for the buildings to cool down after the sun sets before using the telescopes.

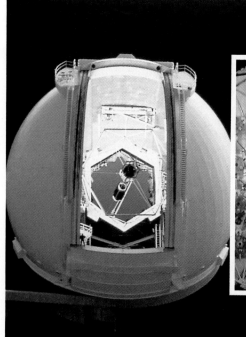

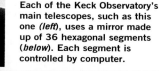

Each of the Keck Observatory's main telescopes, such as this one (*left*), uses a mirror made up of 36 hexagonal segments (*below*). Each segment is controlled by computer.

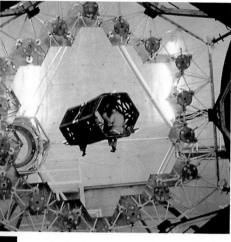

Solar Observatories

Astronomers using solar observatories specialize in studying the sun. The telescopes in these observatories are usually kept in long tunnels or placed on high towers. This is because the sun's heat creates currents of hot air near the ground that can blur images of the sun when viewed through a telescope. Some solar telescopes cannot be pivoted (turned) or moved. Instead, sunlight is directed to them by mirrors that follow the sun as it moves across the sky. There is a solar telescope at Kitt Peak National Observatory in Arizona.

Radio-Astronomy Observatories

Another type of observatory is the radio-astronomy observatory, which looks very different from other observatories. Its radio telescopes frequently consist of huge antennas, usually bowl- or dish-shaped, and a radio receiver. These antennas are used to collect radiation in the form of radio waves from planets, stars, galaxies, and other objects in space. These radio waves are reflected off the antennas' huge surfaces and focused into a narrower area. The receiver picks up the focused radio waves and amplifies them so that they can be studied by astronomers.

Most radio telescopes can be operated both day and night and in all types of weather. There are limitations, however, to where they can be operated. Since radio signals from distant objects are millions of times fainter than radio waves generated on Earth, radio telescopes can be affected by radio signals from places such as cars, houses, and factories. Even small amounts of radio energy from these sources can cause interference with the radio telescope. For this reason, radio-astronomy observatories are usually located in areas far from people and cities.

Because they are less delicate than optical telescopes and less affected by weather, radio telescopes are usually out in the open. This is just as well, for most radio telescopes are far too large to be housed in an observatory dome. The largest single-dish radio telescope in the world is 1,000 feet (305 meters) in diameter. It is located in a mountain valley near Arecibo, Puerto Rico. Other large radio observatories are located at Parkes, Australia; Green Bank, West Virginia; and elsewhere.

It is possible to connect two or more radio telescopes together to produce clearer and more detailed images than images produced by a single radio telescope. This has been done by the National Radio Astronomy Observatory, which has a series of 27 radio telescopes connected together. This grouping of telescopes, known as the Very Large Array, is located near Socorro, New Mexico. Such a network of telescopes working together is called an **interferometer**.

Airborne Observatories

Some astronomical observatories consist of telescopes and other specialized instruments

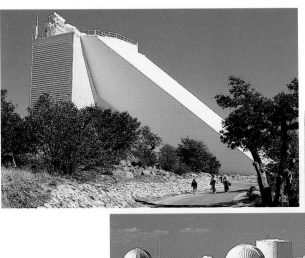

Kitt Peak National Observatory (*below*) is home to several types of telescopes. The McMath-Pierce solar telescope at Kitt (*left*) is used for studying the sun.

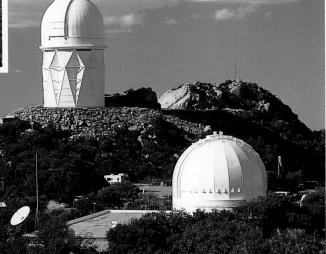

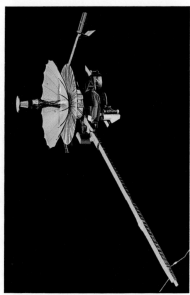

The Very Large Array (*left*) in New Mexico receives radiation in the form of radio waves to map objects in space. Spacecraft such as the U.S. *Galileo* (*right*) capture other kinds of radiation to send information about the solar system back to Earth.

mounted in airplanes. The largest airborne observatory will be the Stratospheric Observatory for Infrared Astronomy, or SOFIA, which is scheduled for launch in 2005 and will feature an 8-foot (2.5-meter) reflecting telescope. Water vapor in the atmosphere absorbs most infrared radiation coming from space before it reaches the Earth's surface. A telescope used to study infrared rays must therefore be above most of the water vapor in the atmosphere. Carried in a modified Boeing 747SP jet, SOFIA will be high enough to detect such rays.

SOFIA's predecessor, the Kuiper Airborne Observatory, consisted of a 3-foot (1-meter) telescope and flew from 1971 to 1995.

Observatories in Space

Astronomical observatories can be located far out in space. Some of these space observatories have been sent to orbit the Earth or to fly past other planets in the solar system. The data gathered by such space observatories is radioed back to Earth.

There is a good reason for sending observatories into space. Certain kinds of radiation in space never reach the surface of the Earth, even at mountain tops, because they are absorbed by the Earth's atmosphere. To observe or detect radiation such as ultraviolet rays, X rays, and gamma rays, astronomers must have telescopes and other specialized instruments

in places where the Earth's atmosphere is very thin or where it does not exist at all.

Spacecraft and Space Probes. Other types of space observatories are spacecraft and space probes. Since the 1960's, such devices have transmitted vital information to astronomers. For example, the *Mariner* and *Pioneer* spacecraft sent to Mercury, Venus, Mars, Jupiter, and Saturn by the United States have provided information about the atmosphere, surface, and structure of these planets. The *Venera* probes of the former Soviet Union have landed on Venus and sent back pictures of its surface. The U.S. *Viking, Pathfinder, Spirit,* and *Opportunity* probes have landed on Mars to examine its soil and to search for evidence of conditions necessary for life. The U.S. *Voyager 1* and *Voyager 2* spacecraft have taken pictures of Jupiter and its moons and have also provided close-up images of the rings and moons of Saturn, Uranus, and Neptune. *Voyager 2* has also sent back information about Uranus and Neptune. The *Galileo* spacecraft has sent detailed images of Jupiter and its moons. And the *Cassini-Huygens* spacecraft reached Saturn in 2004, beginning a four-year mission to study the planet, its rings, and its moons.

Orbiting Observatories. Since the 1970's, a number of observatories have been placed in orbit around the Earth to study distant stars, galaxies, and other objects. These orbiting observatories are free of interference from the Earth's atmosphere as well as from clouds, pollution, city lights, and other conditions that can hinder the data they detect. The Infrared Astronomical Satellite, sent into space in 1983, is an example of an orbiting observatory that has sent information back to astronomers on Earth.

Astronomers do not have to travel into space to use observatories. Instead, they can use research facilities on Earth that receive radio signals from the observatories in space. Images and data developed from these radio signals are viewed and then analyzed by computers that can be located at the research facilities or even at astronomers' offices.

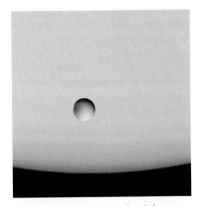

This image taken by the *Cassini* space probe in 2004 shows the icy moon Dione in orbit around Saturn.

The Great Observatories. During the 1980's, the National Aeronautics and Space Administration (NASA) drew up plans for four Great Observatories to orbit in space and send information back to Earth for many years. Each of these orbital observatories has equipment designed to study the different types of radiation that will give astronomers important information about the universe and how it has evolved since its beginnings.

Hubble Space Telescope

The first of the Great Observatories was the Hubble Space Telescope (HST). Launched in April 1990, the HST is designed to detect visible light as well as ultraviolet and infrared radiation coming from distant objects. Soon after the telescope was launched, astronomers discovered a flaw in its primary mirror that resulted in blurry pictures. This problem was resolved in 1993. The repaired Hubble has observed comets, supernovas, nebulas, distant planets, black holes, and colliding galaxies.

The second observatory was the Compton Gamma-Ray Observatory, launched in April 1991. The Compton was designed to detect gamma rays, a high-energy form of electromagnetic radiation. It studied cosmic rays and solar flares, detected mysterious bursts of gamma radiation from deep space, and discovered a new class of high-energy gamma-ray sources called gamma-ray quasars. The Compton's mission ended when it re-entered the Earth's atmosphere and burned up in June 2000.

The third observatory, the Chandra X-Ray Observatory, was launched in July 1999. It is designed to detect and study X rays that are emitted by distant objects, such as black holes, supernovas, and dark matter—invisible mass in galaxies and galaxy clusters. Chandra also studied the formation and evolution of galaxies.

A supernova remnant is revealed in different kinds of light by three space observatories (*left to right*): visible light, by the Hubble; X rays, by the Chandra; and infrared, by the Spitzer.

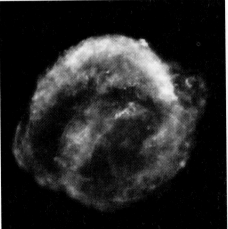
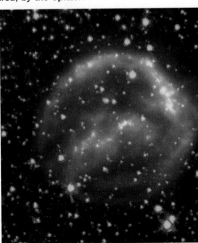

The fourth and final of the Great Observatories is the Spitzer Space Telescope (formerly, the Space Infrared Telescope Facility, or SIRTF), launched in August 2003 to detect the infrared radiation emitted by objects in space. The Spitzer can see through clouds of dust and gas that optical telescopes cannot, studying objects such as cool, dim stars and distant planets.

For more information, see SPACE TELESCOPES in Volume S.

Future Observatories. Several space-based observatories are scheduled for launch in the near future. Among these are the Gamma-Ray Large Area Space Telescope (GLAST) and the James Webb Space Telescope (JWST). The GLAST, due to launch in 2006, will study the gamma-ray radiation produced by massive black holes, colliding neutron stars, and other phenomena. The JWST, previously known as the Next Generation Space Telescope, will succeed the Hubble Space Telescope. Scheduled for launch in 2011, this telescope will be the most powerful ever built and will allow astronomers to study very old and distant galaxies and learn about the formation of galaxies, solar systems, and planets.

▶ **TOOLS USED IN OBSERVATORIES**

Astronomers use many kinds of instruments in their work. The telescope, of course, is one of the most important.

Astronomers rarely spend much time looking through telescopes, however. This is because the human eye is not as sensitive as other instruments that detect and analyze visible light and other types of radiation. Astronomers sometimes use special cameras to take pictures of objects in space. When film is exposed to light, it forms an image of the object emitting the light. Up to a point, a longer exposure allows more light to build up on the film and allows it to "see" and record very faint objects. Most cameras used today are equipped with charge-coupled devices (CCD's), which can produce images or data faster than film and can be reused. These CCD's are similar to devices used in digital cameras, except that they are much more sensitive to light. The images obtained with CCD's are fed into computers and adjusted to reveal different details. CCD's can be used to study visible light as well as ultraviolet and infrared radiation.

Another important instrument is the **spectrograph**, which splits up light from objects in space into the various colors of the spectrum. (This is the way a prism divides white light into a band of colors.) The spectrograph, which is attached to the telescope, usually records the spectrum on a CCD. Because different chemical elements have unique patterns of light in the spectrum, a spectrograph enables astronomers to determine the chemical composition of objects. It can also reveal such data as the temperature of objects, the strength of their magnetic fields, the speeds of the rotations of stars, and whether objects in space are moving toward the Earth or away from the Earth.

Astronomers also use instruments that measure the brightness of stars and other objects in space. Known as **photometers**, these devices are very sensitive light meters. In a photometer, light usually passes through different color filters before it is measured and its intensity is recorded.

In their work, astronomers perform many complicated mathematical calculations. Today most of these calculations are done by computers and supercomputers. Computers can also control the operations of one or more telescopes; gather information from telescopes, spectrographs, photometers, and other instruments; and store this information until it is needed. This leaves astronomers more time to do the kind of work only the human brain can do—study and evaluate images and data, decide what calculations are needed, and draw conclusions from all of the information that is gathered.

In addition to observing objects in space, an astronomer analyzes data, writes scientific reports, attends meetings and conferences, reads about the work of other astronomers, and applies for money to do further research. All these activities help the astronomer expand our knowledge of the universe.

WILLIAM A. GUTSCH, JR.
President, The Challenger Center for
Space Science Education

See also ASTRONOMY; LIGHT; PLANETARIUMS AND SPACE MUSEUMS; RADIO AND RADAR ASTRONOMY; SATELLITES, ARTIFICIAL; SPACE EXPLORATION AND TRAVEL; SPACE PROBES; SPACE TELESCOPES; TELESCOPES.

OBSIDIAN. See ROCKS (Igneous Rock).

OCCUPATION, CHOICE OF. See GUIDANCE COUNSELING; VOCATIONS.

OCCUPATIONAL HEALTH AND SAFETY

The field of occupational health and safety is concerned with lessening the dangers people are exposed to while at work—dangers that threaten health and sometimes life. Various professionals work in this field, including doctors, chemists, and safety engineers. They try to find ways to reduce or eliminate accidents and diseases that are common to certain kinds of work.

About 400 B.C., the Greek physician Hippocrates identified the first cases of lead poisoning among miners. But the first real study of occupational hazards was published in 1700 by Bernardino Ramazzini, an Italian doctor. He observed that the effects of many of these hazards developed gradually. (The term **latent period** is now used to describe the time between exposure to the danger and the appearance of symptoms.) He was also the first to describe brown lung, a disease that affects workers exposed to cotton dust. The first link between an occupation and cancer was established in the late 1700's when Percival Pott, an English surgeon, noticed many cases of cancer among chimney sweeps.

In the factories and mines of the 1800's, workers were exposed to many job-related hazards. As the factory system spread and machinery became more complicated, accidents were common. Yet employers were not considered responsible. In the late 1800's, laws were passed that required employers to make sure that workplaces were safe.

Much progress has been made since this time. During the early 1900's, American physician Alice Hamilton pioneered investigations of the causes of industrial diseases; her work helped bring about legislation that improved conditions at unsafe factories. In 1970 the U.S. Congress passed the Occupational Safety and Health Act. Employers covered by the law must comply with safety and health standards, and employees must comply with standards that apply to their own actions.

Standards are set and enforced by the Occupational Safety and Health Administration (OSHA) and the Mine Safety and Health Administration (MSHA), both divisions of the U.S. Department of Labor. The National Institute for Occupational Safety and Health (NIOSH), within the Department of Health

A worker wears protective clothing while spraying pesticide. Proper safety gear and thorough training help prevent work-related illnesses and injuries.

and Human Services, conducts research, develops recommendations, and provides funds for professional training.

As technology advances, new hazards emerge. The largest problem facing workers today involves bone and muscle injuries; these include computer-related repetitive stress injuries (RSI's) such as carpal tunnel syndrome, which may develop as a result of long hours of typing. Physical and mental stress is created by high-speed automated processes and noise. And exposure to radiation and thousands of hazardous chemicals raises workers' risk of cancers and other serious diseases. Long latent periods are still a problem in the detection of these occupational diseases.

To deal with these issues, employers must keep up to date on all safety concerns. Office furniture is increasingly being designed for maximum comfort of the human body in order to improve worker efficiency. More built-in safeguards can be added to machinery, and protective eyewear and clothing provided for employees. Information on hazardous substances and conditions present in a workplace should be made available. Few jobs are free of danger. But with proper training, equipment, and care, many accidents and work-related problems can be prevented.

Reviewed by PAUL A. SCHULTE
Centers for Disease Control and Prevention

See also SAFETY; WORKERS' COMPENSATION.

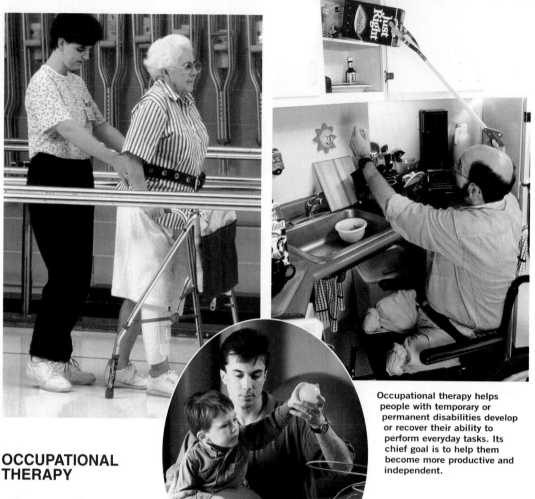

Occupational therapy helps people with temporary or permanent disabilities develop or recover their ability to perform everyday tasks. Its chief goal is to help them become more productive and independent.

OCCUPATIONAL THERAPY

Some people have disabilities, either temporary or permanent, that prevent them from performing everyday tasks. They may be unable to dress or feed themselves or to walk across a room. Occupational therapy is a form of treatment that helps people improve their ability to perform such activities so that they can lead independent, productive, and satisfying lives.

The professionals who provide occupational therapy are called occupational therapists (OT's). They work with people of all ages and with various types of disabilities—physical, mental, and emotional—in many different settings. Some work in schools to help students with learning disabilities or behavioral problems. Others work with children who have cerebral palsy, Down syndrome, or other disabilities. Occupational therapists and occupational therapy assistants also work with people who have traumatic injuries (from car accidents, for example), Alzheimer's disease, and mental health problems, and those who have been disabled by strokes. Care may be provided at community centers, rehabilitation hospitals, and nursing homes or in the patients' homes.

▶ TREATMENT AND TECHNIQUES

Planning the Program. Occupational therapy is prescribed by a physician. Before beginning treatment, the occupational therapist must evaluate a patient's physical and emotional condition. This includes assessing his or her strength, sight, hearing, coordination, and ability to perform everyday activities. The occupational therapist may also consider the patient's support system, relationships with others, and leisure interests. A treatment program is then worked out with the patient, family members or partner, and other members of the patient's health care team, such as doctors, nurses, and social workers. This joint planning helps ensure that the patient's needs will be met.

For people with physical disabilities, the therapist's first goal is to help them develop or recover their ability to perform critical daily activities, such as eating and grooming. Once these skills are mastered, therapy may then focus on other areas. For an adult, this might include developing the skills needed to drive a car, care for a home and family, or seek and hold a job. A child might be helped to participate more fully in educational and recreational activities.

Therapy goals for those with mental disabilities can be similar. These, too, focus on developing or recovering the skills needed to be independent. The treatment program may emphasize methods of working and communicating with others, time management techniques, and leisure activities.

Treatment. Occupational therapists train patients to perform tasks by breaking them down into small, simple steps. As the patient learns each step, more difficult steps are gradually added until the activity can be done independently. A therapist who is teaching someone how to prepare a meal, for instance, might begin by showing the patient techniques for pouring liquid into a glass or cutting food with a knife.

Sometimes occupational therapists will suggest aids and equipment to make physical activities easier. For example, if a child has a disability that makes it difficult to sit up and do homework, the therapist might recommend a special chair to improve sitting balance and an adjustable reading table. If an elderly person with arthritis (a disease that affects the joints) cannot grasp small objects with the fingers, the therapist might recommend adaptive equipment, such as eating utensils with large handles.

Occupational therapists recommend activities as treatment, too. Examples include working with clay to strengthen weak hand muscles, sawing wood to loosen up a stiff shoulder, and playing games such as checkers to improve coordination.

▶ **HISTORY OF OCCUPATIONAL THERAPY**

Occupational therapy began during World War I (1914–18), when thousands of wounded soldiers needed help with physical and emotional problems. The American Occupational Therapy Association (AOTA) was founded in 1917 and became the profession's official organization. Today it represents more than 40,000 occupational therapists, occupational therapy assistants, and students studying occupational therapy.

The AOTA has helped promote greater understanding of people with disabilities. It educates the public and advances the profession by providing resources, setting standards, and serving as an advocate for improved health care. It has also pressed for more laws to benefit the disabled, such as the Americans with Disabilities Act (ADA), enacted in 1990. Such laws have increased public recognition of the occupational therapy profession.

▶ **CAREERS IN OCCUPATIONAL THERAPY**

There are more than 300 occupational therapy and occupational therapy assistant educational programs in the United States. Students must usually take courses in the biological and behavioral sciences. Most programs also require volunteer or observation experience with disabled people.

Occupational therapists may have a bachelor's degree, a master's degree, or a doctorate. Many work as members of rehabilitation teams, while others choose careers in private practice, consulting, management, teaching, or research. **Occupational therapy assistants** have a two-year associate's degree from technical programs. Under the supervision of occupational therapists, occupational therapy assistants provide hands-on services to children and adults.

In addition to earning a degree, occupational therapists and occupational therapy assistants must complete fieldwork training, pass a national examination, and become licensed in the state where they plan to work.

The need for occupational therapy is expected to increase as improvements in health care enable more people with disabilities to live longer. Areas that are becoming more important in this field include making buildings and homes more accessible for the disabled and promoting health and wellness.

FRANK E. GAINER
The American Occupational
Therapy Association, Inc.

See also BLINDNESS; DEAFNESS; DISABLED PEOPLE; OLD AGE.

The Atlantic, Pacific, Indian, and Arctic oceans are actually one huge interconnected body of salt water covering nearly three quarters of the surface of the earth.

OCEAN

Almost 71 percent of the earth's surface is covered by seawater. Under this vast, watery surface are the tallest peaks and deepest valleys on this planet. The greatest variety of organisms lives beneath the sea. And some of the most valuable resources for human life, such as food and energy sources, are found in the ocean depths.

But how did the oceans first form? Why is ocean water salty? How deep is the ocean? What unusual creatures live there? These are the kinds of questions people have asked for centuries. But because the world's oceans are so vast, it has not been easy to discover the answers.

Today we know many, many things about the ocean. Modern research tools and years of investigation have uncovered some of the answers. But we have yet to stop asking questions about the sea. Its many mysteries will keep us interested for centuries to come.

▶ORIGIN OF THE OCEANS

Several theories explain the origin and location of our oceans. The most widely accepted theory was proposed by Alfred Wegener, a German meteorologist, in 1912. This theory is known as **continental drift.**

The continental drift theory assumes that continents and the ocean floor are part of large plates making up the earth's crust. These plates slide over the earth's soft inner layer, or mantle. Movement of these plates also moves the continents and the ocean floor.

Most scientists believe that more than 200 million years ago the continents were united as a single land mass called Pangaea. Continental drift caused the land masses making up Pangaea to separate into northern and southern halves. The northern half was known as Laurasia and included the land areas that now make up North America, Europe, and Asia. Gondwanaland was the southern half, which included the present-day continents of South America, Africa, and Antarctica.

These masses eventually broke into pieces to form the continents we know today. The continents drifted slowly over the earth's surface to their present locations. Here they form the boundaries of today's ocean basins.

There are theories that explain the origin of water in our oceans. One theory suggests that millions of years ago the earth and a surrounding cloud layer slowly cooled. This cooling process caused the clouds to rain vast quantities of water into the ocean basins.

A second theory states that water vapor was once released from very hot rocks in the earth's crust. This vapor cooled and helped to fill the ocean basins.

▶ OCEAN WATER

Seawater, also known as salt water, makes up 85 percent of all the water on earth. This amounts to 328,000,000 cubic miles (more than one billion cubic kilometers) of water in the sea.

Salts and Salinity

Seawater is really pure water in which compounds have dissolved. Salts account for most of these dissolved substances. The total amount of salts dissolved in seawater is known as the **salinity,** which is measured as the number of parts of salt in a thousand parts of water. For example, a 1,000-gram sample of seawater will usually contain 35 grams of dissolved salts and, as a result, has a salinity of 35 parts per thousand.

Salinity levels range from near zero at river mouths (where freshwater is flowing into the ocean) to more than 40 parts per thousand in the Red Sea and Persian Gulf. (Salinity can be even greater in lakes. Great Salt Lake and the Dead Sea are lakes in which the salt content is extremely high.) You can read more about them in the article LAKES in Volume L. Dissolved salts allow us to float more easily in seawater than in freshwater. The higher the salinity of the water, the more buoyancy (ability to float) it provides.

Seawater contains all the dissolved substances necessary for the growth and well-being of plant and animal life. These substances include inorganic salts, compounds derived from living organisms, and dissolved gases. More than 99 percent of these materials are inorganic salts present as ions. (Ions are atoms or groups of atoms that carry an electric charge.) Major ions in ocean water include chlorine, sodium, sulfur, magnesium, calcium, and potassium.

Dissolved Gases

Nitrogen, carbon dioxide, and oxygen are the most abundant dissolved gases in seawa-

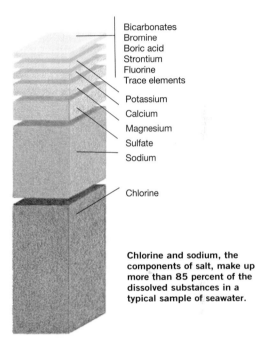

Bicarbonates
Bromine
Boric acid
Strontium
Fluorine
Trace elements

Potassium

Calcium

Magnesium

Sulfate

Sodium

Chlorine

Chlorine

Chlorine and sodium, the components of salt, make up more than 85 percent of the dissolved substances in a typical sample of seawater.

ter. Although nitrogen is not involved in the life processes of most marine organisms, carbon dioxide and oxygen are essential to life in the sea. Green plants in the sea require carbon dioxide to carry out photosynthesis. Marine plants and animals use oxygen from the water to breathe.

Other Substances

Other important dissolved substances are nitrates and phosphates, which are needed by plants for photosynthesis. Silicon dioxide is important in the building of skeletal material in some marine organisms. Trace elements essential to marine life include iron, manganese, cobalt, and copper.

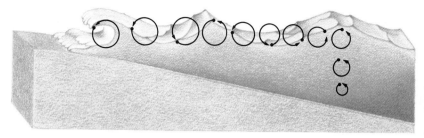

Left: Water particles on the ocean's surface move in a circle as a wave passes. Despite appearances, they are not carried along with the wave. *Right:* A breaking wave advances toward shore where it is met by the backwash from a previous wave (a–c). After the wave breaks and washes onto land (d–f), it also becomes backwash and the cycle repeats.

▶ MOVEMENT OF OCEAN WATER

Ocean water is in continual motion. This water movement helps to provide a nearly constant environment for marine organisms. Water circulation helps disperse swimming and floating organisms, carries body wastes away from marine animals, and replenishes food, nutrients, and essential elements.

Movement of the upper layers of ocean water is usually caused by winds blowing steadily across the sea surface. Other causes include sudden shifts in the earth's crust and the gravitational pull of the moon and the sun.

Waves and Currents

Creation of waves depends on the wind's speed, duration, and the size of the area over which the wind blows. Ocean waves range in height from fractions of an inch to almost 100 feet (30 meters) high.

Winds also produce surface currents. These are large-scale horizontal movements of surface waters caused by winds of constant direction and speed. As a result, these currents are semi-permanent features of the world's oceans.

Currents have a tremendous effect on the climate because they carry warm water into cold regions and cool water into tropical re-

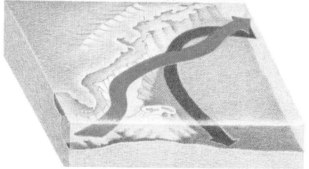

The Gulf Stream, a surface current, flows north along the eastern coast of the United States. Beneath it a deep-water current flows in the opposite direction.

gions. This mix of temperatures creates many kinds of weather patterns. And without currents, the oceans would stagnate and could not support their great abundance of life.

Navigators rely on currents because the water movement helps ships speed along their paths. The Gulf Stream is a strong ocean current that was important to early travelers in exploring and settling the New World. (See the article GULF STREAM in Volume G.) Other strong currents include the Peru Current and the Japan Current in the Pacific Ocean as well as the Labrador Current and the Brazil Current in the Atlantic Ocean.

Winds known as the trade winds, westerlies, and polar easterlies help propel most ocean surface currents. (More information can be found in the article WINDS in Volume W-Z.) Below these surface currents are deeper, cool-water currents that flow in opposite directions to those above. Their movements result from changes in seawater density.

Upwelling and El Niño

Ocean water masses can also move vertically in a process called **upwelling.** As winds blow warm surface water away from a coastline, cold water—rich in nutrients—moves up from the ocean depths. Upwelling brings nutrients and food to shallow ocean areas. As a result, areas of upwelling such as the Pacific coast of North America have rich fishing grounds.

Sometimes winds weaken so much that upwelling cannot take place. For example, when westward-blowing trade winds over the Pacific Ocean diminish near the equator, warm water surges eastward and stops upwelling along the northwestern coast of South America. This phenomenon, called **El Niño,** can have catastrophic consequences. Large populations of fish can die, and weather patterns can be disrupted around the world. (See the Wonder Question, What is El Niño? in the article WEATHER in Volume W-Z.)

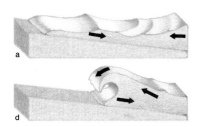
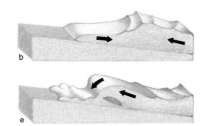
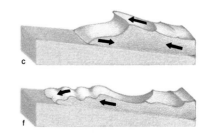

Tides

Ocean waters can also be put into motion by tides. These are very long waves that cause a rise and fall of the ocean surface. The maximum height of this rise is called a high tide and is followed by a fall in sea level known as the low tide. As many as two high and two low tides may occur along a coastline in each 24-hour period.

Tides that result from the gravitational pull of the moon are called **lunar tides.** Strong gravitational pull on the side of the earth facing the moon causes the ocean to rise up or bulge. This produces a high tide. On the opposite side of the earth, the gravitational pull of the moon on the water is weak. However, the earth mass is still attracted toward the moon, leaving the oceans on the far side of the earth slightly behind. The result is the same—a high tide.

The gravitational pull of the sun (in addition to that of the moon) produces solar tides known as **spring tides** and **neap tides.** A spring tide occurs during the full and new moons when the sun, moon, and earth are in a straight line. This combined gravitational pull of the sun and moon causes extra-high high tides and very-low low tides.

A neap tide happens when the sun and moon are at right angles to one another. The gravitational pull is not very strong, so these tides are not very high or very low. Two sets of spring and neap tides occur each month.

Tsunamis

The highest ocean waves are caused not by powerful winds but rather by sudden movements in the earth's crust. These waves are called **tsunamis.** Although sometimes called tidal waves, they have nothing to do with tides. Instead, they happen as a result of earthquakes, volcanic eruptions, and underwater landslides. Though rare, they occur most commonly in the Pacific Ocean. The huge waves of tsunamis move across the ocean very rapidly and can destroy entire coastal communities.

Effects of Ocean Movements

Waves, currents, and tides may influence marine plants and animals and their habitats. Waves, especially those created by storms, may cause the erosion of land masses, move-

Ocean shorelines are constantly changing, sometimes causing damage to coastal communities. This California roadway was washed away by the pounding of ocean waves.

Surtsey (*left*) is a volcanic island that formed off the southwest coast of Iceland in the 1960's. It is one of the few places where features of the ocean floor (*diagramed below*) project above the water's surface.

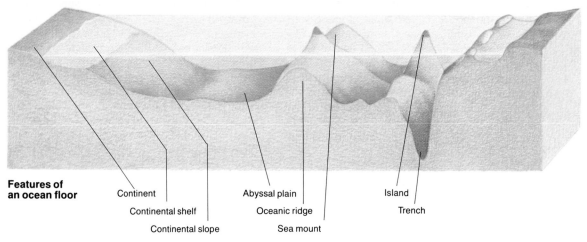

Features of an ocean floor

Continent
Continental shelf
Continental slope

Abyssal plain
Oceanic ridge
Sea mount

Island
Trench

ment of large volumes of ocean-floor sediment, and the relocation or destruction of marine life. The movement of sediment during coastline erosion may build up sandbars along the shore and fill harbors with sand and mud, thus preventing the passage of ships. Sediments carried by currents may bury feeding areas and spawning grounds important to the survival of marine organisms.

▶ **OCEAN FLOOR**

Many of the most exciting mysteries of the ocean are contained deep below its surface along the ocean floor. One of the best ways of describing the ocean floor is to begin with its landward connection and proceed seaward to the dark mysterious areas along the deep ocean bottom. (The floors of the four major ocean basins—the Pacific, Atlantic, Indian,

and Arctic—have similar features and can be grouped together by their characteristics.)

The Continental Shelf

The ocean floor begins as a shallow underwater extension of a major land mass. This seaward extension is known as the **continental shelf** because of its connection to continents. The shelf is relatively flat and is covered with mud, silt, and other material carried from land.

Most continental shelves slope gently seaward to depths ranging from 400 to 650 feet (about 120 to 200 meters). The width of continental shelves varies from a few miles off the Pacific coast of North America to more than 250 miles (400 kilometers) off eastern Canada. This part of the seafloor accounts for 7 to 8 percent of the total ocean area, or nearly one sixth of the earth's total land area. Some of the world's most important fishing grounds and largest oil deposits are found here.

The Continental Slope

At the outer edge of the continental shelf is the shelf break, where the ocean floor abruptly steepens to become the **continental slope.** The slope acts as a boundary between the continental mass and the deep ocean basins. The ocean floor drops very rapidly here to depths ranging from 2 to 2½ miles (3 to 4 kilometers).

Plains, Ridges, and Trenches

Beginning near the outer margins of the continental slope is the **abyssal plain.** Most abyssal plains are flat, monotonous, sediment-covered areas. They account for the majority of the ocean floor at depths of 2 to 3 miles (3 to 5 kilometers). The abyssal plain is interrupted in several places by **oceanic ridges.** These ridges are essentially a continuous underwater mountain chain within each ocean basin. They cover more than 30 percent of the ocean basin area.

The best-known ridge is the Mid-Atlantic Ridge that divides the Atlantic Ocean into east and west basins. Occasionally, isolated ridge peaks extend above sea level to form islands such as the Azores and Ascension islands. The ridge system and its islands are often the sites of volcanic activity.

Abyssal plains are also broken in several areas by deep, narrow troughs called **trenches.** Most trenches are deeper than 20,000 feet (6,100 meters) below sea level and border the Pacific Ocean islands and continents. The greatest known ocean depth, 36,198 feet (11,033 meters) below sea level, is the Mariana Trench in the western North Pacific. Trenches constitute less than 2 percent of the ocean bottom but are important because of the extreme temperatures and pressures found there.

The floor of the abyssal plain and trenches is covered by layers of mud. These layers may be hundreds of feet deep in some places. Mud along the ocean floor often contains large quantities of plant and animal material. These muds are known as **oozes.** Their contents and location are of great interest to oceanographers for a number of reasons, including that they serve as feeding areas for very unusual deep-sea organisms.

Islands and Sea Mounts

Thousands of individual islands and underwater **sea mounts** have been formed by volcanic action on the ocean floor. Islands are volcanic peaks that extend above sea level.

OCEAN DEPTHS OF THE WORLD

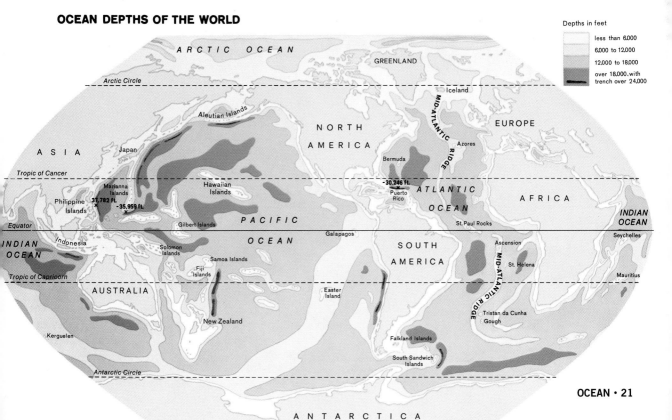

phytoplankton

flying fish

conger eel

green moray eel

coralfish

pipefish

shrimps

zooplankton

cow-nosed ray

triggerfish

pearly nautilus

nutrient upwelling

killer whale

sardines

tuna

gulper

glass sponge

thornback ray

squid

viperfish

crinoids

swallower

tuna

mackerel

gray shark

scarlet prawns

gulper

blackfish

marlin

Portuguese man-of-war

coelacanth

deep-sea angler fish

crinoids

brittle stars

great barracuda

hatchet fish

jellyfish

luminous shark

sperm whale

giant squid

photic zone

mesopelagic zone

bathypelagic zone

benthic zone

Arrows in this ocean scene indicate the path of food resources to bottom-dwelling organisms. Upwelling along the coast returns nutrients to the surface.

Sea mounts are those below sea level. In tropical areas coral builds up around these islands to form ring-shaped reefs called coral atolls.

▶OCEAN LIFE

Several hundred thousand kinds of plants and animals live in the ocean. Some organisms are found near the ocean surface, others prefer middle depths, and still others are found only on the ocean floor.

But depth is not the only thing that determines where ocean life is found. Such factors as ocean size, temperature, currents, and water pressure influence where certain marine plants or animals can live. The abundance of nutrients, the amount of light, and the characteristics of the seafloor are also important.

Habitat Zones

To classify and better understand the different regions in the ocean that support life, scientists have divided the ocean into **habitat zones.** These zones are based on such features as water depth, temperature, and light penetration. Marine organisms are then classified according to the zones in which they live.

The amount of sunlight able to penetrate the water determines the **photic** and **aphotic habitat zones.** The photic (lighted) zone includes the upper ocean layers where there is enough light for plant growth. The permanently dark water mass below the photic zone is termed the aphotic (unlighted) zone.

The photic zone usually extends to depths ranging from 160 to 330 feet (50 to 100 meters). The depth depends on conditions that affect the amount of light able to pass through seawater. Light-scattering sources such as suspended material, or dense patches of microscopic plants limit light penetration. Therefore the photic zone extends much deeper in clear tropical waters than in murky coastal waters.

The ocean environment can be further subdivided both vertically and horizontally. Vertically, the ocean consists of two broad environments: the **pelagic** or water environment and the **benthic** or bottom environment. Pelagic organisms are those that live in the open water away from the sea bottom, while benthic organisms live on or in the sea bottom.

The pelagic environment is made up of two zones: 1) the neritic zone, which includes all waters over the continental shelves, and 2) the oceanic zone, which includes waters beyond the shelves.

The benthic environment is divided into three zones according to depth of the ocean floor. Ocean bottoms encompassing the continental slope down to about 13,000 feet (4,000 meters) represent the **bathyl zone.** Between 13,000 and 20,000 feet (4,000 and 6,000 meters) are the broad abyssal plains of ocean basins that make up the **abyssal zone.** The **hadal zone** includes the trench areas and ocean bottoms below 20,000 feet (6,000 meters). These three zones in the benthic environment constitute most of the aphotic areas of the ocean about which little is known.

The Plankton

One of the largest groups of organisms in the world's oceans is the plankton. The term plankton is derived from the Greek word *planktos*, which means "to wander." The plankton were given this name because they are those ocean plants and animals that have little or no swimming ability. The plankton float and are carried by water currents and tides. Most plankton are so tiny they cannot be seen with the naked eye, although some varieties such as the jellyfishes are quite large.

Plankton are interesting in that they may exhibit different life-styles. Some organisms spend their entire life in the plankton stage. Other organisms spend only a part of their lives as plankton. Examples are the eggs and young of fishes that develop into free-swimming adults and the young stages of crabs, snails, and clams that later live on the sea bottom.

Phytoplankton. Plant members of the plankton are called **phytoplankton.** These plants are generally very small and live in the photic zone. Phytoplankton use the energy of sunlight in the photic zone to make energy-rich organic compounds for food. The phytoplankton in turn become a food source for many other forms of ocean life.

Oceanic phytoplankton are largely composed of two major groups—**diatoms** and **dinoflagellates.** Diatoms are easily distinguished from dinoflagellates by their overlapping glasslike cell walls that give them a boxlike appearance.

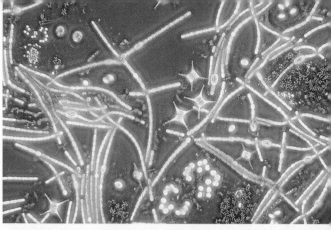

A jellyfish (*above*), a cluster of phytoplankton magnified 80 times (*above right*), and a school of damselfish (*right*) represent just three of the many thousands of kinds of marine organisms.

All living matter in diatoms is enclosed within a box constructed of silicon dioxide, the same material from which glass is made. Diatoms may occur singly or in chains of various designs. In contrast to the dinoflagellates, diatoms have no visible means of locomotion.

Dinoflagellates are recognized by their two whiplike tails, or flagella, which they use to propel themselves through water. They lack the silicon skeleton of diatoms but are often covered with stiff segments made of cellulose.

Most dinoflagellates exist as individual units and rarely join together to form chains such as those made by the diatoms. Some dinoflagellates produce poison substances in seawater that are capable of killing fish and invertebrates. Other dinoflagellates are **bioluminescent** (light producing), and when present in large numbers, they actually light up the wakes of boats, schools of fish, or waves breaking on the beach.

Zooplankton. **Zooplankton** are the animal members of the plankton community. Although less abundant, zooplankton are a much more diverse group than are the phytoplankton. Zooplankton consist of a varied array of juvenile and adult stages representing most of the animal groups found in the ocean. These range in size from microscopic, single-celled animals such as the protozoa to large multicellular organisms such as the jellyfish.

Virtually all marine animals are part of the zooplankton during some time in their life. The group known as copepods dominates the zooplankton throughout the world's oceans. Their importance is discussed in the section on ocean food chains.

Some colorful and interesting ocean dwellers include the peppermint lobster (*above left*), the purple anemone (*left*), and the northern elephant seal (*above*).

The Nekton

In contrast to the small, weak-swimming plankton are the larger, actively swimming marine animals known as the **nekton.** These animals are predominantly vertebrates (animals with backbones), whereas the plankton are dominated by invertebrates (animals without backbones). Oceanic nekton include a wide variety of bony fishes, sharks, rays, marine mammals, and reptiles. These nektonic organisms typically spend all or part of their lives in the pelagic zone.

Fishes constitute a large portion of oceanic nekton. Species such as the thresher sharks, flying fishes, tunas, marlins, and swordfishes spend their entire life in the pelagic zone and are most abundant in surface waters of the tropics. Other fishes such as herring, whale shark, and dolphin spend only their adult life in the deep ocean. Some nektonic fishes such as the tunas, herrings, and anchovies sustain major fishing industries.

Nektonic reptiles are almost entirely turtles and sea snakes. The marine sea turtles are one of several animal groups in danger of becoming extinct. There are several varieties of sea snakes, some of which have a very poisonous venom. These snakes usually do not attack humans unless they are provoked.

Marine mammals are a popular nekton group. Nektonic marine mammals include the whales, dolphins, porpoises, seals, and sea lions. Considerable public controversy has existed over the killing of marine mammals such as whales and seals. The number of whales has been drastically reduced in recent years. For this reason, laws have been passed to stop the killing of whales and other marine mammals.

Deep-sea giant worms live 8,000 feet (2,400 meters) below the ocean surface. Discovered in 1977, these unusual creatures are more than 8 feet (2.5 meters) long.

The Benthos

The third major group of marine organisms is the **benthos.** These are plants and animals living on the ocean bottom or in the sediment of the ocean floor. Benthic animals can live anywhere along the ocean bottom. However, benthic plants occur only along the ocean floor in the photic zone.

The benthos generally depend on the seafloor for food and shelter. The benthos include many kinds of fishes and other animals that can swim but are usually found near the ocean bottom. Eels and shrimp are good examples of these benthos because they feed on other organisms on the seafloor and burrow into soft muds along the bottom. Other benthic organisms attach themselves permanently to the bottom by means of roots or holdfast structures. These organisms are referred to as the sessile benthos. (Sessile means fixed in place or permanently attached.)

Benthic plants such as large kelp or brown algae cement themselves to the seafloor. Sponges and corals are dominant members of benthic communities in tropical oceans. Other abundant benthic groups are the marine worms and mollusks (chitons, snails, clams, oysters, and scallops) and arthropods (crabs, shrimp, and barnacles).

The Food Chain

Besides oxygen, food is the most vital requirement of marine organisms. Feeding among marine organisms is basically what oceanographers describe as the predator-prey relationship. This is simply a description of what an organism eats and what eats the organism.

To understand this relationship, we can construct a food chain, or a feeding pyramid, divided into three levels—each level containing a particular group of marine organisms. The first or lowest feeding level is the largest and contains plants, both phytoplankton and larger benthic algae. Plants occupy this first level because they are so numerous and can produce their own food. They are referred to as primary producers, because organisms in the other two higher levels cannot make their own food and are directly or indirectly dependent on the plants.

The second and third feeding levels get progressively smaller than the first because they contain fewer organisms. Animals, usually zooplankton, that are adapted to feeding on plants occupy the second feeding level and are called herbivores. These animals are preyed on by animals in the third feeding level.

A typical oceanic food chain would show microscopic diatoms being eaten by larger copepods. These would in turn become food for herring.

Such a food chain can of course extend further. Larger fish such as haddock may prey on the herring. Human beings even become part of the chain when they catch the haddock and eat it as food.

Deep-Sea Life

Some of the most mysterious organisms in the world's oceans live in the deep sea. The deep sea is that part of the ocean beyond the continental shelves and below the photic zone. As such, the deep sea is a very harsh environment of permanently cold, dark water that contains little food.

Deep-sea organisms possess a number of adaptations that allow them to survive in their stressful environment. Modified eyes are common adaptations to the lack of light in the deep sea. Fishes in the upper parts of the deep sea often have very large eyes. These large eyes give fishes great light-collecting ability in areas where light levels are very low. On the other hand, fishes living on the bottom of the deep sea often have very small or no eyes at all. Others have tube-shaped eyes. Certain deep-sea squids have one eye larger than the other—an unusual characteristic that is not well understood by biologists.

Lack of available food is another reason for bizarre physical features among some deep-sea organisms. Most deep-sea fishes are very small in size so that they need less food to survive. Many deep-sea fishes have extremely large mouths with very long teeth. These fishes can open their mouths wider than their own bodies and swallow prey larger than themselves.

Other fishes, such as the anglerfish, have modified fins that act as lures to attract prey. These lures may have a luminescent (light-producing) organ that the fish flashes on and off to attract prey.

Light-producing organs called photophores are a very common adaptation among deep-sea organisms. Photophores consist of either specialized cells or bacteria that can produce light. Fishes and squids use specially placed photophores to camouflage their bodies and thus avoid being eaten. Other fishes use photophores to produce a flash of light and "blind" potential predators. Photophores may also be used to light an area in order to find food.

▶ USES OF THE OCEAN

Oceans represent the last frontier on this planet where human beings may explore and find new resources. Recent advances in ocean navigation and engineering have allowed us to venture into all parts of the sea. Increases in human population have forced us to explore the ocean for new resources such as food and energy sources.

The Fishing Industry

One of the oldest and most important uses of the ocean is the harvest of marine organisms for food and other products. Most major fishing grounds of the world are located over the continental shelves. The only major fishing industries that operate in oceanic waters are those for tuna and whales.

Fishes constitute the greatest harvest from the sea. Herrings, sardines, and anchovies account for the largest harvests. Other important fish groups are the cods, hakes, mackerels,

Two of the ocean's most valuable resources are food and energy. Fishermen (*above*) haul in a big catch; a drilling platform (*below*) is needed to recover petroleum.

and tunas. Invertebrates such as shrimp, crabs, lobsters, squids, oysters, and clams are economically valuable and command high prices.

In addition to fish, mammals are also harvested from the sea. The major fishery for marine mammals has concentrated on harvesting whales. However, the overfishing of whales has virtually destroyed this industry. Seals and sea lions continue to be harvested.

Smaller industries harvest various species of algae or seaweed. The Japanese use algae for food. Algae and seaweed are also used to make industrial and medical products.

The decline in natural populations of marine organisms due to overfishing has resulted in humans culturing various plant and animal species. This farming of the seas is known as **mariculture.** (The term "aquaculture" describes all types of farming underwater, though it is also often used to mean just freshwater farming.) In the science of mariculture, marine plants and animals are grown under controlled conditions. Fishes that are grown commercially include Pacific salmon, mullet, soles, and yellowtail grouper. Invertebrates such as shrimps, prawns, oysters, mussels, and abalone also are cultured intensively.

Energy Sources

Great natural resources are present beneath the ocean floor. Important among these are the energy-related resources or the fossil fuels including oil and natural gas. These resources are drilled from the continental margins of such places as the Gulf of Mexico, California, and Alaska. A valuable by-product of oil exploration is the sulfur produced from many salt domes under the ocean floor.

A second energy-related use of the oceans is to produce electricity. Ocean waters are used to turn generators that make electricity.

Minerals

Several mineral resources lie on the ocean floor and in solution above it. Salt, magnesium, and bromine are the principal minerals being removed commercially. Magnesium is probably the most valuable. It is used to make alloys of lightweight metals and as a catalyst to speed chemical reactions. Two thirds of the world's bromine comes from the sea. Bromine is used as a gasoline additive, an insecticide, and for medicinal purposes.

The most immediately recoverable mineral resources are manganese and phosphate nodules (Nodules are small, rounded lumps of minerals.) Many attempts have been made to mine the trace quantities of gold that are found in the ocean, but these efforts are very expensive.The sea is also being used as a source of freshwater for industrial and domestic use. Desalination plants remove salt from seawater to produce freshwater.

Other Uses

The ocean has been a source of transportation ever since people learned to sail. Ocean-going vessels transport most of the world's food, machinery, and oil. The ocean floor is lined with telephone and telegraph cables. These serve as communication links between continents.

Recreation is another expanding use of the oceans. Boating, surfing, fishing, swimming, snorkeling, and diving are popular recreational uses of the ocean.

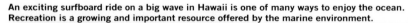

An exciting surfboard ride on a big wave in Hawaii is one of many ways to enjoy the ocean. Recreation is a growing and important resource offered by the marine environment.

Oil spills and oil fires are sometimes the unfortunate result of ocean drilling and ocean transport of fuels. Cleanup measures, such as those being used on this spill in the Gulf of Mexico, can help limit the damaging impact on the marine environment.

▶POLLUTION

For centuries the world's oceans have been used as a dumping ground. During the past 50 years, the oceans have received a wide variety of especially harmful pollutants. Well-known examples are oil pollution resulting from crude oil spilled at sea, the discharge of raw or poorly treated sewage, and the release of toxic chemicals such as DDT and PCB by industrialized countries.

More recent pollutants include the discharge of heated water from power plants located along the coast and the dumping of radioactive wastes in the deep. Despite theories to the contrary, oceans are not capable of absorbing all of these wastes.

Some effects of dumping wastes in the ocean may be seen easily, while others may require more time before distinct changes are noticed. Nevertheless, many pollutants have the ability to harm marine life. This harm may result in some marine organisms being eliminated or forced to move to more favorable areas. Other organisms may have their feeding and spawning grounds destroyed. Still others may not grow to maturity or may lose the ability to have young.

At present, our oceans remain in relatively good condition. We cannot permit the resources of the sea to be over-exploited or polluted. As a result, many countries such as the United States have laws that control the use of the seas and restrict the destruction of marine resources through overharvesting and pollution.

Technological advances have also enabled us to prevent many harmful effects of pollution. Toxic wastes can be burned aboard incineration ships at sea to avoid the dangers of burying these chemicals on land. New knowledge and special equipment have helped to contain most oil and chemical spills on the ocean and have reduced the damage they usually inflict on coastlines.

Limiting the amount of seafood harvested from the oceans has allowed fish and valuable invertebrates to reproduce and therefore restore their depleted populations. Recent advances in mariculture enable us to boost fisheries' stocks to keep food resources high.

These preventive measures and others will continue to help us improve the condition of our oceans. They will also protect the ocean's bountiful resources for generations to come.

ANDRE M. LANDRY
Texas A & M University

See also EARTH; ENERGY SUPPLY; FISHING INDUSTRY; GEOLOGY; OCEANOGRAPHY; OCEANS AND SEAS OF THE WORLD; PLANKTON; TIDES; UNDERWATER EXPLORATION; WATER POLLUTION; articles on individual marine animals.

OCEANIA. See PACIFIC OCEAN AND ISLANDS.

OCEAN LINERS

Ocean liners remain one of the most glamorous and luxurious means of transportation, although most people generally choose to use air travel when they want to reach their destinations quickly.

An ocean liner is a large ship that carries passengers across seas. Some ocean liners are built to carry just passengers and their belongings. Others carry cargo but allow a small number of passengers aboard.

The first half of the 1900's was the golden age of the luxury ocean liner. Britain, France, the Netherlands, Italy, and the United States each tried to outdo the others in attracting transatlantic passengers. To do this, they built and equipped fine ships. As time passed, the ships became larger, faster, and more luxurious.

In the late 1940's a change in transoceanic travel began to take place. Speeding airplanes were spanning the Atlantic and the Pacific in hours instead of days at a cost far lower than that of a sea voyage. A leisurely ocean crossing on a luxury liner began to lose some of its charm.

Great numbers of travelers preferred the advantages of swift, inexpensive air service, and, because of the high cost of operation, shipping lines were unable to meet the competition. One by one the great ocean liners were retired from transoceanic service. Today almost all of the luxury ships are used for vacation cruising, rather than as a means of crossing the ocean. Many cruise liners make ocean crossings as part of long cruises. These transoceanic voyages are sold to persons wishing to travel by ship. Sometimes these trips are called ''positioning voyages,'' because passengers take the cruise ship from one cruising area to another. For example, some ships that cruise the Caribbean Sea area in the winter also cruise the Mediterranean Sea in the summer. Their positioning cruises would take place in spring and fall.

Cruises may last anywhere from one day to three months. The most popular cruises are for one week. A ship may head for a single port or travel around the world with stops in many countries on many continents. Once in port, the ship becomes a hotel for its passengers. They leave it for sightseeing during the day and return to it at night.

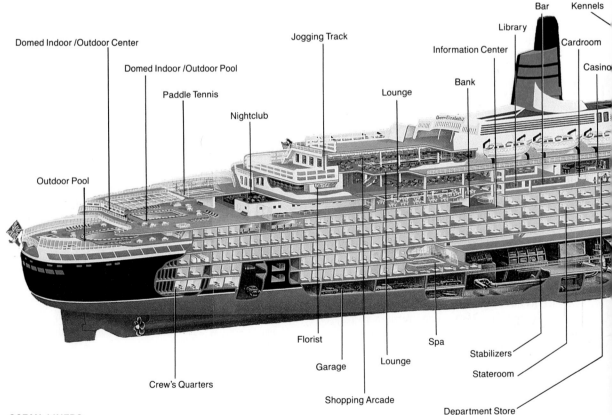

Domed Indoor /Outdoor Center
Domed Indoor /Outdoor Pool
Paddle Tennis
Nightclub
Outdoor Pool
Crew's Quarters
Jogging Track
Lounge
Florist
Garage
Shopping Arcade
Lounge
Spa
Bank
Information Center
Library
Bar
Kennels
Cardroom
Casino
Stabilizers
Stateroom
Department Store

GREAT OCEAN LINERS

In 1967 the Cunard Line of Britain launched the *Queen Elizabeth 2,* a 66,000-ton superliner that became the first great ship of the cruising era. The *QE2,* as it is popularly called, made its maiden voyage in 1969. The great liner is used for transatlantic crossings during the summer months. For the remainder of the year it is a luxury cruise ship.

The *QE2* represented the latest in ocean superliner design and construction. It is 294 meters (963 feet) long and can carry 2,000 passengers and a crew of almost half that number. About 160 crew members are needed just to staff the three dining rooms. There are four swimming pools, a theater, libraries, bars, lounges, a nightclub, shops, and a children's playroom.

The *QE2* is in the tradition of the great ocean liners of the past. Stories of transatlantic voyages aboard those luxury ships have become legend. Among the best-known vessels that made regular crossings were France's *Normandie* and Britain's sister ships, the *Queen Mary* and the *Queen Elizabeth,* all launched during the 1930's. These ships could cross the Atlantic in a little over four days.

During the height of the popularity of ocean travel, there was much rivalry among ships for speed. Greatly sought after was a trophy called the Blue Riband (ribbon). This trophy was awarded to the liner making the fastest Atlantic crossing. Every time the *Normandie* or the *Queen Mary* set a new speed record, the other would break it. The trophy was passed back and forth between them several times.

In the 1950's a new star appeared—the *United States.* On its maiden voyage in July, 1952, it took the Blue Riband for the United States fleet for the first time in 100 years. It made the eastbound crossing in 3 days, 10 hours, and 40 minutes, and the westbound trip in 3 days, 12 hours, and 12 minutes. The average speed for the round trip was 35 knots, a little more than 64 kilometers (40

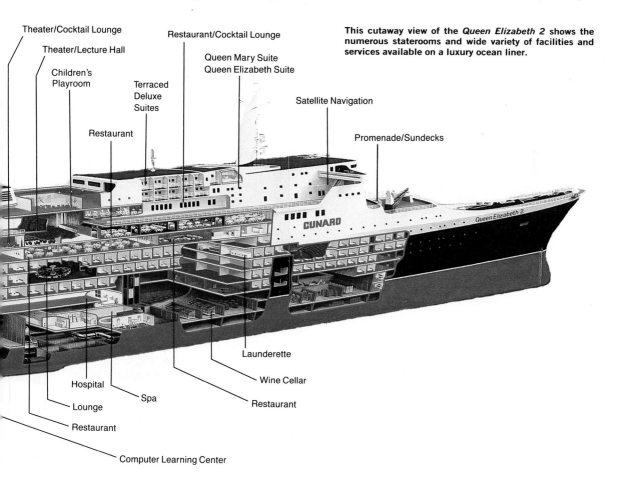

Theater/Cocktail Lounge
Theater/Lecture Hall
Children's Playroom
Restaurant
Terraced Deluxe Suites
Restaurant/Cocktail Lounge
Queen Mary Suite
Queen Elizabeth Suite
Satellite Navigation
Promenade/Sundecks
Launderette
Wine Cellar
Restaurant
Hospital
Spa
Lounge
Restaurant
Computer Learning Center

This cutaway view of the *Queen Elizabeth 2* shows the numerous staterooms and wide variety of facilities and services available on a luxury ocean liner.

miles) per hour. (A knot is 1 nautical mile, or 1,852 meters, per hour.)

As with other great ships of the time, the *United States* was designed to carry passengers in three classes—first, cabin, and tourist. First class was the most luxurious and expensive. Most cruise ships carry only one class, and the *United States* could not be adapted to modern needs. After 17 years of being the unchallenged queen of the seas, it was towed to a pier in Norfolk, Virginia, and retired from service.

Life on a Cruise Liner

A modern cruise ship is like a floating hotel. Besides the many cabins and staterooms where passengers sleep, there are lounges, dining rooms, kitchens, recreation rooms, shops, swimming pools, gymnasiums, a

The *Sun Princess* ocean liner is like a floating hotel. It is shown here moored for the evening off the scenic coast of an island in the Caribbean Sea.

movie theater, a hospital, a garage, and even a kennel for pets. Elevators carry the passengers from one deck to another.

Feeding several thousand people for a number of days requires huge quantities of food. Large liners carry tons of meat, poultry, fish, vegetables, eggs, and other foods.

A large ship needs hundreds of crew members to run it and tend to passengers. Room stewards clean the cabins and perform personal services for the passengers. Dining-room stewards wait on tables. Deck stewards set up deck chairs and serve food and drink to passengers on deck.

A ship's officers are in charge of running the ship and are responsible for the safety of all. The chief officer is the captain, who has authority over officers, crew, and passengers. In an emergency such as a storm or serious accident, the captain decides what action must be taken.

Soon after a liner sails, all passengers are required to attend a lifeboat drill. During the drill passengers must put on their life jackets and report to their assigned lifeboat station.

The Bridge and the Engine Room

Two places are especially important on a liner—the bridge and the engine room. The bridge, set high above the main deck, houses steering controls and navigation equipment. From the bridge the ship is guided to its destination.

Far below the decks is the engine room. Here large engines and dynamos generate the power to move the ship and to provide electricity for the liner's lights, heaters, air conditioners, radios, kitchen ranges, and other equipment.

▶ HISTORY OF OCEAN LINERS

In 1816, the first ocean liners began crossing the Atlantic, carrying mail and passengers. Compared to modern liners, these early sailing ships were not very comfortable. First-class passengers had only small cabins, and travelers in the cheapest class, called the steerage, had no cabins at all. They slept on wooden bunks stacked three deep in low, narrow spaces below deck. Starvation and illnesses that spread from steerage over the whole ship were not unusual.

Sailing ships had to face the problem of not being able to move if there was no wind. The ship might be becalmed for hours or even days. Steam-powered ships, however, did not have this problem. A steam engine could turn the ship's paddle anytime. In 1819 the American paddle-wheel steamship *Savannah* was the first steam-powered ship to cross the Atlantic, completing the trip in 29 days.

During the 1870's and 1880's, ocean liner service grew rapidly. This was chiefly because

What caused the *Titanic* tragedy?

The British ocean liner *Titanic* was the largest, most luxurious, and supposedly safest ship of its day. It was widely believed to be "unsinkable"—a belief that proved to be terribly wrong on the vessel's maiden voyage from Southampton, England, to New York City. Shortly before midnight on April 14, 1912, the *Titanic* struck an iceberg about 400 miles (650 kilometers) south of Newfoundland. Less than three hours later, the magnificent ship went down in the frigid Atlantic waters, taking with it more than 1,500 lives.

Why did the great ship sink and most of its roughly 2,200 passengers and crew perish? Experts say that human error was largely to blame for the disaster. Despite warnings of ice ahead, the crew increased speed in hopes of arriving early in New York. Too few lifeboats were aboard, and several were filled to less than half capacity when people started to evacuate the ship. And although distress calls were radioed, nearby ships failed to respond quickly.

New insights into the *Titanic* tragedy came in 1985, when a U.S.-French team of oceanographers located the long-lost ship, upright and in two large pieces on the ocean floor, nearly $2^1/_2$ miles (4 kilometers) below sea level. Later undersea expeditions found evidence that the construction of the *Titanic* may have also contributed to the tragedy.

Most experts originally believed that the iceberg must have ripped a huge gash along the mighty liner's steel hull. In 1997, however,

Too few lifeboats were aboard the *Titanic* when it hit an iceberg and sank in the Atlantic Ocean in 1912, as shown in this scene from the 1997 movie about the tragedy.

explorations of the wreck revealed only six narrow tears toward the bow. The total damage was less than the area of two sidewalk squares, but it spanned six watertight holds. This discovery suggested that the *Titanic* sank because of the unlucky locations of the tears, which let water flood the holds and spill into the rest of the forward hull.

Whatever the reasons for the tragedy, the *Titanic* continues to captivate the interest of researchers and the public. Camera-equipped submersibles have retrieved pieces of the eerie wreck, captured spectacular footage of it, and featured it in films, including one released in 1997 entitled *Titanic*, which attracted the largest box-office crowds in history.

of the large number of emigrants traveling from Europe to America. Luxury ocean liners were introduced at this time, each one larger, faster, and more luxurious than its predecessors.

The British Cunard ships *Lusitania* and *Mauretania*, each 240 meters (790 feet) long, were launched in 1907. They were the first ships to cross the Atlantic in less than five days. The *Lusitania* was torpedoed and sunk off the coast of Ireland by a German submarine early in World War I.

Ocean liners became so big and powerful that safety did not seem to be a problem. However, after the liner *Titanic* struck an iceberg and sank in 1912, international sea safety rules were adopted.

Traveling on ocean liners today is very safe. Modern navigation, communications, and fire-fighting equipment, as well as highly trained captains and crews, minimize the chance of accidents.

The day of the great liner is far from over. In 2004, the Cunard Line launched the *Queen Mary 2* (*QM2*). Measuring 345 meters (1,132 feet) and weighing 150,000 tons, the *QM2* is the largest passenger ship ever built. This liner and those that follow it will continue to provide people with safe and relaxing ocean voyages for years to come.

FRANK O. BRAYNARD
Curator, American Merchant Marine Museum

See also BOATS AND BOATING; ICEBERGS; SHIPS AND SHIPPING; TRANSPORTATION.

OCEANOGRAPHY

Oceanography is the study of the oceans, ocean floors, and air above the oceans. Oceans, often called seas, are huge bodies of water. Together they cover nearly three-fourths of the Earth's surface. Scientists, engineers, and technicians who study the oceans are called oceanographers.

The work of oceanographers is very important. Humans depend on the oceans for fish and other food. Just as the land has become overcrowded and polluted, the oceans have become more polluted and overfished. Oceanographers try to understand what controls the size of fish stocks and help govern-

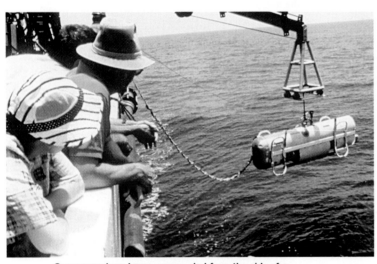

Oceanographers lower a sonar sled from the side of a research ship. The sled will be towed through the water to gather data on the composition of the seafloor.

ments decide how many fish can be caught each year.

The oceans help determine what weather will occur around the world each day. Oceans also influence Earth's climate. Climate is the weather that occurs over a long period. Changes in ocean temperature and ocean currents have a big effect on climate. They may help us understand global warming caused by the greenhouse effect.

Study of the ocean floors gives scientists information about Earth's past. Sediment or mud in the ocean floors contains the remains of plants and animals that lived in the seas long ago. It contains ash from ancient vol-

canic eruptions and a record of disasters in which asteroids smashed into our planet, killing the dinosaurs and other life. The ocean floors also give scientists information about the causes of earthquakes and the structure of Earth.

Yet scientists know less about the oceans than about the land surface. The oceans are the most mysterious places on Earth. Almost all of Earth's land has been explored, but big areas of the ocean have never been studied. Oceanographers still discover strange new creatures living deep in the oceans. People have explored mainly the pleasant parts of the ocean, where the water is warm, clear, and shallow. Most of the sea is cold, dark, and deep. The Arctic and Antarctic areas are the coldest and stormiest. These regions have been explored very little, even though they have a great influence on Earth's climate.

▶ WAYS OF STUDYING THE OCEAN

Scientists study the oceans in different ways. Some spend long months at sea on special science ships called oceanographic research vessels. These ships are floating laboratories equipped with scientific instruments and computers. Oceanographers use the ships to collect and test water samples, measure ocean currents, study ocean animals and plants, and gather samples and other data from deep beneath the ocean floors. Some oceanographers even go into the seas in special submarines or scuba gear.

Other oceanographers never go to sea. Instead, they work mainly in laboratories, often studying the oceans with computers and information collected by satellites that orbit Earth. Ocean scientists often work closely with ocean technicians and engineers, who have important roles in operating and designing oceanography equipment.

Branches of Oceanography

Most oceanographers specialize in one of the four major branches of the science. The four branches deal with the physics, chemistry, geology, and biology of the sea. Scientists who work in these branches are called physical oceanographers, chemical oceanographers, geological oceanographers, and biological oceanographers.

Physical oceanographers study the physics of the sea. They are concerned with the forces that move seawater, affect its temperature, and change it in other ways. Some, for instance, study how the wind and sun cause waves and currents and how waves and currents move the water. (Currents are huge movements of water that flow in specific directions through the oceans.) Others study the rise and fall of tides or the flow of water below the surface.

Chemical oceanographers are concerned with the chemistry of seawater. They study the kinds and amounts of chemicals dissolved in seawater and changes that occur in the chemicals. The amount of salt, or salinity, in seawater is especially important. It decides what plants and animals can live in an area of water, and affects the water in other ways. Chemical oceanographers may study pollutants and other chemicals that people put into the sea. Some of these are washed into the oceans from rivers. Chemicals also enter the ocean from the atmosphere. Oceanographers use some of these chemicals as identification tags, or tracers, to understand how the water is moving.

Geological oceanographers study the sediments and rocks found under the sea. They sometimes are called marine geologists. Some determine where the sediments came from and how they got to their resting places on the seafloor. Sediments may contain the remains of ancient animals that once lived in the ocean. By knowing the temperature and salinity that these animals needed to live, scientists can figure out how the ocean and the air above it have changed over thousands or millions of years.

Geological oceanographers also study movement of the huge plates of rock that make up Earth's crust. The crust is Earth's solid outer layer. All the continents sit on these plates and move with them. The movement causes earthquakes. Research by geological oceanographers thus helps us understand the causes of earthquakes. Other geological oceanographers study the way the whole Earth has changed since its birth 4.5 billion years ago. Still others study how erosion is changing beaches and coastlines.

Marine life, such as this coral in Australia's Great Barrier Reef, is studied by biological oceanographers, also known as marine biologists.

Biological oceanographers study life in the sea. They also are known as marine ecologists or marine biologists. Some are interested in microscopic plants, corals, and other animals that live in the sunlit upper waters. These organisms often are sensitive to ultraviolet (UV) light from the sun. More UV light is reaching the surface now because of damage to the ozone layer in the atmosphere. Biological oceanographers study UV light's effects on ocean life, especially the microscopic plants, or plankton, that supply food for almost all other ocean life. Others study the larger animals, such as fish and whales, some of which provide food for people.

Animals and plants also live in the dark, cold environment on the seafloor. Biological oceanographers have discovered a whole new group of creatures that live around hydrothermal vents. These are hot springs that spurt warm water, rich in chemicals, from Earth's interior. Communities of living things around hydrothermal vents have worked out a way of getting energy from the hot spring chemicals. Unlike life elsewhere on Earth, they do not rely on sunlight for life.

This article is an overview of the science of oceanography. The article OCEAN describes the physical characteristics of the ocean as well as ocean life. The article UNDERWATER EXPLORATION provides more detail on the ships, instruments, and other technology used in studying the oceans. The article UNDERWATER ARCHAEOLOGY discusses discoveries about ancient shipwrecks and cities submerged below the oceans.

Working Together

Most oceanographers specialize in just one of these branches. Yet they must know about the other areas of oceanography. Biologists need to be aware of changes in water chemistry and circulation patterns and how these might influence living creatures. Geologists must understand the effects of waves, tides, and currents on the shoreline and seabed. Physical oceanographers need to know how chemicals come into the oceans in rivers and rainfall, and how they are changed by chemical reactions.

There often are not sharp dividing lines between branches of oceanography. A physical oceanographer, for instance, may do studies that involve a lot of chemistry. A chemical oceanographer may study how water chemistry affects ocean plants and animals.

Understanding the oceans often takes teams of scientists from different disciplines, or fields. This is called interdisciplinary research. Each scientist on an interdisciplinary team studies a problem with his or her own skills. Then they put all the knowledge together to find answers.

▶ OCEANS AND CLIMATE

Interdisciplinary research is especially important in understanding complex problems such as how the oceans affect Earth's climate and weather. Scientists know the oceans play a big role in global climate change caused by the greenhouse effect. The greenhouse effect is a slow warming of the Earth due to the release of carbon dioxide and other gases into the air by cars, factories, and farming. Carbon dioxide traps heat just like the panes of glass in a greenhouse or in a car parked in the sun.

The oceans are one of the major sinks, or natural disposal sites, for carbon dioxide. They take in huge amounts of carbon dioxide from the atmosphere. Ocean plants trap some of the carbon dioxide in their bodies during photosynthesis. Ocean animals trap some in their shells. When plants and animals die,

they sink to the ocean floor, trapping the carbon dioxide. The amount of carbon dioxide the oceans trap depends on ocean temperature, waves, currents, ice cover, and other factors. Oceanographers want to know how all these factors work together as a system—actually a climate control system. It could help scientists predict the future climate.

Earth's oceans are as important as the atmosphere in deciding weather conditions. For instance, a warming of Pacific Ocean waters, called El Niño, may bring unusually cold, wet, stormy weather to some parts of the United States. El Niño may mean a mild, dry, easy winter for other areas.

▶ MAPPING AND MEASURING THE OCEAN

People have measured the ocean since ancient times. Old maps of the world show the coastline, where ocean meets land. This tells the size of the ocean's surface area. Oceanographers need to make many other measurements in order to understand the ocean. Some of the most important are ocean depth, salinity, pressure, density, temperature, acoustics, and optics. They also need to mea-

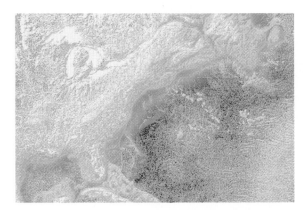

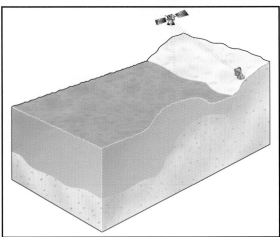

Several instruments are used to map the seafloor. *Left to right:* Satellites can detect variations in the ocean's surface height. Multibeam sonar emits sound waves from an array of sources mounted on a ship's hull. The time it takes for the sound waves to bounce back from the ocean bottom is used to determine depth. Side-scan sonar equipment, towed behind a ship, uses sound waves to provide information about the contours of the ocean floor.

sure ocean circulation, which is the flow of water from one part of the ocean to another. Measurements of the seafloor also are very important.

Some measurements can be done with cameras and sensors on satellites orbiting high above Earth's surface. For others, oceanographers have to obtain actual samples of seawater or sediment from the ocean floor. Oceanographers often measure big areas of the sea with instrument packages lowered from or towed behind research ships. The packages have several different electronic sensors and other instruments that send information through a cable for storage in the ship's computers.

Measuring Depth

Ocean depth varies from a few inches near the shore to almost 6.6 miles (10.6 kilometers) in deep-sea trenches. Oceanographers find water's depth by sounding, or taking a sounding. At one time, sounding was done with markers spaced 1 fathom (6 feet or 1.8 meters) apart on a long rope. The rope had a heavy weight at one end and was lowered into the water. A person could tell the depth by lowering the rope and feeling when the weight touched the bottom. Counting the number of markers then told the depth. This was very difficult to do in deep water, so scientists knew very little about the bottom of the ocean.

Sounding is now done with sound waves, or sonar (SOund Navigation And Ranging). Scientists use a device called an echo sounder that is located on the bottom hull of a ship. It makes a continuing series of sounds that echo or reflect off the ocean bottom. Sound waves travel through water at a speed of about 4,800 feet (1,460 meters) per second in water. By measuring the time needed for the sound to reach the ocean floor and return, scientists can figure out the water's depth. Some echo sounders scan back and forth in front of a ship. Scientists can use the resulting data to produce a map of the bottom.

Sounding also can produce an outline or profile of the ocean floor. As a ship moves along, it makes a continuous record of depth. By collecting these records from the many ships that have crisscrossed the ocean, geolo-

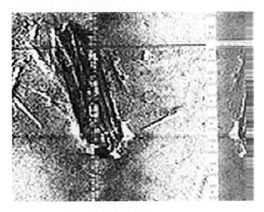

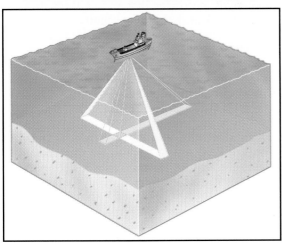

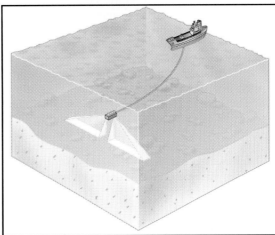

A CTD is lowered over the side of an oceanographic research ship with a crane. The instrument will measure the conductivity, temperature, and depth of the water.

canoes than near undersea valleys. The stronger gravity pulls more water toward big undersea formations. Water level above a huge seafloor mountain may be 5 feet (1.5 meters) higher than the average ocean level. Oceanographers use sea level measurement to make maps of the ocean bottom in far greater detail than is possible with echo sounding by ships. This technique has revealed features of the ocean bottom, such as underwater mountains called seamounts, which had not been seen before with echo sounders.

Sampling Water Chemistry and Temperature

Oceanographers can learn much about the ocean by checking its chemical properties and temperature.

Two of the most important measurements for oceanographers are the water's temperature and salinity. These measurements are important because temperature and salinity help determine how water circulates, or flows from one part of the ocean to another. Together, temperature and salinity also determine water's density, or weight. Cold, salty water is denser than warm water that is fresher or has less salt. Masses of cold, salty water in the ocean thus will sink, causing layers of water below to move out of the way. These movements are the power behind ocean currents and upward flow of water containing nutrients for fish and other marine life. Oceanographers can even learn something about the movement of the water from the temperature and salinity structure alone using the laws of physics.

Oceanographers check salinity and temperature with an electronic instrument called a CTD. It measures water's conductivity, temperature, and depth. Conductivity is the amount of electricity that passes through a material. Scientists can find salinity from this measurement because more electricity flows through salty water than fresh water. Other important properties of seawater, such as oxygen content and clarity, also are measured with electronic instruments.

The CTD is a large instrument that is lowered over the side of an oceanographic research ship with a crane and winch. Data from the CTD travels back to the ship's computers through an electric cable. CTD's also collect water samples in special containers

gists have made detailed charts of the ocean bottom. They show high mountain ranges, flat plains, volcanoes, and deep valleys or trenches. Echo sounding also can be used to study the thickness and other properties of sediments just below the ocean floor. Another kind of echo sounder is anchored to the ocean bottom and sends pings of sound toward the surface. The speed of sound in water changes with temperature, salinity, and other factors. By analyzing signals from the inverted echo sounder, scientists can see how water temperature and other traits change over long periods.

Remote sensing instruments on satellites help oceanographers map the ocean floor. They do so by measuring the surface height of the oceans. Although the sea surface may seem almost flat, its height varies by hundreds of yards over great distances. The differences occur because the pull of gravity is stronger near underwater mountains and vol-

called Nishkin Bottles. They are arranged around the CTD on a special circular framework called a rosette sampler. Actual samples of water are necessary for taking other chemical measurements of ocean water.

Geological Sampling

Oceanographers have several ways of collecting samples of sediment, rock, and other material from the ocean floor. The kind of instrument depends on whether the bottom is hard or soft.

Above: The *JOIDES Resolution* is outfitted for deep-sea drilling. *Right:* Crew members prepare the drill, which will collect core samples of the seafloor. *Bottom right:* In the ship's laboratory, scientists study a core sample of seafloor material that has been split in half lengthwise.

A coring tube can be used when the seafloor consists of soft mud. The tube is a long section of pipe several inches in diameter. It is sharp on one end and has heavy weights on the other. The coring tube is lowered over the side of a research ship on a wire until it is near the bottom. Then it is allowed to fall free, and its weights drive it into the seabed. The bottom sediments are trapped within the pipe. When the sampler is hauled back on board ship, the sediments are pushed out of the tube and analyzed. Another tool is the hydraulic piston corer. It uses seawater at high pressure to drive a hollow steel tube through sediment. To penetrate harder sediment and rock, drill bits may be attached to the corer to cut through the sediment.

Other samples can be taken with a rock dredge. This is a long basket made of wire or chain, with a sharp cutting edge. It is lowered to the bottom, and the ship moves ahead slowly, dragging the dredge along the sea bottom. Fragments of rock are broken off and collected in the basket. When the instrument is brought on board, the scientist can examine the rocks and determine the geology of that piece of the seafloor. The echo sounder, which is used to determine the ocean's depth, can also be used to observe the structure of the solid material under the bottom.

Sampling the seafloor in deep water takes very expensive equipment. Scientists from around the world have joined in the Ocean Drilling Program (ODP) to share the equipment for deep-sea drilling. Since 1985, ODP scientists have used a drill ship called the *JOIDES Resolution*. It is named for the group of universities that sponsor ODP, the Joint Oceanographic Institutions for Deep Sea Drilling. The *Resolution* can bring up samples of the seafloor in water depths up to about 5 miles (8.2 kilometers). Some of the cores of seafloor material are about 29 feet (9.5 meters) long. Information from the *JOIDES Resolution* has allowed scientists to reconstruct a picture of how Earth's surface and climate have changed over billions of years.

Biological Sampling

Biological oceanographers often need samples of plants and animals that live in the sea. Some of the plants and animals swim or float through the water. Others live attached to the seafloor or burrow into it. Different sampling techniques are needed to catch these two biological populations. Scientists use special nets to catch floating or swimming forms of life. Many of the floating creatures, called plankton, are so small they can only be seen under a microscope. A very fine net is required to catch them. The net is put over the side of a ship and lowered to the proper depth. The ship moves ahead slowly, pulling the net through the water and catching the plankton.

Dr. Robert Ballard points out the features of *Jason*, an unmanned submersible, which can be sent to the seafloor to take pictures and collect samples and other data.

When the net is brought on board, the biological oceanographer can examine the catch under a microscope and determine what is living in the ocean at that place. Drag nets are used to catch creatures that live on the seafloor or burrow into it. These are special nets that cut into the sediment as they are dragged along the bottom. They catch creatures swimming near the bottom, such as fish, and those living in the sediment, such as clams and worms. In addition, scientists now can ride down to the bottom of the sea in small submarines called submersibles. The submersibles have special tools that can collect animals and plants and bring them to the surface for laboratory study. Unmanned submersibles equipped with television cameras and tools for collecting samples also are sent to the seafloor. Scientists control these robot vehicles remotely from a ship.

▶ MONITORING OCEAN CHANGES

In order to really understand the oceans, scientists must take repeated measurements of temperature, salinity, currents, and other conditions over long periods. This long-term watch on changing ocean conditions is called monitoring. It is especially important to find out how the oceans affect Earth's climate.

Scientists monitor the oceans with packages of scientific instruments sometimes called ocean observatories. They are put into the ocean by research ships and anchored to the seafloor. The instruments collect and record information for months or years at a time. Scientists may get the information from ocean observatories in several ways. For instance, they may run electric cables from the observatory along the ocean floor to ground receiving stations. Sometimes the observatory stores data in a recorder. Scientists haul the observatory to the surface and remove the recorder. Sometimes a submersible is used to retrieve the data and install a new recorder.

One instrument used to study ocean currents rises to the ocean surface every few weeks. While rising through the water, it measures temperature, salinity, and other conditions. At the surface, it reports to the laboratory by satellite. In the future, the ocean may be seeded with thousands of such devices all cycling up and down and sending their information back to the scientists on a routine basis. This will bring oceanographers much closer to meteorologists in their ability to routinely monitor the ocean conditions.

Oceanographers may also make long-term observations by living on the seafloor in laboratories. The first underwater laboratory went into use in 1997. Located off the coast of Florida, it allows crews of six scientists to do research missions lasting up to ten days.

Satellites orbiting Earth also monitor ocean conditions with cameras, radar, and other sensors. This information is especially valuable because satellites gather information from huge areas of the ocean. The information from satellites also is quickly available for scientists to analyze.

▶ HISTORY OF OCEANOGRAPHY

People began to explore the oceans thousands of years ago. Ancient Phoenicians and Greeks were skilled shipbuilders and sailors. They used the seas as highways to travel from one place to another, as a source of food, and to trade with distant lands. For the most part, however, ancient sailors stayed within sight of the shore. They could not navigate, or find their way, on the open seas, and feared getting lost. Most of the sea was a great mystery.

The scientific study of the oceans began in the 1700's, when many of the early voyages of exploration included scientists. Members of the expedition would explore the lands they found and the oceans they crossed. Typical of these expeditions were the voyages of British sea captain James Cook aboard his ship *Endeavour*. For eleven years, starting in 1768, he explored the South Pacific, discovering many new lands and charting the seas as he traveled. Much of New Zealand and Australia were mapped for the first time.

About the same time as Cook's voyages, American statesman and inventor Benjamin Franklin published a map of the Gulf Stream, the great current that flows along the east coast of the United States. This helped ships that were sailing between the United States and Europe. Another early contributor to knowledge of the oceans was Lieutenant Matthew Maury, an American naval officer. He took meteorological and oceanographic data from the logbooks of ships and consolidated them into a book, *The Physical Geography of the Sea* (1855). This was one of the first good books written about the new science of oceanography.

The first expedition with the sole purpose of studying the sea was that of the H.M.S. *Challenger*. In 1872, this British warship was supplied with the best available equipment for measuring oceanic factors and for taking samples of the water, sediments, and living creatures. The *Challenger* traveled around the world, sailing 69,000 miles (111,000 kilometers) in three and a half years. More than 4,700 new types of marine life were discovered at 500 sampling locations. The voyage

The British ship H.M.S. *Challenger* helped open the modern era of oceanography with an around-the-world expedition completed in 1876.

was completed in 1876, and the results of the expedition filled 50 large books.

In the 50 years following the *Challenger* expedition, many governments sent out research expeditions. Some of these sailed to distant parts of the world. Others studied the coastline and nearby waters that were of special interest to sailors and fishermen.

During World War II (1939–45), interest in the oceans increased. It was recognized that oceanic factors affect the operations of warships and submarines.

Since then, the science of oceanography has continued to grow. Ships have been designed especially for research on the seas. Research submarines and diving equipment have been developed that allow scientists to descend to the bottom of the ocean. Scientists can remotely guide small unmanned submersibles to take pictures and collect data, and they can retrieve core samples from the seafloor using powerful drills. New instruments are continually being developed that allow scientists to observe and sample the ocean and its inhabitants in novel and revealing ways.

Joint international efforts in ocean research include programs designed to give a global view of how the ocean works and how it affects life on land. One such program in the 1990's, called the World Ocean Circulation Experiment (WOCE), involved scientists from about 30 countries. They worked together to develop a more accurate picture of

Is there a new source of energy in the oceans?

Oceanographers have discovered a fantastic new form of energy deep in the oceans. It is ice that "burns." Scientists call the material gas hydrates. Chunks of hydrates look just like dirty ice. When pieces are brought to the surface, they sizzle, pop, sputter, and jump around like bacon in a hot frying pan. If someone lights a match, the chunks will burst into flame.

Gas hydrates are not ordinary water ice. Rather, they are made from gases such as methane. Methane is the main material in natural gas. These gases constantly leak from the seafloor. If the conditions are right, ice forms and molecules of the gas are trapped inside. It takes just the right temperature and pressure for gas hydrates to form. When brought to the surface, where the pressure is lower, the gas sizzles out of the ice like bubbles of carbon dioxide from a bottle of soft drink. If lit, the escaping gas burns with a clean blue flame.

Huge deposits of gas hydrates exist in the seafloor in many parts of the world. Off the United States coast alone, there may be 35 times more methane in gas hydrates than the entire world's supply of methane in natural gas. One gas hydrate deposit off the coast of North Carolina and South Carolina could supply the entire country for more than 50 years.

Can gas hydrates be used as an energy source? The big problem is finding a way to mine gas hydrates and bring them to the surface. Gas hydrates often are mixed with ocean floor sediments at water depths greater than 1,000 feet (300 meters). It would be very expensive to dig up the icy chunks and bring them to the surface. Once on the surface, gas hydrates immediately start to break down. The valuable methane gas sizzles out of the ice. The ice itself starts to melt, releasing more gas.

Oceanographers are trying to find inexpensive ways to mine gas hydrates. If they succeed, the world could have an abundant new source of energy from the oceans.

▶ **CAREERS IN OCEANOGRAPHY**

Oceanography can be an exciting and challenging career. Ocean scientists, ocean engineers, and ocean technicians work for universities, government agencies, oceanographic research institutes, petroleum and natural gas companies, and other organizations. Many ocean scientists teach at universities in addition to doing their own research.

A person interested in a career in oceanography usually takes science and mathematics courses in college. Many ocean scientists major in a subject related to one of the fields of ocean chemistry. They get degrees in biology, chemistry, physics, or geology. Others major in meteorology, mathematics, engineering, or other fields. Hundreds of colleges and universities offer undergraduate degrees in these fields. Students usually get an undergraduate degree after their first four years in college.

After finishing undergraduate study, most oceanographers continue in graduate school. They study for a graduate, or advanced, degree in oceanography. Some get a master's degree or a doctorate degree. A number of universities offer graduate degrees in oceanography.

Engineers and technicians often work with ocean scientists and have important roles in oceanography. Engineers design towers that must stand on the seafloor, drilling equipment, and many kinds of instruments used in studying the oceans. Some ocean engineers also do research on the movement of water, ocean sediments, and other topics. Ocean engineers usually have an undergraduate degree in an engineering field. They may take undergraduate or advanced courses in oceanography.

Ocean technicians operate equipment, collect data, and conduct experiments. Without them, little research in oceanography would be possible. Ocean technicians often have undergraduate or associate degrees in a technical or scientific field.

The world will rely on ocean scientists in the future for solutions to practical problems. Important areas of study include global climate change, preventing further declines in fish populations, and protecting the oceans from pollution.

NELSON G. HOGG, PH.D.
Woods Hole Oceanographic Institution

how the ocean circulates. Scientists recognize that the ocean and atmosphere are forever changing because of natural causes and human activity. Oceanography became more important in the late 1990's as scientists realized that ocean conditions influence the global climate.

OCEANS AND SEAS OF THE WORLD

Oceans and seas cover nearly three-fourths of the Earth's surface. Although the words "ocean" and "sea" are often interchanged, they can also differ in meaning. The word "ocean" is generally included in the names of only five bodies of water—the Atlantic, Pacific, Indian, Arctic, and Antarctic. They are the major bodies of salt water that extend between the continents. Seas are smaller than oceans. Most seas, in fact, are small sections of an ocean. Gulfs and bays are small sections of oceans that border land.

The Adriatic Sea is an arm of the Mediterranean Sea between Italy and the Balkan Peninsula. See the article MEDITERRANEAN SEA in Volume M.

The Aegean Sea is an arm of the Mediterranean Sea between Greece and Turkey. See the article MEDITERRANEAN SEA in Volume M.

The Andaman Sea is an arm of the Indian Ocean between the Andaman Islands and the Malay Peninsula. Ships pass through it on their way from India and Myanmar to Singapore and the China seas. Yangon, the capital of Myanmar, is one of its leading seaports.

The Antarctic Ocean is the name sometimes used when referring to southern parts of the Atlantic, Pacific, and Indian oceans that surround the continent of Antarctica. For more information about this southern ocean, see the article ANTARCTICA in Volume A.

The Arabian Sea is part of the Indian Ocean between India and the Arabian Peninsula. Petroleum from countries bordering the Persian Gulf and the Gulf of Oman is transported by tankers across the Arabian Sea to other parts of the world. The waters of this sea are very warm because almost all of the Arabian Sea lies between 10 degrees north latitude and the Tropic of Cancer.

The Aral Sea. See the article LAKES in Volume L.

The Arctic Ocean is an almost landlocked sea extending from the North Pole to about 70 degrees north latitude. Many Canadian and Siberian islands lie in the shallow seas fringing the deep Arctic basin. The Arctic is mostly covered by ice. The salinity (salt content) is lower than that of any other ocean. For more information about the Arctic Ocean, see the article ARCTIC in Volume A.

The Atlantic Ocean is a huge body of water that extends from the Arctic to the Antarctic regions and from Europe and Africa on the east to the Americas on the west. See the article ATLANTIC OCEAN in Volume A.

The Sea of Azov is an inland sea located south of Ukraine. It is connected to the Black Sea by the Kerch Strait. Fishing for sturgeon, carp, pike, and herring is important. Seaports are Kerch, Taganrog, Rostov, and Zhdanov.

The Baltic Sea in northern Europe is bordered by Denmark, Sweden, Finland, Poland, Germany, Estonia, Latvia, Lithuania, and parts of Russia. The gulfs of Bothnia, Finland, and Riga are arms of the Baltic Sea.

Much of the Baltic is frozen for three to five months each year. Navigation is limited to the ice-free months. The Baltic receives the waters of many rivers, including the Neva, Narva, Western Dvina, Neman, Oder, and Vistula. These freshwater rivers keep the salinity of the Baltic low in comparison to other seas. This accounts for the Baltic's long period of freezing. Chief ports are Helsinki (Finland), Copenhagen (Denmark), Stockholm (Sweden), St. Petersburg (Russia), Riga (Latvia), Szczecin and Gdansk (Poland), and Kiel (Germany).

The Barents Sea is an arm of the Arctic Ocean north of Norway and Russia. The North Atlantic Drift (an extension of the Gulf Stream) keeps Murmansk, the chief seaport, ice-free in winter when other Russian ports are frozen in. The Barents Sea is an important commercial fishing ground. The sea was named for William Barents, a Dutch navigator of the 1500's.

The Beaufort Sea is part of the Arctic Ocean lying north of Alaska and west of the Arctic Archipelago.

The Bering Sea is the northern part of the Pacific Ocean between Siberia and Alaska. It is a region of storms, cold, and fog. The Bering Sea is connected to the Arctic Ocean by the Bering Strait. This narrow strait is only 56 miles (90 kilometers) wide. The Pribilof Islands in the Bering Sea are the breeding ground for fur seals. Fishing and whaling are also important. Nome (Alaska) and Anadyr (Siberia) are the main ports. Between 1728 and 1741, the sea was explored by Danish navigator Vitus Bering, after whom the sea was eventually named.

The Bismarck Sea is a southwestern arm of the Pacific Ocean between New Guinea and the Bismarck Archipelago. The first Europeans to discover the Bismarck Sea were William Van Schouten and Jacob Lemaire, Dutch explorers who rounded the southern tip of South America and crossed the Pacific Ocean in 1616.

The Black Sea is a large inland sea between Europe and Asia. Bulgaria, Romania, Ukraine, Russia, Moldova, Georgia, and Turkey are bordering countries. The Black Sea is connected to the Mediterranean Sea by a series of straits—the Bosporus, the Sea of Marmara, and the Dardanelles. The Dnieper and Danube rivers, as well as many other European rivers, empty into the Black Sea. The sea is nearly ice-free all year. Its principal ports are Odesa and Sevastopol (Ukraine), Varna (Bulgaria), Constanta (Romania), and Trabzon (Turkey). Some fishing is carried on, principally for herring, carp, and sturgeon. Because of a pleasant subtropical climate, the European shores of the Black Sea have long been popular resort areas. However, its waters have become increasingly polluted by oil tankers and other industrial shipping vessels.

The Caribbean Sea is an arm of the Atlantic Ocean surrounded by Central America, the West Indies, and northern South America. See the article CARIBBEAN SEA AND ISLANDS in Volume C.

The Caspian Sea. See the article LAKES in Volume L.

The China Sea borders on continental China. Taiwan divides the China Sea into the East China Sea and the South China Sea. The East China Sea lies between the eastern coast of China and the Ryukyu Islands. China's largest river, the Yangtze (Chang), empties into the East China Sea. Shanghai is its major seaport. The South China Sea is located between the Southeast Asian mainland and Indonesia and the Philippine islands. The southern half of the sea is only about 600 feet (180 meters) deep. In the north, parts of the sea are more than 15,000 feet (4,570 meters) deep. The South China Sea is subject to violent typhoons. Its main seaports are Singapore, Ho Chi Minh City, Guangzhou, Hong Kong, Bangkok, and Manila.

The Chukchi Sea is a branch of the Arctic Ocean lying north of the Bering Strait. Because it lies so far north, the Chukchi is frozen or blocked by ice for most of the year. It is navigable only in August and September.

The Coral Sea lies between Australia and the Solomon Islands and Vanuatu. The sea is dotted with many coral islands and bordered by the Great Barrier Reef of Australia. In 1942, during World War II, a major battle between the U.S. and Japanese fleets took place there.

The Dead Sea. See the article LAKES in Volume L.

The Sea of Galilee. See the article LAKES in Volume L.

The Indian Ocean is the world's third largest ocean. It touches Asia, Australia, Antarctica, and Africa and forms two large indentations in the southern coast of Asia: the Arabian Sea and the Bay of Bengal. Many rivers empty into the Indian Ocean—the Indus, Ganges, Irrawaddy, Brahmaputra, and Shatt al Arab from Asia and the Zambezi and Limpopo from Africa. See the article INDIAN OCEAN in Volume I.

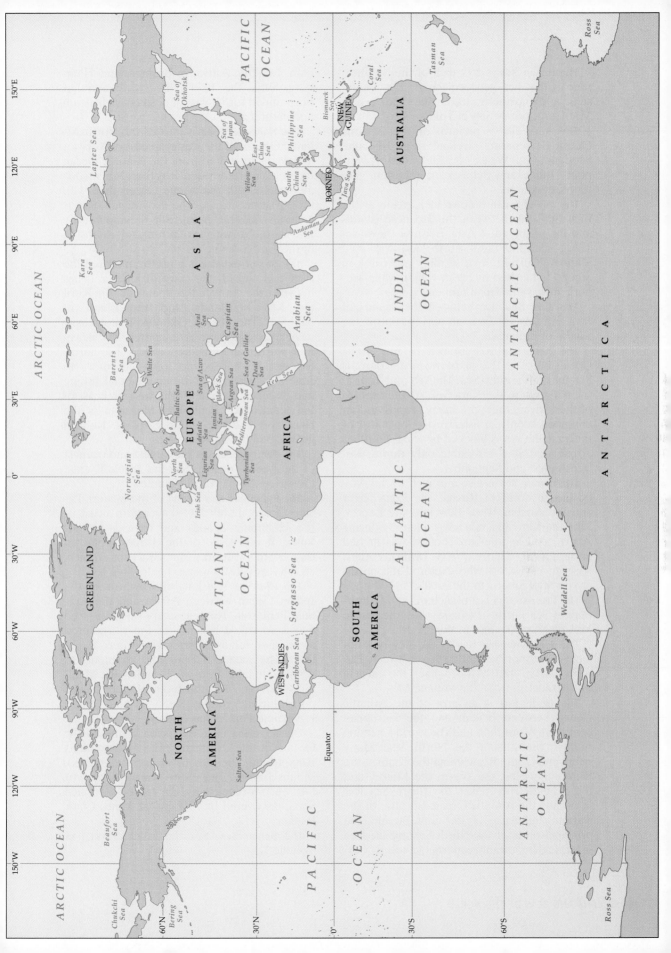

The Ionian Sea is a branch of the Mediterranean that lies between the Balkan Peninsula and northern Italy. See the article MEDITERRANEAN SEA in Volume M.

The Irish Sea is an arm of the Atlantic Ocean. It separates Ireland from England, Scotland, and Wales. Its chief ports (Liverpool, Dublin, and Belfast) are important centers of commerce.

The Sea of Japan (known by Koreans as the East Sea) lies between the Japanese islands and the mainland of Asia. Because the warm Japan Current flows north and the cold Okhotsk Current flows south, Vladivostok in Siberia is blocked by ice in winter while seaports in western Japan remain ice-free.

The Java Sea lies between the islands of Java and Borneo. Its main port is Jakarta, the capital of Indonesia.

The Kara Sea is a branch of the Arctic Ocean north of Russia, between the Barents Sea and the Laptev Sea. The Ob and Yenisei rivers flow into the Kara Sea. At the mouths of these rivers there are many islands and an abundant supply of fish. Throughout most of the year the sea is blocked by ice. Like other Arctic seas, it is navigable only during ice-free August and September.

The Laptev Sea is also a branch of the Arctic Ocean north of Russia. The Lena River and the Anabar River flow into the Laptev. Like the Kara Sea, it is navigable only during August and September. The sea was named in honor of Khariton and Dmitri Laptev, Russian navigators who explored the northern coast of Siberia in the 1700's.

The Ligurian Sea is a branch of the Mediterranean Sea north of Corsica. See the article MEDITERRANEAN SEA in Volume M.

The Mediterranean Sea is the nearly landlocked body of water that lies between Europe, Asia, and Africa. See the article MEDITERRANEAN SEA in Volume M.

The North Sea is an arm of the Atlantic Ocean between Britain and the European continent. More than half the world's herring supply comes from the North Sea. Many rivers empty into it, including the Thames, the Rhine, the Elbe, the Weser, the Meuse, and the Scheldt. This makes the North Sea less salty than the Atlantic Ocean. Because of the warming influence of the Gulf Stream, the principal ports of the North Sea are ice-free in winter. Important seaports include Rotterdam, London, Antwerp, Bremen, and Hamburg. Since the 1970's, the North Sea has been mined for its vast deposits of petroleum and natural gas.

The Norwegian Sea is part of the North Atlantic Ocean off the western coast of Norway. The sea is separated from the Atlantic Ocean by an underwater ridge. It is therefore associated more with the Arctic Ocean than with the Atlantic Ocean. The Norwegian Sea is generally ice-free because it is tempered by the warm Norwegian Current, an extension of the Gulf Stream.

The Sea of Okhotsk is a northern arm of the Pacific Ocean off the coast of Siberia. It lies between the Kamchatka Peninsula, the Kuril (or Kurile) Islands, and the island of Sakhalin. The Sea of Okhotsk is not easily navigable. Shipping is hindered by heavy fogs, storms, and floating icebergs. The northern section is icebound from November to June. Nevertheless, some commercial fishing and crabbing is done off the western coast of the Kamchatka Peninsula. Magadan is the chief port and the entrance to the Kolyma gold region of Russia.

The Pacific Ocean is the largest and deepest of the world's oceans. See the article PACIFIC OCEAN AND ISLANDS in Volume P.

The Philippine Sea is part of the western Pacific Ocean. It borders the eastern coast of the Philippine Islands and extends toward Japan. It is the site of the deepest point on the Earth's surface: the Mariana Trench, 36,198 feet (11,033 meters) below sea level.

The Red Sea is a long, narrow arm of the Indian Ocean between Africa and the Arabian Peninsula. The sea is very salty. The Red Sea is so called because of the red-colored algae and reddish coral formations found there. The Suez Canal provides an important shipping link between the Red Sea, the Mediterranean Sea, and the Indian Ocean. Major ports include Jidda, Saudi Arabia; Suez, Egypt; and Port Sudan, Sudan.

The Ross Sea is an extension of the Pacific Ocean in the Antarctic. The sea contains Ross Island, the site of an active volcano, Mount Erebus. The entire southern part of the sea is occupied by the frozen Ross Ice Shelf, discovered in 1841 by Sir James Clark Ross.

The Salton Sea. See the article LAKES in Volume L.

The **Sargasso Sea** is the name given to the part of the Atlantic Ocean lying between the West Indies and the Azores. See the article ATLANTIC OCEAN in Volume A.

The **Tasman Sea** is a branch of the South Pacific Ocean between Australia and Tasmania on the west and New Zealand on the east. The sea was named for the Dutch navigator Abel Janszoon Tasman in 1642.

The **Tyrrhenian Sea** is a branch of the Mediterranean Sea between the west coast of Italy and the islands of Corsica, Sardinia, and Sicily. See the article MEDITERRANEAN SEA in Volume M.

The **Weddell Sea** is an extension of the South Atlantic Ocean near Antarctica. The sea was discovered in 1829 by James Weddell, a British navigator.

The **White Sea** is an arm of the Barents Sea situated off the northern coast of Russia. The sea abounds in fish, especially cod and herring. The main port of this sea is Arkhangel'sk, located at the mouth of the Northern Dvina River. This port is essential for the export of Russian lumber and forest products. Shipping on the White Sea is carried on only in summer, since the sea is frozen from the months of September to June. The sea is connected to the Baltic Sea by the White Sea-Baltic Canal. The White Sea was discovered by a Norwegian explorer, Ottar, in the 800's.

The **Yellow Sea** (known as Huang Hai in China) is a branch of the Pacific Ocean between the eastern Chinese mainland and the Korean Peninsula. The main port on the Yellow Sea is Dalian (or Lüta), an important Chinese naval station.

Reviewed by JEREMY BLACK
University of Exeter

OCHOA, ESTEVAN. See ARIZONA (Famous People).

O'CONNELL, DANIEL (1775–1847)

Daniel O'Connell, called the Liberator, was a beloved figure in Ireland's fight for independence from England. O'Connell was born on August 6, 1775, in County Kerry. He went to school in France and England before becoming a lawyer.

The Irish, and particularly the Irish Catholics, had many grievances against England. In 1801 the Act of Union dissolved the Irish Parliament and made Ireland part of the United Kingdom. Catholics had to pay taxes to the (Protestant) Church of England, and only Protestants were allowed to sit in the British Parliament. Catholics bitterly resented these and many other injustices.

O'Connell, a devout, peace-loving Catholic, was soon giving most of his time to the struggle for freedom. A forceful speaker, he addressed meetings and rallied thousands of people to his cause. In 1823, O'Connell formed the Catholic Association for the purpose of winning Catholic equality. Soon there were branches of this organization in all of Ireland's large cities. Although the government tried to stop the movement, O'Connell and his followers kept the association active.

In 1828, O'Connell became a candidate for Parliament. He was elected by a large majority but as a Catholic could not legally take office. The British government, fearing the anger of the Irish, was forced to take action. In 1829 the Catholic Emancipation Act was passed, which removed restrictions on the civil rights of Catholics. The next year O'Connell took his seat in the House of Commons.

Protests against English rule continued. Much Irish land belonged to Englishmen, and Irish peasants were very poor. In 1840, O'Connell formed a Repeal Association for the purpose of forcing England to repeal the Act of Union. The movement received enormous support, but its goal, home rule for Ireland, was not won in O'Connell's lifetime.

In 1843, O'Connell was arrested on a charge of conspiracy. After serving a term in prison, he was released by an action of the House of Lords. But by this time he was a sick man. Young militant followers deserted him because they thought his methods too mild.

In 1847, O'Connell set out on a journey to Rome. He died in Genoa on May 15.

DOROTHY MARSHALL
University College of South Wales

O'CONNOR, FLANNERY. See GEORGIA (Famous People).

O'CONNOR, SANDRA DAY. See SUPREME COURT OF THE UNITED STATES (Famous People).

October

October received its name from the ancient Romans. "October" comes from a Latin word meaning "eight." It was the eighth month of the year in the old Roman calendar.

Place in year: 10th month.
Number of days: 31.
Flowers: Cosmos and calendula.
Birthstone: Opal or tourmaline.
Zodiac signs: Libra, the Scales (September 23–October 22), and Scorpio, the Scorpion (October 23–November 21).

1
- James Earl Carter, Jr., born 1924
- First free rural delivery of mail in U.S., 1896
- Model T Ford introduced, 1908
- International Atomic Energy Agency's first conference opened, Vienna, 1957
- National holiday in Cyprus; Nigeria; People's Republic of China; Tuvalu

2
- Mohandas Gandhi born 1869
- Wallace Stevens born 1879
- First Pan-American conference, Washington, D.C., 1889
- National holiday in Guinea

4
- Rutherford B. Hayes born 1822
- First artificial satellite launched by the U.S.S.R., 1957
- Independence Day in Lesotho

5
- Chester Alan Arthur born 1829
- Robert Goddard born 1882
- Gregorian calendar established, 1582
- President Truman delivered first presidential address telecast from White House, 1947.

6
- George Westinghouse born 1846
- Le Corbusier born 1887
- American Library Association founded, 1876

7
- Niels Bohr born 1885

8
- Jesse Jackson born 1941
- Chicago fire started and burned for 27 hours, 1871

9
- Alfred Dreyfus born 1859
- Leif Ericson in Iceland
- National holiday in Uganda

10
- **Giuseppe Verdi** born 1813
- U.S. Naval Academy opened at Annapolis, 1845
- *Oklahoma Historical Day*
- National holiday in Taiwan

11
- **Eleanor Roosevelt** born 1884
- *Pulaski Day*

12
- Columbus landed in America, 1492
- National holiday in Equatorial Guinea; Spain

13
- **Margaret Thatcher** born 1925
- White house cornerstone laid, 1792

14
- **William Penn** born 1644
- **Dwight D. Eisenhower** born 1890
- William the Conqueror won the Battle of Hastings, 1066

15
- **Vergil** born 90 B.C.
- **Noah Webster** born 1758
- **Oscar Wilde** born 1854
- **David Ben-Gurion** born 1886
- **Eugene O'Neill** born 1888
- John Brown and others attacked U.S. arsenal in a raiding party at Harpers Ferry, Virginia (now in West Virginia), 1859
- Cardinal Karol Wojtyla became Pope John Paul II, 1978

17
- General John Burgoyne surrendered to Americans at Saratoga, 1777

18
- **Pierre Elliott Trudeau** born 1919
- Russia formally transferred Alaska to the U.S., 1867

19
- First general court in New England held in Boston, 1630
- General Charles Cornwallis surrendered to Americans at Yorktown, 1781

20
- **Christopher Wren** born 1632
- **John Dewey** born 1859
- **Charles Ives** born 1874

21
- **Alfred Nobel** born 1833
- Ferdinand Magellan sailed into the strait that bears his name, 1520
- "Old Ironsides" (USS *Constitution*) launched, 1797
- Admiral Horatio Nelson killed in Battle of Trafalgar, 1805
- Thomas Edison demonstrated the first practical electric light, 1879
- Revolution Day in Somalia

22
- **Franz Liszt** born 1811
- Sam Houston inaugurated as first president of the Republic of Texas, 1836

23
- **Pelé** born 1940

24
- **Anton van Leeuwenhoek** born 1632
- First transcontinental telegram sent, 1861
- *Pennsylvania Day*
- *United Nations Day*
- National holiday in Zambia

25
- **Johann Strauss, Jr.,** born 1825
- **Pablo Picasso** born 1881
- **Richard Evelyn Byrd** born 1888
- Henry V of England defeated French at Agincourt in the Hundred Years' War, 1415

26
- Erie Canal opened to traffic, 1825
- National holiday in Austria

27
- **James Cook** born 1728
- **Theodore Roosevelt** born 1858
- *Navy Day*
- National holiday in Saint Vincent and the Grenadines

28
- Harvard College founded, 1636
- Statue of Liberty dedicated, 1886

29
- "Black Tuesday," darkest day of the great stock market crash, 1929
- Republic Day in Turkey

30
- **John Adams** born 1735
- **Fëdor Dostoevski** born 1821

31
- **Jan Vermeer** born 1632
- **John Keats** born 1795
- **Chiang Kai-shek** born 1887
- Nevada became the 36th state, 1864
- *Halloween*
- *UNICEF Day* (on behalf of United Nations Children's Fund)

Last Sunday in October: Daylight Savings Time ends for much of the United States. **First Monday in October:** *Missouri Day; Child Health Day.* **Second Monday in October:** *Columbus Day;* Thanksgiving Day in Canada. **Holidays that may occur in either October or September:** *Rosh Hashanah* (Jewish New Year); *Yom Kippur* (Jewish Day of Atonement).

The calendar listing identifies people who were born on the indicated day in boldface type, **like this.** You will find a biography of each of these birthday people in *The New Book of Knowledge.* In addition to citing some historical events and historical firsts, the calendar also lists the holidays and some of the festivals celebrated in the United States. These holidays are printed in italic type, *like this.* See the article HOLIDAYS for more information.

Many holidays and festivals of nations around the world are included in the calendar as well. When the term "national holiday" is used, it means that the nation celebrates an important patriotic event on that day—in most cases the winning of independence. Consult *The New Book of Knowledge* article on the individual nation for further information on its national holiday.

OCTOPUSES, SQUIDS, AND OTHER CEPHALOPODS

Octopuses, squids, and similar animals are members of a group of ocean invertebrates (animals with no backbone) called **cephalopods**. Cephalopods are a kind of mollusk, a group of animals that also includes clams, oysters, and snails. The name "cephalopod" means "head-foot," which refers to the fact that the limbs of these animals are attached to their head.

Cephalopods live throughout the world's oceans, from surface waters to depths of more than 4 miles (7 kilometers). About 700 different species (types) exist. The largest is the giant squid, which measures up to 60 feet (18 meters) long. The smallest is the pygmy squid, which measures just ½ inch (1.27 centimeters) long.

All cephalopods have at least eight arms, and sometimes two or more feeding tentacles. The arms are usually covered with powerful suckers, while the longer tentacles may have suckers all along their length or only at their tips. These suckers help the animals catch fish and other prey. All cephalopods have a beak, similar to a bird's beak, that is used to bite prey. Cephalopods have well-developed eyes, and some species use their keen vision to hunt for food.

Expert hunters, cephalopods are also skilled at avoiding predators. Their skin is covered with **chromatophores**, pigment-filled sacs that contract or expand to change the animal's color to match its surroundings. (Cephalopods also communicate with each other by changing color.) Many cephalopods squirt a black, ink-like substance into the water to confuse predators.

A cephalopod's internal organs, which include three hearts, are protected by a fleshy covering called the **mantle**. Inside the mantle is the **mantle cavity**, where gills pick up oxygen from the water. After the water passes over the gills, it can be ejected forcefully from the mantle cavity through a funnel. This propels the animal through the water.

▶ KINDS OF CEPHALOPODS

Among the many different kinds of cephalopods, five groups are the most notable. In addition to octopuses and squids, the other groups are the nautiluses, the cuttlefishes, and the vampire squid.

Octopuses. Octopuses are found in every ocean, and there are more than 100 species. They use their eight muscular arms to crawl along the ocean floor. They lack feeding tentacles, and most lack fins. The giant octopus may weigh more than 220 pounds (100 kilograms) and measure about 15 feet (5 meters) from the tip of one arm to the tip of the opposite arm.

Octopuses hide in cracks and crevices in the rocks or in burrows in sand and mud. Seizing their prey with their arms, they inject it with a paralyzing toxin before eating it. This toxin also starts the process of digestion. A female octopus attaches her eggs to rocks and guards them until they hatch; then she dies. Octopuses have well-developed brains,

Octopuses (*left*) and other cephalopods have at least eight arms that are usually covered on the underside with powerful suckers (*below*). These help the animals catch fish, crabs, and other prey.

and they are considered the most intelligent invertebrate.

Squids. Squids have eight arms, two long feeding tentacles, and a fin on each side of their body. They are found in every ocean and spend their lives swimming, floating, or sometimes resting on the bottom. Squids that live in shallow water are slender and streamlined, and they are fast and active hunters. Deepwater squids tend to be more delicate and more sluggish; they spend most of their time floating in the dark, waiting for food to come to them. Although squids can move by shooting water from their mantle cavity, they also use their two fins to swim.

Some species of squids attach their egg masses to the ocean floor, while others lay egg masses that float. One deepwater species carries its eggs in its arms until they hatch. Most squids die after laying their first batch of eggs.

Nautiluses. The chambered, or pearly, nautilus is a shelled cephalopod. Five species live in the tropical waters of the Indian and Pacific oceans. Nautiluses have about 90 arms, none of which have suckers. They rest in deep water during the day, but at night they rise into shallow water to feed. Although most cephalopods live for only a short time, nautiluses may live as long as 20 years. Their beautiful, coiled shells are popular with collectors.

Cuttlefishes. There are more than 100 species of cuttlefishes, which live in the Mediterranean Sea and in many oceans of the world. Like squids, these animals have eight arms, fins on each side of their body, and two tentacles. Cuttlefishes are usually less active than squids. They live on the ocean floor or float just above it in shallow water. Cuttlebone, a chalky, shell-like structure inside the body, helps cuttlefishes float.

Vampire Squids. There is only one known species of vampire squid, which is not a true squid. It lives in deep waters around the

Cuttlefishes, like squids, have fins and feeding tentacles. They live along the ocean floor or just above it in shallow water.

world. This animal is named for its black skin and for the webbing between its arms that looks like a vampire's cape. It lacks feeding tentacles. The vampire squid is about 15 inches (38 centimeters) long and has the largest eyes of any animal in relation to the size of its body. Vampire squids are very sluggish swimmers, primarily using their paddle-shaped fins to move through the water. They have an unusual trick for confusing predators: When they are disturbed, special organs near their fins and at the tips of their arms produce light, through a chemical process called **bioluminescence**.

▶ **CEPHALOPODS AND PEOPLE**

Most cephalopods are not dangerous to people. There are some notable exceptions, however. The venom of the blue-ringed octopus can be fatal to humans. The Humboldt squid, which can grow as long as 6 feet (2 meters), will attack scuba divers, although no serious injuries have occurred.

Humans, on the other hand, can be very dangerous to cephalopods. Octopuses, cuttlefishes, and squids are popular food items in many parts of the world and support large commercial fisheries. If too many of these animals are caught before they can reproduce, their populations could decline very rapidly.

BRAD SEIBEL
University of Rhode Island

The chambered nautilus is a shelled cephalopod. It rests in deep water during the day and rises at night to feed in shallow water.

ODES

The lyric poem has many forms, one of which is the ode. The ode is dignified in style and noble in sentiment and pays tribute to someone or something. "Ode" comes from a contraction of the Greek word *aoide*, which means "song."

Odes have simple and complex forms. In English the irregular (complex) form imitates the odes of the poet Pindar, of ancient Greece. **Pindaric odes** were written to be sung and danced to, and they celebrated athletic victories at religious festivals. The poems began with a **strophe**—literally "a turning"— lines the chorus sang as it turned to one side of the stage. Moving to the other side, the chorus sang the **antistrophe**, or counterturn. Then followed the **epode**, or lines the chorus sang while standing still.

In contrast there is the Horatian ode. This form, popularized by the poet Horace, of ancient Rome, employs a simple sequence of stanzas, as in "Ode to Evening" (1746), 13 unrhymed stanzas by English poet William Collins. Neither the Horatian ode nor the Pindaric ode as adapted by the English poets was ever intended to be sung, although John Dryden wrote two odes that remain important exceptions—"Song for St. Cecilia's Day" (1687) and "Alexander's Feast" (1697).

In the 1600's, Abraham Cowley tried to establish the Pindaric odes in English. Unfortunately he failed to understand Pindar's structure and technique, and his English odes are not truly Pindaric. Yet later poets used Cowley's irregular form. Dryden gave it a dignity and brilliance not again achieved until 1852, when Alfred, Lord Tennyson's masterful "Ode on the Death of the Duke of Wellington" appeared.

Of all the many odes in English literature, however, the imitations of the simple Horatian odes—particularly those written by John Keats and Percy Bysshe Shelley—are best known. But Samuel Taylor Coleridge wrote three odes: "France: an Ode" (1798), "Ode to Tranquility" (1800), and "Dejection: an Ode" (1802); and these must be classed as irregular (Pindaric), the first one most of all. William Wordsworth wrote a number of odes, including the Pindaric one with the famous long title "Ode: Intimations of Immortality from Recollections of Early Childhood" (1807).

This ode still stands as one of the great poems of the English language.

Keats wrote a number of odes, all of them fairly brief. Four of them are famous: "Ode on a Grecian Urn," "Ode to a Nightingale," "Ode to Autumn," and "Ode on Melancholy" (all 1819). Keats composed "Ode to a Nightingale" in only two to three hours while sitting under a plum tree. A nightingale had nested nearby, and its song had given the poet "a tranquil and continual joy." After reading the poem's 80 lines, even people poor at memorizing verse will surely remember something of the following passage:

Thou wast not born for death, immortal Bird!
  No hungry generations tread thee down;
The voice I hear this passing night was heard
  In ancient days by emperor and clown:
Perhaps the self-same song that found a path
  Through the sad heart of Ruth, when, sick for
      home,
    She stood in tears amid the alien corn;
      The same that oft-times hath
  Charmed magic casements, opening on the foam
    Of perilous seas, in faery lands forlorn.

Shelley's "Ode to the West Wind" (also written in 1819)—a sonnet sequence in form—rises to the level of Keats's "Ode to a Nightingale." It was Shelley's special gift to write with lightly accented stress syllables, and this ability keeps his "Ode to the West Wind" in perpetual motion. Here are the closing lines:

Drive my dead thoughts over the universe
Like withered leaves to quicken a new birth!
And, by the incantation of this verse,

Scatter, as from an unextinguished hearth
Ashes and sparks, my words among mankind!
Be through my lips to unawakened earth

The trumpet of a prophecy! O Wind,
If Winter comes, can Spring be far behind?

Since the time of Keats and Shelley, not many poets have turned their talents to the ode form. And very few of their odes are memorable. Two are outstanding: the American poet Allen Tate's "Ode to the Confederate Dead" (1932) and the British-American poet W. H. Auden's "Ode; to my Pupils" (1936).

DAVID MCCORD
Poet and essayist

ODIN. See NORSE MYTHOLOGY (Profiles).

ODYSSEY

Most people believe that the *Odyssey* was composed by Homer, just as the *Iliad* was. The *Odyssey*, like the *Iliad*, is an epic poem in 24 books. It deals with some of the same people. However, it differs in tone.

The *Odyssey* is named after its hero, Odysseus (Ulysses). The poem tells of the adventures Odysseus had in getting home to his kingdom of Ithaca after the Trojan War, and of the problems that faced him when he arrived there. It also tells of his son, Telemachus, who searches for his long-lost father. And it tells of Odysseus' wife, Penelope, who has waited 20 years for her husband to return. These three stories are interwoven into an exciting tale. If it had not been written as poetry, it would be the world's first novel.

We see Odysseus first on an island belonging to Calypso, a beautiful goddess. Odysseus has stayed with her for seven years. She offered to make him immortal, but he preferred to return home. Zeus sends down Hermes to order Calypso to let Odysseus go.

Odysseus had lost all his ships and all his companions long before. He now makes himself a boat and sets off. He arrives in the land of the Phaeacians and is discovered by the Princess Nausicaa. In the palace of her father Alcinous, he tells the Phaeacians all that happened to him since he left Troy. The most exciting of these adventures are the following.

The travelers arrived in the land of the Lotus-Eaters. The men tasted the lotus plant, forgot their past, and wanted to stay and eat more lotus. Odysseus dragged them off.

They next met the Cyclops, a monster whose single eye was in the middle of its forehead. The Cyclops, named Polyphemus, made a meal of two of Odysseus' men twice a day. But Odysseus made the Cyclops drunk. Then he and his men heated a huge stake in the fire, and with it they blinded the Cyclops.

Odysseus and his men left Polyphemus' cave by another trick. Three sheep were tied together, with a man tied beneath the middle sheep. As the blind Cyclops felt the backs of the sheep, he did not notice the men.

Aeolus, the god of the winds, gave Odysseus a bag. All the winds were tied up inside, except the one they needed to sail. But his men thought there was a treasure, and that they were being cheated. So they opened the bag and were promptly driven back.

Odysseus then came to Circe, a witch, who turned the men into swine. When Odysseus heard this, he went to Circe's house. The god Hermes gave him a plant called moly. This plant had magical powers that helped him to resist Circe's charms. He persuaded her to release his men.

Odysseus then had encounters with the Sirens and with Scylla and Charybdis. The Sirens were beautiful women who sang so enchantingly that sailors would kill themselves to get to them. Odysseus put wax into the ears of his sailors. He himself was tied to the mast, so that he could hear the music without jumping overboard. Scylla was a sea monster something like a giant octopus. Charybdis was a whirlpool that could suck down a whole ship. Odysseus managed to pass the whirlpool, but Scylla caught six sailors and ate them.

This Roman mosaic shows Odysseus tied to the mast of his ship so that he cannot jump overboard to join the Sirens. The Sirens were beautiful women whose songs lured sailors to destruction.

Back in Ithaca at last, Odysseus is disguised as a beggar. He goes to the hut of the swineherd Eumaeus, one of the few people who stayed loyal to him. Telemachus also appears there, and father and son recognize each other. Together they plot revenge against the men who courted Penelope while Odysseus was away and wasted Odysseus' property.

Odysseus receives shameful treatment from the suitors. Only Argus and Eurycleia recognize him. Argus is the dog he left behind. Eurycleia is his old nurse, who, while washing his feet, recognizes Odysseus by a scar.

Penelope announces that she will marry the suitor who can handle Odysseus' bow. None can. Odysseus himself wants to try. The suitors laugh at him. He does try, and he succeeds. Then he starts shooting down the suitors. When they get hold of weapons and attack him, he is helped by Telemachus, Eumaeus, and one other faithful servant. In a fierce battle they kill all the suitors.

Odysseus then reveals himself to Penelope. She will not believe that he really is her husband. He proves it by reminding her of some carpentry work he did on their bed—making one of the bedposts out of a growing tree. This had been known only to Penelope and Odysseus. Penelope always had her wits about her, as is shown by the story of her web. She had promised to marry one of her suitors as soon as she finished some weaving. But each night she unraveled what she had woven during the day.

Homer is a wonderful storyteller. The *Odyssey* is perfectly constructed, moves rapidly, and is gripping throughout. Its happy ending makes it a romantic story. Odysseus endures many reverses, but he is tremendously resourceful, courageous—and lucky.

The *Odyssey*, like the *Iliad*, has enormously influenced world literature. Odysseus appears again in many poems and plays, sometimes as a clever crook, sometimes as a daring explorer. Authors—from Greek dramatists, through Vergil and Dante, down to James Joyce in his *Ulysses*—have been intrigued by his character and his adventures.

URSULA SCHOENHEIM
Queens College
Reviewed by GILBERT HIGHET
Formerly, Columbia University

OFFENBACH, JACQUES (1819–1880)

Jacques Offenbach, the famous composer of French operettas, was born in Cologne, Germany, on June 20, 1819. His father was the cantor of the Cologne synagogue. When he was 14, Jacques went to France to study music at the Paris Conservatory. By the age of 15, Jacques was supporting himself as a cellist at the Opéra-Comique.

In 1844, Offenbach married Herminie de Alcain. Three years later he became a conductor of the Théâtre Français.

Offenbach's first compositions were cello pieces and songs. When one of his songs became a popular success in 1850, he was convinced that his real talent was for writing operettas and other stage pieces.

In 1855 he opened a theater of his own, the Bouffes-Parisiens, in Paris. He wrote most of the works presented there. His first great success was *Orpheus in the Underworld* (1858). It was immediately popular for its lively music and dancing and because it poked fun at the attitudes of the time. Offenbach was a witty man with a gift for satire. *Orpheus* made him a great celebrity.

Offenbach wrote several new stage works every year. Among the most successful were *La belle Hélène* (1864), *La vie parisienne* (1866), and *La Périchole* (1868). During these years he also visited Germany, Austria, and England. In 1876 he made a visit to the United States.

Offenbach wanted to be remembered as a serious composer, and so near the end of his life he began a grand opera, *The Tales of Hoffmann.* But he died in Paris on October 5, 1880, before he had finished it. The score was completed and arranged by another composer. When the opera was presented at the Opéra-Comique in 1881, it was an enormous success. The "Barcarole" song from this work has become world famous. Of Offenbach's more than 100 stage works, *The Tales of Hoffmann* is performed most often today.

Reviewed by WILLIAM ASHBROOK
Philadelphia College of the Performing Arts

OFFICE MACHINES

Office machines are devices designed to help office workers gather, record, store, and distribute the information needed to operate a business. By helping office workers process information more rapidly and accurately, office machines save businesses time and money. Most office machines do jobs with words, numbers, sound, and graphics (pictorial information). The most common office machines include telephones, computers, calculators, typewriters, and copiers.

▶ COMPUTERS

One of the most important office machines used today is the computer, an electronic machine that can follow a set of instructions (called a program), automatically process information, and quickly solve problems. Although many kinds of computers are used in offices, they all work the same way: by using digits (numbers) as a code for all letters, numbers, and symbols.

Businesses use computers for many jobs formerly performed by an office staff. These tasks include accounting, payroll, billing, purchasing, inventory control (keeping track of a company's merchandise), and creation of letters and other documents.

In 1947, John von Neumann, an American mathematician, created the first true computer, called EDVAC (Electronic Discrete Variable Automatic Computer). Its program was stored internally. EDVAC was one of the first commercially available computers.

There are several sizes of computers. General categories include supercomputers (giant computers, such as those used for a government census), mainframe computers (large business and scientific computers), workstation or minicomputers (medium-sized computers), microcomputers (small computers, also called personal computers), notebook computers (also called laptops), and palmtop (handheld) computers. Some microcomputers do one job at a time, but most computers, regardless of size, can easily perform several jobs simultaneously.

Computers handle information in four stages: input, storage, processing, and output. Information is most often entered (input) on a keyboard. (The operator can see it displayed on a monitor.) Another important

In many offices today, computers are used to process, store, and distribute information, allowing workers to perform their tasks accurately and efficiently.

way to enter information into a computer is with an optical character recognition (OCR) device (scanner). A scanner can "look" at typed pages and translate the words and numbers into computer code. Information stored magnetically on tape or disks is invisible to the naked eye and can only be read electronically. Information can also be stored optically by using a laser to burn the information onto the face of an optical disk. The code marks, made up of rough and smooth spots, are so small that a disk about the size of a CD can hold more than half a gigabyte. (A whole gigabyte consists of 1,073,741,824 bits of information.)

The central processor, or CPU, is the electronic brain of a computer and is what performs the work. A program and the information to be worked on are recorded into the memory. Depending upon the program, the computer will do mathematics, filter or sort data, print out a report, or do other jobs. When the work is finished, it is "output" (put out of the central processor). The program tells the computer where to output the information, such as storing it on a disk, sending it to another computer over telephone lines, or printing it on paper.

Many types of printers are used in offices. The most common kinds are called **laser**, **ink jet**, and **dot matrix**. They differ in terms of

Co-workers in different locations can see and hear each other using videoconferencing systems, which are computers equipped with microphones and cameras.

how they run, the kind of letters or graphics that will appear, and speed. Some printers print in color.

Another important business use of computers is statistical graphics. A computer can draw line graphs, bar graphs, pie charts, and other graphics in black-and-white or color.

Today's computers have come a long way since EDVAC and are many times faster. For example, IBM's ASCI White computer does 12.3 trillion calculations per second. It is 30,000 times more powerful than a personal computer and fills a room the size of two basketball courts.

Additional information on computers and how they operate can be found in the article COMPUTERS in Volume C.

Other office machines that feature computer technology include **point-of-sale (POS) devices**. POS devices are really cash registers with laser scanners; the POS machines either have a microcomputer inside them or act as terminals connected to a computer. The scanners "read" the Universal Product Codes (UPC codes) found on packages and labels, look up the prices in the computer memory, then add them. The computer can then figure out how many items are left in stock and whether to re-order them, and can also prepare sales reports. Like cash registers, POS devices have money drawers.

▶ SPECIAL COMPUTERIZED TOOLS

Computers can be programmed to do jobs other office machines cannot. That includes communicating via **electronic mail** (e-mail). Using a personal computer or terminal, person A can write and transmit an electronic letter to person B, storing it in a computer. Person B uses his computer to retrieve the message. He can then send a copy of that message to person C and still keep a copy for himself on a computer disk. E-mail is a relatively new and important way to communicate, especially when many people live and work in different time zones, because messages can be sent quickly and read at any time.

Electronic calendar systems help schedule meetings. The names of the participants and the date and time for the meeting are put into the computer. The computer, which stores everyone's activity schedule on a disk, checks to see when everyone has free time. It will write the name, date, time, and place of the meeting on everyone's electronic calendar for them to see.

Using **word-processing software**, many people also write letters and create other documents on their computers, or revise existing documents by adding or deleting material and moving text around. The word-processing program can direct documents to a printer, sort lists into alphabetical order, and add up a column of figures in a business letter. These sophisticated programs can take

Computers can be used to create and display many types of graphics, including charts, maps, and illustrations, for sales and marketing presentations.

one copy of a letter and a list of names and addresses and automatically print a letter to each person.

Word-processing programs can check to make sure all words in a document are spelled correctly. Others enable users to draw graphs or pictures and print them on the same page with the text of a report. Also, printers can "type" many times faster than a person using an electric typewriter, making as many copies as needed.

Computers can be used for **desktop publishing** as well. This is the production of newsletters, brochures, books, flyers, and other professional-quality printed material on a personal computer. To create these items, a program is used that combines text and graphics. These and many other important uses for the computer make it one of the most important inventions of all time.

In the late 1800's, typewriters modernized office procedures and brought more women into the business workforce.

▶ **TYPEWRITERS**

The typewriter was introduced as an inexpensive substitute for the costly process of setting movable type when only a few copies had to be printed. Soon, people realized it was also a fast, neat way to prepare letters and documents.

Some typewriters have print characters engraved on the ends of hinged steel bars. When a key is pressed, the bar is forcefully swung forward, pinching an inked ribbon against the paper and leaving the symbol impression on the sheet of paper while the paper is held in position against a hard rubber cylinder. Other typewriters have characters engraved on a small metal sphere. When a key is pressed, the sphere rotates to bring the correct character into position and then is propelled forward like a type bar.

There are many kinds of typewriters. Some have special characters such as mathematical characters or musical notes. Some are compact portables. Others are specially made for typing on extra-wide paper. Braille typewriters prepare documents for the blind, and large-type typewriters create documents for those with poor eyesight. Audio-response typewriters pronounce words and say numbers out loud as they are typed, to verify typing accuracy by blind typists. Voice-recognition typewriters recognize spoken words and then type them on paper.

Some electronic typewriters can store up to 100 pages of typing, which can be used over and over again for forms such as thank-you letters. To send one, the typist types a name and address, then the electronic typewriter types the main part of the letter automatically.

Early machines were called "blind" typewriters, because the typist could not see the section of the paper being typed on. In the early 1900's, Edward B. Hess patented a typewriter that allowed the typist to see what was being typed. It also solved the problem of the keys being hard to press down. The action of the keys was reversed so that when a typist pressed on a key, the type bar (with the letter on one end) was pulled up to strike the paper, instead of being pushed down. This gave the typewriter a light, "fast" touch.

The first electrically powered typewriter was introduced in 1908, but electric typewriters did not become popular until the late 1940's, probably because most offices did not have enough typing work to justify the cost. Early models also had many mechanical flaws. After World War II, increased paperwork in offices and improvement in electric typewriter design stirred public interest.

▶ **AUDIO MACHINES**

The need to communicate over long distances has led to many inventions, including the telegraph (1837) and the telephone (1876).

The most widely used office machine in the world is the **telephone**. Originally, calls were placed by operators working at telephone company offices called exchanges. Today, special-purpose computers called **Private Branch**

Exchanges (PBX's) are installed in business offices and perform many of the functions formerly handled by operators. They can be used to connect many telephones so that people in different locations can hold meetings without leaving their offices. Called teleconferences, these meetings save time and travel costs. PBX's can do more than 100 specialized tasks, including connecting displays to computers.

There are several special types of telephones, including telephone headsets, like those used by airplane pilots. These, along with speakerphones, which have built-in microphones and speakers, allow people to use both hands for other things while talking on the phone. Speakerphones are commonly used for teleconferencing, as well as regular telephone calls. Other communications devices include cellular ("cell") phones and pagers. Both of these are wireless, which means people can use them to communicate without being connected by telephone wires. Although cell phones function like regular telephones, pagers only allow people to send or receive messages.

A telephone's **speed dialer** can record and store up to several hundred telephone numbers and redial any stored number with the touch of one or two buttons. Another common device is a **telephone answering machine**, which can answer a telephone, play a taped announcement to callers, and then record callers' messages.

A **teletypewriter** is a kind of electronic typewriter that sends signals over telephone lines to other similar machines, which can print messages on paper. Facsimile devices, or **fax machines**, can be thought of as long-distance photocopiers. A document is scanned by a beam of light or a low-powered laser beam, then the light and dark areas are translated into signals and sent over telephone lines. Hundreds of miles away, the receiver interprets the signals and makes a duplicate copy of the original. Faxes are used extensively by general business, by law enforcement agencies, and by news services to transmit photographs to newspapers.

Another office tool is the **dictation machine**, which records sound. The first, called the Graphophone, was developed in 1887 by Alexander Graham Bell. The machine had a cylinder on which voice patterns were scratched in much the same way as they are on phonograph records. The cylinder was later played back by a typist, who typed a dictated letter.

Cylinders were ultimately replaced by belts, tapes, disks, and digital memory voice recordings; today most dictating machines use audiocassettes. In addition to individual desk-model dictation machines, there are large, centrally located machines and battery-powered portables. Any push-button telephone can be used to dial and dictate to a central machine. Some portables, powered by batteries, can be easily carried and operated anywhere. The advantage of dictation machines is that they can record dictation at the convenience of the user, for later transcription by a typist.

Voice mail systems are sophisticated audio systems in which a person uses a telephone to call a computer that stores spoken messages for an individual or group of people. All users of such systems periodically call the computer to find out whether they have messages and to listen to them. Voice mail messages can be saved, played over and over, copied, and sent to others.

▶ GRAPHIC AND COPYING MACHINES

Duplicating and **copying** machines are used to make copies of letters and documents. In 1887 an American named A. B. Dick developed a duplicating machine that used a soft, wax-coated paper stencil on which a typist

With its built-in microphone and speaker, a speakerphone lets several people in one office hold a conference call with people in an outside office.

Fax machines, which send and receive documents over telephone lines, are often used by businesses, news organizations, and law enforcement agencies.

ing functions such as printing different sizes of type on the same page, printing sideways, printing special symbols, and many other functions. They accept computer code as input, rather than original documents.

In 1839 **microphotography** was invented, which led to micrographics, the miniaturized photographic storage of information. The most common kinds of micrographic films are 16 millimeter (the size of 110 camera film) and 35 millimeter roll film (the same as most motion pictures), and microfiche. **Micro-fiche** are flat sheets of film, about 4 by 6 inches (12 by 15 centimeters) in size. A single standard microfiche can hold photographs of more than 1,000 typewritten pages. A viewer (a projector with a built-in screen) is used to read the information. **Holofiche** use a holographic (three-dimensional) recording technique and can store the equivalent of up to 20,000 typewritten pages on a single 4- by 6-inch piece of film. Holofiche are read with a special display. Because of the way in which information is recorded on holofiche, the information can be read even if a holofiche sheet is punctured, torn, or even partially burned. The chief advantages of micrographics are that they are more compact than paper and are less expensive to mail. Electronic storage of text and graphics is most common.

▶ **ADDERS AND CALCULATORS**

The forerunner of today's electronic adders and calculators—the **abacus**—is actually one of the first office machines ever invented. This piece of equipment, which is still used in some parts of the world, was introduced as travel and trade developed and record keeping became necessary. Early people had counted on their fingers, with pebbles, by scratches on stones, or by notches on sticks, but as merchants bought and sold items by the hundreds or thousands, numbers became too large to count in those ways.

Originally, the abacus was a flat stone with parallel grooves into which small pebbles were placed to keep count. The modern abacus, attributed to the Chinese, is a series of movable beads on rods, mounted in a frame. (See the article ABACUS in Volume A.) Calculating on an abacus is still a very fast way to do mathematics. Shortly after World War II a Japanese bank clerk, using an abacus, was

could type—or mark in some other way—to leave cuts in the waxed surface. The stencil was then placed over an inked drum, rolled against plain paper, and ink passed through the cuts and marked the paper. Though the **mimeograph** (stencil-ink duplicator) is still occasionally used, there are now other methods of doing the same job. An offset-method duplicator uses a typed master sheet onto which information is typed. The typing is then etched onto the surface of the master, put onto the drum of a duplicating machine, and inked. Since the master is a positive image, it first prints onto a blank roller (making a negative image), which in turn prints a positive image onto the paper.

In addition, there are now photocopy machines that reproduce one or more copies of ordinary (not master) documents. Most use the **xerographic** (pronounced "zero-graphic") process called **xerography**, developed in 1937. Some copiers employ ink-jet technology. **Collators** collect and arrange and sometimes staple the copies as they come out of the machine. Some kinds of copiers make clean, flat copies of bulky originals like books and ledgers. Others make copies in color or in reduced or enlarged sizes.

Intelligent copiers are really sophisticated computer printers. They combine a laser copier with a microcomputer or a minicomputer, enabling them to perform special print-

matched against an American soldier using a calculator. Performing identical business work that required addition, subtraction, multiplication, and division, the Japanese clerk with his abacus won every contest.

An adding device that more closely resembled today's calculators was invented in 1642 by Blaise Pascal, a 19-year-old French genius. Pascal was bored with the job of adding long columns of figures in his father's office, so he invented a shoe-box-sized adding machine. It was operated by turning a series of wheels that had the numbers 0 through 9 painted on the edge of their rims. As the first wheel counted beyond nine, its zero again came into

Before the development of electric and electronic office equipment, procedures such as payroll processing, billing, and inventory control took much longer to perform.

view, and the mechanism moved the wheel to the left up one number. In this way, the machine could carry over tens. When the second wheel from the right made one full revolution, and its zero came into view, the next wheel to the left moved up one number, carrying over 100's. Totals were shown through small windows in the machine's cover. By 1671, Gottfried Wilhelm von Leibniz expanded on Pascal's machine by inventing one that could multiply, divide, and compute square roots.

Mechanical **calculators** closely resembling Pascal's remained in use through the 1960's,

when faster and quieter electronic calculators came into popular use. Numbers were displayed on small screens, and some calculators could also print on paper tape. As transistors came into use, calculators became smaller. Office calculators are electrically powered; pocket calculators are usually battery operated. The smallest calculators are the size of a plastic credit card and solar powered. Any light source, such as a room light, will operate them; they have no batteries.

Special machines that combine the functions of calculators and typewriters are called **bookkeeping machines.** They are used by small businesses and banks for preparing forms and documents and making entries in the bank books of depositors.

▶ **SPECIAL-PURPOSE MACHINES**

There are many special machines used in offices. **Folders** fold letters and advertising material in preparation for mailing. **Inserters** take folded materials, insert them into envelopes, and seal the flaps shut. **Mailing machines**, which are large postage meters, print postage directly onto envelopes. Banks and other businesses use machines that can count paper money and other papers. Special cameras attached to computers can make color slides, color prints, and motion pictures. (Some animated films are now made in this manner.) **Bursters** separate continuous forms printed by computers. And when documents are no longer needed, **shredders** destroy them by chewing them to bits to prevent anyone from reading private information. For almost every job in an office, there is one or more special machines to help people get more work accomplished easily and efficiently.

DAVID BARCOMB
Author, *Office Automation:*
A Survey of Tools and Technology
Reviewed by NICK MANWELL
Technician, Hewlett Packard

See also ABACUS; COMPUTERS; TELECOMMUNICATIONS; TYPEWRITERS.

OGLETHORPE, JAMES (1696–1785)

James Edward Oglethorpe, the founder of Georgia, was born in London on December 22, 1696. He attended Oxford University and then, while still in his teens, joined the Army. On the death of his older brother he became head of the family estates. Like many country gentlemen he entered Parliament.

The turning point in Oglethorpe's life came when a friend of his was imprisoned for debt. Eighteenth-century English law was very harsh toward people who could not pay their debts. When his friend died in prison of smallpox, Oglethorpe was deeply shocked. He began a campaign in Parliament to improve prison conditions and to obtain the release of poor debtors imprisoned for owing small sums. However, it was not much use getting poor people out of prison if they had no means of earning a livelihood. So Oglethorpe decided to establish a colony in America for them. In 1732 he received from King George II a grant of land. The new colony was to be called Georgia, after King George.

In 1732 Oglethorpe sailed for America with about 120 settlers. He made his first settlement at Savannah. Soon more colonists arrived. Not all were debtors. New settlements were established. Oglethorpe governed firmly but kindly. Rum and slavery were forbidden. Religious toleration was practiced, and relations with the Indians were peaceful.

War between Spain and England increased hostilities between Georgia and the Spanish in Florida. The protection of Georgia rested mainly on Oglethorpe's leadership and personal bravery. He received little support from the British Government and had pledged his own credit to help pay for the defense of the colony. This led to charges of financial irregularities against him. In 1743 he returned to England and was cleared. Soon after, he married. He served as a general in the Army and again sat in Parliament. But partly because of difficulties with the British Government he never returned to Georgia. He died in England on July 1, 1785.

DOROTHY MARSHALL
Author, *Eighteenth Century England*

O. HENRY. See HENRY, O.

O'HIGGINS, BERNARDO (1778–1842)

Bernardo O'Higgins, hero of Chile's struggle for independence, was born on August 20, 1778, in Chillán, Chile, then under Spanish rule. Bernardo's father, Ambrose O'Higgins, had come to Chile from Ireland. Bernardo's mother was of Spanish descent.

Bernardo was sent to school in England. There he met a Venezuelan patriot, Francisco Miranda (1750?–1816). After a journey to Spain, where he met José de San Martín, O'Higgins returned home a convinced republican. In 1810 he joined a group of Chilean liberals, who rebelled against Spain and established the first National Congress. In 1813 O'Higgins was given command of the republican forces. But Spain's royalist forces defeated him in 1814, and O'Higgins had to flee with his broken army into free Argentinian territory. There he joined San Martín. After 3 years of preparation an army of some 5,000 Chileans and Argentinians, under the command of O'Higgins and San Martín, marched across the Andes. In 1817 they won a victory at the battle of Chacabuco. San Martín was appointed supreme director of Chile. But he declined in favor of O'Higgins.

On February 12, 1818, O'Higgins declared the independence of Chile. After a final victory over the Spaniards, at Maipu, he put into effect the first constitution for his country. He aided San Martín in the liberation of Peru. In Chile, O'Higgins founded schools, imported teachers from England, and started public works. He abolished slavery and titles of nobility. He instituted freedom of worship and taxed the church and the aristocracy.

But these liberal reforms turned Chile's conservatives against him. In 1823 he was made to resign. O'Higgins left Chile for Peru. In 1839 the Chilean Senate asked him back. But old and sick, O'Higgins first refused and then was unable to return. He died in Lima, Peru, on October 24, 1842.

Reviewed by HUMBERTO DÍAZ-CASANUEVA
Minister Plenipotentiary of Chile to the UN

See also SAN MARTÍN, JOSÉ DE.

OHIO

The state of Ohio was named for the Ohio River. Native Americans called it O-he-o, *or* O-y-o, *which probably meant "great water."*

Ohio acquired its nickname, the Buckeye State, from early settlers, who found the buckeye tree both useful and plentiful. Again, they borrowed the name from Native Americans, who called this tree hetuck *("eye of a buck") because the tree's round, shiny seeds reminded them of a deer's eye.*

State flag

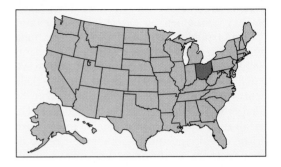

Ohio is one of the East North Central states, located north of the Ohio River and south of Lake Erie, about midway between the Atlantic coast and the Mississippi River. Its land varies from the rugged ridges and ravines in the south and east to the level lake plains in the north and the rolling till plains in the west.

A leading industrial state, Ohio ranks second in the automotive industry, second in steel, and among the nation's top producers of electrical equipment and machine tools. Corn, soybeans, wheat, livestock, and dairy products dominate Ohio's thriving agricultural industry. Nevertheless, two out of every three wage earners in Ohio are employed in the rapidly growing service industries.

Ohio is heavily populated. Most of its people live in urban areas, which are well distributed across the state. Ohio's population is mostly concentrated in a broad band extending from greater Cleveland in the northeast, through Columbus, the state capital, in central Ohio, to Cincinnati in the southwest. The southeastern and south central regions are the least populous, although they were among the first to be settled by pioneers.

Ohio once belonged to a vast frontier region known as the Northwest Territory, acquired in the Louisiana Purchase of 1803. After the Revolutionary War (1775–83), Ohio's rich lands attracted not only people from every settled part of the nation but European immigrants as well. Admitted to the Union in 1803, Ohio became the first state carved from the Northwest Territory.

By 1840, Ohio had the nation's third largest population. Many of its men and women played major roles in the antislavery, women's rights, and temperance movements and were also key contributors to the Union

victory in the Civil War (1861–65). In the sixty years following the war, seven native sons—Ulysses S. Grant, Rutherford B. Hayes, James A. Garfield, Benjamin Harrison, William McKinley, William Howard Taft, and Warren G. Harding—were elected president of the United States.

During the industrial age, Ohio's developing cities were filled with immigrants from eastern, central, and southern Europe as well as migrants from Appalachia and the rural South. The latter group included the state's first major wave of African Americans, who came from the South to fill industrial jobs in northern cities.

Ohio made major economic gains during both world wars, but it also suffered setbacks during periods of economic depression. Beginning in the 1930's, tensions between workers and management led to the organization in Ohio of several powerful labor unions. Loss of jobs slowed Ohio's economy after the mid-1960's, but reorganization of the industrial base and the booming service economy created renewed optimism toward the end of the 1900's.

Opposite page, clockwise from top left: **Built in the shape of a snake, the Great Serpent Mound, near Hillsboro, is one of North America's most impressive Indian burial mounds. Holiday parades are popular among Ohioans. Cleveland, situated on Lake Erie, is a leading industrial center of the Midwest and Ohio's second most populous city.**

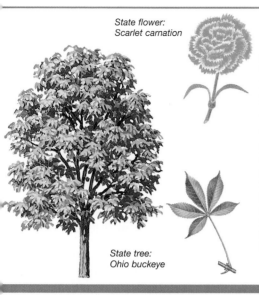

State flower:
Scarlet carnation

State tree:
Ohio buckeye

FACTS AND FIGURES

Location: East north central United States; bordered on the north by Michigan and Lake Erie, on the east by Pennsylvania and West Virginia, on the south by West Virginia and Kentucky, and on the west by Indiana.

Area: 44,828 sq mi (116,103 km²); rank, 34th.

Population: 11,353,140 (2000 census); rank, 7th.

Elevation: *Highest*—1,550 ft (472 m), at Campbell Hill in Logan County; *lowest*—433 ft (132 m) above sea level, along the Ohio River in Hamilton County.

Capital: Columbus.

Statehood: March 1, 1803; 17th state.

State Motto: *With God, all things are possible.*

State Song: "Beautiful Ohio."

Nickname: Buckeye State.

Abbreviation: OH

State bird:
Cardinal

Above: The Till Plains of west central Ohio are covered with a fertile soil that is perfectly suited to agriculture.
Right: The Ohio River forms the southern boundary of the state. Of all the rivers in the United States, only the Mississippi carries more commercial traffic.

▶ **LAND**

Millions of years ago, parts of present-day Ohio were covered by an inland sea, whose sedimentary deposits now form the underlying and surface rock structure of the state. Sandstone and shale underlie most of eastern Ohio, while limestone underlies the west. Other kinds of rocks, such as granite, were carried into the area by glaciers.

Land Regions

The land surface in Ohio includes parts of three major natural regions of the United States—the Appalachian Plateau, the Central Lowland, and the Interior Low Plateaus.

The Appalachian Plateau, a vast upland region of the eastern United States, covers the eastern half of Ohio, where it is often called the **Allegheny Plateau**. During the Ice Age,

glaciers moved over the northeastern part of the plateau, smoothing off hills and filling in valleys. The rest of the region, in southeastern Ohio, remained unglaciated, leaving steep hills and ridges separated by sharp ravines. Much of the state's timber and mineral resources are located in this rugged region.

The Central Lowland covers the western half of Ohio. Within this region, the **Great Lakes Plain** stretches south of Lake Erie in a narrow band in the east, expanding into a wide lobe in the west. Lake Maumee, a glacial lake, once covered these plains. The rest of the Central Lowland contains the **Till Plains**, where the flat to gently rolling land is covered with deep, fertile soil called till. Agriculture flourishes in this region.

The Interior Low Plateaus cover a small section of south central Ohio, in an area known as the Bluegrass region. This rural region produces much of Ohio's tobacco crop.

Rivers and Lakes

About 70 percent of the state's waterways drain southward into the Ohio River, a major transportation artery and recreational resource that forms the state's southern border. Major tributaries of the Ohio River include the Muskingum, Hocking, Scioto, Little Miami, and Great Miami rivers. Shorter but commercially important streams that drain northward into Lake Erie include the Grand, Cuyahoga, Black, Huron, Sandusky, and Maumee rivers.

Lake Erie supports international trade through the St. Lawrence Seaway and is also a valuable recreational resource. Large reservoirs dot the state. Some, like Grand Lake and Buckeye Lake, were built to maintain canal water levels. Others, like those in the Muskingum Conservancy District, were built for flood control and recreation.

The beautiful Cuyahoga Valley lies within the Appalachian (or Allegheny) Plateau in the northeastern part of the state.

Climate

Ohio temperatures vary from north to south. For the state at large, the temperature averages 31°F (–1°C) in January and 71°F (22°C) in July. Annual precipitation ranges from 32 inches (813 millimeters) in the north to 42 inches (1,067 millimeters) in the south.

Northern Ohio has much cloud cover and a growing season of about 150 days, except near Lake Erie, whose moderating effect extends it. Much of southern Ohio has a 200-day growing season.

Plant and Animal Life

When settlers first came to Ohio, about 95 percent of the land was forested. The remaining land was covered by prairie grasses. Now the grasslands are gone, and much of the forest has been reduced to woodlots. But forestlands are increasing in many areas, especially in the southeast. Oak, hickory, elm, ash, and yellow poplar are among the trees that grow in the valleys. Pine and hemlock grow on the slopes and in the uplands.

Wildlife thrives in much of Ohio. Deer, opossums, squirrels, groundhogs, raccoons, skunks, rabbits, and other small animals have adapted well to suburban life. In recent decades, beavers and a few bears and coyotes have returned to the wild, as have turkeys, bald eagles, and various waterfowl. Pheasants and other game birds, once plentiful in western Ohio, are now limited.

Walleyed pike, yellow perch, and salmon are restoring Lake Erie's reputation as a major fishing center, which was tarnished by years of pollution. Ohio's other lakes and many rivers produce catches of bass, panfish, and muskellunge.

Natural Resources

Productive soils and an abundance of water and various minerals are among Ohio's most valued natural resources. Ohio's most fertile soils are

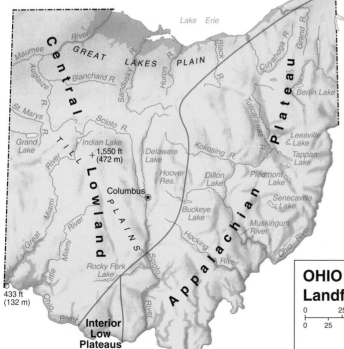

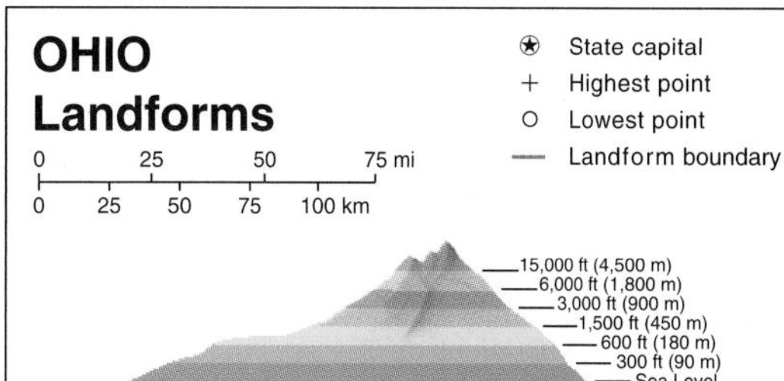

OHIO
Landforms

�	State capital
+	Highest point
O	Lowest point
—	Landform boundary

0   25   50   75 mi
0 25 50 75 100 km

15,000 ft (4,500 m)
6,000 ft (1,800 m)
3,000 ft (900 m)
1,500 ft (450 m)
600 ft (180 m)
300 ft (90 m)
Sea Level
Below

Left: The Cleveland Flats, along the Cuyahoga River, include a popular shopping and entertainment district.

Below: In the warmer months, many fairs are held throughout Ohio, such as Cleveland's Square to Square festival.

found chiefly in the western part of the state. Ohio has large deposits of bituminous coal, which is largely strip-mined. However, its high ash and sulphur content contaminates the air, reducing its attractiveness as a fuel. Local oil and natural gas wells supplement large amounts imported into the state. Clay and salt are still abundant, as are shale, limestone, sandstone, and gypsum. Sand and gravel, essential to the construction industry, are widely available.

▶ PEOPLE

Ohio has long attracted people of diverse cultures. In the early years of white settlement, Ohio's Native American tribes were joined by New Englanders, who came to dominate an area in northeastern Ohio known as the Western Reserve. Kentuckians and upland Southerners, many of Scotch-Irish heritage, settled Ohio's eastern and southern counties, while Pennsylvania Dutch (Germans) favored east central Ohio. Eastern and southern Quakers founded communities in eastern and southern Ohio.

The Germans and the Irish dominated early foreign immigration to Ohio, but significant numbers of English, Scots, Welsh, French, Swiss, and Dutch also came. A free state before the Civil War, Ohio also attracted free blacks and escaped slaves. For many years thereafter, Ohio's great industrial areas continued to attract new residents from other parts of the United States, chiefly Appalachia and the South.

Today 85 percent of Ohioans claim European descent, German being the most common ancestry. About 11.5 percent are African American. Less than 2 percent are Asian or Native American. Nearly 2 percent are culturally Hispanic. Three out of four residents were born in Ohio.

PEOPLE

Population: 11,353,140 (2000 census).

Density: 253 persons per sq mi (98 per km²).

Distribution: 74% urban; 26% rural.

Largest Cities (2000 census):

Columbus 711,470	Akron 217,074
Cleveland 478,403	Dayton 166,179
Cincinnati 331,285	Parma 85,655
Toledo 313,619	Youngstown 82,026

Source: U.S. Bureau of the Census

Persons per sq mi	Persons per km²
over 250	over 100
50-250	20-100
5-50	2-20
0-5	0-2

Toledo • Cleveland
Parma • Youngstown
Akron •
Columbus ★
Dayton •
Cincinnati •

Education

The Land Ordinance of 1785 set aside a section of land in each township to help support public schools. Ohio's first effective law providing for tax support of public education was passed in 1825, but young people who wanted an education beyond the lower grades had to enroll in private academies. In 1853 a new law was passed, authorizing the establishment of public high schools.

Higher education got its start in Ohio soon after statehood. Ohio University in Athens received its charter in 1804; Miami University in Oxford received its charter in 1809. In 1870, Ohio State University (OSU), financed by a land grant, was established in Columbus. Today, OSU branch campuses are located in Lima, Mansfield, Marion, and Newark. Other state universities include Kent State University, Bowling Green State University, the University of Akron, Cleveland State University, the University of Cincinnati, the University of Toledo, Youngstown State University, Central State University in Wilberforce, Wright State University near Dayton, and Shawnee State University in Portsmouth. More than 40 regional campuses, community colleges, and technical colleges are also assisted by the state.

Among the many well-known private senior colleges and universities are Antioch College in Yellow Springs, Denison University in Granville, College of Wooster in Wooster, Hiram College in Hiram, Oberlin College in Oberlin, Case Western Reserve University in Cleveland, Ohio Wesleyan University in Delaware, Marietta College in Marietta, and Kenyon College in Gambier.

Libraries, Museums, and the Arts

Ohio is served by an extensive system of 250 tax-supported libraries, containing more than 40 million volumes. Among the largest are the Cleveland Public Library and the

Above: All of Ohio's major cities have world-class art museums. The Cleveland Museum of Art contains important collections of European and Asian art.
Left: Ohio State University (OSU) in Columbus has one of the largest enrollments of any university in the nation.

Public Library of Cincinnati and Hamilton County.

Ohio has one presidential library—the Rutherford B. Hayes Library and Museum in Fremont, containing not only the president's papers but special collections on the Civil War, African Americans, American railroads, and Ohio and United States history. Other special libraries include the library of the Ohio Historical Center in Columbus, whose collections include early Ohio newspapers and maps. The Ohioana Library, also in Columbus, specializes in books by and about Ohioans. Major historical collections are also found in Cleveland's Western Reserve Historical Society and in the Cincinnati Historical Society.

Cleveland, Cincinnati, and Toledo have world-class art museums, and each major city has collections of special merit. Cincinnati's natural history museum shares quarters in the former Union railroad terminal, providing unique display areas. The Ohio Historical Society in Columbus has an exceptional collection of prehistoric Indian materials and also maintains the National Afro-American

Ohio is the birthplace of professional baseball. Today the state supports two professional baseball teams. The Cleveland Indians play at Jacobs Field (*pictured*); the Cincinnati Reds play at Cinergy Field.

Museum in Wilberforce and the Neil Armstrong Air and Space Museum in Wapakoneta. Ohio also offers the Rock and Roll Hall of Fame and Museum in Cleveland, the Pro Football Hall of Fame in Canton, and Inventure Place, the National Inventors Hall of Fame in Akron.

Ohio supports more than 20 symphony orchestras, including the Cleveland Orchestra, ranked among the world's finest. Opera, theater, and classical dance flourish in the larger cities and on major college campuses.

Sports

Professional baseball was born in Ohio in 1869 with the organization of the Cincinnati Red Stockings. Today, Ohio's baseball fans still support the Cincinnati Reds of the National League and the Cleveland Indians of the American League. The forerunner of the National Football League also had its origins in Ohio, in Canton. Today, Ohioans support the Cincinnati Bengals of the American Football Conference. Basketball is represented by the Cavaliers of the National Basketball Association and the Rockers of the Women's National Basketball Association. In collegiate sports, the Ohio State Buckeyes have powerhouse teams in football, basketball, and several other sports. The University of Cincinnati also has a strong basketball team that enjoys a wide following.

▶ ECONOMY

In the late 1900's, services surpassed heavy industry in Ohio's economic growth, although the state remains a major exporter of manufactured goods.

Services

Services, including government, finance, insurance, real estate, retail and wholesale trade, and other business and social services, account for more than 60 percent of Ohio's economic output, or gross state product (GSP). In many cities, the largest employers are providers of medical, educational, and government services.

PRODUCTS AND INDUSTRIES

Manufacturing: Motor vehicles and other transportation equipment, motor vehicle parts, machinery and machine parts, food products, fabricated metal products, chemicals, steel and other primary metals, electrical equipment, and paper, rubber, clay, and glass products.

Agriculture: Corn, soybeans, beef cattle, wheat, fruits and vegetables, dairy products, hogs, poultry, eggs.

Minerals: Bituminous coal, natural gas, limestone and dolomite, sand and gravel, petroleum, salt, sandstone, clay, gypsum.

Services: Wholesale and retail trade; finance, insurance, and real estate; business, social, and personal services; transportation, communication, and utilities; government.

*Gross state product is the total value of goods and services produced in a year.

Percentage of Gross State Product* by Industry

- Mining 1%
- Manufacturing 27%
- Business, social, and personal services 17%
- Agriculture 1%
- Construction 4%
- Transportation, communication, and utilities 9%
- Government 10%
- Finance, insurance, and real estate 15%
- Wholesale and retail trade 16%

Source: U.S. Bureau of Economic Analysis

Manufacturing

Manufacturing accounts for 27 percent of Ohio's GSP, which is well above the national average. Ohio is one of the nation's foremost manufacturers of cars, trucks, and airplane and motor vehicle parts; machinery and machine parts; processed foods, including packaged meats and cheeses; electrical equipment, such as home appliances and communications equipment; chemicals; and paper, rubber, glass, and clay products. Ohio is also one of the nation's leading producers of steel.

Ohio is committed to high-technology industries. It is also a leading producer of polymers, especially in the Akron-Cleveland area, known as Polymer Valley. Polymers are used to make plastics and other synthetic materials.

Left: Ohio ranks second only to Indiana in the production of steel in the United States. Much of it is produced in Cleveland.

Below: Ohio is a major agricultural state, important in the production of oats (*pictured*), corn, wheat, and soybeans. Field crops account for the largest segment of Ohio's agricultural income.

Agriculture

Corn, soybeans, wheat, fruits and vegetables, beef cattle and dairy products, hogs, poultry, and eggs are Ohio's leading farm products. Most of Ohio's largest farms are located in the central and western regions. A growing portion of the state's agricultural production is in the hands of large companies that often specialize in a single crop or a single type of livestock.

Mining and Construction

Ohio's most profitable mineral resource is bituminous coal, followed by natural gas, limestone and dolomite, sand and gravel, petroleum, salt, sandstone, clay, and gypsum. Ohio's reserves of salt, sandstone, limestone, and shale are among the nation's largest.

Construction accounts for about 3.5 percent of Ohio's GSP, placing it well ahead of farming and mining. Plentiful supplies of sand and gravel, stone, clay, and hardwood lumber are locally available.

Transportation

Ohio's first roads were its waterways. The Ohio River and Lake Erie in particular remain important transportation arteries. Ohio River barge traffic carries coal, oil, chemicals, and building materials. Ports on Lake Erie—Ashtabula, Fairport, Cleveland, Lorain, Sandusky, and Toledo—serve the Great Lakes. Several also serve as

Manufacturing is Ohio's single most important economic activity. One out of every four workers produces commercial and industrial goods, such as tools (*pictured*), machines, motor vehicles, airplanes, chemicals, and building materials.

Places of Interest

Pro Football Hall of Fame, in Canton

Rock and Roll Hall of Fame and Museum, in Cleveland

Campus Martius Museum, in Marietta, is a state memorial dedicated to the study of pioneer life. The museum contains collections of artifacts from Ohio's first permanent settlement.

Cuyahoga Valley National Park occupies 33,000 acres (13,200 hectares) in a densely populated region in the Cuyahoga River valley. Its main attractions include a scenic railroad, biking and hiking trails, and picnic facilities.

Indian Mounds, left behind by the Adena, Hopewell, and Fort Ancient Indians, are numerous in Ohio. **Fort Ancient State Memorial**, southeast of Lebanon, preserves a prehistoric enclosure containing the remains of a village site, burial mounds, and other earthworks. **Great Serpent Mound**, overlooking Brush Run in northern Adams County, features a prehistoric burial mound that was probably used as a ceremonial or religious site. Five feet (1.5 meters) high and nearly $^1/_4$ mile (400 meters) long, it was made to look like a giant snake swallowing an egg. **Mound City Group National Monument**, north of Chillicothe, preserves a group of more than 20 burial mounds built by the Hopewell. A small museum displays carvings and other artifacts.

National Underground Railroad Freedom Center, in Cincinnati, commemorates the pre-Civil War experiences of some 100,000 slaves who used the Underground Railroad to escape slavery in the South. Opened in 2004, the center was built on a bluff overlooking the Ohio River, which was considered the dividing line between

the slave states of the South and the free states of the North.

Perry's Victory and International Peace Memorial is located on South Bass Island in Lake Erie near the site of Oliver Hazard Perry's 1813 victory over a British fleet during the War of 1812. The peace memorial commemorates that victory and the unfortified boundary between the United States and Canada.

Presidential Homes, open to the public, are numerous in Ohio. They include Ulysses S. Grant's birthplace at Point Pleasant; Rutherford B. Hayes's estate, Spiegel Grove, in Fremont; James A. Garfield's home, Lawnfield, in Mentor; and Warren G. Harding's home in Marion. William Howard Taft's home in Cincinnati is preserved as a national historic site. (No homes in Ohio remain for Presidents William Henry Harrison, Benjamin Harrison, or William McKinley.)

The Pro Football Hall of Fame, established in Canton in 1962, honors

Cuyahoga Valley National Park

outstanding football players and maintains a museum of memorabilia, including film clips, equipment, and uniforms.

The Rock and Roll Hall of Fame and Museum, in Cleveland, is one of Ohio's most popular tourist attractions. It features memorabilia, such as musical instruments played by some of history's greatest rock and roll performers.

Schoenbrunn Village State Memorial, near New Philadelphia, is a restoration of a settlement founded in 1772 by a Moravian missionary and his Christian converts, many of them Indians who had come with him from Pennsylvania. The village features a church, a schoolhouse, and several residences.

Sherman State Memorial, in Lancaster, was the birthplace and boyhood home of William Tecumseh Sherman, one of the Union's most famous generals of the Civil War.

Thomas A. Edison Birthplace, in Milan, preserves the birthplace of the famous inventor. (A biography of Edison is included in Volume E.)

Zoar Village State Memorial, in Zoar, preserves a village founded in 1817 by a group of religious "separatists" from Germany who experimented in cooperative living until 1898.

State Areas. The Ohio Department of Natural Resources maintains dozens of recreation areas and places of natural beauty. They include state forests, state beaches, and state parks. For more information, contact the Division of Parks and Recreation, 2045 Morse Road, Building C-3, Columbus, Ohio 43229.

Ohio has six major port cities on Lake Erie. Barge traffic carries coal, oil, chemicals, and other industrial materials to ports on the Atlantic Ocean via the St. Lawrence Seaway.

transfer points to the St. Lawrence Seaway, which gives Ohio direct access to world ports.

Today Ohio has a vast complex of transportation facilities, including major railroads, interstate highways, and airlines. The Ohio Turnpike crosses the northern part of the state and is tied into the interstate highway system, which links Ohio's key cities. All the large cities have modern air terminals, and each of Ohio's counties has at least one modest airport for local traffic. Ohio's busiest airport is Cleveland Hopkins International.

Communication

Ohio's first newspaper—*The Centinel of the North-Western Territory*—was published in Cincinnati in 1793. At present more than 100 newspapers are published in the state, including such well-known dailies as the *Cincinnati Enquirer*, the *Plain Dealer* (Cleveland), *The Columbus Dispatch*, the *Dayton Daily News*, the *Akron Beacon Journal*, and *The Blade* (Toledo). The state has approximately 300 radio stations and 50 commercial and public television stations. It has also been a leader in developing educational computer-linking services.

▶ CITIES

About three-fourths of Ohio's people live in urban centers—communities of 2,500 or more. In keeping with national trends, most of the inner cities have lost population as residents have moved to suburban metropolitan areas and to the rural counties beyond.

Ohio's two most populous urban areas are the Cleveland metropolitan area, with nearly 3 million people, and the Cincinnati metropolitan area, with almost 2 million.

Columbus, named in honor of the explorer Christopher Columbus, is Ohio's state capital and its most populous city. Conveniently located on the Scioto River in the middle of the state, Columbus is a major center of research and education as well as government. An article on Columbus appears in Volume C.

Cleveland, Ohio's second largest city, is located on the shores of Lake Erie at the mouth of the Cuyahoga River. The city is an important regional center for manufacturing, services, and culture. An article on Cleveland appears in Volume C.

Cincinnati, founded as Losantiville in 1788, was renamed in 1790 in honor of the Society of Cincinnati, an organization of Revolutionary War officers. Located on the north bank of the Ohio River, the port city of Cincinnati prospered as trade developed in the Ohio and Miami valleys. It became known as the Queen City of the West. By about 1850, it had become the world's foremost pork-packing center, earning another nickname—Porkopolis.

Now known as the Queen City, Cincinnati remains an important industrial center and river port, known for the production of processed

Columbus, the capital of Ohio, is the state's most populous city. It is a major center of government, research, and education.

Cincinnati, known as the Queen City, is located on the north bank of the Ohio River. A major commercial and industrial center, it is also a port city for traffic between the Ohio and Mississippi rivers.

foods, soaps, machine tools, and aircraft engines. Cincinnati is also an educational and cultural center, supporting many universities and museums as well as symphony, opera, ballet, and theater companies. The Cincinnati Reds play at Great American Ball Park.

Toledo, the commercial and cultural center of northwestern Ohio, is located on the Maumee River at the western end of Lake Erie. Toledo is Ohio's largest St. Lawrence Seaway port in product value and a major manufacturer of automobiles and automotive parts. The Toledo Zoo is a major tourist attraction.

Akron (the Greek word for "high") was founded at the high point of the Ohio and Erie Canal in northeastern Ohio. Once known as the Rubber Capital of the World for its production of tires and tubes, Akron today has a more service-driven economy, although rubber products, chemicals, plastics, and machine tools are produced there. The University of Akron is a world center of polymer research.

▶ GOVERNMENT

The government of Ohio is based on a constitution that was approved in 1851. Amendments made since that time include the adoption of initiative and referendum, direct primaries, and charter government (or "home rule"), which permits each city or village to choose its own form of government.

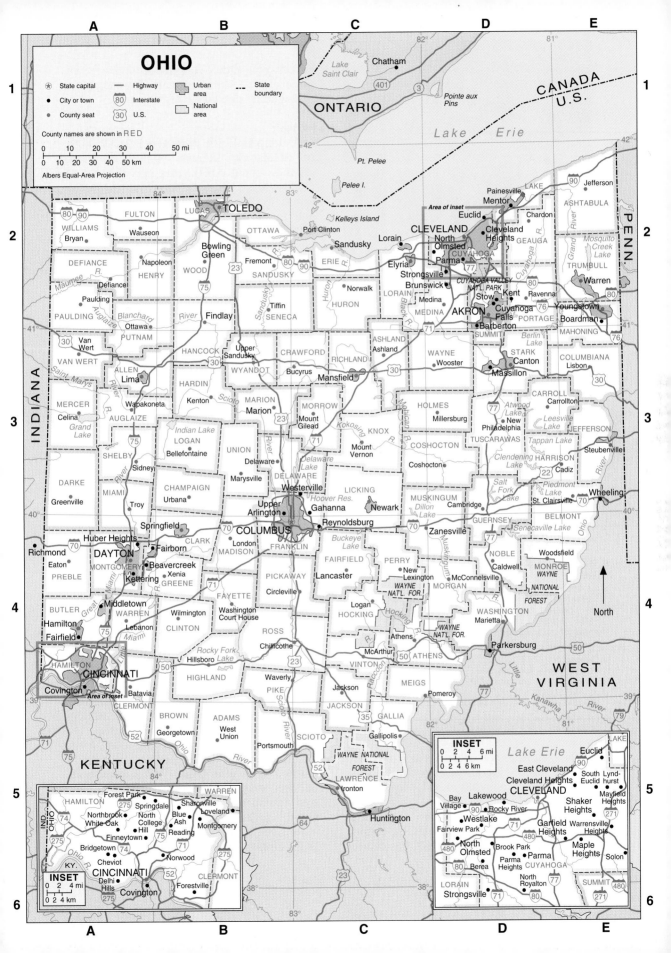

OHIO

State capital ⭑
City or town ●
County seat ●
Highway —
Interstate 80
U.S. 30
Urban area
National area
State boundary

County names are shown in RED

0 10 20 30 40 50 mi
0 10 20 30 40 50 km
Albers Equal-Area Projection

ONTARIO
CANADA
U.S.
Lake Erie

A **B** **C** **D** **E**

Chatham
Lake Saint Clair
Pointe aux Pins
Pt. Pelee
Pelee I.
Kelleys Island

1

PENN.

Jefferson
Painesville
Mentor
LAKE
Euclid
Cleveland Heights
Chardon
ASHTABULA
Area of inset
CLEVELAND
North Olmsted
CUYAHOGA
Parma
GEAUGA
Grand River
Mosquito Creek Lake
TRUMBULL

2

TOLEDO
LUCAS
FULTON
WILLIAMS
Bryan
Wauseon
OTTAWA
Port Clinton
Sandusky
Lorain
Elyria
Strongsville
Brunswick
Medina
ERIE R.
LORAIN
Norwalk
Black R.
CUYAHOGA VALLEY NAT'L PARK
Stow
Kent
Ravenna
Warren
DEFIANCE
Napoleon
HENRY
WOOD
Bowling Green
Fremont
SANDUSKY
90
75
Tiffin
SENECA
Huron R.
HURON
MEDINA
AKRON
Cuyahoga Falls
Barberton
SUMMIT
Berlin Lake
76
Youngstown
Boardman
PORTAGE
MAHONING
Maumee R.
Defiance
Paulding
PAULDING
Blanchard R.
Ottawa
PUTNAM
Findlay
HANCOCK
River
Upper Sandusky
WYANDOT
Bucyrus
CRAWFORD
Mansfield
RICHLAND
Ashland
ASHLAND
WAYNE
Wooster
Millersburg
HOLMES
New Philadelphia
TUSCARAWAS
Atwood Lake
Leesville Lake
CARROLL
Carrollton
Clendening Lake
HARRISON
Steubenville
JEFFERSON
Cadiz
Tappan Lake
22
Piedmont Lake
St. Clairsville
Wheeling
BELMONT
70

3

INDIANA
Van Wert
VAN WERT
30
Lima
ALLEN
Wapakoneta
MERCER
Celina
Grand Lake
AUGLAIZE
Saint Marys River
Kenton
HARDIN
MARION
Marion
23
Mount Gilead
MORROW
KNOX
Mount Vernon
Kokosing R.
Coshocton
COSHOCTON
MUSKINGUM
Cambridge
GUERNSEY
Senecaville Lake
Salt Fork Lake
NOBLE
Woodsfield
MONROE
WAYNE NATIONAL FOREST
Ohio River

4

Indian Lake
LOGAN
Bellefontaine
SHELBY
Sidney
MIAMI
Troy
DARKE
Greenville
Richmond
Eaton
PREBLE
DAYTON
Huber Heights
Fairborn
Beavercreek
Xenia
Kettering
GREENE
MONTGOMERY
UNION
Delaware
DELAWARE
Marysville
CHAMPAIGN
Urbana
Springfield
CLARK
70
London
MADISON
Westerville
Upper Arlington
COLUMBUS
Gahanna
Reynoldsburg
FRANKLIN
Hoover Res.
Delaware R.
Newark
LICKING
Buckeye Lake
Dillon Lake
Zanesville
70
PERRY
New Lexington
McConnelsville
MORGAN
Muskingum R.
WASHINGTON
Marietta
Parkersburg
50
North
WEST VIRGINIA

4

BUTLER
Hamilton
Fairfield
Middletown
Lebanon
WARREN
Wilmington
CLINTON
Washington Court House
FAYETTE
PICKAWAY
Circleville
Lancaster
FAIRFIELD
Logan
HOCKING
Athens
ATHENS
WAYNE NAT'L FOR.
Hocking R.
McArthur
VINTON
50

KENTUCKY
HAMILTON
CINCINNATI
Covington
Area of inset
CLERMONT
Batavia
BROWN
Georgetown
ADAMS
West Union
HIGHLAND
Hillsboro
Rocky Fork Lake
ROSS
Chillicothe
23
Waverly
PIKE
Scioto River
Jackson
JACKSON
GALLIA
Gallipolis
MEIGS
Pomeroy
77
Kanawha River
79

5

Ohio River
Portsmouth
SCIOTO
52
WAYNE NATIONAL FOREST
LAWRENCE
Ironton
64
Huntington

INSET

0 2 4 6 mi
0 2 4 6 km
Lake Erie
Euclid
East Cleveland
Cleveland Heights
South Euclid
Lyndhurst
CLEVELAND
90
Bay Village
Lakewood
Rocky River
Shaker Heights
Mayfield Heights
271
Westlake
Fairview Park
Garfield Heights
Warrensville Heights
480
North Olmsted
Brook Park
Parma
Maple Heights
Solon
80
Berea
Parma Heights
CUYAHOGA
North Royalton
77
LORAIN
Strongsville
71
80
480
SUMMIT
271

5

INSET

0 2 4 mi
0 2 4 km
HAMILTON
WARREN
Forest Park
Springdale
Sharonville
Loveland
275
Northbrook
White Oak
North College Hill
Blue Ash
Reading
Montgomery
IND.
OHIO
Finneytown
75
Bridgetown
74
Cheviot
Norwood
71
275
KY.
CINCINNATI
Delhi Hills
Covington
52
Forestville
CLERMONT

6

A **B** **C** **D** **E**

Ohio's state capitol, built before the Civil War in the classical revival style, is located in Statehouse Square in the heart of Columbus.

The governor, as chief executive, is elected every four years but can serve no more than two consecutive terms. Other elected state executives—the lieutenant governor, secretary of state, treasurer, auditor, and attorney general—are also limited to two consecutive 4-year terms.

The state legislature, known as the General Assembly, is composed of 33 senators and 99 representatives. Legislators are limited to eight years of continuous service.

GOVERNMENT

State Government
Governor: 4-year term
State senators: 33;
    4-year terms
State representatives: 99;
    2-year terms
Number of counties: 88

Federal Government
U.S. senators: 2
U.S. representatives: 18
Number of electoral votes: 20

THE GREAT SEAL OF THE STATE OF OHIO

For the name of the current governor, see STATE GOVERNMENTS in Volume S. For the names of current U.S. senators and representatives, see UNITED STATES, CONGRESS OF THE in Volume U-V.

The state supreme court has seven elected justices. Justices are also elected to the state appeals courts. Ohio has an extensive county and municipal court system.

Cities and counties in Ohio may adopt charter government. Most cities have done so, but only one county, Summit, has charter government. Other counties are managed by three elected commissioners. Townships are managed by elected trustees.

▶ **HISTORY**

As long as 13,000 years ago, Paleo-Indians, or prehistoric Indians, hunted on Ohio ground. About 3,000 years ago, the Adena (1000–100 B.C.) came to the Ohio region, followed by the Hopewell (100 B.C.–A.D. 400) and the Fort Ancient peoples (A.D. 1000–1600?). The Adena and Hopewell became known as the mound builders for the thousands of earthen mounds they constructed for burial and ceremonial purposes.

The Native American tribes of recorded history entered Ohio in the early 1700's. The Miami located in the west; the Wyandot (Hurons) settled in central Ohio and the Sandusky Valley; Seneca and Cayuga occupied the east central region; the Delaware (also known as Lenni-Lenape or Lenape) settled along the Muskingum and Tuscarawas rivers in the east; the Ottawa had villages in the north; and the Shawnee settled in the south. All were semi-nomadic farmers, hunters, and trappers and had long been exposed to European influences.

Exploration and Settlement

French traders and trappers probably were the first Europeans to see Ohio. Robert Cavelier, Sieur de La Salle, is said to have traveled down the Ohio River in 1669–70 as far as present-day Louisville, Kentucky. Later, English traders from the colonies of Virginia and Pennsylvania also came to the valley, and in 1747, land speculators organized the Ohio Company of Virginia.

After the French and Indian War (1754–63), Great Britain took possession of the Ohio region, but trouble with the local Indians began shortly after the peace treaty was signed. Pontiac, chief of the Ottawa, led several tribes in an effort to drive white settlers from the area west of the Alleghenies. He failed, but only after destroying many forts. Conflict between the Indians and the settlers reached its peak in Ohio in 1782 when frontiersmen massacred more than 90 Christianized Indian men, women, and children at Gnadenhutten.

In 1783, at the end of the Revolutionary War, Great Britain ceded to the United

States a vast territory that included Ohio. In 1787 the American Congress of the Confederation passed the Northwest Ordinance and established a system of government for the new territory that prohibited slavery. Marietta, Ohio's first permanent settlement, was established in 1788, followed soon after by Cincinnati, Chillicothe, Gallipolis, Dayton, and Cleveland.

During this time the new territory was threatened by organized Indian attacks. In 1794, General "Mad" Anthony Wayne defeated the Indians in the Battle of Fallen Timbers near present-day Toledo. The Treaty of Greenville, signed in 1795, opened Ohio to peaceful settlement.

Statehood

Early in 1802, Congress passed an act enabling Ohio to prepare for statehood. A state constitution, drawn up at Chillicothe, was approved by Congress on February 19, 1803. Ohio became a functioning state at that time. But through an oversight, Congress neglected to pass an act formally admitting Ohio to the union. Nevertheless, the first state legislature convened on March 1 of that year. Belatedly, on August 7, 1953, Congress passed a resolution formally admitting Ohio to the Union and establishing the date of statehood as March 1, 1803.

The War of 1812: The Tribes Depart

Ohio met an early challenge during the War of 1812 when its northwestern corner was invaded by British troops and their Indian allies, led by the Shawnee warrior Tecumseh. General William Henry Harrison successfully defended Fort Meigs (Perrysburg), and Major George Croghan saved Fort Stephenson (Fremont). Oliver Hazard Perry's capture of a British fleet on Lake Erie was followed by British and Indian retreat through Canada. In 1813, Harrison defeated the British in the Battle of the Thames, during which Tecumseh was killed.

On September 10, 1813, during the War of 1812, Lieutenant Commander Oliver Hazard Perry and his fleet defeated the British at the Battle of Lake Erie. Today, Perry's Victory and Peace Memorial stands at Put-in-Bay, off the Ohio shore. It honors this naval hero, whose famous words to General William Henry Harrison were "We have met the enemy and they are ours." His motto was "Don't give up the ship."

Following the war, Indians who remained in Ohio were confined to tiny reservations, but even those lands were coveted by white settlers. Federal and state authorities hastened to evict the tribes and send them west of the Mississippi River. After 1843, no organized Indian tribes remained in Ohio.

The Toledo War

For a number of years a war of words raged between Ohio and the Michigan Territory. The dispute—sometimes called the Toledo War—involved a strip of land that included the port of Toledo. In the course of the argument, both Ohio and Michigan called out their militia, but no shots were fired. Congress made a peaceful settlement in 1836, giving Ohio the disputed strip of land. As compensation, Michigan received statehood and the area between Lake Superior and Lake Michigan now known as the Upper Peninsula.

Pioneer Ohio

By 1840, Ohio was the nation's third most populous state. Canals fostered growth by opening the interior and giving access to new markets. The Ohio and Erie canal connected Portsmouth on the Ohio with Cleveland on Lake Erie. The Miami and Erie Canal connected Cincinnati and Toledo. Also important was the National Road, completed across the state by 1840. Canals and roads were both

Florence E. Allen (1884–1966), a jurist and feminist, was born in Utah but moved to Cleveland, where she was admitted to the Ohio Bar in 1914. In 1922 she became the first woman ever elected to a state supreme court (Ohio). In 1934, President Franklin D. Roosevelt appointed her a justice of the Sixth United States Circuit Court of Appeals, also a first for a woman. An advocate of human rights, international law, and world peace, Allen also was the first woman awarded New York University's Albert Gallatin Medal for service to humanity (1960).

Sherwood Anderson (1876–1941), born in Camden, spent his early years in Clyde. In 1909, Anderson started writing, partly to overcome his unhappy childhood memories. His short stories and novels describe an American "wasteland" violated by the ravages of industry. His 1919 masterpiece, *Winesburg, Ohio*, which features lonely, disappointed, and eccentric people, reveals Anderson's familiarity with small-town life. A master of narrative and psychological insight into the lives of ordinary people, Anderson influenced the work of Ernest Hemingway and other important 20th-century writers.

Mary Ann Ball Bickerdyke (1817–1901), born in Knox County, was a well-educated nurse who convinced General Ulysses Grant that Union soldiers needed her medical and welfare services. "With muscles of iron, nerves of steel," she cut through army red tape to establish hundreds of hospitals and support facilities for the Union's western armies. Appreciative troops called her Mother Bickerdyke. Others called her the General in Calico. She is buried in Galesburg, Illinois, where she is honored with a monument.

Salmon Portland Chase (1808–73), chief justice of the U.S. Supreme Court (1864–73), was born in Cornish, New Hampshire, but he began his legal career in Cincinnati. An ardent antislavery advocate, he helped form the Liberty Party in 1841 and the Free Soil Party in 1848. As a U.S. senator from Ohio (1849–55) he opposed the extension of slavery into new territories. After serving as governor of Ohio (1856–60), Chase was appointed secretary of the Treasury (1861–64) by President Abraham Lincoln to handle the financing of the Civil War. Lincoln then appointed him chief justice of the U.S. Supreme Court, where he ruled on several important Reconstruction cases and presided at the 1868 impeachment trial of President Andrew Johnson.

Sherwood Anderson

"Mother" Bickerdyke

Carl Stokes

challenged by railroads, and by 1860, Ohio had more miles of track than any other state.

The growing economy supported new schools, academies, colleges, libraries, churches, and other elements of civilized life. Concerned Ohioans fostered social reform movements and soon led the western states in support of women's rights, the temperance movement, and, particularly, the abolition of slavery throughout the nation. As soon as a fugitive slave had crossed the Ohio River into Ohio, he or she could find shelter from abolitionists working on the Underground Railroad.

The Civil War

Ohio actively supported the Union during the Civil War (1861–65). Two of the Union's highest ranking generals—Ulysses S. Grant and William Tecumseh Sherman—were native Ohioans. The state provided more than 345,000 troops to the Union Army, 35,000 of whom died. The only military action in Ohio took place when John Hunt Morgan, a Confederate officer, led a cavalry raid across southern Ohio.

Industry, Labor Unrest, and the World Wars

Industry flourished in post–Civil War Ohio, but politics favored big business while ignoring social and labor reforms. Many workers showed their discontent by striking. Two serious strikes were the railroad strike of 1877 and the Hocking River valley coal strike of 1884. Unemployment was high in the 1890's. In 1894, Jacob S. Coxey of Massillon led a large group of unemployed people—known as Coxey's Army—in a march on Washington, D.C., to demonstrate in favor of a public-works relief program.

After the United States entered World War I in 1917, Ohio sent more than 200,000 men into the armed forces. As a major producer of war materials, Ohio attracted new workers; most were white Appalachians and rural southern blacks.

Rita Frances Dove (1952–), a professor and poet whose work focuses on African American themes, was born in Akron. In 1987 she received the Pulitzer Prize in poetry for *Thomas and Beulah* (1986), the story of her grandparents' migration from the South. Dove served as U.S. poet laureate (1993–95) and in 1996 was awarded the Heinz Prize for individual achievement in the arts and humanities.

Norman Vincent Peale (1898–1993), born in Bowersville, was one of America's best-known ministers. He reached thousands from his pulpit in New York City's Marble Collegiate Church. His 1952 self-help book, *The Power of Positive Thinking*, which emphasized the therapeutic power of positive thoughts, sold more than 15 million copies. The phrase "the power of positive thinking" has since become a common expression.

Carl Burton Stokes (1927–96), born in Cleveland, was the first African American to serve as mayor of a major U.S. city. As mayor of Cleveland (1968–72), Stokes appointed African Americans to jobs, initiated nondiscrimination policies, and started the cleanup of Lake Erie and the Cuyahoga River. On leaving office he became the first African American to anchor a New York television news program (1972–80). He later served as ambassador to the Seychelles (1995–96).

President William Howard Taft and his family

Consult the Index to find more information in *The New Book of Knowledge* about the following people who were either born in Ohio or are otherwise associated with the state:

ARMSTRONG, Neil	HARDING, Warren G.	PERRY, Oliver Hazard
BABBITT, Natalie	HARRISON, Benjamin	ROCKEFELLER, John D.
BROWN, John	HARRISON, William Henry	SHERMAN, William T.
CUSTER, George Armstrong	HAYES, Rutherford B.	SPIELBERG, Steven
DARROW, Clarence	HENDRICKS, Thomas Andrews	STANTON, Edwin McMasters
DAWES, Charles Gates	KETTERING, Charles	STEINEM, Gloria
DUNBAR, Paul Laurence	McCLOSKEY, Robert	TAFT, Robert A.
EDISON, Thomas	McKINLEY, William	TAFT, William Howard
FAIRBANKS, Charles Warren	MORRISON, Toni	TECUMSEH
GABLE, Clark	MOSES, Edwin	THURBER, James
GARFIELD, James A.	NEWMAN, Paul	WOODHULL, Victoria
GISH, Lillian	NICKLAUS, Jack	WRIGHT, Wilbur and Orville
GLENN, John H., Jr.	NORRIS, George W.	YOUNG, Cy
GRANT, Ulysses S.	OAKLEY, Annie	
HAMILTON, Virginia	OWENS, Jesse	

The prosperity and building craze of the late 1920's halted abruptly as America fell into the Great Depression of the 1930's. Many of Ohio's industrial workers, who had suffered extensive and prolonged unemployment, joined what became the Congress of Industrial Organizations (CIO), a labor union targeting the rubber, steel, mining, and automotive industries. The "sit-down" strike, which originated in Ohio, was widely adopted as a tactic in bitter organizational strikes.

In the 1940's, World War II brought economic recovery to Ohio. After 840,000 Ohioans left for war, about 40 percent of the industrial jobs in the state were taken over by women. The war also created better job opportunities for African Americans.

The Late 1900's

For nearly thirty years following World War II, jobs were plentiful, and Ohio's population grew by a million or more each decade. But as Ohio's industrial plants aged and production costs soared, Ohio lost manufacturing jobs to other states and foreign countries.

By the end of the 1960's, social unrest added to Ohio's concerns, heightened by riots in Cleveland and demonstrations against the Vietnam War. Tragedy occurred at Kent State University on May 4, 1970, when Ohio's governor James Rhodes called in the National Guard to suppress antiwar demonstrators. Four unarmed students were killed and nine were injured.

By the 1990's, Ohio had regained its economic strength as more Ohioans sought work in the services and high-technology industries. City renovations and cultural preservation efforts have all helped move the state forward again. In preparation for Ohio's bicentennial celebration in 2003, more than 500 new historical markers recognizing significant places, people, and events in Ohio's history were placed across the state.

GEORGE W. KNEPPER
Author, *Ohio and Its People*

OHIO RIVER

The Ohio River begins at the junction of the Allegheny and Monongahela rivers in Pittsburgh in southwestern Pennsylvania and flows 975 miles (1,569 kilometers) before emptying into the Mississippi River at Cairo, Illinois. Its basin covers 203,900 square miles (528,101 square kilometers) and drains parts of ten states. Of the 69 tributaries within the Ohio River basin, the longest are the Cumberland, Tennessee, Wabash, Green, Allegheny, Licking, Kentucky, and Scioto. The Ohio River also forms the boundary between several states (Ohio and West Virginia; Ohio and Kentucky; Indiana and Kentucky; and Illinois and Kentucky).

An early transportation artery, the river was first used by Native Americans. The first European known to explore the river was the French fur trader Robert Cavelier, Sieur de La Salle. In early colonial days, the Ohio River formed a natural boundary between the Indians and European settlers.

In the mid-1700's, the French began building forts in the Ohio River valley. The French and Indian War (1756–63) resulted from a clash between British and French over the site of present-day Pittsburgh. Soon after this war, colonists flooded into the Ohio River valley, eager to settle the Northwest Territory (land between the Ohio and Mississippi rivers). In the 1800's the river became a natural boundary between "North" and "South."

The Ohio River has long been a major commercial waterway. Keelboats, and later steamboats, carried resources and raw materials to emerging industrial states. The use of steamboats reduced costs of transit and travel time but required modifications in the river. The U.S. Army Corps of Engineers began a series of improvements—dredging and dams that would improve transit possibilities but change the river forever. Dams and other enhancements guaranteed a 9-foot (2.7-meter) channel for navigation, but the changes in depth eliminated some of the shallow areas that had been the habitats of certain plants and animals.

Today barge transport carries about 250 million tons of cargo annually, notably coal and other fossil fuels. Vacationers are attracted to the river's many recreational offerings, including boating and fishing.

NANCY R. BAIN
Department of Geography
Ohio University

OHM, GEORG SIMON. See ELECTRICITY (Ohm's Law).

OIL. See PETROLEUM AND PETROLEUM REFINING.

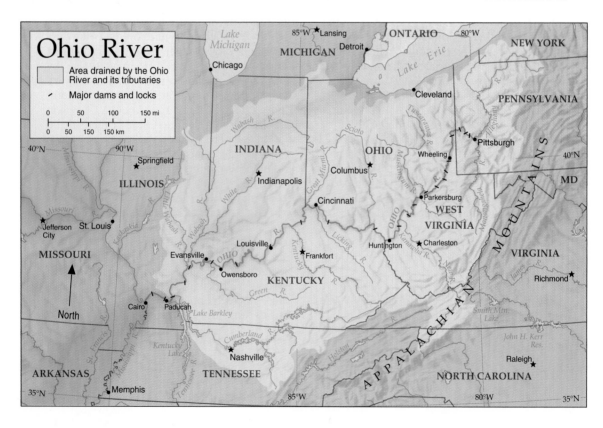

Ohio River

- Area drained by the Ohio River and its tributaries
- Major dams and locks

0 50 100 150 mi
0 50 150 150 km

OILS AND FATS

Oils and fats are an important class of compounds produced by plants and animals. Living things use these compounds as a form of stored energy. And many different products, including food and cleansers, are made from fats and oils.

Oils are liquids that feel greasy to the touch and do not mix with water. The word "oil" can refer to several different substances. Essential oils are compounds obtained from plants; they have the characteristic taste or odor of the plant from which they are obtained and are used in perfumes and flavorings. Mineral oils are made from petroleum and are used chiefly as fuels and lubricants. Another class of oils consists of the liquid fats obtained from plants and animals. This article will focus on these and their relationship to fats.

▶ CHEMISTRY OF OILS AND FATS

In chemistry, a fat is a molecule produced by combining the alcohol **glycerol** (also called **glycerin**) with **fatty acids**. A fat may be either liquid (an oil) or a solid. While all liquid fats are oils, not all oils are fats. For the purposes of this article, we will define "fat" as all compounds, both liquids and solids, formed by combining glycerol with fatty acids.

A molecule of glycerol can react with up to three fatty acid molecules to form one molecule of fat. For this reason, fats are called **triglycerides** ("tri" means "three"). In nature, triglycerides usually contain more than one

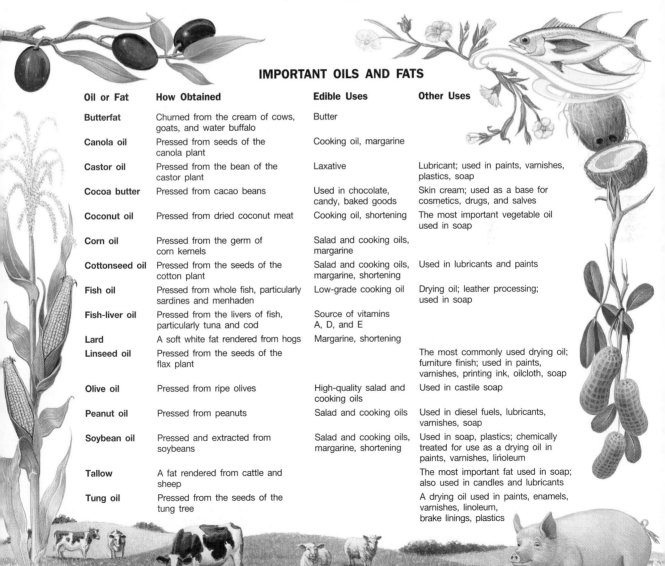

IMPORTANT OILS AND FATS

Oil or Fat	How Obtained	Edible Uses	Other Uses
Butterfat	Churned from the cream of cows, goats, and water buffalo	Butter	
Canola oil	Pressed from seeds of the canola plant	Cooking oil, margarine	
Castor oil	Pressed from the bean of the castor plant	Laxative	Lubricant; used in paints, varnishes, plastics, soap
Cocoa butter	Pressed from cacao beans	Used in chocolate, candy, baked goods	Skin cream; used as a base for cosmetics, drugs, and salves
Coconut oil	Pressed from dried coconut meat	Cooking oil, shortening	The most important vegetable oil used in soap
Corn oil	Pressed from the germ of corn kernels	Salad and cooking oils, margarine	
Cottonseed oil	Pressed from the seeds of the cotton plant	Salad and cooking oils, margarine, shortening	Used in lubricants and paints
Fish oil	Pressed from whole fish, particularly sardines and menhaden	Low-grade cooking oil	Drying oil; leather processing; used in soap
Fish-liver oil	Pressed from the livers of fish, particularly tuna and cod	Source of vitamins A, D, and E	
Lard	A soft white fat rendered from hogs	Margarine, shortening	
Linseed oil	Pressed from the seeds of the flax plant		The most commonly used drying oil; furniture finish; used in paints, varnishes, printing ink, oilcloth, soap
Olive oil	Pressed from ripe olives	High-quality salad and cooking oils	Used in castile soap
Peanut oil	Pressed from peanuts	Salad and cooking oils	Used in diesel fuels, lubricants, varnishes, soap
Soybean oil	Pressed and extracted from soybeans	Salad and cooking oils, margarine, shortening	Used in soap, plastics; chemically treated for use as a drying oil in paints, varnishes, linoleum
Tallow	A fat rendered from cattle and sheep		The most important fat used in soap; also used in candles and lubricants
Tung oil	Pressed from the seeds of the tung tree		A drying oil used in paints, enamels, varnishes, linoleum, brake linings, plastics

kind of fatty acids. Since there are many different fatty acids, there are many different triglycerides. These differences determine the characteristics of the different fats.

For each fatty acid molecule that reacts with a glycerol molecule, a molecule of water is released. This reaction is reversible. Fats react with water to produce fatty acids and glycerol in a process called **hydrolysis**. Fatty acids are an important fuel source for living organisms, but they are not stored like fats. When the body needs fuel, triglycerides are hydrolyzed to release fatty acids.

Because the body stores fat, eating too much fat will make a person gain weight. While eating some fat is necessary for good health, having too much body fat leads to a condition called obesity. Obese people have many health problems, the most common of which are diabetes, cardiovascular disease, and an increased risk of some cancers.

▶ SATURATED, UNSATURATED, AND HYDROGENATED FATS

A fatty acid molecule is composed of a long chain of carbon and hydrogen atoms with an acid group on one end. Fatty acids can be either **saturated** or **unsaturated**. In saturated fatty acids, the carbon atoms are bonded to the maximum number of hydrogen atoms possible. If there are double bonds between carbon atoms, then the number of hydrogen atoms present is reduced, and the molecule is unsaturated. Saturated fats are usually solids, while unsaturated fats tend to be oils. A fatty acid with one double bond is **monounsaturated**, while **polyunsaturated** fats have more than one double bond.

To increase the shelf life of oils—and to change liquid oil to a solid or semisolid form—companies **hydrogenate** polyunsaturated fats by adding hydrogen atoms to the carbon-carbon double bonds. During hydrogenation some naturally occurring fatty acids in vegetable oils may be converted into a different kind, called trans-fatty acids.

The small structural differences among the different kinds of fatty acids make them react very differently in the human body. Saturated fats increase the amount of cholesterol in the blood, while unsaturated fats lower blood cholesterol. Trans-fatty acids raise the level of "bad" cholesterol (low-density lipids, or LDL's) in the blood and decrease the level of "good" cholesterol (high-density lipids, or HDL's). High cholesterol levels, especially LDL's, are thought to promote cardiovascular disease.

▶ SOURCES

All plants and animals, including human beings, manufacture their own fats and oils. Besides serving as a fuel source, the fatty tissues where oils and fats are stored in animals serve as cushions to protect some body parts and as insulation against the cold. Some of the familiar animal fats are lard (from hogs), tallow (from cattle and sheep), and butter (from the milk of various animals).

Because dairy fats are high in saturated fats, many milk products have been treated to reduce the fat content. For example, the most common form of whole milk is 4 percent fat, but milk is available with 2 percent, 1 percent, and 0 percent fat.

Fats and oils from plants are found mostly in fruits and seeds. The most important vegetable oils come from soybeans, cottonseed, corn, peanuts, safflower, olives, and coconuts.

▶ PREPARING FATS AND OILS FOR USE

More than 60 percent of the fats in our diet occur in the food we eat. Meat, fish, eggs, dairy products, fruits, nuts, and vegetables all contain fat. But for many purposes—cooking, for example—pure fat is needed. This fat must be extracted from its source. Three common methods of extracting fats from animal tissues and from vegetables are **rendering**, **pressing**, and **solvent extraction**.

In rendering, fat is removed from animal tissues by heating. Animal tissues may also be pressed after rendering to extract any residual fat. But pressing is used mainly in extracting fats and oils from seeds and fruit pulp. First the shells are removed from seeds, and the seeds and fruit pulp are crushed. Then machines called presses squeeze out the oil. Usually the amount of oil that can be obtained is increased by first heating, or hot pressing, the seeds and pulp. If they are not heated first, the process is called cold pressing. The material that remains after pressing is called cake. It is usually rich in proteins and is used for animal feed. In solvent extraction, a solvent is used to dissolve the oil and remove it from the material. The solvent is then evaporated, leaving the pure oil.

▶ OILS AND FATS IN THE DIET

Oils and fats are very important food components. They supply more than twice as much energy as the same amounts of proteins or carbohydrates. Additionally, some oils and fats are sources of vitamins needed for good health and proper growth. Olive oil, for example, is an excellent source of vitamin K.

Many edible products are made from fats and oils. Some products are simply the extracted and purified fat or oil. Lard, salad oil, and cooking oil are examples. Mayonnaise and salad dressings are created by mixing oils with spices and other foods. Butter is prepared by churning cream. Margarine and semisolid shortenings are made from vegetable oils that have been hydrogenated.

▶ OTHER USES OF OILS AND FATS

One of the most important products made from fat is soap. Soap results from the reaction of a fatty acid with lye (also known as sodium hydroxide or caustic soda) or potassium hydroxide. Fat is first hydrolyzed to form glycerol and fatty acids, then the fatty acids are treated with sodium or potassium hydroxide, producing soap.

Certain oils, such as linseed oil and tung oil, are called drying oils. They are used in paints, varnishes, and linoleum and other coverings. They combine with oxygen from the air to create a tough, elastic, waterproof film, which sticks to a surface and protects it.

KENTON H. WHITMIRE
Rice University

See also DETERGENTS AND SOAP; NUTRITION.

O'KEEFFE, GEORGIA (1887–1986)

Bones bleached white by the desert sun, flowers, rolling hills, rocks, trees, and the sky itself are frequent subjects of paintings by the American artist Georgia O'Keeffe. Her works portray nature simply but dramatically, with precise lines and glowing colors.

Georgia O'Keeffe was born on a farm in Sun Prairie, Wisconsin, on November 15, 1887. At the age of 16, she went to study art in Chicago. She later continued her studies in New York City. In 1912 she accepted a posi-

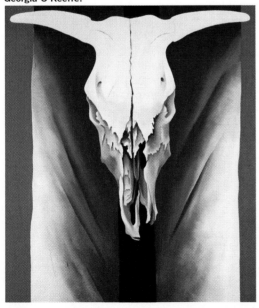

Cow's Skull: Red, White and Blue, painted in 1931 by Georgia O'Keeffe.

tion as an art teacher at a small college in Texas.

A selection of her drawings was exhibited in New York City in 1916, at the gallery of Alfred Stieglitz, the photographer. The drawings were well received. In 1918, O'Keeffe moved to New York to paint. She became friendly with a group of artists who gathered at Stieglitz' gallery, and in 1924 she married Stieglitz and joined him in running the gallery. Some of her most famous works date from this period. In flower studies such as *Black Iris* (1926), she enlarged a flower and painted it in its simplest form by eliminating detail. During the 1920's and 1930's, she also painted many views of the New York City skyline.

After Stieglitz died in 1946, O'Keeffe moved to New Mexico. She settled down near Abiquiu, on the edge of the desert. The wild juniper and aspen trees around her house and the stark hills of the desert became inspirations for her paintings, as did animal bones she found in the desert. In 1984 she moved to Santa Fe, New Mexico, where she lived until her death on March 6, 1986.

In her works, O'Keeffe combined simplicity with strength. She is known as an artist who drew inspiration from nature and made it into an artistic expression wholly her own.

PATRICK STEWART
Williams College

OKLAHOMA

Oklahoma means "red people" in the Choctaw Indian language. In 1866, Choctaw leaders suggested the name for a proposed territory in which the Native American tribes of the area would be united. This did not happen, but the name Territory of Oklahoma was later adopted when portions of the present-day state were opened to non-Indian settlement.

Some of the first white settlers were responsible for Oklahoma's nickname—the Sooner State. In the 1880's and 1890's, the U.S. Congress opened various lands for settlement, leading to what were known as land runs. Some of the would-be settlers slipped across the boundary lines a few days and others a few hours before the official openings. Because they entered the area sooner than allowed by law, they were called Sooners. Citizens of Oklahoma later adopted the label as a state nickname.

Oklahoma is a southwestern state, located largely in the southern plains of the United States. The Ouachita Mountains and the Ozarks cover the eastern third of the state. The remaining portions are relatively flat prairie land and high plains interrupted by occasional hills and mountain systems.

Traditionally, Oklahoma's economy has centered on agriculture and mining. The plains of north central Oklahoma produce the bulk of the state's most important cash crop—wheat. Cattle, cotton, peanuts, soybeans, and pecans are also important products. So, too, are petroleum and natural gas. The first successful oil well was drilled at Bartlesville in 1897, and after the Glenn Pool gusher was struck in 1905, Oklahoma became a leading producer of oil. In recent decades, however, the economy has diversified, with jobs increasing in the manufacturing and service industries. As a result, Oklahoma has become more urbanized. More than half of all Oklahomans now live in two metropolitan areas: Oklahoma City, the state capital, and Tulsa.

Although known as a home for Native Americans, Oklahoma had only a small population of Indians upon the arrival of the first Spanish explorers in 1541. After the United States acquired the region as part of the Louisiana Purchase in 1803, Oklahoma became the home of thousands of Chickasaw,

State flag

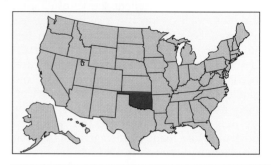

Choctaw, Cherokee, Creek, and Seminole Indians—known as the Five Civilized Tribes—who were removed from their lands in the southeastern states. Following the Civil War, thousands of Plains Indians from reservations in Kansas and Nebraska were also moved to Oklahoma as part of a new federal policy. But beginning in the 1890's, Oklahoma's Indian reservations were dissolved, and Native Americans there received individual allotments of property. Today Oklahoma has the fourth highest percentage of Native American residents, after Alaska, New Mexico, and South Dakota.

▶ LAND

Oklahoma is shaped like a huge saucepan with a long strip called the Panhandle pointing to the west. The land slopes from the highest elevations of the Panhandle in northwestern Oklahoma down to the coastal plains in the southeast. Some mountain systems and other rough terrain occasionally disrupt that general pattern.

Land Regions

Most of Oklahoma is located in the Central Lowland of the United States. The eastern third of the state includes portions of the Coastal Plain, the Ozark Plateau, and the

Opposite page, clockwise from top left: **A Texas longhorn drinks from a stream in western Oklahoma. Many Oklahomans are employed in oil-related industries. The Red Earth Festival in Oklahoma City celebrates the state's Native American population.**

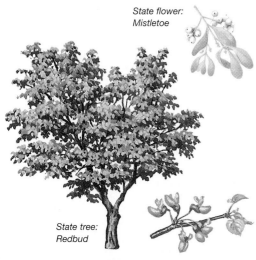

State flower: Mistletoe

State tree: Redbud

FACTS AND FIGURES

Location: West south central United States; bordered on the north by Colorado and Kansas, on the east by Missouri and Arkansas, on the south by Texas, and on the west by Texas and New Mexico.

Area: 69,903 sq mi (181,048 km²); rank, 20th.

Population: 3,450,654 (2000 census); rank, 27th.

Elevation: *Highest*—4,973 ft (1,516 m), at Black Mesa in Cimarron County; *lowest*—287 ft (87 m), along the Little River in McCurtain County.

Capital: Oklahoma City.

Statehood: November 16, 1907; 46th state.

State Motto: *Labor omnia vincit* ("Labor conquers all things").

State Song: "Oklahoma!"

Nickname: Sooner State.

Abbreviations: OK; Okla.

State bird: Scissor-tailed flycatcher

Left: Mount Scott is the highest of the granite peaks that rise in the Wichita Mountains National Wildlife Refuge, in southwestern Oklahoma.

Below: The fertile plains of central and western Oklahoma make the state one of the nation's leading producers of wheat.

Ouachita Mountains. Extreme northwestern Oklahoma lies in the Great Plains.

The Central Lowland, covering central and western Oklahoma, is the state's largest region. The relatively flat terrain of the Central Lowland is often broken by low hills and ridges. The region also includes two ancient, worn mountain systems—the mostly limestone **Arbuckle Mountains** of south central Oklahoma and the granite peaks of the **Wichita Mountains** in the southwest.

The remainder of the Central Lowlands includes areas known as the **Prairie Plains**, the **Sandstone Hills**, the **Red Bed Plains**, and the **Gypsum Hills**. The eastern part of the Central Lowlands is covered with scrub oak, while the central and western areas are largely grasslands.

The Coastal Plain, a low-elevation area that stretches along most of the United States' Atlantic and Gulf coasts, extends into southern Oklahoma, where it is called the Red River Plains. The area consists of grassy prairies alternating with large stands of trees on level and gently rolling land.

The Ozark Plateau, which extends into Oklahoma from southern Missouri and northern Arkansas, is a forested rolling upland. Clear, swiftly flowing streams cut through this rocky uplift.

The Ouachita Mountains, part of a system that extends out of southeastern Arkansas, contain the most rugged terrain in the state. The Ouachita Mountains are a series of rough ridges and deep, narrow valleys, running east to west. Kiamichi Mountain and Winding Stair Mountain are among the highest ridges. The Arkansas River, which is sur-

rounded by steep-sided hills and rolling valleys, flows through the northern part of the mountain system.

The Great Plains, which extend through the midsection of the United States, include the Oklahoma Panhandle and the northwestern corner of the state. Windblown and semi-arid, Oklahoma's Great Plains area contains the state's highest elevations. Black Mesa, the state's highest point, rises to 4,973 feet (1,516 meters) in this region.

Rivers and Lakes

Oklahoma is drained by two principal river systems—the Arkansas River and the Red River. The Arkansas River system drains the northern two-thirds of the state. Chief tributaries include the Verdigris, Cimarron, and Canadian rivers. The Red River system covers much of southern Oklahoma and forms the state's boundary with Texas. Its main tributaries are the Washita, Boggy Creek, and Little rivers and the North Fork of the Red River.

Dams built on many of the rivers in eastern Oklahoma have created numerous reservoirs, the largest of which is Eufaula Lake. These lakes provide flood control, hydroelectric power, domestic water storage, and recreational facilities.

Climate

Oklahoma's climate is classified as humid subtropical, but the high plains of the northwest approach a dry continental climate. Winters are generally mild. Temperatures in January, the coldest month, average 47°F (8°C). Summers are hot, with temperatures averaging 82°F (28°C) in July. The growing season ranges from 170 days in the Panhandle to 240 days in the south central region.

The state receives an average of 33 inches (838 millimeters) of precipitation per year, but the amount varies widely. Portions of the Panhandle average less than 16 inches (406 millimeters) annually, whereas areas in the southeast can average more than 54 inches (1,372 millimeters).

Most of Oklahoma's rainfall occurs during the spring, which is also the time when tornadoes are likely to occur, particularly on the plains, when warm air from the Gulf of Mexico clashes with cool air from the north. Oklahoma experiences more tornadoes each year than most other states.

Plant and Animal Life

Forests dominate the eastern sections of Oklahoma. Hardwoods, mostly oak and hickory, cover the Ozark Plateau, while mixed pine and oak trees are characteristic of the Ouachita Mountains. Hardwoods also thrive along the state's rivers. The remainder of eastern Oklahoma as well as portions of central Oklahoma are located in a savanna-woodland zone, where trees and grasslands are intermixed. Westward, tall grass prairies give way to the short grasses of the plains.

Large game animals, such as white-tailed deer, mule deer, elk, and pronghorn antelope, are either native to Oklahoma or have been introduced in recent years. Bison and black bears, once plentiful, now exist only in managed areas. Small animals include raccoons, opossums, rabbits, squirrels, beavers, wild turkeys, quail, and numerous songbirds and waterfowl. Both eastern and western subspecies of various birds and other animals are found in the state.

Natural Resources

Since the early 1900's, Oklahoma has been among the top five producers of petroleum and natural gas. Eastern Oklahoma has enor-

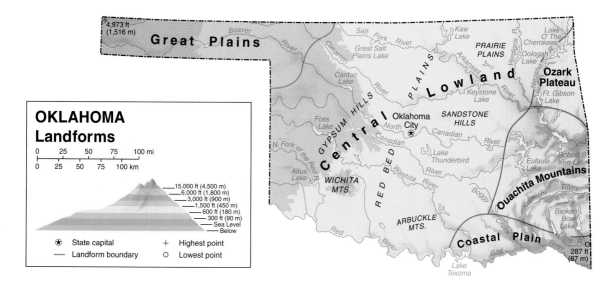

**OKLAHOMA
Landforms**

0   25   50   75   100 mi

0   25   50   75   100 km

— 15,000 ft (4,500 m)
— 6,000 ft (1,800 m)
— 3,000 ft (900 m)
— 1,500 ft (450 m)
— 600 ft (180 m)
— 300 ft (90 m)
— Sea Level
— Below

⊛ State capital   + Highest point
— Landform boundary   ○ Lowest point

Above: A Native American father and son sell handicrafts at an outdoor market.
Left: Crowds in Norman enjoy a Juneteenth Celebration, a festival featuring jazz, blues, and gospel music.

mous coal deposits. The state also contains large quantities of gypsum, clay, crushed stone, glass sand, tripoli, and iodine.

The large reservoirs of eastern Oklahoma offer one of the most important resources for the state. Water from these lakes is used for hydroelectric production, drinking water, and recreation. The forests of eastern Oklahoma are also a major resource. More than 140 native species of trees grow in the state, including oak, cottonwood, walnut, pecan, sweet gum, and short leaf and loblolly pine. Many are harvested to produce pulp for paper, utility poles, charcoal, and wood for furniture.

▶ **PEOPLE**

When the first European explorers arrived in what is now Oklahoma, the Quapaw, Caddo, Wichita, and Plains Apache were among the Native American tribes that lived or hunted there. In the 1820's and 1830's, the federal government moved thousands of Chickasaw, Choctaw, Cherokee, Creek, and Seminole Indians into Oklahoma. They were known as the Five Civilized Tribes because whites considered their societies more advanced than those of other tribes. After the Civil War (1861–65), the government confiscated the western half of the Five Civilized Tribes' lands to make room for thousands of additional Indians from dozens of Plains and Woodlands tribes.

Today almost 8 percent of Oklahoma residents are Native Americans. African Americans make up nearly 8 percent of the population. Some are descended from slaves held by the Five Civilized Tribes before the Civil War. Others moved there after the Civil War or were among the settlers during the land runs of the late 1800's. Asians make up little more than 1 percent. Of the total population, about 5 percent claim Hispanic heritage.

White settlers began entering Oklahoma in large numbers beginning in 1889, and by 1900 the population of the territory was almost 800,000. When Oklahoma became a state in

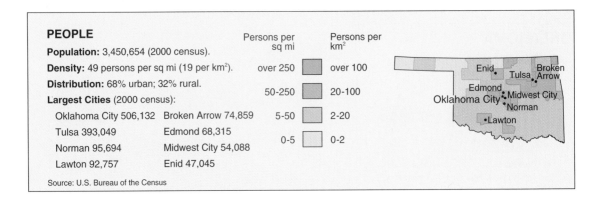

PEOPLE

Population: 3,450,654 (2000 census).

Density: 49 persons per sq mi (19 per km²).

Distribution: 68% urban; 32% rural.

Largest Cities (2000 census):

Oklahoma City 506,132	Broken Arrow 74,859
Tulsa 393,049	Edmond 68,315
Norman 95,694	Midwest City 54,088
Lawton 92,757	Enid 47,045

Source: U.S. Bureau of the Census

Persons per sq mi	Persons per km²
over 250	over 100
50-250	20-100
5-50	2-20
0-5	0-2

Enid · Tulsa · Broken Arrow
Edmond · Midwest City
Oklahoma City · Norman
· Lawton

1907, the population had expanded to more than 1.4 million. The period between 1907 and 1920 saw continued rapid growth. Newcomers represented almost every state in the Union, as well as many European countries. In 1910, at the peak of European immigration, small numbers of Germans and Czechs settled in the wheat-growing areas. Italians, Poles, Lithuanians, Britons, Germans, and others settled in the coal-mining regions in the southeast.

Education

When the Five Civilized Tribes settled in Oklahoma in the early 1800's, they established schools and eventually built several academies or seminaries for advanced learning. Christian missions helped support these institutions. In the 1890's, non-Indians also began establishing public schools and colleges.

After statehood, Oklahoma established additional colleges and created a system of public education. Today the state has about 500 local public school districts and has 13 public universities.

The University of Oklahoma in Norman and Oklahoma State University in Stillwater are the largest state-sponsored universities. Others are located in Edmond, Durant, Ada, Tahlequah, Alva, Weatherford, Lawton, Langston, Goodwell, Chickasha, and Tulsa.

The state also has 13 public junior and community colleges.

The University of Tulsa is the state's largest private university. Twelve additional private two-year and four-year colleges or universities are located throughout the state.

Libraries, Museums, and the Arts

There are almost 200 public libraries in Oklahoma. The State Department of Libraries houses the state archives. It also serves the various state agencies as a research center and coordinates services for public libraries statewide.

The state's largest library, located at the University of Oklahoma in Norman, includes an outstanding history of science collection, the Western History Collections, and the Carl Albert Congressional Archives. Libraries at Oklahoma State University in Stillwater and the University of Tulsa also contain large holdings and have significant archival records. The Oklahoma Historical Society in Oklahoma City includes both a library and an archives and manuscripts division with official papers of various Indian tribes.

Oklahoma also has many locally and privately funded museums. Tulsa is the home of two significant museums originally funded by wealthy oil men. The Thomas Gilcrease Insti-

Above: Visitors enjoy exhibits at the National Cowboy Hall of Fame and Western Heritage Center in Oklahoma City. *Left:* Oklahoma State University in Stillwater is the state's second largest public university.

tute of American History and Art, also known as the Gilcrease Museum, contains works on the American West and Native Americans. The Philbrook Museum of Art includes Native American artwork and Italian Renaissance paintings and sculptures. In Oklahoma City, the National Cowboy Hall of Fame and Western Heritage Center commemorates men and women important to the development of the American West.

The Oklahoma Museum of Natural History, on the campus of the University of Oklahoma in Norman, houses an impressive collection of prehistoric fossils and modern species displayed in natural surroundings. One of the state's most popular museums is the Will Rogers Memorial in Claremore, commemorating the cowboy-humorist, Oklahoma's best-known native son.

Numerous communities support seasonal arts, theater, and music festivals. In Oklahoma City, theatrical and musical productions take place at Stage Center and at the Civic Center Music Hall, which is also home for the Oklahoma City Philharmonic Orchestra. Cultural activities in Tulsa include the Tulsa Ballet Theatre and Tulsa Opera. The Greenwood Cultural Center also sponsors events.

▶ ECONOMY

Long dependent on petroleum, natural gas, and agriculture, Oklahoma's economy widened its scope in the late 1900's. Today's developing service industries produce the most revenue.

Services

Service industries employ about 70 percent of Oklahoma's workforce and account for approximately 70 percent of the total gross state product (GSP). Federal, state, and local government make up the largest service segment.

In recent years Oklahoma has seen a major increase in business services. Several car rental companies established their reservations headquarters in Oklahoma City and Tulsa. These two metropolitan areas are also centers for computer-operations assistance. Other service industries employing large numbers of Oklahomans include health-care, financial, transportation, and communication services, followed by wholesale and retail trade.

Manufacturing

Manufacturing industries employ about 13 percent of Oklahoma's workforce. Fabricated metal products and industrial machinery are the most important products, followed by petroleum and coal products and transportation equipment. Food processing has become increasingly profitable with the establishment of poultry plants in eastern Oklahoma and pork processing plants in the western part of the state. Electronic and electrical equipment are also important.

Mining and Construction

Oklahoma is a major producer of natural gas and oil. However, the mining sector has become less important as oil and gas reserves have declined. Coal production remains steady but small. The state's nonfuel minerals include gypsum, limestone, granite, sand, and clay.

Construction in Oklahoma is most active in the two major urban areas. The building of homes and businesses are the main activities. Government-sponsored road building also accounts for a major segment of the construction business.

Oil derricks are a familiar sight on the plains of central Oklahoma. Despite a decline in oil reserves, Oklahoma remains an important oil-producing state.

Above: Oklahomans manufacture a significant amount of electronic and electrical products.

Left: Oklahoma City stockyards hold cattle headed for market. Cattle account for about half of the state's agricultural income.

Agriculture

Following the national pattern, Oklahoma's agricultural sector now has a smaller share of the overall economic output than in previous decades. It amounts to just under 3 percent of the GSP. About one-half the value of agricultural output comes from beef cattle. Grazing areas are located throughout the state, with the most important concentrations in the hills north of Tulsa, portions of western Oklahoma, and various mountainous areas.

Other livestock, mostly poultry and hogs, are also important. Hog production has increased significantly in recent years, and the state is now among the top ten producers of pork. Dairy farms are also numerous.

Wheat is by far the most important crop, accounting for about one-third of all cash crops. North central and northwestern Oklahoma produce the bulk of the wheat crop. Substantial amounts of cotton are produced, particularly in the irrigated lands in the southwest. Other important crops include peanuts, soybeans, pecans, hay, and sorghum.

Transportation

Tulsa International Airport and Will Rogers World Air Port in Oklahoma City are the state's largest air centers. Facilities in Lawton, Enid, and Ponca City also provide airline service.

There is no railroad passenger service in Oklahoma, but about 20 railway companies provide freight service over almost 4,000 miles (6,400 kilometers) of tracks. Controlling the most mileage of tracks are the Union Pacific and Burlington Northern/Santa Fe railroad companies.

Trucks and buses provide freight service on Oklahoma's 1,000 miles (1,600 kilometers) of interstate highways. Three bus lines offer passenger service.

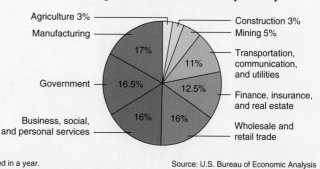

PRODUCTS AND INDUSTRIES

Manufacturing: Industrial machinery and equipment, fabricated metal products, petroleum and coal products, motor vehicles and equipment, electronic and electric equipment, rubber and plastics products, food products.

Agriculture: Cattle, wheat.

Minerals: Petroleum, natural gas.

Services: Wholesale and retail trade; finance, insurance, and real estate; business, social, and personal services; transportation, communication, and utilities; government.

*Gross state product is the total value of goods and services produced in a year.

Percentage of Gross State Product* by Industry

Agriculture 3%
Manufacturing 17%
Government 16.5%
Business, social, and personal services 16%
Wholesale and retail trade 16%
Finance, insurance, and real estate 12.5%
Transportation, communication, and utilities 11%
Mining 5%
Construction 3%

Source: U.S. Bureau of Economic Analysis

Places of Interest

Cherokee Heritage Center and National Museum, south of Tahlequah at Park Hill, offers permanent museum displays and an annual pageant depicting the Trail of Tears. The Tsa-La-Gi Ancient Village in the complex is a re-creation of a Cherokee settlement from the 1500's. Historical cemeteries, where Cherokee leaders are buried, are located nearby.

Cherokee Heritage Center, at Park Hill

Fort Gibson, in the town of Fort Gibson, is a replica of Oklahoma's first military post. Established in the 1820's, it ceased to be an active fort in 1890. During the fort's heyday, soldiers kept peace among the tribes in the area and also played a pivotal role during the Civil War. Many of the houses in the residential area adjacent to the site are actually old fort buildings.

Fort Sill, north of Lawton, houses the U.S. Army Field Artillery and Fort Sill Museum. The museum displays numerous pieces of artillery and depicts the conflicts with the southern plains tribes. A number of historic sites are located there, including cemeteries where the Comanche chief Quanah Parker and the Apache leader Geronimo are buried. Established in 1869, the fort remains an active post and principal center for U.S. Army artillery training.

Guthrie, the territorial and first state capital of Oklahoma, today is the largest urban historical preservation district in the United States. Numerous shops, restaurants, bed and breakfast lodges, and museums, all housed in about 400 city blocks of Victorian-style buildings, make the town a unique site. The Territorial Museum displays artifacts of pre-statehood history. The State Capital Publishing Museum has an outstanding collection of printing equipment from the 1800's.

International Gymnastics Hall of Fame moved to Oklahoma City in 1996. It includes a gymnastics museum and a library that contains a large collection of books as well as videos and films of major gymnastics events dating back to the 1930's.

National Cowboy Hall of Fame and Western Heritage Center, in Oklahoma City, celebrates the history of the cowboy and the American West. Sponsored by 17 western states, it includes paintings, artifacts, and memorials to famous rodeo cowboys as well as to a number of actors who made significant western films.

Old Route 66, once called America's Main Street, passes through Oklahoma from the northeast to the southwest. The state at one time contained 392 miles (631 kilometers) of the highway, which from the 1920's to the 1970's was traveled by countless thousands of migrants and tourists. Although abandoned by the U.S. highway system in the 1980's, much of the old highway in Oklahoma still exists, along with dozens of colorful diners, gas stations, and souvenir shops. The Oklahoma Route 66 Museum in Clinton is a highlight on the old highway.

Ouachita National Forest, in southeastern Oklahoma, provides dozens of recreation areas, hiking trails, and horseback riding camps. Talimena Scenic Drive follows the crest of Winding Stair Mountain and is especially popular during the fall foliage season.

Tallgrass Prairie Preserve, north of Pawhuska, protects 35,000 acres (14,000 hectares) of the tallgrass ecosystem. A

Guthrie

road through the preserve provides a look at bison and hundreds of other species of animals and plants.

Wichita Mountains Wildlife Refuge is a sanctuary for a variety of wildlife, including bison, elk, and longhorn cattle. Located north of Lawton among granite peaks, the refuge offers hiking, camping, fishing, rock climbing, and other activities.

State Recreation Areas. Oklahoma has more than 50 state parks and dozens of state museums and historic sites. Among them are Alabaster Caverns State Park, near Freedom, with its large gypsum caves; Great Salt Plains State Park near Cherokee, where white salt plains dazzle visitors; Robbers Cave State Park, north of Wilburton, where outlaws reportedly hid from lawmen; and Spiro Mounds Archaeological Park, site of large earthen mounds of the ancient Mississippian Indian culture. For more information on state parks and places of interest, contact the Oklahoma Tourism and Recreation Department, 15 N. Robinson, Suite 100, Oklahoma City, Oklahoma 73102.

The Route 66 Museum, in Clinton

The McClellan-Kerr Arkansas River Navigation system, which opened in 1971, links Tulsa and other river ports with the Mississippi River and the Gulf Coast.

Communication

About 175 weekly and 50 daily newspapers are published throughout Oklahoma. Oklahoma City's *Daily Oklahoman* and the *Tulsa World* have the largest daily circulations. Approximately 20 television and 150 radio stations broadcast throughout the state, mostly from Oklahoma City or Tulsa.

▶ CITIES

Seven cities in Oklahoma have more than 50,000 residents. Six of them are located within the Oklahoma City and Tulsa metropolitan areas.

Oklahoma City, the largest city and the state capital, is located on the North Canadian River in the center of the state. The city was settled within a few hours of the first land run on April 22, 1889. Its role as the center of government and retail trade sped its growth. Later, manufacturing and livestock marketing and processing became important. In recent years service industries, electronics, and governmental operations have also supported its workforce. Tinker Air Force Base and the Monroney Federal Aviation Administration Center are located there.

Three suburbs of Oklahoma City have more than 50,000 residents: **Norman**, home of the University of Oklahoma; **Midwest City**, located near Tinker Air Force Base; and **Edmond**, site of the University of Central Oklahoma. A separate article on Oklahoma City follows this article.

Tulsa, the state's second largest city, is located on the Arkansas River in the northeastern part of the state. Originally a small Creek Indian village, Tulsa became the center of oil financing and refining in the region after the discovery of petroleum in nearby areas. As a result, early in the 1900's, it came to be known as the Oil Capital of the World. Manufacturing of oil-field equipment, oil refining, and banking remain important economic activities, as do services, retail trade, and aircraft maintenance. The University of Tulsa is located in the city, which is also a regional cultural center. **Broken Arrow**, a suburb of Tulsa, has been one of the fastest-growing towns in

Bartlett Square in downtown Tulsa is a pleasant place to relax in the city. Tulsa, Oklahoma's second largest city, is a center of the oil industry.

Oklahoma in recent decades. A separate article on Tulsa appears in Volume T.

Lawton, Oklahoma's fourth largest city, is located on Cache Creek in southwestern Oklahoma. It came into being during a unique lottery of Indian lands in 1901. Adjacent to the city is Fort Sill, the leading artillery training center for the U.S. Army. Also nearby is the Wichita Mountains Wildlife Refuge. Stone quarries, petroleum production, and manufacturing are important elements of the area's economy.

▶ GOVERNMENT

Oklahoma has operated under the same constitution since statehood in 1907. Written during an era of reform, it included the initiative and referendum—devices of direct democracy that allow citizens to bring proposed laws and constitutional amendments to a vote of the people. The constitution also placed restrictions on the governor, who cannot serve successive terms and may easily be removed from office. And it provided for a commission to protect consumers from abuses by utilities and railroad companies.

GOVERNMENT

State Government
Governor: 4-year term
State senators: 48; 4-year
   terms
State representatives: 101;
   2-year terms
Number of counties: 77

Federal Government
U.S. senators: 2
U.S. representatives: 5
Number of electoral votes: 7

For the name of the current governor, see STATE GOVERNMENTS in Volume S. For the names of current U.S. senators and representatives, see UNITED STATES, CONGRESS OF THE in Volume U-V.

The government is made up of three branches. The executive branch is headed by the governor. Other state-level elected officials include the lieutenant governor, auditor and inspector, attorney general, treasurer, and labor commissioner. The legislative branch, known as the Oklahoma Legislature, consists of a house of representatives and a senate. The judicial branch is headed by a state supreme court, which hears all civil appeals, and a state court of criminal appeals. Judges from these two high courts are appointed by the governor, then retained by a vote of the people every six years. Below the two high courts are district courts, operated by the state, and various municipal courts, overseen by local governments.

Oklahoma City replaced Guthrie as the state capital in 1910. A statue of a Native American now graces the entrance to the state capitol building.

INDEX TO OKLAHOMA MAP

● County Seat   Counties in parentheses   ★ State Capital

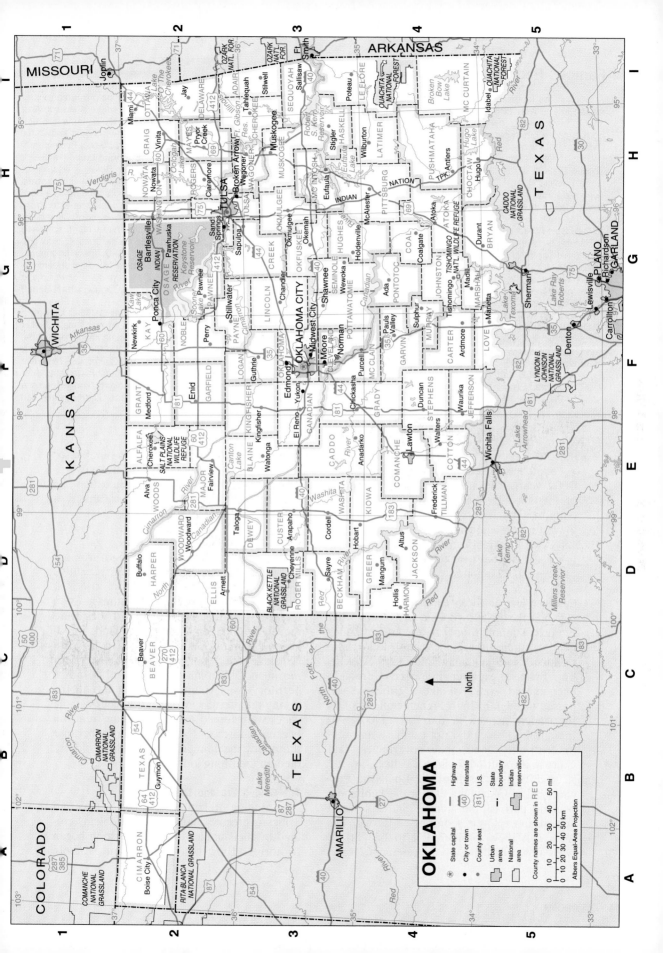

OKLAHOMA

County names are shown in RED

	State capital
	City or town
	County seat
	Urban area
	National area

Highway
Interstate
U.S.
State boundary
Indian reservation

0 10 20 30 40 50 mi
0 10 20 30 40 50 km

Albers Equal-Area Projection

North

Famous People

Consult the Index to find more information in *The New Book of Knowledge* about the following people who were born in or are otherwise associated with Oklahoma: Cherokee linguist Sequoya (1770?–1843); Olympic athlete Jim Thorpe (1888–1953); historian John Hope Franklin (1915–); mystery writer Tony Hillerman (1925–); political scientist Jeane Kirkpatrick (1926–); and baseball great Mickey Mantle (1931–95).

Carl Bert Albert (1908–2000), born in McAlester, was an Oklahoma Democrat who served in the U.S. House of Representatives for thirty years (1947–77). Albert was a strong supporter of civil rights programs during the 1960's. He served as Speaker of the House from 1971 until his retirement.

Daniel Joseph Boorstin (1914–), born in Atlanta, Georgia, but raised in Tulsa, is an award-winning historian. Two of his works, *The Americans: The Colonial Experience* (1958) and *The Americans: The Democratic Experience* (1973), won National Book Awards; the latter also won a Pulitzer Prize (1974). Boorstin taught history at a number of universities and colleges. He also served as librarian of Congress (1975–87).

Ralph Waldo Ellison (1914–94), born in Oklahoma City, was Oklahoma's most celebrated novelist. His most famous work, *The Invisible Man* (1952), won a National Book Award and is viewed as one of the most important works concerning racism. Ellison also published two collections of essays, *Shadow and Act* (1964) and *Going to the Territory* (1986).

Woodrow Wilson (Woody) Guthrie (1912–67), born in Okemah, was an influential folk singer, guitarist, and composer whose songs often focused on social injustice. "This Land Is Your Land" is among his best-known compositions. In the 1940's, he joined with singer Pete Seeger and his Almanac Singers, often

Ralph Ellison

singing before unions and migrant workers. His son **Arlo Guthrie** (1947–), a folk-rock performer, is best known for his song "Alice's Restaurant."

Shannon Lucid (1943–), raised in Bethany, was one of America's first six female astronauts. She holds a doctorate in biochemistry from the University of Oklahoma. Lucid made her first space voyage in 1985 on the shuttle *Discovery*. In 1996 she set a U.S. space endurance record by spending 188 days aboard the Russian space station *Mir*, for which she was awarded the Congressional Space Medal of Honor.

Wilma Mankiller (1945–), born in Adair County, was the first female chief of the Western Cherokee nation, part of the largest tribal group in the United States. While living in California, Mankiller became a community activist after observing urban poverty, and in 1969 she participated in the Native American

---

▶ HISTORY

People have lived in Oklahoma for at least 8,000 years. The skeletal remains of mammoths killed by the region's earliest inhabitants have been uncovered by archaeologists in western Oklahoma. Between A.D. 1200 and 1500, Native American farmers built a large town and mounds near the Arkansas River in east central Oklahoma.

European and American Exploration

When the first Europeans arrived in what is now Oklahoma, only a few Indian tribes lived or hunted there, including the Wichita, Caddo, Pawnee, Quapaw, and Plains Apache. The Spanish explorer Francisco Coronado encountered some of these tribes as he passed through in 1541. French explorers and fur traders arrived in the early 1700's. Although the French did not establish any permanent settlements, they nevertheless laid claim to the entire Mississippi Valley.

In 1803, as a result of the Louisiana Purchase, all of Oklahoma except the Panhandle became part of the United States. Several American explorers soon passed through the area. But they considered it to be part of what was called the Great American Desert and therefore did not think it was suitable for agricultural settlement. The federal government later chose the area as a relocation site for large numbers of Native Americans from the southeastern United States.

Removal of the Southeastern Tribes

During the 1820's, the federal government began buying land from Oklahoma's native Indians to make room for more tribes it wished to remove from the Southeast. Soon members of the Five Civilized Tribes were moved to Oklahoma from their lands in Alabama, Florida, Georgia, Mississippi, North Carolina, and Tennessee. At first, Indian removal to Oklahoma (then known as Indian Territory) was voluntary. But in the 1830's, during the presidency of Andrew Jackson, the tribes were forced out. The Indians' removal became known as the Trail of Tears because thousands, including children and the elderly, died on their long journey.

The Golden Era and the Civil War

In Indian Territory, the Five Civilized Tribes overcame many of the problems created by their upheaval, and they soon began to thrive. They built homes and schools,

Wilma Mankiller

protest occupation of Alcatraz Island. She later returned to Oklahoma and became involved in tribal politics. As principal chief (1985–95), she worked to bring self-sufficiency to the Cherokee people.

Shannon Miller (1977–), who grew up in Edmond, became the most highly decorated American gymnast in history. In the 1990's she won two consecutive all-around World Championship titles, the only American to do so. At the Olympics in Barcelona in 1992, she won two silver and three bronze medals. She was also part of the team that won two gold medals at the 1996 Olympics in Atlanta.

William Penn Adair (Will) Rogers (1879–1935), born near Oologah, was an actor, lecturer, humorist, and newspaper writer. Rogers first performed in 1905 as a trick rope artist in vaudeville shows. He began telling colorful stories during his act, and he soon became known for his humorous monologues. Rogers later appeared in the Ziegfeld Follies and in motion pictures. His syndicated newspaper column gained national popularity during the 1920's. One of

Will Rogers

his most famous quotations was "I never met a man I didn't like." The Will Rogers Memorial in Claremore is dedicated to his memory.

Maria Tallchief (1925–), born in Fairfax, was a noted ballerina of Osage descent. A principal dancer with the New York City Ballet (1947–65), she later served as artistic director for the Lyric Opera Ballet in Chicago and helped found the Chicago City Ballet (1980). In 1996 she received a Kennedy Center award for lifetime achievement in the arts. Her sister, **Marjorie Tallchief** (1927–), also a talented ballerina, danced for the Paris Opéra Ballet (1957-62).

planted crops, and developed a cotton-plantation culture similar to other areas of the South. Some even had slaves of African descent. The Cherokee had invented a written form of their own language before removal. Missionaries now worked to create written forms of other tribal languages. But this golden era in the lives of Oklahoma's Native Americans was soon interrupted by the Civil War (1861-65).

As the Civil War approached, the Five Civilized Tribes were divided in their loyalties, but they eventually allied themselves with the Confederacy. Members of the five tribes fought in dozens of battles and skirmishes in Indian Territory and neighboring states. One of their leaders, Stand Watie, a Cherokee, became a Confederate general. After the war, the U.S. government punished the Five Civilized Tribes for siding with the Confederacy by forcing them to sign new, unfavorable treaties.

The Land Runs

The new treaties forced the Five Civilized Tribes to give up the western half of their lands so that other Indians could be relocated there. Most of these new tribes came from reservations in Kansas and Nebraska, but they also included such nomadic southern plains tribes as the Comanche, Kiowa, Plains Apache, Southern Cheyenne, Osage, and Arapaho. The federal government hoped that all of the tribes would form an all-Indian territorial government.

By the early 1870's, however, coal was being mined in the McAlester area in southeastern Oklahoma; Texas ranchers were driving herds of cattle through the territory; and people from the surrounding states began demanding that much of the Indian land be opened to white settlement. In 1889, when Congress allowed the opening of a portion of central Oklahoma to white settlement, so many people arrived for the event that it turned into the first of several land runs. On May 2, 1890, the area in which these people settled, together with the Panhandle, was organized as a U.S. territory. It was named the Territory of Oklahoma, with the capital at Guthrie. Other land runs followed in 1891, 1892, 1893, and 1895. These lands were also added to Oklahoma Territory.

The eastern half of the present state remained as Indian Territory, under the tribes' own governments. But white sharecroppers,

An 1889 photograph shows settlers racing into central Oklahoma to stake land claims the minute the U.S. Congress first authorized opening up the territory to white settlement. Those who slipped in sooner than allowed by law gave Oklahoma its present nickname, the Sooner State.

railroad workers, miners, and other non-Indians continued to drift into the area. During the 1890's, Congress created the Dawes Commission to negotiate with the Five Civilized Tribes and convince them to break up their lands and take individual allotments. By 1902, all five tribes had agreed to do so. They also agreed to join Indian Territory with Oklahoma Territory.

Statehood

Delegates from both territories met at Guthrie in 1906 to write a state constitution. The constitution was approved by popular vote, and on November 16, 1907, President Theodore Roosevelt proclaimed Oklahoma the 46th state.

The first two decades after statehood saw both growth and turbulence. Giant oil fields opened, but the boom-and-bust petroleum economy did not provide wealth equally to all. Farmers struggled to stay in business, and tenant farming remained highly active. The Socialist Party thrived in this environment. Following World War I (1914–18), the Ku Klux Klan spread throughout the state, and a race riot in Tulsa in 1921 revealed tense race relations.

The 1930's brought difficult times to Oklahoma. The nation suffered a severe financial depression. Farm prices were low, and dust storms and drought added greatly to the plight of Oklahoma's farmers. The Panhandle and other northwestern areas became part of the Dust Bowl. Some of the people moved to towns and cities in the state. Others joined the migration to California, hoping to find work there. The residents of California called most Dust Bowl refugees Okies—a negative label most Oklahomans have since tried to overcome. The life of these migrants was described by John Steinbeck in his novel *The Grapes of Wrath*, published in 1939, and in the many folk songs of Woody Guthrie, a native Oklahoman.

During World War II (1939–45), even more Oklahomans left the state to work in war-related industries. From 1930 to 1950, the state's population declined.

Modern Times

Since World War II, improving and diversifying the economy has been a key goal of state leaders. They have worked to attract new businesses and to create an economy that is less dependent on oil and agriculture.

Minorities and women have also made significant gains. Court cases that originated in Oklahoma in the 1940's opened the way for people of all backgrounds to be admitted to law and other graduate schools. Native Americans, who were allowed to organize tribal business groups in the 1930's, have made tremendous economic advancement in recent years.

On April 19, 1995, the world's attention turned to Oklahoma City when a terrorist's bomb exploded outside the Murrah Federal Building, killing 168 men, women, and children. The bombing united Oklahomans and revealed their strength and spirit of community. That strength and spirit, along with Oklahoma's abundant resources, have helped this progressive state continue to thrive.

KENNY L. BROWN
University of Central Oklahoma

OKLAHOMA CITY

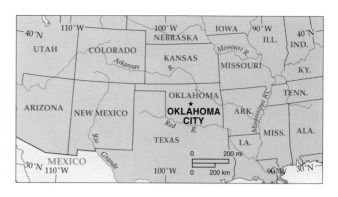

Oklahoma City is the capital of Oklahoma and the state's most populous city. Located on the North Canadian River in the central part of the state, the city covers more than 608 square miles (1,575 square kilometers). Approximately 506,000 people live in the city proper. More than 1 million live in the greater metropolitan area.

Oklahoma City's economy is based on a wide variety of enterprises. Among the most important activities are agriculture and its related businesses, government and military defense services, health care, retail sales, automobile assembly, and the manufacture of electronic equipment, construction equipment, and petroleum products.

There are many interesting places to visit in Oklahoma City. Among them are the National Cowboy Hall of Fame and Western Heritage Center, the Oklahoma City Art Museum, the International Gymnastics Hall of Fame, the National Softball Hall of Fame, and the State Museum of History. Other popular attractions include Frontier City Theme Park, Myriad Botanical Gardens, Will Rogers Park, Remington Park Race Track, and the Oklahoma City Zoo, located in Lincoln Park, the largest of the city's many public parks.

Education and culture are also important to the life of the city. Oklahoma City University, Southern Nazarene University, and the University of Science and Arts of Oklahoma are all located within the city limits. The University of Central Oklahoma in Edmond and the University of Oklahoma in Norman are found in the greater metropolitan area. The city supports the Oklahoma City Philharmonic Orchestra, two dance companies—Ballet Oklahoma and the Prairie Dance Theatre—and several dramatic-arts theaters. Popular annual events include the Spring Arts Festival and the Red Earth Native American Cultural Festival, featuring the crafts, dances, and folk art of the region's many Native American tribes.

In 1889 a great land rush occurred on the nation's southern prairies when the U.S. government opened up thousands of acres of "unassigned lands" to settlement. On April 22, ten thousand settlers staked claims in what is now Oklahoma City, and overnight the community was born. The city was officially incorporated the following year, when Oklahoma became a U.S. territory. Oklahoma City became the state capital in 1910.

The discovery of the Oklahoma City Oil Field in 1928 contributed significantly to the city's growth. For two decades it was one of the nation's most important sources of petroleum. In the 1940's, during World War II, Tinker Air Force Base and Air Logistics Center opened, bringing highly technical industries—and a more diversified economy—to the metropolitan region.

On April 19, 1995, Oklahoma City suffered one of the worst terrorist attacks in the nation's history when a bomb exploded outside the Alfred P. Murrah Federal Building, killing 168 men, women, and children. Timothy J. McVeigh, a former U.S. soldier, was convicted of the crime and put to death in 2001.

HOWARD MEREDITH
University of Science and Arts of Oklahoma

Oklahoma City is the capital of Oklahoma and the heart of the state's largest metropolitan area. The city serves as a regional center for industry, education, culture, and recreation.

More and more people today are able to enjoy active lifestyles well into their older years. The number of older Americans is growing rapidly, a trend that is expected to continue in the future.

OLD AGE

Old age means different things to different people. Although it is universally viewed as the final stage of life, definitions vary according to culture, time, and place.

Among many traditional and nonindustrial societies, for example, old age is determined by changes in appearance, social roles, or physical abilities. That is, people are considered old when they have wrinkles and gray hair, have grandchildren, or can no longer perform certain physical tasks.

Among cultures that define old age chronologically, people are considered old when they reach a certain age. In the United States, age 65 has long been considered the beginning of old age, since it is when many people leave the paid workforce and become eligible for retirement benefits. However, as people live longer, 65 is increasingly considered middle age. In fact, a person aged 65 in the year 2000 could expect to live, on average, almost two more decades.

Regardless of how it is defined, old age is experienced by more people, and for a longer time, than ever before. In 1900 only 4 percent of the U.S. population was over the age of 65, and almost no one reached age 85. In 2000, 13 percent of the U.S. population was 65 or older and 2 percent was 85 or older.

This means that the older population is also getting larger. In 1900 only 3 million people were age 65 or older. Today that number has grown to 35 million. There are also more than 50,000 people in the United States who are over 100—an achievement few could have dreamed of fifty years ago.

The number of older Americans will grow even more as "baby boomers" age. Those in this group—76 million people born between 1946 and 1964—will add greatly to the ranks of those 65 or older in the coming years.

Although the United States has the greatest number of older people (also called senior citizens), it has the lowest percentage among industrialized nations. Italy, Japan, Germany, and France have the highest percentages of older persons in their populations.

Increases in longevity (life span) in the United States, Canada, Japan, and Europe are remarkably similar. In all these nations, life expectancy increased from about 67 years in 1965 to about 75 years in 2000. While estimates of longevity in developing nations vary, life expectancy is much shorter because of harsher living conditions, less advanced medical care, political strife, and more disease.

Despite their growing numbers, older people in the United States, Europe, and Japan face significant challenges. These include chronic (long-term) illnesses, inadequate financial resources, and difficulty maintaining their independence. Older people in developing nations face these same challenges, as well as poverty and poor health care.

Negative attitudes toward older people and aging can also be a challenge. Although some cultures regard their elders as wiser and more experienced, others—particularly Western societies—emphasize the advantages of youth. Also, in cultures where status is linked to one's job and income, retired people may feel that they are less valued.

▶HEALTH

As people age, many develop health problems that restrict their physical abilities and daily activities. In the United States, more than half of people over age 75 say they are limited because of a chronic illness, and almost three-fourths over 80 report having at least one disability. The most common chronic conditions among the elderly are arthritis, hypertension, heart disease, hearing and visual impairments, and diabetes. The branch of medicine specializing in these and other problems of aging is called **geriatrics**.

Chronic conditions often result in higher medical expenses. Despite coverage by Medicare and other supplemental health insurance policies, older Americans spend about twice as much money on health care as the rest of the population. Health care for the elderly has improved, however, and people now survive ailments that would once have killed them. But survival may come at a cost; living with chronic health conditions can mean a reduced quality of life.

Still, disability rates among older Americans have declined, along with the percentage of older people residing in nursing homes. Currently, only a small percentage of the elderly are in nursing homes—usually those who are sickest and who have the fewest family resources.

▶FINANCES

The financial status of older Americans varies according to several factors, including age, gender, race, ethnic group, marital status, and the type of assets owned. Older women are more likely than older men to be poor, and older African Americans are more than twice as likely as older whites to be poor. Married people, homeowners, and those who have access to health care are more financially secure in old age than those who do not have these benefits.

Although many older people have income from

Although many older people lead independent lives, others may develop health problems that restrict their activities and require them to seek support services.

99

A senior volunteer tutors high school students. After retirement, many older people serve their communities.

savings and other assets, as well as pensions from previous employers, Social Security is the primary source of income for more than half of all retired workers. It pays benefits to 90 percent of people age 65 and older. The amount of the monthly payment received varies based on the money that has been paid into the Social Security system (a fixed percentage of one's salary) and the number of years worked.

Without Social Security, about half of all older Americans would be considered poor. Currently only about 10 percent are considered poor, or living at or below the poverty level. Living at the poverty level means that a person earns or consumes less than the amount considered necessary to meet minimum adequate levels of nutrition, shelter, and other necessities.

Still, even those who are not considered poor face challenges. Many older people receive just enough money to live on and may be unable to afford any added or unexpected expenses. And the rising costs of necessities such as food, clothing, housing, and medical care are difficult to meet on a fixed income.

▶ HOUSING

Housing is important to the well being of the older population. Older people clearly prefer to remain in their own homes, or "age in place." One way to enable this is through home design. A movement called **universal design** seeks to create homes that are usable by people of all ages and abilities. Homes can be built or remodeled to accommodate

wheelchairs, for example, or to include safety features such as handrails and non-skid surfaces, making it easier for older people to live where they wish.

Most older persons eventually need support services to remain independent. These include delivered meals, transportation for those who do not drive, in-home health care, and help with personal care and housekeeping. Such services are often available through community programs and organizations.

For those who do not remain in their homes, **assisted living**—special housing that includes support services—has become an increasingly popular option. During the 1990's, the number of assisted living facilities in the United States rose by almost 50 percent.

▶ LOOKING AHEAD

The interests and activities of older persons vary considerably, but spending time with friends and family, reading, and pursuing spiritual or religious interests are favored activities. Many older people are also involved in their communities; they vote at higher percentages than people in other age groups and often serve as volunteers. Some predict that as the U.S. population ages, there will be an increase in the number of older volunteers, who will deal with critical social issues as never before.

Older people may also delay retirement in the coming years. Although most people now over 65 are not employed, surveys suggest that this will change as baby boomers age; many may work into their 70's. However, this will depend on the level of health care available and on continued medical advances in the treatment of chronic illness.

JEFFREY LOVE
AARP

See also AGING; INFLATION AND DEFLATION; SOCIAL SECURITY.

OLD TESTAMENT. See BIBLE.

OLINGOS. See RACCOONS AND THEIR RELATIVES.

OLIVE

The olive is the fruit of a type of evergreen tree found in warm, temperate regions. One of the earliest foods cultivated, the olive is believed to have originated in southwestern Asia. Later the trees spread to all the lands bordering the Mediterranean Sea. Olives and olive oil were an important source of food and trade among ancient peoples. The remains of storerooms that held jars of olive oil dating back to 2000 B.C. have been found on the island of Crete.

The Spanish first brought olives to the Americas. The trees thrived in the warm, dry climate of California. Today California produces almost all the olives grown in the United States. Spain and Italy, the leading olive-producing countries, provide about half the world's supply. Greece is also a major olive producer.

There are hundreds of varieties of olives, most of which are grown for their oil. Only four varieties are grown commercially for eating—the Mission, Manzanillo, Servillano, and Ascolano.

▶ THE OLIVE TREE

Olive trees are usually reproduced from cuttings. A cutting is the part of a tree that can grow into a new tree if properly planted. Olive cuttings are grown in nursery rows for two years before being planted in orchards. In April and May the trees bear great numbers of flowers. Pollen from the flowers is carried by the wind to the flowers of other olive trees, as well as to those on the parent tree. Usually, olive trees bear a light crop one season, followed by a heavy crop the next.

The olive tree has a long life and can live through long dry periods because of its wide-spreading roots. But the trees do best when they are irrigated and fertilized.

▶ HARVESTING AND PROCESSING OLIVES

Methods of harvesting the olive crop depend on how the fruit is to be used. Olives for oil are left on the tree until they are fully ripe and have the largest possible amount of oil. Oil is obtained by squeezing the fruit between presses. The oil is then clarified (made clear and pure). Oil content ranges from 15 to 30 percent of the weight of the olive. Olives that are to be processed for eating

Olives have been a source of food since ancient times. Once carried to distant markets by caravan, today they are grown in many temperate parts of the world.

must be harvested carefully. The fruit should not be bruised, and it must be picked at the right stage of maturity. The olives are graded according to size. The smallest olives are usually called Standard. The grades of the bigger olives generally range from Large to Mammoth, Jumbo, and Colossal. The price paid for the Colossal grade may be five or six times that paid for Standard-size fruit.

Before olives can be eaten, their naturally bitter taste must be removed by treatment with lye or salt. Several methods are used commercially. Each method gives the olives a characteristic taste. To produce **green pickled olives**, the olives are left in a lye solution until it has penetrated almost to the pit. Lye removes the bitter taste and softens the skin of the olive. The olives are then washed and stored in barrels for several months while a chemical process called fermentation takes place. This is called the Spanish method.

Black ripe olives are produced by treating the fruit with lye solution and then washing it in water. Air is then blown through the olives while they are covered with the water. The forced air (aeration) helps the olives turn black. If the olives are to be canned, they are sterilized for 60 minutes at 240°F (115°C).

The fruit for making **green ripe olives** is processed soon after harvesting. It is treated with lye but not put through forced aeration. Some olives are marketed with the pit removed. The cavity is left empty or is filled with pimiento or other ingredients.

IRA J. CONDIT
University of California—Riverside

OLYMPIA. See WASHINGTON (Cities).

The opening and closing ceremonies of the modern Olympic Games are spectacular celebrations of the world's greatest international athletic competition.

OLYMPIC GAMES

Every two years, athletes from all over the world gather in one place to compete against each other in the greatest of all sporting events: the Olympic Games. This tradition has its origins in the ancient past. Today the Olympic Games continue to bring together people of different nationalities, races, and religions in peaceful athletic competition.

▶ ORIGIN AND HISTORY OF THE ANCIENT OLYMPIC GAMES

The Rise of the Games

The Olympic Games originated long ago in ancient Greece. Exactly when the Games were first held and what circumstances led to their creation is uncertain. We do know, however, that the Games were a direct outgrowth of the values and beliefs of Greek society. The Greeks idealized physical fitness and mental discipline, and they believed that excellence in those areas honored Zeus, the greatest of all their gods.

One legend about the origin of the Olympic Games revolves around Zeus. It was said Zeus once fought his father, Kronos, for control of the world. They battled atop a mountain that overlooked a valley in southwestern Greece. After Zeus defeated his father, a temple and immense statue were built in the valley below to honor him. This valley was called Olympia, and soon religious festivals developed there as people came to worship Zeus and to approach as nearly as possible his great strength. It is believed that these religious festivals eventually led to the famed Games of the Olympics.

Although we do not know just when the Games were first played, the earliest recorded Olympic competition occurred in 776 B.C. It had only one event, the one-stade (approximately 630-foot or 192-meter) race, which was won by a cook named Coroebus. This was the start of the first Olympiad, the four-year period by which the Greeks recorded their history.

Athletic competition became so important to the Greeks that the Olympic festivals were a peaceful influence on the warlike city-states. Sparta was famous for the strict military training of its citizens. But it would wait until the Games were over before sending fighters into battle. Other cities followed this example.

For the first 13 Olympic Games, the only event was the one-stade run. But over the years, new sports were added to the Games. The hoplitodrome, for instance, was a footrace the athletes ran wearing full armor. The pentathlon, in which the athletes competed in five events (jumping, javelin, sprint, discus, and wrestling) was added to the Games in 708 B.C. The pancration was introduced in 648 B.C. This brutal sport had no rules and combined boxing and wrestling. A winner was named only when one man raised his hand in defeat or lay unconscious on the ground.

In addition to the pre-existing religious shrines and altars, a vast complex of buildings and structures was constructed at Olympia to accommodate the growing number of sports and athletes. Chariot races, first run in 680 B.C., were held in the hippodrome. Boxers and wrestlers trained in the Palaestra, which was adjacent to the gymnasium. The Leonidaion housed the athletes.

Generally, only freeborn men and boys could take part in the Olympic Games (servants and slaves were allowed to participate only in the horse races). Women were forbidden, on penalty of death, even to see the Games. In 396 B.C., however, a woman from Rhodes successfully defied the death penalty. When her husband died, she continued the training of their son, a boxer. She attended the Games disguised as a man and was not recognized until she shouted with joy over her son's victory. Her life was spared because of the special circumstances and the fact that her father and brothers had been Olympians.

At first, the Games were strictly for Greek citizens. Eventually, however, athletes from all over the Roman Empire (which covered the entire Mediterranean region) were permitted to participate.

All athletes were required to take an oath that they would observe all the rules and standards. In spite of the luxurious facilities offered to athletes, all had to remain amateurs. That is, they had to pay their own expenses, and they could receive no monetary awards.

Winners of the Games were crowned with wreaths of olive leaves and hailed as heroes. They were showered with material gifts, and sometimes a special entrance was cut in the wall surrounding their home city just for them to pass through—a symbol that the people of the city felt well protected with an Olympic champion living among them.

One of the most exciting competitions of the ancient Olympic Games was the chariot race, which was held in an arena called the hippodrome.

Ancient Olympia (*left*) was an important religious and athletic center for the citizens of Greece. Scattered ruins, such as this stone archway (*above*), are all that remain of Olympia today.

Perhaps the greatest athlete of the ancient Games was Milo of Croton, a wrestler who lived in the 500's B.C. He won the wrestling crown six times, and he was said to be so powerful that he could carry a full-grown bull on his shoulders.

The ancient Olympic Games also honored, and inspired, artists. The poet Pindar wrote many odes in praise of the Games' winners. The Olympic buildings were prime examples of the beauty of Greek architecture, and the remains of Zeus' great statue bear the signature of the famous Athenian sculptor and architect Phidias. Like the athletic champions, artistic champions were awarded olive wreaths and great acclaim.

The Decline of the Games

After Rome conquered Greece in the 100's B.C., Olympic standards began to decline. Competition for the common good was ignored by the glory hunters, who were willing to use any trick or deceit to win. For instance, in A.D. 67 the emperor Nero brought his own cheering section and competed in events himself. Even though he fell from his chariot during the race, he was named the champion. In A.D. 394 the Roman emperor Theodosius I, a Christian who considered the Games a pagan festival, ordered them stopped.

Olympia then began to crumble. The great statue of Zeus was taken away to Constantinople, where it was destroyed in a fire. In 426, Roman emperor Theodosius II ordered all the temples destroyed. Earthquakes later helped finish what human hands had started, as well as flooding caused by a change in the course of the river that flowed through Olympia. The once-great city was eventually buried.

In 1829, German archaeologists began uncovering Olympia. Today, the site of the ancient Olympic Games is only a shadow of its former glory. Many of the building foundations remain, but few walls and pillars still stand, and the stadium where footraces were held long ago is now just a broad stretch of barren ground.

▶ THE MODERN OLYMPIC GAMES

The revival of the Olympic Games began with Baron Pierre de Coubertin (1863–1937) of France. Coubertin was greatly interested in education, and he firmly believed that the best way to develop the minds of young people was to develop their bodies as well; learning and athletics should go together. After he visited the ruins of ancient Olympia, it occurred to Coubertin that perhaps the best way to generate widespread acceptance of his theory was to resurrect the Olympic Games. He hoped the new Games would bring back the ideals of physical, mental, and spiritual excellence displayed in the ancient Games, as well as build courage, endurance, and a sense of fair play in all who participated. In addition, he hoped the Games would turn the tide he saw worldwide of the growing commercialism of sports.

In 1892, Coubertin first introduced the idea of starting the Olympic Games again. Few people were ready to accept his idea. But in 1894 Coubertin founded the International Olympic Committee (IOC) and began planning the first modern Olympiad.

The first modern Olympic Games were held in 1896 in Athens, Greece—a fitting place to rekindle the spirit of the early Greek Games. Coubertin remained president of the International Olympic Committee until 1925. In this office he directed the course the Games were to take. He wrote the Olympic Charter, protocol, and athletes' oath, and he also planned the ceremonies.

Although the modern Olympic Games are patterned after the ancient Greek Games, there are important differences. Unlike ancient Greece, modern nations have not stopped wars for peaceful athletic competition. Because of World War I, Games were not held in 1916. Nor were they held in 1940 and 1944, during World War II.

The original Olympics were always held at Olympia. Almost every modern Olympiad is celebrated in or near a different city of the world. The earlier Games were open only to Greek citizens and athletes from other Mediterranean countries. The modern Games encourage all nations to compete. A person may enter if his or her country has a National Olympic Committee (NOC) that is recognized by the International Olympic Committee. Events for women have become a major interest in the modern Games, and the winners receive honors equal to those given the male winners.

The ancient Greeks furthered culture by giving honors for cultural achievements at the

Baron Pierre de Coubertin of France revived the Olympic Games in 1896, more than 1,500 years after their demise. He believed that athletic competition improved the minds as well as the bodies of all who participated.

Olympic Games. The modern Olympics hold an arts festival, where the culture of the host country is showcased in various art forms.

Footraces, jumping, discus and javelin throwing, boxing, wrestling, and some other events were carried over from the original Olympic Games. But such present Olympic contests as cycling, canoeing and sailing, football (soccer), basketball, judo, rifle shooting, and water polo were unknown in early times. The modern pentathlon tests an athlete's all-around ability in swimming (300-meter freestyle), cross-country running (4,000 meters), fencing with the épée, horse show jumping, and shooting with a target pistol at 10 meters.

One of the most grueling events of the modern Olympics is the marathon. This footrace over a distance of 26 miles, 385 yards (42.195 kilometers) is a supreme test of the runners' endurance. The marathon was not run at Olympia, but it has its origin in ancient

DATES AND SITES OF THE MODERN OLYMPIC GAMES

Summer Games		Winter Games	
Year	**Site**	**Year**	**Site**
1896	Athens, Greece	1924	Chamonix, France
1900	Paris, France	1928	St. Moritz, Switzerland
1904	St. Louis, United States	1932	Lake Placid, United States
1908	London, United Kingdom	1936	Garmisch-Partenkirchen, Germany
1912	Stockholm, Sweden	1948	St. Moritz, Switzerland
1920	Antwerp, Belgium	1952	Oslo, Norway
1924	Paris, France	1956	Cortina d'Ampezzo, Italy
1928	Amsterdam, the Netherlands	1960	Squaw Valley, United States
1932	Los Angeles, United States	1964	Innsbruck, Austria
1936	Berlin, Germany	1968	Grenoble, France
1948	London, United Kingdom	1972	Sapporo, Japan
1952	Helsinki, Finland	1976	Innsbruck, Austria
1956	Melbourne, Australia	1980	Lake Placid, United States
1960	Rome, Italy	1984	Sarajevo, Yugoslavia
1964	Tokyo, Japan	1988	Calgary, Canada
1968	Mexico City, Mexico	1992	Albertville, France
1972	Munich, West Germany	1994	Lillehammer, Norway
1976	Montreal, Canada	1998	Nagano, Japan
1980	Moscow, U.S.S.R.	2002	Salt Lake City, United States
1984	Los Angeles, United States	2006	Torino, Italy
1988	Seoul, South Korea	2010	Vancouver, Canada
1992	Barcelona, Spain		
1996	Atlanta, United States		
2000	Sydney, Australia		
2004	Athens, Greece		
2008	Beijing, China		
2012	London, United Kingdom		

For information on other athletes with outstanding Olympic achievements, see the articles ICE-SKATING (Profiles); OWENS, JESSE; SWIMMING (Great Swimmers); THORPE, JAMES FRANCIS (JIM); and TRACK AND FIELD (Great Athletes).

Nadia Comaneci (1961–), born in Onesti, Romania, began performing gymnastics at the age of 6. At the 1976 Olympics, Comaneci became the first gymnast in the history of the Games

Nadia Comaneci

Olga Korbut

to receive a perfect score of ten—which she did six more times. She went on to win gold medals in the balance beam, uneven parallel bars, and individual all-around performance. She also won a silver medal in the team competition and a bronze medal in the floor exercise. At the 1980 Games, she won gold medals in the floor exercise and the balance beam and silver medals in the team competition and individual all-around. She retired in 1984, defected to the United States in 1989, and married gymnast Bart Connor in 1996. She was inducted into the International Gymnastics Hall of Fame in 1997.

Bruce Jenner (1949–), born in Mount Kisco, New York, was an excellent high school athlete. He began training for the decathlon in college. At his first Olympics in 1972, he finished in tenth place. Four years later, however, he set a world record by winning the Olympic decathlon with 8,618 points. He was named Athlete

of the Year in 1976 by the Associated Press. After he retired from competition, Jenner was elected to the National Track and Field Hall of Fame in 1980 and the United States Olympic Committee Hall of Fame in 1986.

Olga Korbut (1955–) was born in Grodno, Belorussia, a republic of the former Soviet Union. Korbut's appealing personality and revolutionary routines brought wide popularity to gymnastics. At her first Olympic Games in 1972, she won gold medals in the floor, balance beam, and team event and a silver medal in the uneven parallel bars. That same year, she was named Female Athlete of the Year by the Associated Press—the first athlete from a Communist nation to be so honored. A recurrent ankle injury hampered Korbut's performance at the 1976 Olympic Games, but she did win a silver medal in the balance beam. She retired in 1977 and was inducted into the International Gymnastics Hall of Fame in 1997.

Fred Carlton (Carl) Lewis (1961–), born in Birmingham, Alabama, won four gold medals (100- and 200-meter dash, long jump, 400-meter relay) at his first Olympic Games in 1984, matching the record set by Jesse Owens for most track-and-field gold medals won in a single Olympics. He won additional Olympic gold medals in 1988 (100-meter dash, long jump) and in 1992 (long jump, 400-meter relay). He also won a silver medal in the 200-meter dash at the 1988 Games. He won his ninth gold medal, in the long jump, at the 1996 Games. In addition to his Olympic triumphs, Lewis was also world long-jump champion twice (1983, 1987), world 100-meter dash champion once (1983), U.S. long-jump champion six times (1981–83, 1986–87, 1991), and U.S. 100-meter dash champion five times (1981–83, 1986, 1990). Lewis was inducted into the National Track and Field Hall of Fame in 2001.

Greg Louganis (1960–), born in San Diego, California, is considered one of the best divers of all time. He began diving at the age of 10, and he won his first Olympic medal (a silver in the platform dive) just six years later at the 1976 Games. At the 1984 and 1988 Games, he won the gold medal in both the platform and springboard events. Louganis was also world platform diving champion three times (1978, 1982, 1986) and world 3-meter springboard champion twice (1982, 1986). In 1984 he won the Sullivan Award as the top amateur athlete in the

Greece. In 490 B.C. the Athenians defeated an army of invading Persians at Marathon, which is northeast of Athens. From there, Pheidippides, a champion runner in the Olympic Games, carried the news of victory to the people of Athens. To do this he had to run a great distance. Once he reached Athens and gasped out his news of victory, he died. It is in his honor that the marathon race is run.

In 1924, the Winter Games became a new feature of the modern Olympics. Such cold-weather sports as pair and figure skating, ice

Norway's Jacob Tullin soars in the high jump during the first Winter Olympic Games, held in Chamonix, France, in 1924.

Greg Louganis

United States. He was elected to the United States Olympic Committee Hall of Fame in 1985. In 1993, he was also inducted into the International Swimming Hall of Fame. After retiring from diving, Louganis became an actor and author.

Bob Mathias (1930–) was born in Tulare, California. Mathias was only 17 years old when he triumphed in the decathlon at the 1948 Games, and he remains the youngest male gold-medal-winner in Olympic history. For his accomplishment, he received the Sullivan Award that same year. At the next Olympics in 1952, he set a world record of 7,887 points as he once again won the decathlon. No other Olympic athlete has won that Olympic event twice. He retired afterward, undefeated in every decathlon he had entered, and later had a successful career in politics. Mathias was inducted into the United States Olympic Committee Hall of Fame in 1983.

Jenny Thompson (1973–) was born in Dover, New Hampshire. She is the most honored swimmer in Olympic history, with more medals (twelve) than any other swimmer. At the 1992 Olympic Games, she won two gold medals (400-meter freestyle relay, 400-meter medley relay) and one silver medal (100-meter freestyle). At the 1996 Games, she repeated in the 400-meter freestyle and medley relays and won her fifth gold medal in the 800-meter freestyle relay. At the 2000 Games, Thompson won her sixth gold medal in the 400-meter freestyle relay and her seventh in the 800-meter freestyle relay. After she tied teammate Dara Torres for the 100-meter freestyle bronze medal and won the 400-meter medley relay at the same Games, she had won ten medals—more than any other woman swimmer in the history of the Olympic Games. At her fourth and final Olympic Games in 2004, Thompson won silver medals in the 400-meter freestyle and medley relays. Thompson was also a world champion swimmer, triumphing in many individual and team races. *Sports Illustrated* named her among the 100 greatest female athletes of the 20th century.

Jayne Torvill (1957–) and **Christopher Dean** (1958–), both born in Nottingham, England, were one of the most captivating skating pairs in the history of ice dancing. Before they began skating together in 1975, Torvill had been a British national pairs champion and Dean had been a British Junior (ice) dance champion. During their amateur career, they were four-time world (1981–84) and European (1981–82, 1984, 1994) champions and seven-time British national champions (1978–83, 1994). After they turned professional, Torvill and Dean were also world professional champions five times (1984–85, 1990, 1995–96). It was at the Olympic Games, however, that the team made their greatest impact on the world of ice dancing. At the 1984 Games in Los Angeles, they performed a freestyle routine that was a significant departure from the usual "ballroom" style so common to the sport at the time. Every judge on the panel awarded Torvill and Dean a perfect score, and the pair went on to win the gold medal. Torvill and Dean returned to the Olympic Games in 1994 and won the bronze medal in ice dancing. They were inducted into the World Figure Skating Hall of Fame in 1989.

Torvill and Dean

hockey, bobsledding, and the biathlon (rifle shooting on a cross-country ski course) could never have developed in the warm climate of Greece (although figure and pair skating and ice hockey had been included in previous modern Games). Until 1992, the Winter Games were held in the same year as the Summer Games. Beginning in 1994, the Winter and Summer Games were held two years apart, on separate four-year cycles.

▶ **HOW THE OLYMPIC GAMES ARE ORGANIZED AND OPERATED**

The International Olympic Committee continues to govern the Games. It works with national committees and with international sports federations, establishing rules and arrangements for each new Olympic Games celebration.

A National Olympic Committee governs Olympic sports in each country that takes part. It includes representatives of all the groups in a country that govern sports in the Olympic program. It must also include members of the IOC for that country. A National Olympic Committee must avoid any political, commercial, or religious interference.

Each sport is governed by an International Federation, which oversees the selection of athletes to the Olympic Games. The National Olympic Committee sees to the welfare of its country's athletes on their way to and from the Games, as well as during their stay in the city where the Games are being held. Most athletes are housed in a complex called the Olympic Village.

To qualify for Olympic competition, an athlete must be a citizen of his or her country and must abide by the rules of the IOC and of the International Federation for his or her sport. Athletes must also be amateurs—they cannot have received money or material benefit from their participation in sports. This qualification has been relaxed in recent years, since some athletes require financial support to train full-time.

In 1984, professional soccer players were allowed to participate in the Games for the first time. Today, professional athletes are also permitted to compete in basketball, ice hockey, and tennis.

The total number of athletes that a nation may enter in the Games is limited by competition rules approved by the IOC. There have been one-member teams as well as teams made up of several hundred athletes.

▶ THE OLYMPIC PRINCIPLES AND TRADITIONS

Over time, the IOC has established official symbols, statements, and philosophies that represent the ideals of the Games. These include the Olympic creed, motto, and symbol; the Olympic flame; the athletes' oath; and the Olympic Movement.

The Olympic Creed

The creed, or guiding principle, of the modern Olympic Games is a quote by Baron de Coubertin: "The most important thing in the Olympic Games is not to win but to take part, just as the most important thing in life is not the triumph but the struggle. The essential thing is not to have conquered but to have fought well."

The Olympic Motto

The Olympic motto consists of the Latin words *Citius, Altius, Fortius*, which means "Swifter, Higher, Stronger." The motto, introduced in 1924, is meant to spur the athletes to embrace the Olympic spirit and perform to the best of their abilities.

The Olympic Symbol

The official symbol of the modern Olympic Games is five colored rings linked together. These rings represent the continents of North and South America, Africa, Asia, Australia, and Europe. They also symbolize the uniting of athletes from all over the world to compete at the Olympic Games. The Olympic flag, first used at the Antwerp Games in 1920, has the Olympic symbol in the center of a white field.

The Olympic Flame

The Olympic flame symbolizes the continuity between the ancient and modern Games. Modern Games are opened officially by runners carrying a burning torch brought from the Temple of Zeus at Olympia. Except where travel by ship or plane is necessary, the torch is carried overland from Greece by a relay of athletes. At the site of the Games, the torch is used to light the flame in a giant torch, or cauldron,

The modern Games are opened officially with the dramatic lighting of the Olympic flame. The flame is lit from a burning torch brought all the way from Olympia, Greece, by a relay of runners.

OLYMPIC SPORTS

More than thirty sports are recognized by the International Olympic Committee. Some have contests for men only; others have separate contests for men and women.

Track and field

Swimming

Snowboarding

Summer Sports

Archery
Athletics (track and field)
Badminton[5]
Baseball[1]
Basketball
Boxing[1]
Canoe/Kayak
Cycling
Diving
Equestrian[2]
Fencing
Field hockey
Football (soccer)
Gymnastics (artistic,
    rhythmic, trampoline)
Handball
Judo
Modern pentathlon
Rowing
Sailing[3]
Shooting
Softball[4]
Swimming

Synchronized
    swimming[4]
Table tennis
Taekwondo
Tennis
Triathlon
Volleyball
Water polo
Weight lifting
Wrestling

Winter Sports

Biathlon
Bobsled
Curling
Figure skating[5]
Ice hockey
Luge
Skeleton
Skiing (includes
    snowboarding)
Speed skating

Gymnastics (artistic)

Speed skating

[1] Only men compete in this sport.
[2] There are no separate events for men and women in this sport.
[3] There are both separate events for men and women and events in which men and women compete against each other in this sport.
[4] Only women compete in this sport.
[5] There are both separate events for men and women and events in which men and women compete together in pairs in this sport.

Equestrian

Luge

which burns for the duration of the Games. The flame was first used at the 1928 Games.

The Athletes' Oath

At the opening ceremonies, an athlete from the host country takes the following oath on behalf of all the athletes: "In the name of all the competitors I promise that we shall take part in these Olympic Games, respecting and abiding by the rules which govern them, committing ourselves to a sport without doping and without drugs, in the true spirit of sportsmanship, for the glory of sport and the honour of our teams." Like the

Olympic symbol, the oath was first used at the 1920 Games.

The Olympic Movement

The Olympic Movement is a philosophy created and promoted by the International Olympic Committee. This philosophy advocates using sport not just as a physical activity but also as a means of educating people.

According to this philosophy, the good sportsmanship, sense of fair play, and respect for fellow athletes that is developed through participation in sports teaches men and women of different races, religions, and nationalities to work peacefully together in competition toward common goals. The Olympic Movement works to expand such lessons beyond the sports arena in the hope of promoting peace and a sense of brotherhood throughout the world.

The most prominent way the IOC promotes the Olympic Movement is through the Olympic Games. But the Movement's ideals are practiced in other ways, including the promotion of environmental issues, fighting drug use among athletes, and providing financial and educational aid.

▶ OLYMPIC AWARDS

Like the ancient Greek athlete who won an olive wreath, modern Olympic winners also receive awards. The winner receives a diploma with a gold medal as first-place prize. A diploma and a silver medal are awarded for second place, and a diploma and bronze medal for third place. At the awards ceremony, the three medal winners stand on platforms as their medals are placed around their necks. The national anthem of the gold medalist's country is played, or the Olympic Hymn may be played instead if the winner's country wishes. Athletes placing fourth, fifth, and sixth receive diplomas. Each participant receives a commemorative medal.

The IOC does not recognize any nation as winner of any Olympic Games. Only winning individuals and teams are credited with victory. But newspapers publish tables indicating the numbers of medals won by each country. These figures have been used to stress the leading roles played by countries like the United States and Russia and to emphasize the competition between them.

The top three finishers in an Olympic competition are awarded medals (*above*): gold for first place, silver for second, and bronze for third. During the awards ceremony (*right*), the national anthem of the gold medalist's country is played as the top three athletes stand on platforms.

POLITICS AND THE OLYMPICS

The IOC tries to maintain the Olympic ideals and hold Games that are free of political conflict. However, politics have occasionally intruded into the Games.

For instance, host countries have tried to use the Games as a showcase for the merits of their political systems. The most glaring example of this was at the 1936 Games in Berlin, Germany. Adolf Hitler, dictator of Nazi Germany, tried to make the Games a Nazi propaganda show. He believed Germans belonged to a "master race" and that German athletes were superior to all others, especially blacks and Jews. But to Hitler's embarrassment, a group of African American track-and-field athletes won eight gold, three silver, and two bronze medals. Foremost among them was Jesse Owens, a sprinter and long jumper. He won four gold medals; no other male track-and-field athlete in these Games won more than one.

At the 1968 Summer Olympics in Mexico City, Americans politicized the Games. Two African American athletes, Tommie Smith and John Carlos, placed first and third, respectively, in the 200-meter dash. As the national anthem played during their medal ceremony, each man raised a clenched fist above his head in support of the Black Power movement and to protest racism in the United States. They were suspended from the Games and expelled from the Olympic Village.

Boycotts

Over the years, numerous countries have boycotted (refused to participate in) the Olympic Games, usually for political reasons.

The 1956 Summer Games in Melbourne, Australia, were boycotted by seven nations. Egypt, Iraq, and Lebanon refused to participate because of a dispute over the Suez Canal. Spain, Switzerland, and the Netherlands boycotted the Games in protest over the Soviet Union's invasion of Hungary. And China (The People's Republic of China) boycotted the Games after a flag for Taiwan (The Republic of China) was raised in the Olympic Village.

The outstanding performances of Jesse Owens (*left*) and other African American track-and-field athletes at the 1936 Games in Berlin, Germany, were a blow to the racist beliefs of Adolf Hitler and his Nazi Party.

Twenty countries, most from Africa, boycotted the 1976 Summer Games in Montreal, Canada, because the IOC refused to ban New Zealand from the Games. A New Zealand rugby team had played in South Africa, which had been banned from the Olympics since 1964 for its policies of racial segregation. The track-and-field competition was especially affected because some excellent runners were from the boycotting African nations.

More than sixty nations invited to the 1980 Summer Games in Moscow did not take part as a protest against the host country's military incursion into Afghanistan. Among the boycotters were countries with traditionally strong teams, including Canada, Japan, West Germany, and the United States. The Soviet

Americans Tommie Smith and John Carlos used their medal ceremony at the 1968 Games to salute Black Power and protest racism in the United States.

The first modern Olympic Games

1896 The first modern Olympic Games were held in Athens, Greece, with 311 athletes from 13 countries participating. James Connolly of the United States won the very first competition (triple jump).

1900 Women competed for the first time in the Olympic Games. A total of eleven women participated, and Great Britain's Charlotte Cooper became the first champion (tennis). Margaret Abbot became the first American woman to win an Olympic gold medal (golf).

1920 Finnish long-distance runner Paavo Nurmi, called the "flying Finn," won the first three of his nine career gold medals. The Olympic oath and flag were introduced this year.

1924 The first Winter Games were held in Chamonix, France (figure and pair skating had been included in the 1908 Games, and ice hockey had been

included in the 1920 Games). The Olympic motto, *Citius, Altius, Fortius* ("Swifter, Higher, Stronger") was introduced.

1928 The Olympic flame made its first appearance, at the Summer Games in Amsterdam, the Netherlands.

1932 African American women competed in the Olympics for the first time, represented by track-and-field athletes Louise Stokes and Tydia Pickett. Other firsts included an Olympic Village for the male athletes, automatic timers, and cameras for photofinishes.

1936 The Olympic torch was carried by relay from Olympia, Greece, to the site of the Games for the first time. At these Games, American track-and-field star Jesse Owens won four gold medals. Ice skater Sonja Henie of Norway became the first athlete to win the same event three times.

Charlotte Cooper

Paavo Nurmi

Union and 16 other nations (mostly Communist) then boycotted the 1984 Summer Games in Los Angeles, the official reason being a fear over the lack of security provided.

In 1988, North Korea objected to its neighbor South Korea hosting the Games, so it boycotted. In support of North Korea, Cuba also declined to participate.

Terrorism

The worst intrusion of politics into the Games occurred at the Summer Games of 1972 in Munich, Germany. In the early morning of September 5, eight Arab terrorists

slipped into the Olympic Village. The terrorists were members of a militant group who sought freedom for Palestinians jailed in Israel. They broke into the sleeping quarters of the Israeli team and killed two athletes who tried to resist them. For

Arab terrorists invaded the 1972 Summer Games in Munich, Germany, killing eleven Israeli athletes.

Eric Heiden

Carl Lewis

Joan Benoit

1948 Fanny Blankers-Koen of the Netherlands set a record for women by winning four gold medals in track and field. American Bob Mathias won the decathlon and became the youngest male gold medal winner in modern Olympic history.

1972 Arab terrorists killed eleven Israeli athletes in the Olympic Village. American swimmer Mark Spitz won seven gold medals.

1976 Nadia Comaneci, a 14-year-old Romanian, became the first athlete in Olympic history to achieve a perfect score of 10 in gymnastics.

1980 American speed-skater Eric Heiden became the first athlete to win five individual gold medals in one Olympics. Soviet gymnast Aleksandr Dityatin became the first athlete to win eight medals in one Olympics.

1984 American athlete Carl Lewis matched Jesse Owens' record by winning four track-and-field gold medals in one Olympics. The first Olympic marathon

Karl Malone

for women was held and was won by Joan Benoit of the United States.

1996 At the 100th anniversary of the modern Olympic Games, a bomb exploded at Olympic Park in Atlanta, Georgia. Famed American boxer Muhammad Ali lit the torch at the opening ceremonies.

2004 The Olympics returned to Greece for the first time since 1896, the year the Games were reborn. Medal winners were crowned with wreaths of olive leaves, just as athletes of the ancient Games had been. American swimmer Michael Phelps tied an Olympic record by winning eight gold medals at a single Games.

the next 24 hours, the terrorists held nine Israelis hostage. German officials tried to negotiate their release. But all nine hostages, five of the terrorists, and a German police officer were killed during a shootout.

Olympic competition had been suspended while the negotiations were going on. Because of the massacre, many people wanted the Games to stop altogether. But after a memorial service for the slain Israelis, the Games were resumed at the request of the Israeli government.

At the 1996 Games in Atlanta, Georgia, a small bomb exploded in the middle of Centennial Olympic Park during a concert. One person was killed and 111 were injured. The person responsible for this and other acts of terrorism was finally brought to justice in 2005.

▶ **OLYMPIC CONTROVERSIES**

Even when politics and violence do not mar the Games, winning in the Olympics has not always been a simple matter. Throughout the history of the modern Olympic Games, there have been occasional disputes.

An early example of this came in the 1908 Games. About 400 yards before the finish line of the 26-mile marathon, Dorando Pietri of Italy collapsed several times from exhaustion. Officials helped him to his feet each time and eventually guided him across the finish line first. Since Pietri did not finish the race under his own power, protests were made and the victory was finally awarded to the second-place runner, the United States' John Hayes.

The Olympic achievements of the great American athlete Jim Thorpe were long disqualified. A year after he won both the pentathlon and the decathlon at the 1912 Games, it was discovered that Thorpe had played semiprofessional baseball. In other words, he had been paid to play a sport and thus was ineligible to participate in the Olympics. Thorpe's gold medals were taken from him. Sixty-nine years later, however, the International Olympic Committee reinstated Thorpe's achievements and returned his gold medals to his children.

Doping

Doping is the use of prohibited drugs by an athlete to enhance his or her performance in a sport, and it has become a major concern at the Olympic Games. The need for strict control of doping was realized at the 1960 Games when a cyclist died due to taking

American athlete Jim Thorpe was stripped of his gold medals in the pentathlon and decathlon after the 1912 Games for having previously played semiprofessional baseball. Today, the rules regarding the participation of professional athletes in the Games are not as strict.

stimulants. Since then, many athletes have been accused of doping, and some have even had their medals taken from them because they tested positive for some kind of prohibited drug. For instance, at the 1988 Summer Games, Carl Lewis of the United States at first lost track-and-field's 100-meter dash to Ben Johnson of Canada. However, Johnson later failed a drug test and the gold medal was instead awarded to Lewis.

There are five basic types of drugs that are banned from the Olympic Games, each meant to improve an athlete's performance in a different manner. Not only is the use of these drugs unfair to the other competitors, it is also potentially unsafe for the user.

• **Stimulants** provide increased energy to the body. However, these drugs can sometimes overstimulate the body, pushing it beyond its natural level of endurance and causing severe damage to various systems and internal organs.

Did you know that...

some sports and events at the Olympic Games have been discontinued over the years? Sports that are no longer part of the Games include cricket, croquet, motor boating, rugby, and the tug of war (pictured). The standing long jump and the stone throw are events no longer included in track and field, and rope climbing and club swinging have been eliminated from the gymnastics program. There was even a 100-meter freestyle swimming event just for sailors in the Greek navy, which was held only once, in 1896.

THE PARALYMPIC GAMES

The Paralympic Games are an international athletic competition for people with physical disabilities. They are called "Paralympic" because they are *parallel* to—that is, held in the same year and usually at the same location as—the regular Olympic Games.

The idea for the Paralympics dates back to 1944. Ludwig Guttman, a British doctor, discovered that athletic activity was an excellent form of physical rehabilitation for soldiers with spinal cord injuries. What began as mere physical therapy, however, soon turned into a recreational and then a competitive pastime. The first organized competition, featuring athletes confined to

Although the athletes in the Paralympic Games have various kinds of physical disabilities, they must train just as hard and be as physically fit as their counterparts in the regular Olympics.

wheelchairs, was held in 1948 and was called the Stoke Mandeville Games (named for the hospital where Guttman worked). The competition became international in 1952, and Games patterned after the Olympics were first held in 1960 in Rome, Italy. Beginning in 1976, the competitions began including athletes with various forms of physical disability. The first Paralympic Winter Games were held in Sweden that same year.

Athletes who compete in the Paralympics must possess any one of the following physical disabilities: visual impairment (including total blindness); impairment of movement or some degree of paralysis due to cerebral palsy (a form of brain damage that affects the use of the muscles), disease, injury, or natural defect of the spinal cord; or amputation (part or all of an arm or leg missing). However, even though they have some form of physical disability, these athletes engage in the same kind of intensive training and trials as regular Olympic athletes do.

Like their counterpart, the Paralympics comprise Winter and Summer Games in which both men and women compete. Both Games also share some of the same sports, including archery, fencing, cycling, swimming, track and field, and skiing. Some Paralympic sports are broken down into events for each kind of disability, and events may be further divided into classes based on the degree to which the disability affects the athlete.

Other sports are unique to the Paralympics. Boccia is similar to the game of horseshoes, but instead of tossing horseshoes at rings, the players toss, kick, or otherwise move a leather ball as close to a target ball

as possible. In sledge racing, the athletes sit on a sledge (or sled) and push themselves with poles along an ice rink. Goalball is a team sport for visually impaired athletes in which the ball used has bells inside it so the players can find and throw it.

The Paralympics are governed by the International Paralympic Committee (IPC), a member organization of the International Olympic Committee (IOC). Established in 1989, the IPC is made up of 160 National Committees and five International Federations. The IPC official symbol consists of three teardrop shapes, one colored green, one red, and one blue, which represent the three elements of the IPC motto: "Mind, Body, Spirit."

Participation has grown steadily during the short history of the Paralympics. At the first Games, 400 athletes from 23 nations participated. At the 2000 Games, more than 3,500 athletes from 122 nations competed for glory.

THE OLYMPIC MUSEUM

The Olympic Museum, located in Lausanne, Switzerland, celebrates the history of the Olympic Games and the accomplishments of the Olympic athletes.

A special museum for the Olympics was first conceived in 1915 by Pierre de Coubertin, the founder of the modern Olympic Games. The realization of Baron de Coubertin's dream did not come true until 1988, however, when construction

One of Eric Heiden's speed skates from the 1980 Games.

of the museum finally began. The museum officially opened on June 23, 1993.

Displayed in the museum are many pieces of equipment that played vital roles in the performances of Olympic athletes. Exhibits include the skis, boots, and helmet worn by France's Jean-Claude Killy when he won the downhill, slalom, and giant slalom at the 1968 Winter Games; the ice skates worn by American Eric Heiden at the 1980 Winter Games, where he won every speed-skating event in

record-setting times; and one pair of track shoes used by American athlete Carl Lewis at the 1984 Summer Games, where he matched the record of Jesse Owens by winning four track-and-field gold medals.

Other exhibits include examples of the many stamps and coins that have been issued over the years commemorating the modern Olympic Games. The first stamps were issued for the 1896 Games, and the funds they generated helped complete the Olympic facilities in Athens, Greece. The first coins were issued for the 1952 Games in Helsinki, Finland. Some coins are made of solid gold or silver.

The museum is also home to the Olympic Studies Centre (OSC), which contains vast amounts of historical print, audio, and visual archives relating to the Games and the Olympic Movement. Access to much of this material requires special permission. A research library, with over 17,000 volumes of printed material, is part of the Studies Centre and is open to the general public.

• **Steroids** develop muscle in the body at an accelerated rate, making an athlete stronger more quickly. Steroids have been shown to inhibit natural body growth in young users, and there have been cases in which these drugs have caused liver and kidney cancer.

• Strong **pain-killers** may mask a severe physical injury, allowing an athlete to continue competing while making the injury even worse. These kinds of prohibited drugs can also be especially addictive.

• **Beta-blockers** slow the rate of the athlete's heartbeat, creating a state of artificial relaxation. However, these drugs can slow the heart's beating until it stops completely.

• **Diuretics** help remove water from the body, thus reducing an athlete's weight. If too

much water is removed from the body, however, dehydration will result.

In 1967 the International Olympic Committee created the Medical Commission to address the issue of doping. Its aims were to ensure equality and health among the athletes as well as to uphold medical and athletic ethics. The World Anti-Doping Agency (WADA), an independent organization, was established in 1999 to combat the use of prohibited drugs in sports worldwide. At the 2000 Games in Sydney, Australia, WADA began monitoring the entire process of routine drug testing performed by the International Olympic Committee's Medical Commission. Because of this increased vigilance, many potential Olympic athletes have been disqualified and banned from the Games even before they have competed.

The 2002 Winter Games, held in Salt Lake City, Utah, were among the more controversial Olympic competitions in recent years. Despite many superb athletic performances, the Games were marred by complaints of biased judging.

The greatest controversy of the Games was in figure skating's pairs competition. Initially, Elena Berezhnaya and Anton Sikharulidze of Russia won the gold, Jamie Salé and David Pelletier of Canada won the silver, and Shen Xue and Zhao Hongbo of China won the bronze. However, many spectators believed the Canadian pair delivered a flawless performance and deserved the gold medal over the Russian pair, who committed some obvious mistakes during their routine. After the competition, a French judge admitted—but later denied—being pressured to vote the Russians first. An investigation was launched, and eventually both the Russian and Canadian pairs were awarded gold medals.

In women's individual figure skating, the focus was on American favorite Michelle Kwan. Kwan had come close to winning the gold medal at the 1998 Games but lost to 15-year-old Tara Lipinski. This time, Americans Sarah Hughes and Sasha Cohen and Russian Irina Slutskaya posed the greatest obstacle to her finally winning the gold. In the end, 16-year-old Hughes won the gold, Slutskaya the silver, and Kwan the bronze medal.

Because of a judging controversy, two pairs of figure skaters—Canada's Jamie Salé and David Pelletier (left) and Russia's Elena Berezhnaya and Anton Sikharulidze (right)—won gold medals at the 2002 Winter Games.

The skeleton competition, in which the athlete rides a small sled (which looks like the "skeleton" of a bobsled) head-first down a winding course of ice, was held for the first time in 54 years. Americans Tristan Gale and Jim Shea took the golds.

Croatia's Janica Kostelic became the first athlete to win four medals in Alpine skiing at one Olympics. She won the gold medal in the women's slalom, giant slalom, and combined, and won the silver medal in the Super-G. Kjetil Andre Aamodt of Norway won gold medals in the men's Super-G and combined, setting a record for ca-

In the skeleton, held for the first time since the 1948 Games, the rider races head-first down an icy course on a small sled.

Janica Kostelic of Croatia (*left*) was the first skier to win four Alpine gold medals at one Olympics. The exciting sport of short-track speed skating (*below*) was very popular at the 2002 Winter Games.

reer Olympic medals won in Alpine skiing (seven). Bode Miller of the United States won silver medals in the giant slalom and combined.

In the Olympic debut of the women's bobsled competition, the United States team of Jill Bakken and Vonetta Flowers won the gold medal ahead of the favored German teams. In the men's bobsled, the German teams won both the two- and four-man competitions.

American athletes took all the medals in the men's halfpipe in snowboarding, with Ross Powers winning the gold. Another American, Kelly Clark, won the gold medal in the women's halfpipe.

Controversy also touched the short-track speed-skating competition, which is held on a 111-meter course. South Korea protested when their skater, Kim Dong-Sung, was disqualified in the 1,500-meter race for interfering with the American skater Apolo Anton Ohno. Although Kim finished first, second-place Ohno was awarded the gold. When most of the other skaters fell in the 1,000-meter race, Steven Bradbury came from last

place to win Australia's first gold medal in the Winter Games. China won its first Winter Olympic gold medal when Yang Yang A triumphed in the women's 500-meter race.

In long-track (400-meter) speed-skating, Germany's Claudia Pechstein won the women's 5,000-meter race with a world-record time of 6 minutes, 46.91 seconds, as well as the 3,000-meter race with a world record of 3 minutes, 55.70 seconds. The Netherlands' Jochem Uytdehaage set world records as he won gold medals in the men's 5,000-meter (6 minutes, 14.66 seconds) and 10,000-meter (12 minutes, 58.92 seconds) races. He also won a silver medal in the 1,500-meter race.

Norway's Ole Einar Bjoerndalen was the star of the men's biathlon competition, winning the gold in every individual event (10-, 12.5-, and 20-kilometer) and as a member of the 30-kilometer relay team. He was the first athlete to win four biathlon gold medals at one Olympics. Sweden's Magdalena Forsberg won bronze medals in the women's 7.5- and 15-kilometer biathlon events.

Ice hockey was dominated by Canada. Its teams won the gold medals in both the men's and women's competitions.

FINAL MEDAL STANDINGS (TOP THREE) FOR 2002 GAMES

COUNTRY	GOLD	SILVER	BRONZE	TOTAL
Germany	12	16	7	35
United States	10	13	11	34
Norway	11	7	6	24

The 2004 Summer Olympic Games were held in Greece, the country where they originated centuries ago and where they were reborn in 1896. Athletes from 202 nations—the most of any Games—participated. In honor of the Games' homecoming, triumphant athletes were not only awarded medals but were crowned with wreaths of olive leaves, just as the athletes of the ancient Games had been.

These Games marked the first Olympic appearance of freestyle wrestling for women, who competed in four weight categories. Women also competed in fencing's sabre event for the first time.

The most successful athlete of the Games was the American swimmer Michael Phelps, who tied a record by winning eight medals at a single Olympics. He won gold in the 100- and 200-meter butterflies, the 200- and 400-meter medleys, the 400-meter medley relay, and the 800-meter freestyle relay; and bronze in the 200-meter freestyle and 400-meter freestyle relay. Fellow American Aaron Peirsol won three golds (400-meter medley relay, 100- and 200-meter backstrokes), and Japan's Kosuke Kitajima won two golds (100- and 200-meter breaststrokes) and a bronze (400-meter medley relay). Australia's Ian Thorpe won two gold medals (200- and 400-meter freestyles), a silver (800-meter freestyle relay), and a bronze (100-meter freestyle).

Two Australians were among the top winners in women's swimming: Petria Thomas won three golds (400-meter freestyle and medley relays, 100-meter butterfly) and one silver (200-meter butterfly), and Jodie Henry won three golds (400-meter freestyle and medley relays, 100-meter freestyle). Natalie Coughlin of the United States won two golds (100-meter backstroke and 800-meter freestyle relay), two silvers (400-meter freestyle and medley relays), and one bronze (100-meter freestyle). Inge de Bruijn of the Netherlands won one gold (50-meter freestyle), one silver (100-meter freestyle), and two bronzes (100-meter butterfly and 400-meter freestyle relay). In her fourth and final Olympics, American Jenny Thompson won two more medals (silvers, 400-meter freestyle and medley relays) to give her a career total of 12 Olympic medals—the most of any swimmer in the history of the Games.

Chinese athletes won all but two events in the diving competition. Multiple medal winners among the women included Guo Jingjing (gold medals, 3-meter springboard and synchronized 3-meter springboard), Lao Lishi (gold medal, synchronized 10-meter platform; silver medal, 10-meter platform), and Wu Minxia (gold medal, synchronized 3-meter springboard; silver medal, 3-meter springboard). Chantelle Newbery of Australia won the 10-meter platform and placed third in the synchronized 3-meter springboard. Tian Liang was the top men's diver, winning gold in the synchronized 10-meter platform and a bronze in the 10-meter platform. (In synchronized diving, two divers jump at the same time and

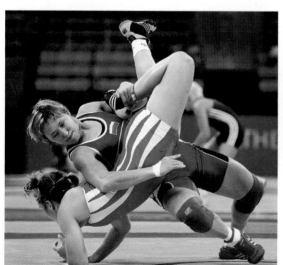

Left: Women's wrestling was a new Olympic event at the 2004 Games. *Below:* American swimmer Michael Phelps was the star of the Games, winning a total of eight medals.

attempt to mirror each other's movements exactly.)

The Games' greatest controversy occurred in the gymnastics competition. After Paul Hamm of the United States was awarded the gold medal in the men's individual all-around competition, it was discovered that the judges had made a scoring error on South Korean bronze-medalist Yang Tae Young's routine on the parallel bars. Without the scoring error, Yang Tae Young might have received the gold medal. The South Koreans filed a protest, but the scores remained final. Hamm also won silver medals in the team competition and on the horizontal bar.

The top female gymnast was Romania's Catalina Ponor, winner of three gold medals (balance beam, floor exercise, team competition). Monica Rosu, also of Romania, won gold in the team competition and in the vault. The women's individual all-around event was won by American Carly Patterson, who also won silver medals on the balance beam and in the team competition.

Although no one athlete dominated track and field, there were several notable performances. Morocco's Hicham El Guerrouj won the men's 1,500- and 5,000-meter races, the first man to win both in one Games since the Finnish runner Paavo Nurmi in

Top: The shot-put competition was held at Olympia, the site of the ancient Games. *Above:* American gymnast Paul Hamm (center) won a controversial gold medal in the men's all-around competition. Like all medalists at the 2004 Games, he was crowned with a wreath of olive leaves.

1924. Poland's Robert Korzeniowski won his third consecutive gold medal in the 50-kilometer walk (he also won the 20-kilometer walk at the 2000 Summer Games). Athletes from Kenya swept the medals in the men's 3,000-meter steeplechase: Ezekiel Kemboi won the gold, Brimin Kipruto won the silver, and Paul Kipsiele Koech won the bronze. And in another acknowledgement of the Games' return to Greece, the shot-put competition was held on the field at Olympia, the site of the ancient Olympic Games. Yuriy Bilonog of the Ukraine won the men's gold and Yumileidi Cumba of Cuba won the women's gold.

In women's track and field, Jamaica's Veronica Campbell won gold medals in the 200-meter race and the 400-meter relay, and a bronze in the 100-meter race. Great Britain's Kelly Holmes won the 800- and 1,500-meter races, and Yelena Isinbayeva of Russia won the pole vault with a new world record of 16 feet, 1.3 inches.

In other competition, 42-year-old Birgit Fischer of Germany won her eighth career gold medal in kayaking when she and her teammates won the four-person crew 500-meter race; Fischer also won a silver in the two-person crew 500-meter race. The Korean women's team won their eleventh straight gold medal in archery. And the American women's softball team won its third consecutive gold medal.

Reviewed by United States Olympic Committee
OMAHA. See NEBRASKA (Cities).

FINAL MEDAL STANDINGS (TOP THREE) FOR 2004 SUMMER OLYMPIC GAMES

COUNTRY	GOLD	SILVER	BRONZE	TOTAL
United States	35	39	29	103
Russia	27	27	38	92
China	32	17	14	63

OMAN

The Sultanate of Oman (formerly Muscat and Oman), a nation in the Middle East, has been called one of "the least known and least visited places on Earth." For many years its rulers resisted outside influences and discouraged change. But the discovery of oil and the ambitious modernization program of a new sultan helped end its isolation.

People. Most Omanis are Arabs. The non-Arab population is largely of Iranian, Indian, and Pakistani ancestry. Most of the people are Muslims. The chief cities are Masqat, the capital and largest city, and Maṭrah, both located on the coast of the Gulf of Oman.

Land. Oman lies in a wide curve along the southeastern coast of the Arabian Peninsula. There are two main fertile regions—the Batina, a narrow coastal plain in the northeast, and the Dhofar area in the south. The interior of Oman consists largely of mountains and desert. The climate is dry and hot, with temperatures reaching as high as 130°F (54°C). Only a few areas are suitable for farming.

Economy. Until oil was discovered in the 1960's, most Omanis farmed and raised livestock. Dates, fruits, and grains are the chief crops. But oil now dominates the economy and is by far the leading export. Because many people have left the land for jobs in the cities, Oman must now import food.

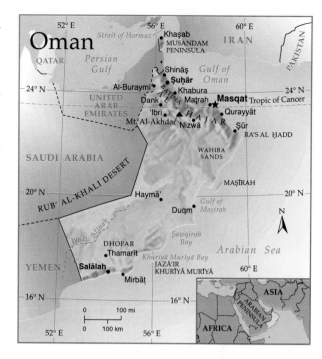

FACTS and figures

SULTANATE OF OMAN is the official name of the country.

LOCATION: Southeastern Arabian Peninsula.

AREA: 82,031 sq mi (212,460km²).

POPULATION: 2,700,000 (estimate).

CAPITAL AND LARGEST CITY: Masqat (Muscat).

MAJOR LANGUAGE: Arabic (official).

MAJOR RELIGIOUS GROUP: Ibadhi Muslim.

GOVERNMENT: Monarchy. **Head of state and government**—sultan. **Legislature**—Majlis Oman.

CHIEF PRODUCTS: Agricultural—dates, limes, bananas, alfalfa, vegetables, livestock. **Mineral**—oil.

MONETARY UNIT: Omani rial (1 riyal = 1,000 baiza).

History and Government. Little is known of Oman's early history. Its first contact with the West came in the 1500's, when the Portuguese conquered parts of the coast. The Omanis expelled them a century later and began to build their own empire. By the 1800's, Oman was the most powerful state on the Arabian Peninsula, with colonies in Africa and other parts of Asia, the last of which it held until recent times. It also developed a special ongoing relationship with Britain.

Oman has been ruled by a single dynasty, or royal family, since 1749. The sultan governs as an absolute monarch. The legal system is based on Islamic law (Shari'a) as well as local custom. The present sultan, Qaboos bin Said Al Said, came to power in 1970 and began a program of modernization and economic development. He also changed the country's name from Muscat and Oman to simply Oman. He is advised by a consultative council, established in 1991. In 2001, Oman became an important ally of the United States in the international war against terrorism.

Reviewed by WILLIAM OCHSENWALD
Virginia Polytechnic Institute and State University

OMAR KHAYYAM. See MATHEMATICS, HISTORY OF (Profiles).

ONASSIS, JACQUELINE KENNEDY. See FIRST LADIES (Jacqueline Lee Bouvier Kennedy).

O'NEILL, EUGENE (1888–1953)

Eugene O'Neill, America's most important dramatist, was born in New York City on October 16, 1888. He spent most of his childhood in hotel rooms and backstage in theaters. His father, James O'Neill, was a successful actor who toured the United States.

Eugene was not a happy child. His mother was often ill and unable to be with him. His father, who was the manager as well as the star of his company, was too busy to spend much time with him. Eugene's brother, James O'Neill, Jr., was ten years older and away at boarding school.

When he was 7, Eugene was sent to boarding school. He was well cared for there, but lonely. He was with his parents only during summers, in their New London, Connecticut, home. By the time he finished high school, he was a quiet, shy, handsome, and rather gloomy boy who liked to bury himself in books. Because he felt neglected by his parents, he was inclined to brood about the sad and bitter things in life.

Eugene went to Princeton University in 1906, but after a year he left. He decided he could learn more about people and life on his own. After a time in New York he went to sea. He continued to read widely, as well as to study the lives of the people he met.

By the time Eugene was 25 and tired of wandering, he began writing about what he knew best—the sea and sailors. He started writing plays in a sanatorium in Connecticut while he was being cured of tuberculosis. In 1914 he went to Harvard University for a year to study playwriting with Professor George Pierce Baker. Among his earliest works were a series of four one-act sea plays called *S.S. Glencairn.*

In 1916 O'Neill began working with the Provincetown Players in Provincetown, Massachusetts. This group launched O'Neill's career by staging his one-act play, *Bound East for Cardiff.* When the Provincetown Players moved to New York, they produced other O'Neill plays. The most famous were two short plays, *The Emperor Jones* (1920) and *The Hairy Ape* (1921).

In the meantime, O'Neill had also written his first full-length play, *Beyond the Horizon.* It was produced on Broadway in 1920 and was awarded a Pulitzer Prize, establishing O'Neill's reputation as an important and original young playwright.

He began to earn quite a lot of money a year later, when *Anna Christie* became a great success. This play also won a Pulitzer Prize. By this time he was 33 years old, married to a short-story writer named Agnes Boulton, and had a son named Shane. He also had a son, Eugene O'Neill, Jr., from an earlier marriage, which had ended in divorce.

O'Neill's next important play was *Desire Under the Elms* (1924). Some of its characters were very much like O'Neill's own family. From then on his plays got longer and more tragic. They always had traces of his parents and the unhappy life he had had with them.

His married life was not happy either. Three years after the birth of his daughter, Oona, in 1925, O'Neill left his family and went to Europe. He wanted complete peace for writing. Divorced from his second wife, he married a former actress named Carlotta Monterey.

O'Neill wrote a great many more plays. Two others, *Strange Interlude* (1926–27) and *Long Day's Journey Into Night* (1940–41), were awarded Pulitzer Prizes. Other notable works by O'Neill include *Mourning Becomes Electra* (1929–31), *The Iceman Cometh* (1939), and *A Moon for the Misbegotten* (1943).

In 1936 O'Neill won the Nobel Prize for literature. He became ill when he was in his late 50's, and was unable to write. For ten years, from 1943 to his death on November 27, 1953, he could only brood about the real tragedies in his life and the stage tragedies he would have to leave unfinished. At his death, O'Neill left 45 completed plays.

ARTHUR GELB
BARBARA GELB
Coauthors, *O'Neill*

ONION

Onions are vegetables that have been grown for thousands of years in many cultures. They belong to the Liliaceae (or lily) family and are in the genus *Allium*, which also includes chives, garlic, leeks, and shallots. These vegetables are prized for their strong flavor and are used to enliven many food dishes. Their flavor and odor are caused by a form of sulfur in the plant tissues.

Onions probably originated in Central Asia, in the area that is now Iran and west Pakistan. By about 3000 B.C. they were known to the Egyptians, who also used garlic—not only for eating, but also for medicine and embalming.

The best known and most widely grown of this group are the common **bulb onions**. These are **biennial** plants, which means they take two growing seasons to produce seed and complete their life cycle. Bulb onions are primarily grown as *annuals*, or one-year plants, for their bulbs, which form underground in the first season. Their green leaves are hollow.

Onion bulbs may be round, somewhat flat, or oblong and are 1 inch to 6 inches (2.5 to 15 centimeters) across. Under its thin, papery cover, the bulb consists of many layers surrounding one or more growing points. The bulbs may be white, red, pink, yellow, or brown. Mildly flavored onions such as the deep red Bermuda onions and yellow Vidalia onions are often eaten raw in salads or sandwiches. Strongly flavored onions such as White Globe are usually cooked.

Scallions may be bulb onions harvested before the bulb forms, or **bunching onions**, a species that does not form bulbs. Garlic is also grown for its bulbs, which form in segments called **cloves**. Garlic's flavor is distinctive

Onion is a popular flavoring for food in many countries. Onions may be harvested early as scallions (*left*), or later when bulbs (*center*) have formed. If not harvested, they produce flowers (*right*) and seeds the second year.

from that of bulb onions, and it is so strong that one clove may be enough to flavor a whole dish. Shallots produce a cluster of 2 to 15 small bulbs that are brown, reddish, or gray. Their strong flavor resembles that of the onion. Chives, which are grown for their long hollow leaves, are also onion flavored. The mildly flavored leek has a thick white base that is cooked and eaten with its leaves.

Cultivation. Onions are cool-season crops that are grown in temperatures ranging from 55 to 75°F (13 to 24°C). To ensure proper bulb formation, it is necessary to plant varieties that will mature in the available hours of daylight. After harvesting, bulb onions are **field cured**, that is, air-dried in the field or in crates. This prevents rot-causing organisms from entering the bulb.

Storing and Processing. Stored at cool temperatures, bulb onions, shallots, and garlic will keep for several months. Leeks, chives, and scallions remain fresh for a few days if refrigerated. Bulb onions may be pickled, canned, frozen, or dehydrated. Garlic, shallots, and chives also may be dehydrated. Onion and garlic may be made into flavorings in liquid or powdered form.

World production of bulb onions is more than 40 million tons a year and is led by China, India, the United States, Turkey, Iran, Japan, Pakistan, and Russia. California, Oregon, Washington, Indiana, and Colorado are leading U.S. producers.

Reviewed by JAMES E. SIMON
Department of Horticulture
Purdue University

WONDER QUESTION

Why do most people "cry" when chopping onions?

When an onion is cut or crushed, sulfur-containing oils in the tissues turn into vapors. These vapors may be strong enough to irritate the nose and eyes, causing sniffling and tears. Cutting the onion under a stream of cold water reduces the vapors and may prevent tears.

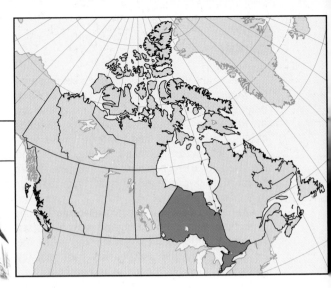

ONTARIO

The British Union Jack on Ontario's flag (above) reflects the province's ties with Great Britain. The coat of arms (opposite page) features a shield with the cross of St. George, patron saint of England, and three gold maple leaves. Also on the coat of arms are a moose, a bear, and a Canadian deer. The official bird of Ontario is the loon (right). The provincial flower is the white trillium (opposite page).

Canada's great central province of Ontario stretches south from Hudson Bay to the Great Lakes and west from Quebec to the plains of Manitoba. Among the provinces, only Quebec exceeds Ontario in land area. Lakes, rivers, and waterfalls spread through Ontario, giving it its Indian name, which means "Land of Beautiful Waters."

▶ THE LAND

Geographically, Ontario is divided into two parts—northern and southern. Northern Ontario, which is six times larger than the southern region, is chiefly mining and timber country. Southern Ontario is the rich industrial and agricultural part of the province.

Northern Ontario. This part of the province extends from lakes Huron and Superior north to Hudson and James bays. It is a rugged, heavily wooded region except for an expanse of low bush and tundra on its northern edge. This expanse is the Hudson Bay Lowland. Most of northern Ontario lies in the vast Canadian, or Precambrian, Shield that sweeps across much of Canada. The Shield consists largely of worn-down mountain ranges. There are also massive rock outcrops, rolling ridges, and granite cliffs. And the ancient glaciers that ground over this land pitted it with lakes and muskeg bogs and etched it with rivers. This made the land ideal for travel by canoe but not easy for roads and railroads to cross.

Southern Ontario. This part lies in a triangle between the Ottawa and upper St. Lawrence rivers and lakes Ontario, Erie, and Huron. The region is part of the Great Lakes–St. Law-

rence Lowland. A wedge of the Canadian Shield juts southeast through the area and forms the central Ontario Highlands. Farther south, the tip of the wedge forms the Thousand Islands. These beautiful, tree-covered islands lie in the broad St. Lawrence River. The international boundary between Canada and the United States passes through them.

Most of the land in southern Ontario is gently rolling country planted to pasture, orchards, and tobacco and field crops. The most prominent physical feature of the area is the Niagara Escarpment. This is a steep limestone ridge that rises like a huge step and runs from the Niagara River northwest to Lake Huron. The spectacular Niagara Falls are formed where the waters of the Niagara River tumble over the escarpment.

Rivers and Lakes. Ontario contains more than 250,000 lakes. The largest lakes are those that Canada shares with the United States. Among these are four of the Great Lakes— Superior, Huron, Erie, and Ontario. The others are Lake St. Clair and Lake of the Woods, which is also partly in Manitoba. Important among the other lakes are Nipigon, Nipissing, Simcoe, Abitibi (part of which is in Quebec), and Rainy (part of which is in the United States). Many of the lakes contain islands, particularly Nipigon and Lake of the Woods. The largest lake island in the world is Manitoulin in Lake Huron.

The Ottawa River, which forms part of the Ontario–Quebec border, flows southeast and merges with the St. Lawrence just west of Montreal. These two great rivers, with their

FACTS AND FIGURES

Location: Central Canada. **Latitude**—41°43′ N to 57°51′ N. **Longitude**—74°21′ W to 95°08′ W.

Joined Canadian Confederation: July 1, 1867, as one of the original provinces.

Population: 11,410,046 (2001 census). **Rank among provinces**—1st.

Capital and Largest City: Toronto, pop. 2,481,494 (2001 census).

Physical Features: Area—415,597 sq mi (1,076,395 km²). **Rank among provinces**—2nd. **Rivers**—St. Lawrence, Albany, Severn, Attawapiskat, Abitibi, Winisk, Mattagami, Missinaibi, Ottawa, Madawaska. **Lakes**—Nipigon, Lake of the Woods, Seul, Nipissing, Abitibi, Rainy, Simcoe. **Bays**—Hudson, James, Georgian. **Highest point**—2,275 ft (693 m), in Timiskaming District.

Industries and Products: Manufacturing; agriculture; mining; forestry and forest products; fishing.

Government: Self-governing province. **Titular head of government**—lieutenant governor, appointed by the governor-general in council. **Actual head of government**—premier, leader of the majority in the legislature. **Provincial representation in federal parliament**—24 appointed senators; 99 elected member(s) of the House of Commons. **Voting age for provincial elections**—18.

Provincial Bird: Common loon (unofficial).

Provincial Flower: White trillium.

Provincial Motto: *Ut incepit fidelis sic permanet* (As loyal she began so she remains).

tributaries, eventually drain into the Gulf of St. Lawrence and the Atlantic Ocean.

The other long rivers of Ontario—such as the Albany, the Severn, the Abitibi, and the Mattagami—rise in the Shield region and drain northward into Hudson and James bays. Shorter but also important rivers—such as the Rainy, the Niagara, and the St. Clair—flow into the Great Lakes.

Climate

There is a variety of climate in Ontario because of differences in latitude and the influence of Hudson Bay and the Great Lakes. In the southern part of the province, summers are warm, averaging between 65°F (18°C) and 75°F (24°C). The winters are fairly mild, averaging between 10°F (–12°C) and 25°F (–4°C). This is because of the moderating effect of the Great Lakes. But in northern Ontario the average winter temperatures of –15°F (–26°C) to 10°F (–12°C) make it one of the coldest regions south of the Arctic zone. Summers in northern Ontario are cool—averaging between 50°F (10°C) and 65°F (18°C)—because of the chilling effect of Hudson Bay. The bay is frozen for most of the year.

Most of the province receives adequate rainfall. In southern Ontario, rainfall varies from about 30 inches (750 millimeters) in the west to 40 inches (1,000 millimeters) in the east. Rainfall is fairly even throughout the year, but sometimes heavy rains and melting snows cause springtime flooding. And in summer, dry spells can damage crops and cause forest fires.

In the northern part of the province, the annual rainfall is between 15 and 40 inches (380 and 1,000 millimeters). Snowfall is heaviest in the southern areas around the Great Lakes, where it averages about 115 inches (290 centimeters) annually.

Natural Resources

Ontario's abundance of natural resources exceeds that of any other Canadian province. Its chief wealth lies in its vast mineral deposits and its extensive forests. The province also has rich soils and plant life, a variety of fur-bearing animals, more freshwater fish than any other province, and large quantities of fresh water.

▶ THE PEOPLE AND THEIR WORK

Ontario has more than 11 million residents—more than one third of Canada's total population. About 50 percent of the people are descendants of the early settlers who came from the British Isles. English is the official language of the province, but about 500,000 Ontarians use French as their first language. There are a number of French-speaking communities along the Quebec border and in northern Ontario. People of French ancestry form the second-largest ethnic group in Ontario, after those of English descent. The next largest groups are people of German, Italian, and Chinese origin. Other sizable groups of Ontarians have come from the Netherlands, Poland, Ukraine, Portugal, Hungary, and Greece. More recent immigrants have come from the Caribbean and Latin

America and from India, the United States, and Vietnam. Ontario also has a native population of more than 190,000—the largest in Canada. Of these, almost 50,000 are métis (people of mixed Indian and European ancestry) and nearly 1,700 are Inuit.

Christians of various Protestant denominations together form the largest religious group in Ontario. But the largest single church is the Roman Catholic Church, which has about 3,000,000 members. The two largest Protestant churches are the United Church, with more than 1,500,000 members, and the Anglican Church, with a membership of more than 1,000,000. Presbyterian, Baptist, and Lutheran denominations are next in order of size. There are about 150,000 Jews and smaller numbers of Muslims, Hindus, Sikhs, and Buddhists.

About 90 percent of Ontario's people live in the southern part of the province. At present about 4,500,000 people live in an arc around the head of Lake Ontario between Niagara Falls and Oshawa, a city that is located northeast of Toronto. This whole area may soon become one huge residential development. There are other smaller, but heavily populated areas throughout the southern region. The occupations and the way of life of the southern Ontarians are much the same as those of their neighbors across the United States border. This is true also for the people who live and work in the port cities along the Great Lakes.

Life is different for the hard-rock miners, loggers, fur trappers, and other inhabitants of northern Ontario. True, a number of sizable towns have been built around the mines and paper mills, and small settlements have grown up around the trading posts and defense bases in the Far North. All these places are in touch with the outside world through radio, and many through television. Some roads have been built, and there are numerous waterways. Pontooned aircraft fly in to the most remote outposts. Most of the towns and settlements have hockey and baseball teams and curling rinks. But these lonely, widely scattered population centers are the only pockets of civilization in the wilderness.

Above: Ontario's ruggedly beautiful north country is heavily forested, with an abundance of lakes and waterways. *Right:* Gently rolling terrain, fertile soil, and moderate climate make southern Ontario well suited to agriculture. Dairies, orchards, and truck farms are most common.

Industries and Products

Once largely agricultural, Ontario today is the most heavily industrialized province in Canada. But it still leads the other provinces in the value of its agricultural products and in the amount of its high-quality farmland. It is second (after Alberta) in mineral production and first as a producer of both furs and fresh-water fish (although these have less importance now than in earlier times). Ontario leads the other provinces in manufacturing production. It ranks second after Quebec in the production of pulp and paper products, and third after British Columbia and Quebec in the production of sawed lumber.

Ontario also leads in service industries, which include advertising and communications, banking and finance, and retailing. It has experienced tremendous growth in the public sector: The centers of federal and provincial government located in Ottawa and Toronto, respectively, employ large numbers of workers. The Metro Toronto system of municipal government is also a major employer.

Agriculture. Ontario's agriculture accounts for more than a quarter of Canada's total farm production. About 90 percent of the province's farm wealth comes from the dairies, orchards, and truck farms of southern Ontario. Beef and dairy cattle, sheep, hogs, processed meats, milk, butter, cheese, poultry, vegetables, and fruits are the leading agricultural products of this fertile region. The Niagara Peninsula is famous for its peaches, grapes, apples, and berries. Soybeans, corn, oats, and tomatoes and other canning vegetables are important farm products, and tobacco—grown chiefly along the shores of Lake Erie—has been a leading specialty crop.

Most of the land in northern Ontario is too rugged, and the climate often too cold, for extensive farming. But there are good agricultural areas near the cities at the heads of lakes Superior and Huron and in the northeastern clay belt. There are dairy and other livestock farms around the mining and paper-milling towns, and truck farming is expanding in these localities.

Left: The truck farms of the south yield tomatoes and other fruits and vegetables for market. *Above left:* Ukrainian dancers in colorful costumes perform at a multicultural festival. Such festivals celebrate the diverse ethnic backgrounds of Ontario's inhabitants. *Above:* Traditional art forms such as totem carving are kept alive by members of Ontario's native Indian population.

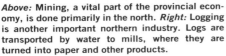
Above: Mining, a vital part of the provincial economy, is done primarily in the north. *Right:* Logging is another important northern industry. Logs are transported by water to mills, where they are turned into paper and other products.

Mining. A great amount of Canada's mineral wealth comes from the mines of northern Ontario. The Sudbury district, long considered the richest mining region in the country, lies north of Georgian Bay, an arm of Lake Huron. About 25 percent of the world's nickel and rich quantities of copper, lead, zinc, platinum, and cobalt come from this region. Uranium ore deposits, among the most extensive on the North American continent, are located in the Blind River and Elliot Lake area on the northern shore of Lake Huron. The main goldmining centers are at Timmins and Kirkland Lake. Iron ore is mined in large quantities at Steep Rock Lake, in the Rainy River district. Silver and cobalt are mined in the Cobalt area near the Ontario–Quebec border. There are deposits of asbestos, calcium, cement, and gravel throughout the province.

Ontario has very little crude oil, although natural-gas deposits found in the southern region were used locally. But oil and gas from Alberta and other sources are transported east to Sarnia, a major refining center. Sarnia is also the center of Ontario's giant petrochemical industry and of synthetic rubber manufacturing.

Forest Industries. Almost two thirds of Ontario's forests are commercially productive. The chief lumbering districts are in northern Ontario, where dense stands of both hardwoods and softwoods cover much of the region. The chief product of the pulp and paper mills is newsprint. Northern Ontario produces more than a tenth of Canada's sawmill products, of which sawed lumber is the most important. Although southern Ontario is no longer heavily forested, lumbering continues on a small scale.

Fishing and Fur-Trapping. Most commercial fishing—smelt, pickerel, and perch—is carried on in the Great Lakes, chiefly in Lake Erie. The inland lakes, which contain more than 100 species of fish in addition to trout, attract many anglers. However, the fish population in some of these smaller lakes has declined greatly due to the effects of acid rain.

About 25 percent of all Canadian furs come from Ontario. In the winter many Indians in the north, like their ancestors, follow lonely traplines, trapping, skinning, and dressing beaver and other fur-bearing animals. Mink is the most valuable fur raised on the many fur farms that are located in southern Ontario.

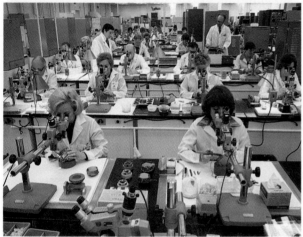

Manufacturing. Ontario produces half the manufactured goods of Canada. This includes the majority of all the motor vehicles and farm machinery made in the country. In addition to its location, there are four important reasons why the province—especially the southern part—is the center of Canada's manufacturing. These are good markets; splendid water transportation, supplied by the Great Lakes and the St. Lawrence, and a fine network of roads and railroads; abundant hydroelectric power from Niagara Falls and many rivers; and a skilled labor force. Most of the factories are located around the arc at the head of Lake Ontario, mainly near Toronto. These factories manufacture a variety of products, including aircraft, iron and steel, heavy and light machinery, pulp and paper, electrical and metal goods, clothing, rubber goods, and processed foods and beverages. Nearby Hamilton is the steel center of Canada. Windsor (opposite Detroit, Michigan) and Oshawa are centers of automobile manufacturing. Diesel locomotives are produced at London.

Ontario also provides more than half of Canada's output of such high-technology products as computers, telecommunications systems, and aerospace products. Most high-technology companies are concentrated in the Ottawa and Toronto areas. One Toronto-based enterprise developed the "Canadarm," a mechanical arm used aboard the United States Space Shuttle orbiter to place and retrieve satellites in space.

Ontario has also been prominent in the field of nuclear energy. The chief Canadian design

Ontario leads all of Canada in manufacturing output. Most of the province's manufacturing is centered in the south. *Top:* Gleaming combines pass along an assembly line at a farm machinery plant in Hamilton. *Above:* The products of high-technology firms such as this Toronto aerospace company are increasingly in demand. *Below:* Traditional heavy industries such as steel production also thrive.

and development center for the nuclear industry is at Chalk River, near the Quebec border. From Chalk River nuclear reactors are exported to power plants around the world. The Ontario government operates a series of huge nuclear power plants, such as that at Pickering, east of Toronto. Today, a substantial portion of the province's electricity is produced by nuclear power.

Transportation and Communication

Ontario's main system of transportation is the Great Lakes–St. Lawrence waterways. The long freighters that sail these inland seas can carry the bulkiest of cargoes. Wheat, brought by rail from the West, is transported by ship from the ports of Lake Superior. Iron and steel from the blast furnaces at Hamilton and automobiles from Oshawa and Windsor plants are other exports shipped from these ports to the markets of the world.

Canals bypass the waterfalls and other natural barriers along the waterways. The Sault Ste. Marie Canals (usually called the Soo Canals) bypass the falls in the St. Marys River between lakes Superior and Huron. The Welland Ship Canal, which has been enlarged many times since it was opened in 1829, bypasses Niagara Falls and links lakes Erie and Ontario. The magnificent St. Lawrence Seaway, a joint Canadian–United States undertaking, completed in 1959, allows ships from the Atlantic to sail into the Great Lakes past the rapids in the upper St. Lawrence River.

Ontario has a well-developed network of railways that covers some 10,000 miles (16,000 kilometers). Most of the railways are concentrated in southern Ontario, focused on the great industrial and shipping center of Toronto. The transcontinental Canadian National and Canadian Pacific railways cut across northern Ontario, tapping the forest and mining areas. The province-owned Ontario Northland railroad runs from North Bay to the port of Moosonee on James Bay.

Ontario's excellent highway system contains more paved roads than any other Canadian province. Many northern roads are graded gravel. A large section of the Trans-Canada Highway crosses Ontario and sweeps along the north shore of Lake Superior. This is one of the most scenic drives in North America. Important expressways include transprovincial Route 401 (Macdonald-Cartier Expressway), which runs from Windsor past Toronto and on to Montreal, and the Queen Elizabeth Way, from Toronto to Fort Erie.

The populated areas of Ontario have a number of radio and television stations. The stations are either privately or publicly owned. The Canadian Broadcasting Corporation's radio programs are an important source of entertainment, as well as information, for the scattered northern communities. The government-owned CBC has a television network across the province, to which chains of privately owned stations and cable television systems have been added. Toronto is the center of Canadian English-speaking radio and television. The Ontario government also maintains its own public chain, TV Ontario, with programming in both English and French. French-language television and radio stations are operated in Ontario by the CBC and private organizations.

More than 45 daily newspapers and some 240 weeklies are circulated throughout Ontario. Most are published in Toronto, which is the main publishing and printing center in Canada. The *Globe and Mail,* one of Toronto's three dailies, is read in all of the provinces and territories of Canada.

Ontario has a well-developed system of navigable waterways. The Welland Ship Canal, which is part of the St. Lawrence Seaway, links Lake Erie with Lake Ontario.

Top: The University of Toronto, founded by royal charter in 1827, is the largest university in Canada. *Above:* Festival Theatre, in Stratford, Ontario, is the home of the Stratford Festival, which specializes in productions of the plays of William Shakespeare.

▶ **EDUCATION AND CULTURE**

Public schooling in Ontario is free, and children must attend school until the age of 16. Many, especially those who intend to go on to college, remain through Grade 13, or the fifth year of secondary schooling. However, this final year is being phased out in favor of a four-year program. Schooling is provided in French for students who have that language as a mother tongue. And there are province-supported "separate" schools, chiefly for Roman Catholic pupils. The province also provides funds for a series of universities. Notable among them are the University of Toronto, Canada's largest institution of higher learning;

Queen's University at Kingston; the University of Western Ontario at London; McMaster University at Hamilton; and the University of Ottawa. After World War II, soaring increases in the school-age population led to the establishment of a number of new universities and community colleges. These new universities included Carleton at Ottawa, York at Toronto, Brock at St. Catharines, Trent at Peterborough, Laurentian at Sudbury, and Lakehead at Thunder Bay.

Ontario has a well-developed system of public libraries, and colleges and universities also have extensive library collections. The research collection at the University of Toronto,

Right: The Canadian, or Horseshoe, Falls at Niagara Falls are both a scenic attraction and a source of hydroelectric power. *Below:* Visitors to Old Fort Henry, in Kingston, can watch a re-enactment of a military drill from pre-Confederation days. *Below right:* The Thousand Islands lie in the St. Lawrence River. About half the islands are in Canada and half in the United States. Several are part of a Canadian national park.

with more than 4,000,000 volumes, is the largest in Canada and one of the ten largest in North America. The province also has many museums, art galleries, and centers for performing arts. In Toronto are the Art Gallery of Ontario, the Royal Ontario Museum, and the Ontario Science Centre. Ottawa is the home of the National Gallery of Canada and the National Arts Centre, which has performances of opera, theater, and the national symphony orchestra. Toronto and Hamilton also have outstanding symphony orchestras. Other cultural features include the National Ballet in Toronto, the renowned Shakespearean festival held yearly in Stratford, and an annual theater festival in Niagara-on-the-Lake featuring the plays of George Bernard Shaw.

▶ PLACES OF INTEREST

Algonquin Park, northwest of Ottawa, is the largest of Ontario's 82 provincial parks and its most popular vacationland. A wildlife sanctuary, the park contains 2,900 square miles (7,511 square kilometers) of woodlands, campsites, beaches, lakes, and streams. Wild animals and birds are everywhere, and the lakes swarm with game fish.

Bell Homestead, near Brantford, is where Alexander Graham Bell worked on his invention of the telephone. A biography of Bell appears in Volume B.

Martyrs' Shrine, near Midland, is a memorial to the Jesuit missionaries slain by the Iroquois Indians in 1649. The shrine overlooks the ruins of old Fort Sainte Marie, the first white settlement in Ontario.

National Parks are Georgian Bay Islands National Park; Point Pelee National Park; and the St. Lawrence Islands National Park, located on the mainland of Ontario and on several of the Thousand Islands.

Niagara Frontier Parks are located on both the Canadian and United States shores of the Niagara River, near the falls. The area has historic houses, restored forts, and battlegrounds.

Old Fort Henry, at Kingston, is known as The Citadel of Upper Canada. Dating from the 1830's, it is a fully preserved old stone fort where the Fort Henry Guard performs an authentic drill from pre-Confederation times.

Ontario Science Centre, in Toronto, houses a multimedia science exhibition and stresses visitor participation.

Quetico Provincial Park, in the Rainy River district west of Lake Superior, is a famous fishing area. The park contains a large tract of wilderness and more than 1,000 lakes and waterways.

Upper Canada Village, near Morrisburg, on the St. Lawrence River north of Kingston, is a replica of an early Ontario settlement.

▶ CITIES

With more than 80 percent of its people living in urban centers, Ontario is the most highly urbanized province in Canada. The principal cities of northern Ontario include **Thunder Bay**, a merger of Fort William and Port Arthur, the great wheat ports at the head of Lake Superior. This combined city contains paper, pulp, and lumber mills, machine shops, and foundries. There are also grain elevators and shipyards. Other important northern cities are **Sudbury**, the rail-transportation and mining center; **Sault Ste. Marie**, the busy port and steel center on the St. Marys River; and **Timmins** and **Kirkland Lake**, the main gold-mining towns.

The leading cities in southern Ontario are considerably larger. These cities are Toronto, Ottawa, Hamilton, London, and Windsor—all important industrial centers.

Toronto is the capital of Ontario and the financial headquarters of the nation. The population of the Toronto metropolitan area is about 5 million. The Toronto Stock Exchange is the world's largest market for mining shares. Because of the St. Lawrence Seaway, Toronto is a leading port for both oceangoing and lake boats. And with its universities, its publishing and communications, its theater, music, and art, and its celebrated Royal Ontario Museum, it is the center of English Canadian culture. An article on Toronto appears in Volume T.

Ottawa is the seat of Canada's federal government. Although the city is located in Ontario, the national capital region extends across the Ottawa River into the city of Hull in the province of Quebec. The population of the Ottawa-Hull metropolitan area is more than

Toronto, the capital of Ontario, is also Canada's largest city. It is a leading port on the St. Lawrence Seaway, as well as a center of business, education, and culture.

The federal Parliament building occupies a prominent spot on Parliament Hill in Ottawa. The city is the national capital and the seat of Canadian government.

1 million. Among Ottawa's features are the stately Gothic towers of the federal Parliament buildings, standing high on a cliff above the rushing Ottawa River.

Ottawa is also an industrial city, but its main concern is government and public affairs. The city contains impressive public buildings, foreign embassies, Canada's fine National Gallery, and many parks and gardens. There is also Rideau Hall, a handsome old mansion on beautiful grounds, set aside for the governor-general. The governor-general is chosen by the federal government to represent the historic dignity of the Crown in the Commonwealth of Nations. An article on Ottawa appears elsewhere in this volume.

Hamilton, with a population of approximately 662,000 in its metropolitan area, is located at the western end of Lake Ontario. The city's excellent harbor and transportation connections have helped to make it an industrial center. It is often called the Pittsburgh of Canada because of its large steel and iron industry. Textiles, electrical equipment, and finance also are important. Hamilton is home to McMaster University and Dundurn Castle, and the Royal Botanical Gardens attract thousands of visitors annually.

London, on the Thames River, is the major city of a rich agricultural region in the southern part of the province. A plan in the late 1700's to establish it as the capital of Upper Canada failed, and about 60 years passed before London became a city. Greater London, which has a population of just over 430,000, is now a center of manufacturing, distributing, and finance.

Windsor, located south of Detroit, Michigan (across the Detroit River), is a major automobile center. Windsor is Canada's busiest port of entry for visitors from the United States. Settled by the French in the 1700's, the city is today a major industrial center. Almost 308,000 people live in and around Windsor.

Other sizable manufacturing cities in the south are **St. Catharines**, the twin cities **Kitchener and Waterloo**, **Oshawa**, **Kingston**, **Brantford**, **Sarnia**, and **Niagara Falls**.

▶ **GOVERNMENT**

The titular head of Ontario's provincial government is the lieutenant governor, who is named by the governor-general of Canada. But the duties of the lieutenant governor are only formal. Actual power lies in the democratically elected House of Assembly and its cabinet of ministers. The leader of the cabinet is the premier. The premier is the real head of the provincial government as long as the administration receives the support of the provincial legislature and the people.

▶FAMOUS PEOPLE

Robert Baldwin (1804–58), Canadian political leader, was born in York (now Toronto). Baldwin is called the Founder of Responsible Government in Canada. He was the leader of the Reform Party of Upper Canada during the 1840's. He helped to form the first Canadian administration (1842) based on responsible government, in which the executive branch was responsible to an elected legislature. Baldwin retired from politics when his moderate views clashed with the more radical views of the majority of his party (1851).

Sir Frederick Grant Banting (1891–1941), Canadian doctor and scientist, found a way to extract insulin from the pancreas glands of animals and thus revolutionized the treatment of diabetics. A biography of Banting appears in Volume B.

Sir Mackenzie Bowell (1823–1917), Canadian statesman, was born in Suffolk, England, and went to Upper Canada with his parents in 1833. He had long service as a Conservative cabinet minister and was briefly prime minister, from 1894 to 1896.

Sir Isaac Brock (1769–1812), British soldier, was born on the island of Guernsey. In 1802, while he was serving with the British Army, his regiment was ordered to Canada, where he later assumed command of the troops in Upper Canada. He was promoted to major general and appointed provisional lieutenant governor of Upper Canada (1811). He fought brilliantly in the War of 1812, capturing the American general William Hull and his army at Detroit. He was killed on the battlefield at Queenston Heights a few months later.

George Brown (1818–80), Canadian journalist and political leader, was one of the Founders of Canadian Confederation. His biography appears in Volume B.

Mazo de la Roche (1879–1961), Canadian writer, was born in Toronto. She is best known for her "Jalna" series of romantic novels set in the Ontario countryside.

John George Diefenbaker (1895–1979), Canadian political leader, served as Conservative Party leader and prime minister. His biography appears in Volume D.

Sir Sandford Fleming (1827–1915), Canadian engineer, was born in Kirkcaldy, Scotland, and went to Canada in 1845. He was engineer-in-chief of surveyors for the Intercolonial Railway and chief engineer (1871) for the Canadian Pacific Railway. He worked on the Pacific cable (completed in 1902) between Canada and Australia. He was chancellor of Queen's University at Kingston, Ontario (1880–1915) and president of the Royal Society of Canada.

Glenn Herbert Gould (1932–82), Canadian pianist, was born in Toronto. He was educated at Toronto's Royal Conservatory of Music and was a concert soloist with the Toronto Symphony at age 14. He soon gained international recognition, especially for his interpretations of the music of Bach. He retired from the concert stage in 1964 and concentrated on studio recording.

Clarence Decatur Howe (1886–1960), Canadian engineer and political leader, was born in Massachusetts and was educated at the Massachusetts Institute of Technology. He moved to Port Arthur (now Thunder Bay), Ontario, and became one of the world's leading consulting engineers. In 1935 he joined Mackenzie King's Liberal government. During World War II, he presided over Canada's industrial war effort. Howe was responsible for establishing a nationally owned airline and for encouraging extensive national economic development.

William Lyon Mackenzie King (1874–1950) was Canada's prime minister for more than 21 years. A biography of Mackenzie King appears in Volume K.

John George Lambton, 1st earl of Durham (1792–1840), English political leader, was born in London. A member of Parliament (1813), he was created earl of Durham in 1833. He served as governor-general of Canada (1838). He worked to establish a union of Upper and Lower Canada and recommended ''responsible government,'' to allow Canadians to manage their own internal affairs.

Stephen Butler Leacock (1869–1944), Canadian economist, political scientist, and humorist, was born in Swanmore, England. Educated at the universities of Toronto and Chicago, he taught at McGill University (1903–36), where he was chairman of the political science department (1908–36). A prolific and versatile author, he wrote works on economics, political science, and history, as well as numerous popular humorous works. His books include *Elements of Political Science, Winsome Winnie, Literary Lapses,* and *Sunshine Sketches of a Little Town.*

Sir John Alexander Macdonald (1815–91), a Conservative Party leader, is called the Founder of Canadian Confederation. His biography appears in Volume M.

Alexander Mackenzie (1822–92), Canadian political leader, was born in Logierait, Scotland. He emigrated to Canada (1842), where he was a newspaper editor. After his election to the Cana-

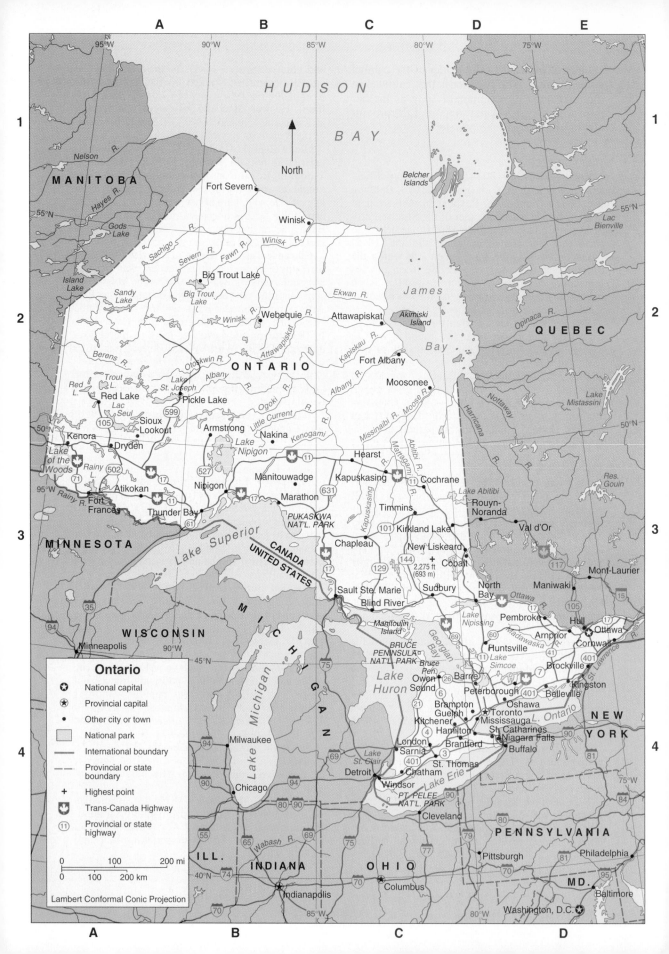

INDEX TO ONTARIO MAP

dian House of Commons (1867) and brief service in the Ontario legislative assembly (1871–72), he became the first Liberal prime minister of Canada, also assuming the post of minister of public works (1873–78).

William Lyon Mackenzie (1795–1861), political reformer and first mayor of Toronto, led an unsuccessful rebellion against the Canadian Government in 1837. His biography appears in Volume M.

Agnes Campbell Macphail (1890–1954), Canadian politician, was born in Proton Township, Ontario. In 1921 she became the first woman elected to the Canadian Parliament, in which she served until 1940. She later served in the Ontario legislature (1943–45 and 1948–51). In both offices she supported farmers' causes and social reform issues.

Sir William Osler (1849–1919), famous physician and teacher, was born in Bond Head, Ontario. His biography appears elsewhere in this volume.

Lester Bowles Pearson (1897–1972), statesman and Liberal Party leader, was Canada's 14th prime minister. His biography appears in Volume P.

Pierre Esprit Radisson (1636–1710?), French explorer, was probably born in Paris. He went to Canada (1651?) and explored the Lake Superior and upper Mississippi River regions (1659–60). He was influential in the establishment of the Hudson's Bay Company (1670). His travel accounts, though inaccurate as to dates and places, give valuable descriptions of Indian life.

Adolphus Egerton Ryerson (1803–82), Methodist minister and educator, was born in Charlotteville, Upper Canada. He developed the public educational system of Upper Canada based on school systems in Britain, Europe, and the United States.

John Graves Simcoe (1752–1806), British army officer and colonial governor, was born at Cotterstock, England. He became the first lieutenant governor of Upper Canada (1791–96). He encouraged settlement of building roads and offering land grants. The city of Simcoe, Ontario, is named for him.

John Strachan (1778–1867), Canadian educator and first Anglican bishop of Toronto, was born in Aberdeen, Scotland. He was curate at Cornwall and then rector of a parish in York (now Toronto). In 1939 he became bishop of the diocese of Toronto. He served as the first president of King's College (now the University of Toronto) and founded the University of Trinity College.

Thomas John Thomson (1877–1917), Canadian artist, was born in Claremont, Ontario. He worked as an engraver and a designer before beginning to paint with oils in 1906. He is best known as a painter of the rugged Canadian wilderness. Many of his paintings depict scenes in Ontario's Algonquin Park, where he worked as a ranger.

▶ **HISTORY**

French explorers, beginning with Samuel de Champlain in 1613, were the first white people to enter the region that is now Ontario. The French developed a fur trade and sent Jesuit missionaries to the Huron Indians near Georgian Bay. But they did not settle the land. In fact, the mission established near Midland, on Georgian Bay, perished tragically when the devout Jesuits and their Huron followers were killed by the hostile Iroquois. When Canada came under British rule in 1763, Ontario was still almost uninhabited except for a few trading posts and a little French settlement on the Detroit River.

Real settlement began at the close of the American Revolutionary War in 1783. United Empire Loyalists, who had supported the British cause during the Revolution, left the United States and migrated to British-held lands north of the upper St. Lawrence River and the Great Lakes. Some 7,000 Loyalists came originally, and more followed. In 1791 the new province of Upper Canada was set up to give these settlers a government. Upper Canada included all of what is now Ontario.

1613–15	Samuel de Champlain explored what is now Ontario.
1668	Médart Chouart, Sieur des Groseilliers, built Rupert's House, the first Hudson's Bay Company fur-trading station, on James Bay.
1783	Loyalists from the United States settled in the Ontario region following the American Revolutionary War.
1791	Upper Canada (Ontario) was separated from Lower Canada (Quebec), and both were granted representative government.
1812–14	American forces invaded the Ontario region during the War of 1812.
1837	A rebellion, led by William Lyon Mackenzie, broke out but was put down.
1842	Queen's University founded at Kingston.
1857	Ottawa was selected by Queen Victoria as the capital of Canada.
1867	Ontario joined Canadian Confederation as one of the four original provinces.
1883	Nickel ores were discovered near Sudbury.
1912	The northern boundaries of Ontario were extended to Hudson Bay.
1959	St. Lawrence Seaway was opened.
1960	Ontario section of the Trans-Canada Highway was opened.
1962	First electric power station in Canada powered by nuclear energy began operations at Rolphton.
1982	Ontario Court of Appeal Judge Bertha Wilson became the first woman appointed to the Supreme Court of Canada.
1986	John C. Polanyi, of the University of Toronto, won the Nobel Prize for chemistry.
1994	Bertram N. Brockhouse, formerly of McMaster University, Hamilton, won the Nobel Prize for physics.
1999	The Progressive Conservative Party and its leader, Premier Ernie Eves, were re-elected.
2003	The Liberal Party won a parliamentary majority; Dalton McGuinty became premier.

After that, many more immigrants came from the United States to take up free lands in the frontier areas the Loyalists had opened.

The War of 1812 put an end to immigration from the United States and forced Americans living in the province to choose their loyalties. During the war, American forces invaded Upper Canada and briefly seized its capital at York, now Toronto. But British regulars and Loyalist militia drove back these assaults. With time, most of the Americans in the province had become loyal Upper Canadians.

After the war a new wave of immigration and settlement began, this time from Britain. English, Irish, and Scots poured in. By 1850, Upper Canada had a population of nearly 1,000,000. The pioneer farming stage had passed, the railway age had opened, and industries had begun operating. In 1867 the Canadian colonies in North America, which were by then self-governing, became part of a federal union, or confederation. Upper Canada became the province of Ontario—one of the four original provinces to join the Canadian Confederation.

In the early 1880's, as the Canadian Pacific Railway was extended westward through Ontario, rich deposits of copper and nickel were discovered around Sudbury. Later, in 1903, there was a silver strike at Cobalt. Discoveries of gold followed. This era marked the opening up of northern Ontario. French and English Canadians, Finns, and Russians moved to the booming mining camps and to the growing lumber and paper and pulp mills.

After World War I, immigration recommenced, but at a slower pace. Mining expanded in the north, and highway construction and automobile manufacturing began in the south. Factories sprang up; cities spread out. Then the growth of the province was slowed by the Depression of the 1930's. But the demands of World War II created rapid industrial expansion. After the war ended, another wave of immigration began. It continued into the 1960's, at first consisting mainly of people from Italy and other southern and eastern European countries. Later arrivals came from the West Indies, Southeast Asia, China, and Korea. These new immigrants gave Ontario a decidedly multicultural character, which was especially noticeable in its large cities and industrial centers.

Beginning in the early 1960's, Ontario's cities grew rapidly. This growth was particularly apparent in Toronto, the capital and chief business center, and in nearby cities situated around the western end of Lake Ontario. Today, nearly half the population of Ontario lives in this area, nicknamed the "Golden Horseshoe." New suburban communities, too, have multiplied in this most populous and powerful of the Canadian provinces.

Yet despite growth and prosperity, as Ontario faces the future it must also meet challenges. These include the impact of worldwide economic trends, the strains of regional differences in Canada, and the problems of living half surrounded by a giant, though friendly, economic power—the United States.

J. M. S. CARELESS
University Professor Emeritus, History
University of Toronto
Author, *Canada, A Story of Challenge*

ONTARIO, LAKE. See GREAT LAKES.

OPEC. See ORGANIZATION OF PETROLEUM EXPORTING COUNTRIES (OPEC).

Elaborate costumes, scenery, and staging can add to the effect of opera, a form of theater that combines music and drama. This scene shows the triumphal march from Verdi's *Aïda*.

OPERA

The word "opera" comes from the Italian phrase *opera in musica* ("work in music"). "Opera" is the term most widely used for a drama set to music. The type of music it uses and its seriousness of purpose distinguish opera from other forms of musical theater.

How Opera Began

Opera was born in Florence, Italy, late in the 16th century. The coming together of a popular Italian style of poetry, called *pastorale,* and a new type of music made the first operas possible.

The poets, musicians, and aristocrats of Florence wanted to replace polyphony (two or more melodies sung or played at the same time) with monody-homophony (a single line of melody with accompaniment). And they wanted to perform plays in what they supposed was the ancient Greek way of building up dramatic effect through music. These aims led directly to the first operas. *Dafne,* a play by Ottavio Rinuccini (1562–1621) with music by Jacopo Peri (1561–1633), was sung in Florence in 1597. The music cannot be found, however, so the opera given the honor of being the first is *Euridice* (1600), also by Peri.

The earliest operas were made up of recitatives (sung dialogue) accompanied by a small ensemble of instruments. The melodies were very close to the rhythms and accents of the text words. The aim was for dramatic expression rather than musical effect. A few passages, often for dancing, were of a more lyrical, musical nature.

The first Florentine operas were musically weak. Their composers were more interested in presenting their texts than in creating musical effects. But the new dramatic-musical form contained rich possibilities for change. Further development was essential for a more satisfactory drama with music. It was provided very quickly.

Development of Italian Opera

A group of composers in Rome adopted the techniques of the Florentines but did not entirely do away with polyphony. They also loved singing for its own sake. The first Roman opera was sung in 1620. It was much richer in musical texture than *Euridice.* One Roman opera—*Il Sant' Alessio* (1632), by

Maria Callas (1923–77) was born in New York, New York. A soprano, she was known for the dramatic power she brought to her roles. She studied in Athens and made her debut in 1938 with the National Opera of Greece. In 1954 she made her American debut in Chicago, in *Tosca*. She went on to sing leading roles in most of the world's great opera houses. She gave her last public opera performance at New York's Metropolitan Opera in 1965.

Enrico Caruso (1873–1921) was born in Naples, Italy. A tenor with unusual vocal power and control, he was a legendary figure even during his lifetime. He sang at opera houses throughout the world and was leading tenor with the Metropolitan Opera (1903–21). Caruso sang more than 40 leading roles, most notably in *Rigoletto*, *Tosca*, and *I Pagliacci*.

Feodor Chaliapin (1873–1938) was born in Kazan, Russia. He was known for his character acting as well as for his powerful bass voice. Chaliapin joined a Moscow opera company in 1896 and later toured Europe and the United States. He was a leading singer at New York's Metropolitan Opera (1921–29), becoming famous for title roles in *Boris Godunov*, *Ivan the Terrible*, and *Mefistofele*.

Placido Domingo (1941–   ) was born in Madrid, Spain. A fine lyric tenor with great dramatic range, he sang leading roles with opera companies around the world. He studied singing in Mexico and sang his first major opera role there in 1960. From 1962 to 1965 he was a member of the Israeli National Opera. Domingo made his Metropolitan Opera debut in 1968. He appeared in film versions of *La Traviata* (1983) and *Carmen* (1984).

Placido Domingo

Kirsten Flagstad (1895–1962) was born in Hamar, Norway. A soprano, she made her debut in New York City as Sieglinde in Wagner's *Die Walküre* (1935). A member of the Metropolitan Opera before and after World War II, she was known for her interpretation of Wagnerian roles. She also specialized in lieder (songs).

Marilyn Horne (1934–   ) was born in Bradford, Pennsylvania. Her flexible voice and wide range allowed her to sing both soprano and mezzo-soprano roles. She made her opera debut in Los Angeles in 1954 in *The Bartered Bride* and her first New York Metropolitan Opera appearance in *Norma* in 1970. She showed her versatility in opera productions throughout the world and in many concert performances.

Jessye Norman (1945–   ) was born in Augusta, Georgia. Her strong, warm soprano voice and magnificent stage presence make her an electrifying performer. A first prize in a Munich competition led her to a contract with the Berlin Opera, beginning in 1969. She made her New York debut in 1973. Her recordings were highly acclaimed.

Luciano Pavarotti (1935–   ) was born in Modena, Italy. He gained fame for his fine lyric tenor voice as well as for his pleasing manner on stage. He sang in

Stefano Landi (1590?–1655?)—had the first known instrumental prelude. Landi's opera and those of other composers also included passages for chorus.

The works of Claudio Monteverdi (1567–1643) were more important in the development of opera. Monteverdi's *La Favola d'Orfeo* ("The Fable of Orpheus") (1607) required 36 accompanying instruments, while Peri's *Euridice* had used only six or seven. Monteverdi allowed his musical inventiveness full freedom. *Orfeo* is still staged because of its musical strength and convincing characters. The last of Monteverdi's operas was *L'Incoronazione di Poppea* ("The Coronation of Poppea") (1642). Its vocal melodies, varied characters, and believable action foretold many elements of future opera.

Opera remained the private pleasure of princes and nobles during the first 40 years of its existence. Then, in 1637, the first public opera house, the Teatro di San Cassiano, was opened in Venice. This event transformed opera into entertainment for a paying audience. A Venetian school of opera composers flourished, and Venice soon went opera-mad. The Venetians developed very elaborate scenery and costumes and made highly imaginative use of costly stage machinery. They did not, however, make much use of a chorus. Their arias, or solo songs, foreshadowed the richness of later Italian melody. Venice had 16 opera houses by 1700.

In the 18th century, so-called Neapolitan opera came to the fore. It was popular not only in Italy but also in other countries where Italian and Italian-trained composers worked. At first Neopolitan opera was ruled by the poets who wrote the librettos (opera texts). Two important librettists were Apostolo Zeno (1668–1750) and Pietro Trapassi (1698–1782), who was called Metastasio. Neither Zeno nor Metastasio was a native of Naples. Both worked at the court in Vienna. These poets wrote numerous librettos, dealing almost entirely with myth, legend, and pseudo history (false, or made-up, history). The librettos were usually in three acts and without any comic relief.

Leontyne Price

opera houses throughout the world, appeared on television, and made many recordings. Pavarotti made his professional debut in Italy in 1961, in the role of Rodolfo in *La Bohème*. He repeated this role many times.

Leontyne Price (1927–) was born in Laurel, Mississippi. She made her debut in 1961 at the Metropolitan Opera as Leonora in *Il Trovatore*. Possessing a rich soprano voice of wide range, she sang a variety of leading roles in opera houses throughout Europe and the United States. In 1966 Price sang Cleopatra in the world premier of Samuel Barber's *Antony and Cleopatra*. She retired from operatic singing in 1985 but continued giving recitals until 2000.

Beverly Sills (1929–) was born in Brooklyn, New York. She joined the New York City Opera in 1955. A soprano, she gained worldwide recognition in 1966 for her performance as Cleopatra in Handel's *Julius Caesar*. After retiring from singing in 1979, she served as general director of the New York City Opera (1979–89), chairperson of the Lincoln Center for the Performing Arts (1994–2002), and chairperson of the Metropolitan Opera (2002–05).

Joan Sutherland (1926–) was born in Sydney, Australia. A coloratura soprano, she made her European debut in 1952 at the Royal Opera House, Covent Garden (London), in *The Magic Flute*. Considered one of the most important singers of her time, she was especially acclaimed for her performance of the difficult title role in *Lucia di Lammermoor*.

Kiri Te Kanawa (1944–) was born in Gisborne, New Zealand. A soprano, she studied opera in London. In 1971 she achieved her first major success as the countess in *The Marriage of Figaro* at Covent Garden. She made her New York debut in 1974 in *Otello*. She was seen by millions when she sang at the 1981 wedding of England's Prince of Wales.

Richard Tucker (1914–75) was born in Brooklyn, New York. He was a cantor (religious singer) before making his debut in 1945 with the Metropolitan Opera, where he became a leading tenor. He remained with the company for his entire career, specializing in Italian operas.

Luciano Pavarotti

Their rigid texts did not allow for the dramatic use of a chorus. About 30 of Metastasio's librettos had been used in more than 1,000 operas before 1800.

Notable among the earliest composers of the Neapolitan operatic school was Alessandro Scarlatti (1660–1725). He made use of *recitativo secco* ("dry recitative," with harpsichord accompaniment, used mostly to carry the plot forward), *recitativo stromentato* ("instrumented recitative," a more lyric style), and the fully lyric independent aria. Scarlatti's many operas (approximately 115) had pauses for character development in otherwise uninterrupted dialogue. He standardized the *aria da capo* ("aria from the beginning"— that is, an aria in three parts in which the third part is a repeat of the first)—which became an operatic convention. Scarlatti also expanded the instrumental introduction.

Other leading composers of Neapolitan opera were Nicola Porpora (1686–1768), Leonardo Vinci (1690–1730), and Johann Adolph Hasse (1699–1783). The style reached its height in London with the Italian operas of George Frederick Handel.

Beginning as early as 1619, with Landi's *La Morte d'Orfeo,* comic episodes had crept into serious opera. Comic scenes play an important part in Monteverdi's *L'Incoronazione di Poppea* and in many Venetian operas.

But the strictly stylized operas produced in Naples and other cities finally led to a division of styles. The solemn librettos of Zeno and Metastasio forced comic opera (*opera buffa*) to develop independently from tragic, or serious, opera (*opera seria*). *Opera buffa* had begun as a light, comic entertainment sung between the acts of an *opera seria*. The most famous early comic opera is *La Serva padrona* (1733), by Giovanni Battista Pergolesi (1710–36). In turn the comic form began to borrow elements from *opera seria*, producing masterpieces of mixed nature. These included *Il Barbiere di Siviglia* ("The Barber of Seville") (1782), by Giovanni Paisiello (1740–1816); Mozart's *Le Nozze di Figaro* ("The Marriage of Figaro") (1786); and

One of the world's great opera houses, the Palais Garnier theater was built in the 19th century. It is the home of the Paris Opera, the principal opera company of France.

Il Matrimonio segreto (''The Secret Marriage''), by Domenico Cimarosa (1749–1801).

France

In France ideas something like those of the Florentines led to the *ballet de cour,* a staged pageant with dance and song and a thread of plot. Under influences from Italy the *ballet de cour* became more and more operatic. Complete performances of Italian operas were also sung at the French court. Probably the first opera in French sung in public in Paris was *Pomone* (1671), composed by Robert Cambert (1628?–77).

The first important composer of operas to French texts was a Florentine emigrant, Giovanni Battista Lulli (1632–87), known in France as Jean-Baptiste Lully. He collaborated with the great dramatist Molière on semi-operatic comedy ballets and with the librettist Philippe Quinault (1635–88) on some 12 true operas. Lully's work influenced a later composer, Jean-Philippe Rameau (1683–1764). Rameau's operas, such as *Hippolyte et Aricie* (1733) and *Castor et Pollux* (1737), also preserved the elaborate staging and pantomimic dancing of the older *ballet de cour.*

England

In England the masque, a short dramatic performance by masked actors, flowered in the 17th century. Alfonso Ferrabosco the younger (1575?–1628), born in England of Italian parentage, had composed music for several of Ben Jonson's masques in the early 1600's. The masque dominated English theater, delaying the development of opera. But some later masques were very similar to operas, especially the entertainments of Sir William Davenant (1606–68). His *Siege of Rhodes* (1656) is considered by some to be the first English opera. *Venus and Adonis* (1685?), by John Blow (1649?–1708), was another masque-opera. *Dido and Aeneas* (1698), by the great English composer Henry Purcell (1659?–95) is a masterpiece.

After Blow and Purcell, English opera was overwhelmed by Italian opera. English opera gathered strength again in *The Beggar's Opera* (1728), with a text by John Gay (1685–1732) and a score partly assembled from existing music by John Christopher Pepusch (1667–1752). That bitter comedy enjoyed a popularity that it has never lost. Just as *Dido and Aeneas* adapted many features of Lully's operas, so *The Beggar's Opera* borrowed some of the manners of *opera buffa*. It and its successors, called ballad operas, led to the German form of half-sung, half-spoken opera called Singspiel (from the German *singen,* "to sing," and *Spiel,* "play").

Germany

In 1627 the Rinuccini text that Jacopo Peri had used for his *Dafne* (1597) was translated into German and staged at Torgau as *Daphne.* Its music was written by the great composer Heinrich Schütz (1585–1672). The first Singspiel, *Adam und Eva,* with music by Johann Theile (1646–1724), was staged in Hamburg in 1678. Among the most influential composers at the flourishing Hamburg opera were Johann Mattheson (1681–1764), Reinhard Keiser (1674–1739), and George Frederick Handel. Handel later developed his own version of Neapolitan opera in Italy and London. His first opera, *Almira* (1705), was bilingual: 41 of its numbers were sung in German, 15 in Italian.

Handel and Hasse

The finest creations of Italian opera outside Italy in the 18th century were by two Germans: Handel in England and Hasse in Dresden. By the time their best operas were written, the Italian *opera seria* was losing all dramatic and theatrical vitality. Strict rules determined the distribution of voices and the pattern of arias. Six main characters were the ideal: three female and three male, led by the *prima donna* ("first woman") and *primo uomo* ("first man"). Librettists had to provide roles for exactly these singers, who had to have important arias at certain places in the story. The impresario, or manager, had to have in hand just these singers, who had to be brilliant in displaying vocal gymnastics. At times the singers' influence was greater in deciding the nature of an opera than that of the librettist, composer, and impresario combined. Two of the most celebrated singers were the male soprano Carlo Broschi (1705–82), called Farinelli, and the contralto Faustina Bordoni (1700?–81), Hasse's wife.

In London, between 1711 and 1741, Handel produced more than 30 operas. These works marked the climax of the Neapolitan style and the heyday of the male soprano and contralto. The finest of Handel's operas and the best of Hasse's are masterpieces. But modern opera-goers perhaps would find a Handel or Hasse opera undramatic. The demands of audiences of the 18th-century for vocal display and the willingness of composers to please them took all dramatic vitality out of opera. Opera had strayed far from its original purpose: the combination of music and drama.

Gluck

By the mid-18th century most new serious Italian operas were nothing but concerts sung in costume against handsome stage sets. They were vehicles for the vanity of extremely well-trained singers. The libretto was simply a framework on which to hang arias. The recitative merely provided intervals during which star singers could catch their breath. A satirical pamphlet by the Venetian composer-poet Benedetto Marcello (1686–1739) was a sharp criticism. Then Christoph Willibald Gluck, a German who had had some success as a composer of Italian *opera seria* and of French *opéra comique,* tried to cure the ailing art.

In Vienna in 1762, Gluck set to music the *Orfeo ed Euridice* of Ranieri di Calzabigi (1714–95) in a relatively undecorated, dramatic style. In this work Gluck avoided the worst abuses of Neapolitan *opera seria.* Both *Orfeo* and Gluck's two other Calzabigi operas, *Alceste* (1767) and *Paride ed Elena* ("Paris and Helen") (1770), were in Italian. He later recomposed *Orfeo* and *Alceste* to French translations of his librettos. Vienna had reacted coolly to *Alceste* and *Paride ed Elena,* so Gluck had gone to Paris.

Gluck's success in Paris had been prepared by Lully and Rameau. His reform of opera was in part a return to the ideals of the early Florentines. This is seen particularly in the French versions of *Orfeo* (*Orphée et Eurydice*) (1774) and *Alceste* (1776) and in *Iphigénie en Aulide* ("Iphigenia in Aulis") (1774), *Armide* (1777), and *Iphigénie en Tauride* ("Iphigenia in Tauris") (1779). In all of these works Gluck forced the music and the singers to serve the drama.

Gluck's reforms scarcely outlived him. His greatest operas were followed in Paris by works that failed to live up to his ideals. These include such "heroic" operas as *Dardanus* (1784), by Antonio Sacchini (1730–86); *Les Danaïdes* (1784), by Antonio Salieri (1750–1825); the *Médée* (1797) of Luigi Cherubini (1760–1842); and *La Ves-*

tale ("The Vestal") (1807), by Gaspare Spontini (1774–1851). The French heroic opera led to grand opera, a style completely opposed to Gluck's ideals. Grand opera was introduced by *La Muette de Portici* ("The Dumb Girl of Portici") (1828), by Daniel-François-Esprit Auber (1782–1871), and by the French operas of Gioacchino Rossini (1792–1868), particularly *Guillaume Tell* ("William Tell") (1829).

Mozart

As Handel had summed up early 18th-century Italian *opera seria,* so Wolfgang Amadeus Mozart borrowed from all the manners and styles of his time. Of Mozart's five most important operas, only *Così fan tutte* ("Women Are Like That") (1790) is nearly pure *opera buffa. Le Nozze di Figaro* (1786) contains elements of *opera buffa* and of later drawing-room comedy, but these elements are transformed by a deeply felt humanity. Mozart's *Don Giovanni* (1787) begins as farce and ends as a morality play. Mozart also composed German Singspiel: *Die Entführung aus dem Serail* ("The Abduction from the Seraglio") (1782) and *Die Zauberflöte* ("The Magic Flute") (1791). The latter mixes farce, pantomime, and symbolism with some of the most expressive music ever created. Parts of *Don Giovanni* and *Die Zauberflöte* foreshadowed the romantic opera of the early 19th century.

Romantic Opera

Romanticism, the great literary and artistic movement that emphasized freedom of the imagination and the emotions, put an end to *opera seria* and pure *opera buffa* almost everywhere but in Italy. Opera was changed by the entire intellectual climate of Europe during the French Revolution.

Among the successful post-Revolutionary operas in Paris were several by Cherubini and Spontini. They marked a transition from strict *opera seria* toward grand opera. Cherubini's best operas have an almost Beethovian musical strength. Like Spontini's *La Vestale, Fernando Cortez* (1809), and *Olimpie* (1819), they give importance to ensemble numbers, characteristic orchestral effects, and splendid staging.

French Opéra Comique. French composers began to adjust *opera buffa* to the social and literary atmosphere of Paris. The first result was *opéra comique.* This began as comic opera but developed into a type of musical play, comic or tragic, that included spoken dialogue.

Opéra comique had been preceded by the works of François André Danican-Philidor (1726–95), Pierre-Alexandre Monsigny (1729–1817), the Belgian André Ernest Modest Grétry (1741–1813), and in *Le Devin du village* ("The Village Soothsayer") (1752), by Jean-Jacques Rousseau. Both serious and comic operas were composed by Étienne-Nicolas-Méhul (1763–1817), François Adrien Boieldieu (1775–1834), and Louis Joseph Ferdinand Hérold (1791–1833). The libretto of Boieldieu's *La Dame blanche* ("The White Lady") (1825) is based on two novels by Sir Walter Scott. Hérold's best-known operas are *Zampa* (1831) and *Le Pré aux clercs* ("The Scholars' Field") (1832).

The purely comic side of *opéra comique* was well represented by the operas of Adolphe Adam (1803–56), the operettas of Auber, and the *opéras bouffes,* or comic operas, of Jacques Offenbach (1819–80).

German Opera. One isolated Singspiel, Ludwig van Beethoven's only opera, *Fidelio* (1805), is almost wholly romantic. Its mixture of farce and near-tragedy in a story of the triumph of good over evil is unsatisfying as drama. However, much of the music is magnificent.

The character of much later German opera was established by *Der Freischütz* ("The Marksman") (1821), a folk-based Singspiel by Carl Maria von Weber (1786–1826). Its great success interrupted the career of grand opera in Germany. Weber's *Euryanthe* (1823) and *Oberon* (1826) were less influential. The libretto of *Der Freischütz* was a landmark in romantic music and a link to the early operas of Richard Wagner.

Equally romantic were the operas of Heinrich Marschner (1795–1861) and *Genoveva* (1850), the only opera of Robert Schumann. Lighter, more operetta-like entertainments included *Martha* (1847), by Friedrich von Flotow (1812–83), and *Zar und Zimmermann* ("Czar and Carpenter") (1837), by Albert Lortzing (1801–51). Other light operas included *Die lustigen Weiber von Windsor*

("The Merry Wives of Windsor") (1849), by Otto Nicolai (1801–49), and *Der Barbier von Bagdad* ("The Barber of Bagdad") (1858), by Peter Cornelius (1824–74).

Italian Styles. In Italy operatic composition was divided almost equally between *opera buffa* and a fresh, partly romantic variety of *opera seria*. The first important composers among the many followers of Paisiello and Cimarosa were Gioacchino Rossini, Gaetano Donizetti (1797–1848), and Vincenzo Bellini (1801–35). Rossini created original and successful operas, such as *L'Italiana in Algeri* ("The Italian Girl in Algiers") (1813), *Il Barbiere di Siviglia* ("The Barber of Seville") (1816), and *La Cenerentola* ("Cinderella") (1817). These were in the style of *opera buffa,* lightly tinged by romanticism. Also in demand well into the 1840's were the best of his serious operas, which had absorbed more romanticism.

The melodious operas of Bellini, particularly *La Sonnambula* ("The Sleepwalker") (1831), *Norma* (1831), and *I Puritani* ("The Puritans") (1835), were entirely serious and lyric. These wholly romantic operas rely for dramatic effect upon subtle modifications within their melodies. Their music was designed for the *bel canto* ("beautiful singing") of expressive and skilled singers.

Donizetti's operas include works of dawning romanticism, such as *Lucia di Lammermoor* (1835); comic operas, such as *Don Pasquale* (1843); and wholly romantic scores, such as *Anna Bolena* (1830).

Grand Opera

Lavish operas based on historical subjects, composed for the Paris audience, acquired the label "grand opera." Grand opera emphasizes stage display, ballet, pageantry, and vocal skills for their own sake. Paris saw *La Juive* ("The Jewess") (1835), by Fromental Halévy (1799–1862), and Donizetti's *Dom Sébastien* (1843). The colossal extravaganzas of Giacomo Meyerbeer (1791–1864), such as *Les Huguenots* (1836), *Le Prophète* (1849), and *L'Africaine* (1865), were also written for Paris audiences.

Three Influences

Giuseppe Verdi, Richard Wagner, and the beginnings of Russian opera determined the history of opera in the middle and late 19th century.

Verdi. Verdi began with *Oberto, conte di San Bonifacio* (1839), a lightly romantic *opera seria*. Then he began to develop a vigorous, naturalistic manner. After a number of failures caused by his lack of good librettos, he composed the highly original and successful *Rigoletto* (1851). This was followed in 1853 by *Il Trovatore* ("The Troubadour") and *La Traviata* ("The Wayward One"). Rigoletto, Azucena in *Il Trovatore,* and Violetta in *La Traviata* show Verdi's ability to create operatic characters unparalleled since Mozart. Grand opera surpassed itself in his *Aïda* (1871), perhaps the most popular of all operas. Verdi was an old man when he composed *Otello* (1887) and *Falstaff* (1893) to texts by the composer-librettist Arrigo Boito (1842–1918). *Falstaff* is one of the greatest of all comic operas. In many parts of the world Verdi is the most frequently performed of all opera composers.

Wagner. Wagner started out under the influences of Spontini, Meyerbeer, and Weber. His earliest operas were *Die Feen* ("The Fairies") (not performed until 1888), *Das Liebesverbot* ("The Ban on Love") (1836), and *Rienzi* (1842). They were followed by a folk-based opera, *Der fliegende Holländer* ("The Flying Dutchman") (1843). An avid student, a man of romantic passion and towering egotism, Wagner had begun to evolve his own operatic style. In *Tannhäuser* (1845)

Enrico Caruso (1873–1921) as the Duke in *Rigoletto.*

Kirsten Flagstad (1895–1962) as Kundry in *Parsifal*.

and *Lohengrin* (1850) he began to apply his theories of music drama, which he distinguished from older types of serious opera. He wrote all his own librettos. He used melodic fragments, called leitmotivs (leading motives), to symbolize ideas, individuals, and objects that are important in the drama. He increased the size of the orchestra so much that singers had to make themselves heard over a tremendous volume of instrumental sound.

Perhaps the core of German romanticism was Wagner's first true music drama, *Tristan und Isolde* (1865). Wagner's music for this folk-based story influenced almost all later music. His next work to be staged was *Die Meistersinger von Nürnberg* ("The Mastersingers of Nuremberg") (1868), the foremost German comic opera. *Der Ring des Nibelungen* ("The Ring of the Nibelung"), a four-part operatic cycle, was staged between 1869 and 1876. The gigantic music dramas of the *Ring* cycle—*Das Rheingold* ("The Rhinegold"), *Die Walküre* ("The Valkyrie"), *Siegfried,* and *Götterdämmerung* ("The Twilight of the Gods")—require more than 14 hours of performance time. These complex works are full of symbolic meanings and philosophical, religious, and political ideas. Wagner closed his career with *Parsifal* (1882), a religious-festival drama.

Wagner's influence upon most later music has been great. But his operatic disciples have been few and unimportant. Aside from the fairy-tale opera *Hänsel und Gretel* (1893)

of Engelbert Humperdinck (1854–1921) and *Guntram* (1894), the first opera of Richard Strauss (1864–1949), the Wagnerian imitations were composed chiefly in France. They have all failed to survive.

Russian Opera. Russia was long ruled musically by Italian, French, and German composers. The first native operas of value were composed by Mikhail Glinka (1804–57): *A Life for the Tsar* (1836) and *Russlan and Ludmilla* (1842). Two operas by Alexander Dargomyzhsky (1813–69)—*Russalka* (1856) and *The Stone Guest* (1872)—had more influence upon Russian and, later, foreign operas. Dargomyzhsky sacrificed purely musical effects for faithfulness to the text, or uninterrupted recitative. *The Stone Guest* is a setting wholly in recitative of a dramatic poem by Aleksander Pushkin (1799–1837).

Outstanding among the works of 19th-century Russian composers were two operas by Modest Mussorgsky (1839–81)—*Boris Godunov* (1874) and the unfinished *Khovanshchina* (1886). Another important work, also left incomplete, was *Prince Igor* (1890), by Alexander Borodin (1883–87). *Boris Godunov,* perhaps the finest Russian opera, and the music of Mussorgsky's nationalist colleagues played an important part in the development of 20th-century composition.

Nikolay Rimsky-Korsakov (1884–1908) stood somewhat apart from his nationalist brothers. He composed highly colorful fairy-tale operas, such as *Le Coq d'or* ("The Golden Cockerel") (1909). The operas of Peter Ilyich Tchaikovsky, particularly *Eugene Onegin* (1879) and *The Queen of Spades* (1890), lack theatrical effectiveness. They are full, however, of fine lyric sections.

Russian nationalist opera inspired parallel movements in other countries. In what is now the Czech Republic, notable operas were written, such as the folk comedy *The Bartered Bride* (1866), by Bedřich Smetana (1824–84), and Antonin Dvořák's *The Devil and Kate* (1899) and *Russalka* (1901). The operas of Leoš Janáček (1854–1928), written in a more advanced musical style, frequently have a folk background. *Schwanda the Bagpiper* (1927) is a folk opera by Jaromir Weinberger (1896–196*i*).

Nationalist schools of opera sprang up in Hungary and Poland. Important 20th-century

Hungarian operas have included *Duke Blue-beard's Castle* (1918), by Béla Bartók (1881–1945), and the ballad opera *Háry János* (1926), by Zoltán Kodály (1882–1967). A popular Polish nationalist opera, *Halka* (1858), was written by Stanislaw Moniuszko (1819–72).

French Operas

The three operas of Hector Berlioz (1803–69)—*Benvenuto Cellini* (1838), *Béatrice et Bénédict* (1862), and *Les Troyens* ("The Trojans") (1890)—have not yet entered the international operatic repertory. However, there have been revivals of them in the 20th century, particularly of his masterpiece, *Les Troyens*. Numerous other French operas are signposts on the main path of operatic development. They include *Faust* (1859), by Charles Gounod (1818–93); *Mignon* (1866), by Ambroise Thomas (1811–96); and *Carmen* (1875), by Georges Bizet (1838–75). Others are *Samson et Dalila* (1877), by Camille Saint-Saëns (1835–1921); *Manon* (1884) and *Werther* (1892), by Jules Massenet (1842–1912); and *Louise* (1900), by Gustave Charpentier (1860–1956).

Spain

In Spain the zarzuela, a variety of musical comedy, long tended to prevent the staging of more serious opera. Some short-lived nationalist operas were composed, but the first lasting one was *Goyescas* (1916), by Enrique Granados (1867–1916). Manuel de Falla (1876–1946) composed the opera-ballet *La Vida Breve* ("The Brief Life") (1913) and

Feodor Chaliapin (1873–1938) as Boris Godunov.

the marionette opera *El Retablo de Maese Pedro* ("Master Peter's Puppet Show") (1923).

Naturalism

Verdi's later contemporaries were largely naturalistic, or realistic, composers. The popular *La Gioconda* (1876) of Amilcare Ponchielli (1834–86) stems from Verdi but includes elements of naturalism. The earliest wholly naturalistic operas were *Cavalleria rusticana* ("Rustic Chivalry") (1890), by Pietro Mascagni (1863–1945), and *I Pagliacci* ("The Players") (1892), by Ruggiero Leoncavallo (1858–1919). The most talented of post-Verdi Italian operatic composers was Giacomo Puccini (1858–1924). His finest operas depart from naturalism. He used a theatrically powerful sentimental style to portray pathetic female characters in such

Geraldine Farrar (1882–1967) as Madama Butterfly.

Maria Jeritza (1887–1982) as Floria in *Tosca*.

operas as *La Bohème* (1896) and *Madama Butterfly* (1904). In *Tosca* (1900) he came closer to melodrama. In his incomplete masterpiece *Turandot* (1926) he experimented with harmonic innovations. His one-act *Gianni Schicchi* (1918) is the best Italian comic opera since Verdi's *Falstaff.*

German-Language Composers

After Puccini the most popular operatic composer of the 20th century was Richard Strauss. His third and fourth operas, *Salome* (1905) and *Elektra* (1909), resembled tone poems with voices superimposed. With *Elektra* Strauss began his collaboration with the Austrian writer Hugo von Hofmannsthal (1874–1929). Their second opera was *Der Rosenkavalier* ("The Cavalier of the Rose") (1911), a waltz-filled, bittersweet comedy. Strauss continued to compose operas for 30 years without matching his earlier success or changing his style very much. Some people consider the huge, puzzling allegory *Die Frau ohne Schatten* ("The Woman Without a Shadow") (1919) his greatest opera.

Arnold Schoenberg produced the comic opera *Von Heute auf Morgen* ("From Day to Day") (1930) and an incomplete biblical opera, *Moses und Aron* (first performed in 1957). Widespread public acceptance has been given to the stark, masterly *Wozzeck* (1925) of Alban Berg (1885–1935). Berg left incomplete an equally powerful and shocking opera, *Lulu* (1937).

Many other German-language composers have written modern operas. Ernst Krenek (1900–91) is best known for his jazz opera *Jonny spielt auf* ("Johnny Strikes Up") (1927). Kurt Weill (1900–50) in his *Die Dreigroschenoper* ("The Threepenny Opera") (1928) underlined the bitter satire of the libretto by Bertolt Brecht (1898–1956). The opera has had continued success throughout the years. Paul Hindemith (1895–1963), Carl Orff (1895–1982), and Hans Werner Henze (1926–   ) also composed notable operas.

Russian Composers

Igor Stravinsky wrote several near-operas and three real operas—*The Nightingale* (1914), *Mavra* (1922), and *The Rake's Progress* (1951). Sergei Prokofiev composed many operas. But only *The Flaming Angel* (1919), *Betrothal in a Convent,* or *The Duenna* (1946), and especially *The Love for Three Oranges* (1921) have interested operatic audiences outside Russia. Dmitri Shostakovich (1906–75) composed *Lady Macbeth of the District of Mtsensk* (1934), an opera that gained international fame. It was condemned by the government of the Soviet Union, which was in power at the time, and was later revised by Shostakovich as *Katerina Ismailova.*

French Composers

In France, Claude Debussy (1862–1918) composed the unique *Pelléas et Mélisande* (1902), a setting of a symbolic drama by Maurice Maeterlinck (1862–1949). It is the single operatic masterpiece of musical impressionism. Maurice Ravel (1875–1937) composed one real opera, the farcical *L'Heure espagnole* ("The Spanish Hour") (1911), and an opera-ballet-pantomime to a text by Colette (1873–1954), *L'Enfant et les sortilèges* ("The Child and the Enchantments") (1925). Three operas by Francis Poulenc (1899–1963) have been successful: *Les Mamelles de Tirésias* ("The Breasts of Tiresias") (1947), a setting of hilarious nonsense; *Les Dialogues des Carmélites* ("The Dialogues of the Carmelites") (1957); and the monodrama *La Voix humaine* ("The Human Voice") (1959), with a text by Jean Cocteau (1891–1963).

English Composers

Several operas have been composed by Benjamin Britten (1913–76), including *Peter Grimes* (1945) and *The Turn of the Screw* (1954). Other modern English operas are *Troilus and Cressida* (1954), by Sir William Walton (1902–83), and *The Midsummer Marriage* (1955) and *King Priam* (1962) of Sir Michael Tippett (1905–98).

American Composers

Operas have been composed in the United States since the 1700's. Of them all, only *Porgy and Bess* (1935), by George Gershwin, has held the stage either at home or abroad. Temporary success was won by *Natoma* (1911), by Victor Herbert (1859–1924); *Mona* (1912), by Horatio Parker (1863–1919); *The King's Henchman* (1927) and *Peter Ibbetson* (1931), by Deems Taylor (1885–1966); and

Merry Mount (1934), by Howard Hanson (1896–1981).

A special niche in American opera is filled by *Four Saints in Three Acts* (1934) and *The Mother of Us All* (1947), by Virgil Thomson (1896–1989). These are skillful, deliberately undramatic settings of texts by Gertrude Stein (1874–1946).

Many American composers have written small-scale operas for workshop, student, or amateur staging and for radio and television. The most successful composer of such forms has been the Italian-American Gian Carlo Menotti (1911–   ). Using his own librettos, Menotti has produced such works as *Amelia Goes to the Ball* (1937), *The Medium* (1946), *The Consul* (1950), *Amahl and the Night Visitors* (1951), and *The Last Savage* (1963).

Samuel Barber (1910–81) used a Menotti text for *Vanessa* (1958). To open the new Metropolitan Opera House in New York City in 1966, Barber composed *Antony and Cleopatra* to a libretto based on Shakespeare's play of the same name. Douglas Moore (1893–1969) is best known for *The Devil and Daniel Webster* (1939), *The Ballad of Baby Doe* (1956), and *The Wings of the Dove* (1961).

Other American composers who have composed opera of one sort or another are Roger Sessions (1896–1985), Aaron Copland (1900–90), Marc Blitzstein (1905–64), Hugo Weisgall (1912–97), Norman Dello Joio (1913–   ), Robert Ward (1917–   ), and Lee Hoiby (1926–   ). American opera has not enjoyed the same popularity as American musical comedy. Most attempts to combine the two forms have been unsuccessful. A notable exception is the popular opera *Porgy and Bess,* which contains many features of the Broadway musical.

HERBERT WEINSTOCK
Coauthor, *The World of Opera*

See also BALLET; MUSICAL THEATER; OPERETTA.

Stories of Famous Operas

Aïda, by Giuseppe Verdi, was first performed in Cairo in Italian in 1871. It was written to celebrate the opening of the Suez Canal. The scene is Egypt in the time of the Pharaohs. During one of the wars between Egypt and Ethiopia, the Ethiopian princess Aïda has been taken prisoner. Her rank unknown, she has been given to the Egyptian

A scene from *Porgy and Bess*, the highly popular opera by George Gershwin.

princess Amneris as a slave. Aïda and Radames, a young Egyptian captain, fall in love. The jealous Amneris also loves Radames.

The Ethiopian army is advancing upon the Nile valley again. The goddess Isis announces, through the high priest Ramfis, that Radames will command the Egyptian army. Radames returns victorious. The prisoners are freed at his request, and the grateful King of Egypt declares Radames his successor and the husband-to-be of Amneris.

Amonasro, Aïda's father, is kept as hostage. (The Egyptians are unaware that he is the king of Ethiopia.) Amonasro and Aïda meet secretly. Amonasro confides that the Ethiopians are about to strike again. He forces Aïda to get from Radames the name of the pass the Egyptians are about to march through. Aïda tricks Radames into revealing the secret, but Amneris overhears and denounces Radames as a traitor. She begs him to confess and promises to help him if he will give up Aïda. He refuses and is condemned to be buried alive. As he is sealed in his tomb, Aïda emerges from the shadows. She has stolen into the tomb to die with him.

Amahl and the Night Visitors, by Gian Carlo Menotti, had its world premiere over NBC television in New York City on Christmas Eve, 1951. It was sung in English. The story takes place in Judea at the time of Christ's birth. The Three Wise Men (the kings Kaspar, Melchior, and Balthazar) and their page are on their way to worship at the manger in Bethlehem. They stop for the night at the humble hut of Amahl, a crippled shepherd boy, and his mother.

Amahl and his mother gaze with wonder at the beautiful gifts the kings are taking to the Christ child. In the morning, as the kings prepare to leave, Amahl begs to send his crutch, his most precious possession. As he lifts it, he walks without help. A miracle has happened. With the crutch tied to his back, Amahl gaily joins the three kings in their pilgrimage.

Andrea Chénier, by Umberto Giordano, was first performed in Milan in Italian in 1896. It takes place in Paris before and during the French Revolution. At a ball given by the Countess of Coigny and her daughter, Madeleine, the poet Andrea Chénier recites a poem. The poem is actually an attack on the rich and horrifies the guests. A mob of beggars bursts in, demanding charity. Gérard, a servant with revolutionary sympathies, joins them.

Chénier remains in Paris during the Reign of Terror. An unknown woman has written to him. The writer arrives. It is Madeleine, who is in danger because she is an aristocrat. Chénier and Madeleine avow their love and plan to escape.

Gérard, now a revolutionary leader, is forced to sign an accusation against Chénier, formerly his friend. He, too, is in love with Madeleine and promises to help her, but the revolutionary tribunal sentences Chénier to death. Madeleine wishes to die with her beloved. She bribes a jailer to put her name on the death list. She joins Chénier in prison, and together they go to the guillotine.

The Barber of Seville, by Gioacchino Rossini, was first performed in Rome in Italian in 1816. It is based on a play by Pierre Beaumarchais. The opera takes place in Seville in the 17th century.

Count Almaviva has fallen in love with Rosina, the beautiful ward of Dr. Bartolo. The Count does not want Rosina to be influenced by his high rank, so he pretends to be a poor student. He serenades her, and with the help of Figaro, a barber and jack-of-all-trades, he gains admission to the house in various disguises. He enters as the student Lindoro, as a drunken soldier, and as a substitute for the music teacher, Don Basilio.

Dr. Bartolo wants to marry his rich ward. With Don Basilio's help he has a marriage contract made out. But Figaro and the Count bribe Don Basilio to change the name on the contract, and Almaviva and Rosina are married. Dr. Bartolo accepts it philosophically when he learns that the groom is really Count Almaviva and does not want Rosina's dowry.

The Bartered Bride, by Bedřich Smetana, was first performed in Prague in Czech in 1866. The scene is laid in a Bohemian village in the 19th century. Marie loves Hans, a stranger in the village, but is to marry Wenzel, son of the rich landowner Micha. The marriage was arranged by the marriage broker, Kezal, and Marie's father, Kruschina. The timid, stuttering Wenzel meets Marie without knowing who she is. She warns him against his intended. He forgets his cares when a circus troupe appears and he falls in love with Esmeralda, a tightrope dancer.

Hans meanwhile has received 300 crowns from Kezal as an inducement to give up Marie. He has accepted only on condition that Marie marry Micha's son. Marie is heartbroken when she learns of this agreement. But Micha at length recognizes Hans as his long-absent eldest son. Hans explains that since the contract specifies that Marie must

Opening bars of the Triumphal Chorus from Verdi's opera *Aïda*.

TRIUMPHAL CHORUS

Maestoso

CHO. Glo - ry to E - gypt's might - - y gods,
Glo - ria al E - git - to ad I - - si - de

marry Micha's son, he—Micha's eldest son—will be Marie's husband.

La Bohème, by Giacomo Puccini, was first performed in Turin in Italian in 1896. It takes place in the Latin Quarter of Paris in 1830. Four poor young bohemians share a cold attic room. The poet Rodolfo, the painter Marcello, and the philosopher Colline build a fire with precious possessions in order to keep warm. The musician Schaunard enters, laden with food and fuel. They celebrate, and three of them leave with the landlord, Benoit, while Rodolfo remains. Mimi, a neighbor, comes to ask for a light for her candle. She and Rodolfo decide they are in love and leave to join their friends at the Café Momus.

Musetta, once Marcello's sweetheart, appears with her new admirer, Alcindoro. When she sees Marcello again, she sends Alcindoro on an errand so she can join Marcello.

Mimi and Rodolfo find life difficult. They separate but are reconciled, while Musetta and Marcello quarrel bitterly.

Both couples are separated when Musetta brings the desperately ill Mimi into the attic room. The others leave to find a doctor, and Mimi and Rodolfo recall their past happiness. The others return. While Musetta prays, Mimi dies.

Boris Godunov, by Modest Mussorgsky, was first performed in St. Petersburg (now Leningrad) in Russian in 1874. It is based on actual episodes in Russian history from 1598 to 1605. Dimitri, heir to the Russian throne, has been murdered by order of Boris, regent for the late czar, the feeble-minded Feodor. As the opera opens, crowds kneeling in the square pray that Boris will accept the Russian crown. When he agrees, he is crowned with great pomp and splendor. Boris, however, has secret pangs of conscience.

Meanwhile, the monk Grigory, inspired by the account of Dimitri's murder told to him by the historian Pimen, decides to appear as Dimitri. He escapes from the monastery and reaches the Lithuanian border.

In the Kremlin, Czar Boris sends his children out of the room. Alone, he muses bitterly on the problems he faces and his visions of the murdered Dimitri. Prince Shuisky arrives with a report on the false Dimitri and the rebellion he is organizing. Boris demands

Scene from Gian Carlo Menotti's 1951 opera, *Amahl and the Night Visitors.*

assurance that Dimitri is dead. Shuisky recounts the gory details. Alone again, Boris is in great agony and prays to be purged of his guilt.

In Poland the false Dimitri has fallen in love with Marina. She urges him to lead the attack against Moscow, so he can seize the throne and make her queen.

At a session in the Kremlin, the boyars (Russian noblemen) discuss what judgment shall be meted out to the traitor, the false Dimitri. Boris appears and hears old Pimen tell of a miraculous healing that took place at Dimitri's tomb. Boris recovers from his frenzy and calls for his son Feodor. He counsels Feodor against traitors, designates him as his successor, and dies.

In the forest of Kromy, peasants curse Boris. The false Dimitri appears with his soldiers. The people acclaim him and follow him as he starts for Moscow. Only a simpleton remains, singing dolefully of the coming doom of Russia.

(This is the version in current use at the Metropolitan Opera in New York and at the Bolshoi Opera in Moscow. In other versions, the scene in the forest of Kromy follows the Polish scene, and the opera ends with the death of Boris.)

HABANERA (Carmen)

Allegretto, quasi andantino

Gyp - sy love is a rov - ing rap - ture, A wan - ton

L'a - mour est un oi - seau re - bel - le Que nul ne

bird___ that___ none can tame.

peut___ ap - pri - voi - ser.

The beginning of the "Habanera" from Bizet's *Carmen*.

Carmen, by Georges Bizet, was first performed in Paris in French in 1875. It takes place about 1820 in and near Seville, Spain. Carmen, a fiery gypsy, is attracted by Don José, corporal of the guard outside the factory where she works. She throws him a rose. When she has a fight with a co-worker and is arrested, she induces Don José to untie her bonds and let her go. Don José is sent to prison for allowing Carmen to escape. When he is released, he meets Carmen at a tavern. Now passionately in love with the beautiful gypsy, he deserts the army to join her band of smugglers. Micaela, his childhood sweetheart, finds him and calls him to the bedside of his dying mother.

The fickle Carmen tires of Don José and takes up with the toreador Escamillo. When Don José returns and pleads for her love, she refuses him and he kills her with a dagger.

Cavalleria rusticana (Rustic Chivalry), by Pietro Mascagni, was first performed in Rome in Italian in 1890. It takes place on an Easter morning late in the 19th century, in a Sicilian village. Off stage, Turiddu is heard singing the praises of Lola, his onetime sweetheart, who is now married to Alfio. Santuzza, who is engaged to Turiddu, complains to

Lucia, his mother, that Turiddu is again seeing Lola. Turiddu becomes angry when Santuzza accuses him of infidelity and throws her to the ground. The jealous Santuzza tells Alfio that his wife has been unfaithful. Alfio vows vengeance.

Turiddu invites everyone to have a drink at Mamma Lucia's tavern. Alfio refuses, and Turiddu challenges him to a duel. Bidding his mother farewell and asking her to look after Santuzza, Turiddu goes off to meet Alfio. Moments later a horrified villager exclaims that Turiddu has been murdered, and Santuzza falls fainting to the ground.

La Cenerentola (Cinderella), by Gioacchino Rossini, was first performed in Rome in Italian in 1817. Clorinda and Thisbe, daughters of Don Magnifico, mistreat their stepsister, whom they call Cinderella. The philosopher Alidoro, friend of Prince Ramiro, disguises himself as a beggar and goes to the door of Don Magnifico's ramshackle mansion. The sisters chase him away, but Cinderella gives him food. Alidoro, much taken with Cinderella's beauty and charm, outfits her properly for the ball at which the Prince is to choose his bride.

The Prince changes clothes with his valet, Dandini. Cinderella's stepsisters, certain that Ramiro will choose one of them, swarm all over the disguised Dandini. Cinderella falls in love with his supposed underling and gives him one of her bracelets. Later, when the Prince takes shelter at Magnifico's during a storm, he recognizes the bracelet on Cinderella's arm. The lovers are happily united. The Princess, on her wedding day, forgives her stepsisters and stepfather, who have treated her so badly.

Carmen sings the "Habanera"—one of the best-known arias in the operatic repertory.

Così fan tutte. (Women Are Like That), by Wolfgang Amadeus Mozart, was first performed in Vienna in Italian in 1790. It takes place in Naples in the 18th century. Don Alfonso lays a wager with Ferrando and Guglielmo that their fiancées, Fiordiligi and Dorabella, are no more to be trusted than any other women. He then announces to the girls, who are sisters, that their sweethearts have been ordered off to the wars. There is a touching scene of farewell, though Despina, their maid, pooh-poohs their lamentations.

Enlisting Despina's aid, Don Alfonso introduces two wealthy young "Albanians" (Ferrando and Guglielmo in disguise), who pretend to become enamored of the sisters. Time and again the sisters repulse their foreign suitors. At last Dorabella succumbs to the entreaties of one, and finally Fiordiligi yields to the other. As the double wedding is about to be performed, with Despina, disguised as a notary, officiating, military music is heard. The "Albanians" disappear. Ferrando and Guglielmo return without their disguises, revealing that they were the Albanians. The sisters blame Don Alfonso and Despina for leading them astray. The old philosopher convinces them that what has happened has been for the best, and all ends happily.

Don Carlos, by Giuseppe Verdi, was first performed in Paris in Italian in 1867. A second version was first performed in Milan in 1884. The story takes place in Spain in the 16th century. Don Carlos, son and heir of Philip II, has been betrothed to Elizabeth of Valois. When they meet for the first time, they fall deeply in love, only to learn shortly that for reasons of state Elizabeth must marry Philip. The royal marriage is solemnized, but Don Carlos cannot overcome his love for Elizabeth. His friend Rodrigo advises him to go to Flanders.

Later Carlos appears at the head of a delegation of Flemings to ask the King for mercy. When the King refuses, Carlos draws his sword and vows to be their savior, but Rodrigo disarms him on the King's order. The Princess Eboli, who loves Carlos but whom he has rejected, denounces him to the King, and the Grand Inquisitor insists that Carlos be imprisoned.

Freed from prison, Don Carlos goes to the tomb of Emperor Charles V to meet Elizabeth, but the King discovers them and turns his son over to the Inquisition. A monk dressed in the Emperor's clothes steps out of the tomb and leads Don Carlos to safety.

Don Giovanni, by Wolfgang Amadeus Mozart, was first performed in Prague in Italian in 1787. It takes place in Seville, Spain, in the 17th century. Don Giovanni's life is a series of amorous conquests. He tries to seduce Donna Anna and kills her father, the Commandant, in the scuffle that follows. He encounters Elvira, a former love, while Leporello, his servant, lists his master's conquests. He makes passes at Zerlina, bride of the peasant Masetto, and even goes so far as to exchange clothes with Leporello. But Donna Anna, her fiancé, Don Ottavio, and Elvira, bent on vengeance, harry him into a graveyard near a statue of the late Commandant, which he mockingly invites to dinner. At the dinner the Commandant's statue appears. Since Don Giovanni refuses to mend his ways, the Commandant consigns him to the fiery regions below. Anna, Elvira, Ottavio, and Zerlina rejoice over Don Giovanni's fate.

Eugene Onegin, by Peter Ilyich Tchaikovsky, was first performed in Moscow in Russian in 1879. It is based on a poem by the famous Russian poet Aleksander Pushkin. It takes place in St. Petersburg (now Leningrad) about 1815. Tatiana and Olga are singing to their mother, Madame Larina, when Lenski and Eugene Onegin arrive. Lenski is in love with Olga, and Tatiana with Onegin. Later, Tatiana, sleepless, writes to Onegin, telling him how much she loves him. But Onegin, in responding to the letter, tells Tatiana that he is not the man for her and she must forget him.

At Tatiana's birthday ball Onegin pays attention to Olga. This arouses Lenski's jealousy. The men quarrel, and Lenski challenges Onegin to a duel. The duel takes place, and Lenski is killed.

Six years later, Onegin attends a reception at Prince Gremin's palace and is astonished to learn that the beautiful Princess Gremina is Tatiana. He knows now that he loves her. He sends her a message, and they meet. Onegin pleads for her love. Tatiana wavers, for she is still in love with him, but gains control of herself and sends him away forever.

Falstaff, by Giuseppe Verdi, was first performed in Milan in Italian in 1893. It is based on Shakespeare's *Merry Wives of Windsor* and *Henry IV*. The action takes place in Windsor, England, in the 15th century. Sir John Falstaff, now old and fat, still fancies himself a lady-killer. He sends love letters to two respectable matrons of Windsor, attempting to set up rendezvous with them—separately, of course. Mistress Page and Mistress Ford compare Falstaff's letters and find them identical. They decide to punish Falstaff, with the help of Dame Quickly. Through plots and counterplots, disguises and complicated tricks, they discredit Falstaff. Everyone has a great laugh at the fat knight's expense.

Faust, by Charles Gounod, was first performed in Paris in French in 1859. It is based on a poem by the famous German writer Johann von Goethe. The opera takes place in Germany in the 16th century. The elderly Faust makes a deal with Mephistopheles. In exchange for Faust's soul, his youth will be restored and he will meet the beautiful Marguerite.

At a fair, Valentin, Marguerite's brother, worries about leaving her unprotected while he is in the Army. Siebel, who is in love with her, promises to watch over her. Mephistopheles joins the crowd, performs magic, fights, and withdraws when the soldiers raise their swords in the form of a cross. Faust meets Marguerite, and she loses her heart to him.

When the war is over, Valentin returns and Faust kills him in a duel. Marguerite, conscience-stricken, kills her newborn child and is put into prison to await execution. Faust and Mephistopheles urge her to escape. On the threshold of death, Marguerite prays for forgiveness. She dies, angel voices sing of her redemption, and Mephistopheles drags Faust to his doom.

Fidelio, by Ludwig van Beethoven, was first performed in Vienna in German in 1805. It takes place in a prison near Seville in the 18th century. Florestan, a Spanish nobleman, has been thrown into prison by Pizarro, a political enemy and the prison governor. Florestan is chained to a wall in a deep dungeon and is slowly starving to death. Hoping to save him, his devoted wife, Leonora, disguises herself as a young man. She takes the name Fidelio and becomes the assistant of Rocco, the chief jailer. Rocco's daughter, Marcellina, falls in love with the handsome Fidelio, to the dismay of her suitor, Jacquino, and of Leonora herself.

Learning that the prime minister is about to inspect the prison, Pizarro determines to silence Florestan forever. He sends Rocco and Fidelio to dig a grave for him in the dungeon. Pizarro enters the dungeon, dagger in hand. Fidelio throws herself between him and Florestan and threatens Pizarro with a pistol. At this moment trumpets sound, heralding the arrival of the prime minister. He orders all prisoners released and brought before him. He is shocked to find Florestan there in such a state, but he is full of admiration for Leonora's courage. Pizzaro is arrested and led away in chains while Leonora removes the fetters that bind her husband.

Der fliegende Holländer (The Flying Dutchman), by Richard Wagner, was first performed in Dresden in German in 1843. It takes place in the 18th century on the Norwegian coast, where the Dutchman's ghost ship comes to shore after 7 years at sea. He is condemned to sail the seas forever, unless he can find a woman who will love him. He is permitted to go ashore once every 7 years.

The Dutchman meets Daland, captain of a Norwegian ship, and begs for a night's lodging in his home. Daland's daughter, Senta, has long been obsessed by the legend of the Dutchman. When she sees him, they realize they are destined for each other.

Erik, Senta's fiancé, pleads with her to return to him. The Dutchman, feeling that if Senta can be untrue to Erik she would be false to him too, decides to set sail again. When his ship leaves the harbor, Senta throws herself into the sea. The Dutchman's ship disappears beneath the waves, and he and Senta, clasped in each other's arms, rise slowly out of the sea.

La Forza del destino (The Power of Destiny), by Giuseppe Verdi, was first performed in St. Petersburg (now Leningrad) in Italian in 1862. It takes place in Spain and Italy at the end of the 18th century. Leonora and Alvaro are in love. They are about to elope when her disapproving father, the Marquis, discovers them. Alvaro, submitting to him, throws down his pistol. It explodes, fatally wounding the Marquis, who dies cursing Leonora.

Leonora, disguised as a man, seeks Alvaro in a mountain village. In the crowd she discovers her brother, Carlo, who has sworn to kill her and Alvaro. She flees to a monastery and is given haven in a mountain cave.

Alvaro, under an assumed name, is with the Spanish Army in Italy. He saves Carlo's life, without knowing who he is, and the two men become devoted friends. When Alvaro is wounded in battle, Carlo discovers his identity. As soon as Alvaro has recovered, Carlo insists on a duel, but they are separated by fellow soldiers.

Five years later Carlo has located Alvaro in a monastery. He comes seeking vengeance, demanding that Alvaro fight. Eventually, aroused by Carlo's bitter insults, Alvaro seizes a sword, and they rush out of the monastery. Alvaro wounds Carlo mortally and summons a hermit from a cave. It is Leonora. She rushes to her dying brother, who stabs her in the heart. With her last breath she begs Alvaro to find salvation in religion.

Hansel and Gretel, by Engelbert Humperdinck, was first performed in Weimar in German in 1893. It takes place in a forest in Germany, in the distant past. Hansel and Gretel, children of a poor broom-maker, are hungry. Their mother scolds them for playing instead of working and sends them into the woods to gather strawberries. The children pick strawberries and eat them, but they become lost in the woods as darkness falls. The sandman puts them to sleep while angels watch over them.

In the morning Hansel and Gretel come upon a little gingerbread house and begin to nibble at it. A witch comes out, locks Hansel in a cage, and sets Gretel to doing housework. When the witch tries to shove Gretel into the oven, the children trick her and push her in instead. The oven explodes, and the wicked witch is burned to a crisp. All her victims change from gingerbread back into children. The parents arrive, and all ends happily.

L'Heure espagnole (The Spanish Hour), by Maurice Ravel, was first performed in Paris in French in 1911. It takes place in 18th-century Spain. While Torquemada, a clockmaker, attends to clocks in the town, his wife, Concepcion, entertains a succession of lovers in his shop. When each new lover arrives, Concepcion hides the old one in one of the big grandfather clocks.

When Torquemada returns from his work, he finds two lovers in clocks and another one with Concepcion. He accepts their explanation that they are only customers. The opera ends with everybody in gay spirits, asking the audience to remember that "this is Spain."

Lohengrin, by Richard Wagner, was first performed in Weimar in German in 1850. It is based on medieval legends. It takes place in Antwerp in the early 10th century. King Henry of Germany finds Brabant in turmoil. The regent, Telramund, has accused Elsa of murdering the heir, her brother, Gottfried. Telramund now claims the throne. Elsa denies the accusation. Her champion will be a knight who has appeared in her dreams.

A boat drawn by a swan appears, bearing the knight Lohengrin. He promises to champion Elsa and marry her, on condition that she never ask who he is or where he came from. Lohengrin defeats Telramund but spares his life. Telramund and his wife, Ortrud, scheme to discredit Lohengrin. Elsa assures Lohengrin of her trust, but later, when they are alone, she insists that he reveal his identity. Telramund bursts in. Lohengrin kills him.

Sadly, Lohengrin leads Elsa to King Henry and confesses that he is a knight of the Holy Grail, son of Parsifal. Having revealed his secret, he must now return to Montsalvat, home of the Grail. His swan appears. Ortrud gloats that the swan is Gottfried, transformed by her own black magic. Lohengrin restores the boy to human form and departs in his boat, now drawn by the dove of the Holy Grail.

Lucia di Lammermoor, by Gaetano Donizetti, was first performed in Naples in Italian in 1835. It is based on Sir Walter Scott's novel *The Bride of Lammermoor*. The scene is laid

Opening bars of the aria sung in the Mad Scene in *Lucia di Lammermoor.*

FROM THE **MAD SCENE** (Lucia)

At last— I'm thine, — love,   at   last— thou'rt mine, — love;
Al - fin — son tu - a,   al - fin — sei mi - o,

155

in Scotland in the late 17th or early 18th century. Edgardo of Ravenswood and Lucia Ashton of Lammermoor love each other, though their families are deadly enemies. Before leaving for France, Edgardo wishes to visit Lord Henry, Lucia's brother, and confess their love. Lucia insists this would be useless, and the two pledge eternal fidelity.

Henry Ashton has learned of the affair and is determined to crush it. He forges a letter to convince Lucia that Edgardo is unfaithful and informs her that only if she marries Lord Arthur Bucklaw can their house be saved from ruin. Lucia yields, but when Edgardo returns and curses the whole Lammermoor family, she goes insane. She kills her husband in the bridal chamber and dies in anguish. When Edgardo learns of Lucia's death and of her innocence, he kills himself upon her grave.

Madama Butterfly, by Giacomo Puccini, was first performed in Milan in Italian in 1904. It takes place in Nagasaki, Japan, in the late 19th century. Lieutenant Pinkerton of the United States Navy enters into a Japanese marriage with Cio-Cio-San, Madama Butterfly, despite objections from the American consul, Sharpless. Pinkerton does not take the marriage seriously, but the girl believes it to be binding and has even renounced her religion. They enter their new life happily. Soon, however, Pinkerton has to go back to America.

For 3 years Butterfly is faithful, certain he will return "one fine day." She refuses a rich suitor. When Sharpless tries to tell her that Pinkerton has married an American wife, a cannon announces the arrival of the *Abraham Lincoln,* Pinkerton's ship. Butterfly, her child, and her maid, Suzuki, await Pinkerton. He and Sharpless arrive and tell Suzuki the truth. Butterfly, expecting to see Pinkerton, encounters his American wife, Kate, instead. Butterfly accepts the truth calmly and tells Kate she may have the child in half an hour.

When they return, Butterfly is dead by her own hand.

The Magic Flute, by Wolfgang Amadeus Mozart, was first performed in Vienna in German in 1791. It takes place in ancient Memphis, Egypt.

Sarastro, the wise high priest of Isis and Osiris, has taken Pamina to the temple to release her from the influence of her mother, the evil Queen of the Night. The Queen induces young Prince Tamino to go in search of her daughter and free her from Sarastro. Tamino, accompanied by Papageno, a bird-catcher, accomplishes his task after various trials. But he becomes the friend of Sarastro, whose wisdom and mildness he has learned to admire. Tamino and Pamina are united as the cheers of the multitude hail the triumph of light.

Manon, by Jules Massenet, was first performed in Paris in French in 1884. It is based on a novel by Abbé Prévost. The opera takes place in Amiens and Paris and on the road to Le Havre in 1721. Pretty, flighty Manon Lescaut is destined by her family for a convent. She goes to Amiens to meet her cousin, Lescaut, who will escort her. At the inn she captivates Finance Minister Giullot, but when the Chevalier des Grieux enters, it is love at first sight. They elope in the coach Guillot had offered Manon.

Manon and Des Grieux live happily in Paris, but Count des Grieux, the Chevalier's father, disapproves of their plans to marry. He has his son kidnapped. At a festival the Count reveals that his son is planning to enter the priesthood. The Count is just as much opposed to his son's becoming a priest as he was to his marrying Manon. At the seminary the Count tries to stop his son from entering the Church, but he is unsuccessful. Manon arrives. Des Grieux cannot resist her entreaties, and they leave together.

Later, Des Grieux gambles with fabulous success. Guillot accuses him of cheating and has him and Manon arrested. The Count has him quickly released, but Manon is convicted and sentenced to deportation. Des Grieux and Lescaut bribe the escorting officers to release Manon. Now desperately ill, she tries to respond to the Chevalier's pleas to escape but dies in his arms on the road to Le Havre.

The Marriage of Figaro, by Wolfgang Amadeus Mozart, was first performed in Vienna in Italian in 1786. The events of the story come after those in *The Barber of Seville,* by Gioacchino Rossini. Both are based on plays by Pierre Beaumarchais. The scene is Count Almaviva's castle near Seville, Spain, in the 17th century. The Count and Rosina have been married some years. Figaro, now the

In Act II, Scene 2 of Verdi's *Falstaff*, blustery Sir John Falstaff (*center stage*) soon will be carried away in the large laundry hamper standing near him.

Above: In the second act of Mozart's *The Magic Flute*, Sarastro, the high priest of Isis and Osiris, stands in the temple of wisdom and sings his thanks to the gods for their favors. Right: Joan Sutherland as Lucia, the mad bride, in a key scene from *Lucia di Lammermoor*, by Gaetano Donizetti.

Count's valet, is engaged to marry Susanna, the Countess' maid. But there are complications.

The Count is trying to seduce Susanna. He suspects the Countess of being overfond of her page, Cherubino, whom he orders to join the

A singing contest in Wagner's *Die Meistersinger*. The seated judges are the mastersingers.

A few bars from the song that wins the contest (*above*).

THE PRIZE SONG (Walther)

Moderato

p Bathed in the sun - light __ at __ dawn __ of the day,
Mor - gen - lich leuch - tend __ in __ ro - si - gem Schein,

army. Cherubino jumps out of a window to avoid being discovered in the Countess' bedroom, and Figaro takes the blame.

Marcellina, Dr. Bartolo's housekeeper, is suing Figaro for breach of promise. They discover, however, that Figaro is actually Marcellina's long-lost son. That obstacle removed, Figaro and Susanna are married. Now the Countess and Susanna conspire to trap the straying Count. They exchange clothes to keep a rendezvous. The Count makes love to the Countess, thinking she is Susanna, and Figaro makes love to Susanna, dressed as the Countess, to make the Count jealous. The substitution revealed, the Count apologizes to the Countess, and both couples are happily reunited.

Martha, by Friedrich von Flotow, was first performed in Vienna in German in 1847. The story takes place in Richmond, England, during the reign of Queen Anne (1702–14). Lady Harriet, maid of honor to Queen Anne, is bored. She decides to go to the Richmond Fair with her maid, Nancy, and her cousin, Sir Tristram Mickleford. They dress as peasant girls and a country squire.

At the fair servant girls offer their services to the farmers for a year. Plunkett, a young farmer, and Lionel, his foster brother, hire Harriet and Nancy and take them to their farmhouse. Harriet says her name is Martha. Nancy says hers is Julia. The men try to teach them to spin, and Lionel and Harriet, Plunkett and Nancy, find they are growing fond of each other. During the night Sir Tristram rescues the girls.

The four meet again, by chance, in Richmond Park. Harriet and Nancy are in their fine clothes, which confuses Plunkett and Lionel. Lionel is taken away by the guards for disturbing a lady.

Harriet discovers that Lionel is really the son of the Earl of Derby. She tells Lionel and asks his pardon for what she has done, but he remains angry with her. To win him back, she arranges another Richmond Fair. She and Nancy pretend to be servant girls again, and Lionel and Plunkett hire them—as their wives.

The Masked Ball, by Giuseppe Verdi, was first performed in Rome in Italian in 1859. It is based on a historical incident. King Gustavus III of Sweden was assassinated by Count Anckarström at a masked ball in

Stockholm in 1792. Verdi changed the locale from the Swedish court to colonial Boston. The King became Riccardo, Earl of Warwick, governor of the colony. Anckarström became Renato, the governor's private secretary. Both Boston and Stockholm, and even Naples, have since been used for the setting, but Verdi's substitute names are generally kept.

Riccardo, King of Sweden, is secretly in love with Amelia, wife of his secretary, Renato. Riccardo and Amelia, disguised, each visit Ulrica, the fortune-teller. Ulrica tells Amelia of an herb that will cure her secret love and predicts that Riccardo will be assassinated. As Amelia searches for the magic herb, Riccardo appears. They declare their hopeless love. Renato discovers Amelia with Riccardo. In his jealousy he joins a group of conspirators and assassinates the King at a masked ball. He learns too late of his wife's innocence, but he is forgiven by the dying King.

Die Meistersinger von Nürnberg (The Mastersingers of Nuremberg), by Richard Wagner, was first performed in Munich in German in 1868. It takes place in Nuremberg, Germany, in the mid-16th century. Most of the characters are actual historic persons.

The knight Walther von Stolzing has fallen in love with Eva Pogner. Because her father has promised her hand to the winner of the singing prize, he asks the mastersingers for permission to enter the competition. Beckmesser, the town clerk, who is infatuated with Eva, maliciously marks up so many errors at Walther's trial that the mastersingers refuse to let him enter the contest. Later, when Beckmesser comes to serenade Eva, Hans Sachs, the cobbler, sings and hammers lustily, arousing the neighborhood. The street fills with people. Eva and Walther decide to elope, but Sachs restrains them. He leads Walther into his house, and eventually quiet is restored.

In the morning Walther describes a dream he has had, and Sachs writes it down as Walther sings. Beckmesser finds the paper, and thinking it is by Sachs, pockets it. At the song contest Beckmesser performs from the stolen manuscript and is laughed off the platform. Sachs announces that the song is not his but Walther's. Walther sings it and wins both the mastersingers' laurel and Eva's hand.

Norma, by Vincenzo Bellini, was first performed in Milan in Italian in 1831. It takes place in Gaul during the Roman occupation, about 50 B.C. Norma, high priestess of the Druids, has broken her sacred vows. She loves Pollione, the Roman proconsul, and has borne him two children. Pollione has now tired of Norma. He tells Flavio, his centurion, that his new love is Adalgisa, a lesser priestess. Not knowing this, Norma tries to prevent a war that would place Pollione in danger. She acts against the wishes of her father, Oroveso, the Archdruid.

Adalgisa innocently confesses to Norma her love for a Roman, the faithless Pollione. Norma considers murdering her children, but maternal pity causes her to confide them to Adalgisa's care. Adalgisa refuses, swearing that she has renounced Pollione forever. Pollione refuses to forsake Adalgisa and tries to force her to go away with him.

Norma calls for war. Pollione is caught entering the sacred temple. Norma confesses that she has broken her vows and must be the sacrificial victim. Pollione now understands the depth of her devotion and asks to share her fate. Norma and Pollione mount the funeral pyre together.

Orfeo ed Euridice, by Christoph Willibald Gluck, was first performed in Vienna in Italian in 1762. It is based on an ancient Greek legend.

At the tomb of Euridice, Orfeo, the great musician, and his friends mourn her untimely death. Orfeo prays to the gods to restore his wife and is ready to go to Hades to regain her. Amor, god of love, appears and tells him that the gods have decided to permit him to enter Hades and return with Euridice, on one condition. He must not gaze upon her face until they are safely back.

At the gateway to Hades the Furies are so moved by Orfeo's music that he is allowed through the portals into the Elysian fields. Here he finds Euridice. Taking her by the hand, he begins the journey back. Euridice begs for just one glance, and eventually Orfeo yields. He turns and embraces her. She collapses instantly, lifeless. Orfeo is desperate and is about to plunge a dagger into his heart when Amor appears and stays his hand. Believing that Orfeo has suffered enough, Amor restores Euridice to life.

Otello, by Giuseppe Verdi, was first performed in Milan in Italian in 1887. It is based on Shakespeare's famous play *Othello.* It takes place at a seaport on Cyprus in the late 15th century. Otello, the governor of Cyprus and commander of the Venetian fleet, returns triumphant after defeating the Turkish Navy. He is acclaimed by the crowd, among whom is Otello's aide, Iago. Iago is resentful that Otello has chosen Cassio as his lieutenant. He is determined to destroy Otello. He induces Cassio to drink heavily and duel with Montano, the former governor of the island. Otello removes Cassio from his command. Iago advises Cassio to ask Desdemona, Otello's wife, to intercede for him.

When Otello appears, Iago arouses his jealousy. He arranges for Otello to find one of Desdemona's handkerchiefs in Cassio's possession. Otello takes this as final evidence of Desdemona's unfaithfulness. Desdemona, who loves Otello dearly, protests her innocence. But he is convinced of her guilt and strangles her. Emilia, Iago's wife, reveals Iago's treachery. At last convinced of his wife's innocence, Otello stabs himself and falls dead across Desdemona's body.

I Pagliacci (The Players), by Ruggiero Leoncavallo, was first performed in Milan in Italian in 1892. It takes place in a village in Italy in the 1800's.

Tonio, a clown, explains that he is the Prologue and that the play to be witnessed is a real story about real people. The curtain then opens. Canio, the head of a theatrical troupe, announces a performance for the evening and goes off to the inn, leaving his wife, Nedda, alone. Tonio tries to make love to her and is driven off. Then Silvio, a villager, appears and she promises to elope with him after the show.

When Nedda refuses to tell Canio the identity of her lover, he attacks her with a dagger. Beppe, another member of the troupe, saves her. Canio remarks on his tragic plight. for he must appear in a comedy while his heart is breaking. At the performance Harlequin (Beppe) serenades Columbine (Nedda) and drives Taddeo (Tonio) away. They are interrupted by Columbine's husband, Pagliaccio (Canio), who demands the name of his wife's lover. She refuses to tell him, and he kills her with a dagger. When Silvio tries to help Nedda, Canio slays him, too. Then Canio tells the horrified audience, "The comedy is ended."

Parsifal, by Richard Wagner, was first performed in Bayreuth in German in 1882. It takes place in the Middle Ages in the Pyrenees mountains in northern Spain. The aging King Titurel had entrusted the Holy Grail to his son, Amfortas. But Amfortas has sinned. He succumbed to the wiles of the enchantress Kundry, in the power of the evil sorcerer Klingsor. Klingsor wounded Amfortas with his own sacred spear. Gurnemanz, a knight of the Grail, believes that the wound can be healed only by recovery of the sacred relic.

Parsifal appears in the forest by Montsalvat Castle and is taken into the hall of the Holy Grail to witness the knights at Communion. He watches the ceremony without understanding it, and Gurnemanz drives him away.

In the enchanted garden near Klingsor's castle Parsifal spurns Kundry. When Klingsor hurls the sacred spear at him, Parsifal grasps it and makes the sign of the cross with it, whereupon the garden withers and the castle falls in ruins.

After wandering for many years, Parsifal returns to Montsalvat on Good Friday. He baptizes Kundry and heals Amfortas' wound with the sacred spear, thus redeeming the brotherhood of the Knights of the Grail.

Pelléas et Mélisande, by Claude Debussy, was first performed in Paris in French in 1902. It is set in the mythical kingdom of Allemonde in legendary times. Golaud has met and married Mélisande, a mysterious girl he found wandering in the forest. He takes her home to the gloomy castle of his grandfather, Arkel. As Mélisande and Pelléas, Golaud's brother, sit by a fountain, she tosses her wedding ring in the air and it drops into the water. Golaud misses the ring. Mélisande says she dropped it by the sea. Golaud asks her to find it. She and Pelléas look for it and meet three blind beggars.

At the castle Mélisande's long hair becomes entwined in some vines as she talks with Pelléas. Golaud discovers them and suspects that they are lovers. He sets his son, Yniold, to spy on them. Golaud warns Pelléas to spare Mélisande any excitement, since she is soon to have a child. Pelléas must leave and comes to bid Mélisande farewell. For the first time they declare their love for each other. Golaud finds them, kills Pelléas, and pursues Mélisande. Mélisande gives birth to a daughter prematurely. She forgives Golaud, insists that the love she and Pelléas had for each other was innocent, and dies.

Peter Grimes, by Benjamin Britten, was first performed in London in 1945. It takes place in a small fishing village on the eastern coast of England about 1830.

Peter Grimes, a fisherman, is unpopular in the village. When his apprentice dies, the villagers accuse him of murder. But the verdict of a coroner's court is accidental death. Only Ellen Orford, the schoolteacher, believes in Peter. They love each other, but Peter feels he does not have enough money to marry her.

Peter takes on another apprentice. When the villagers march menacingly on Peter's hut, the boy rushes out of the hut onto the cliff above the sea, loses his footing, and dies.

The gossipy villagers mutter again about murder. Peter is haunted by the death of his two apprentices. He returns to his boat, his only refuge. He sails out to sea and sinks the boat too far out for him to be rescued.

Porgy and Bess, by George Gershwin, was first performed in Boston in English in 1935. It takes place in Catfish Row, Charleston, South Carolina, in the recent past. Crown, a stevedore, quarrels with a man during a crap game and kills him. Crown escapes, while his girl, Bess, takes refuge with Porgy, a crippled beggar.

Bess, completely reformed, is happy with Porgy, but, somewhat against her better judgment, she goes to a lodge picnic at Kittiwah Island. Crown has been hiding on the island and persuades Bess to stay with him. She returns a few days later, delirious and ill. But she recovers and promises Porgy never to leave him.

Crown arrives back in town. He is looking for Bess when Porgy stabs him. The police take in Porgy as a witness, but he is freed a few days later. Meanwhile Sportin' Life, a New York dope peddler, has convinced Bess that Porgy is gone for good and takes her to New York with him. Porgy sets out to find her.

Rigoletto, by Giuseppe Verdi, was first performed in Venice in Italian in 1851. It takes place in Mantua in the 16th century. The Duke of Mantua covets every female he sees. His hunchbacked jester, Rigoletto, assists him in his amorous intrigues and taunts the husbands. The courtiers vow vengeance on the jester, and Count Monterone, whose daughter has been dishonored by the Duke, curses Rigoletto.

Rigoletto's daughter, Gilda, has been kept hidden by her father in a secluded house. The Duke enters and, pretending to be a poor student, makes love to Gilda. Thinking she is Rigoletto's mistress, the hostile noblemen abduct Gilda.

At the palace Rigoletto acknowledges that Gilda is his daughter. Gilda admits her shame but implores Rigoletto to pardon the Duke, whom she loves. Rigoletto shows Gilda the Duke flirting with Maddalena, sister of the bandit Sparafucile, whom Rigoletto has hired to murder the Duke. Dressed as a man, Gilda returns and hears Sparafucile promise Maddalena to spare the Duke if someone takes his place before midnight. Gilda enters. She is stabbed and put in a sack for Rigoletto, as agreed. Rigoletto hears the Duke singing in the distance. He opens the sack and finds the dying Gilda. She asks his pardon and dies. Rigoletto cries out in despair that Count Monterone's curse has been fulfilled.

Der Ring des Nibelungen (The Ring of the Nibelung) is a cycle of four music dramas by Richard Wagner. The characters in the *Ring* cycle are the gods of ancient Germanic folklore. Wotan is the head god and occasionally appears in mortal form. Fricka is his wife and the goddess of marriage. Freya, Fricka's sister, is the goddess of youth and beauty. Loge is the god of fire and deceit. Erda is the goddess of the earth. Donner is the god of thunder. They dwell in Asgard, in a palace called Valhalla. The Valkyries are the nine daughters of Wotan and Erda. They guard the gods and carry slain earthly heroes to Valhalla. The Nibelungs are a race of dwarfs who live underground in the Nibelheim.

Das Rheingold (The Rhinegold) is the first of the four operas and a prelude to the cycle. It was first performed in Munich in German in 1869.

The evil-looking dwarf Alberich, King of the Nibelungs, shouts his renunciation of love and makes off with the magic gold, which the three Rhine maidens had been guarding. His brother, Mime, fashions from it a golden ring whose possessor may rule the world and a magic helmet (Tarnhelm) that allows its wearer to assume any form. The giants Fasolt and Fafner have finished Wotan's and Fricka's palace, Valhalla, and demand Freya in payment. Loge suggests the gold as a substitute. By trickery Wotan secures the Tarnhelm from Alberich and forces the captive dwarf to bring from his caverns all the wealth of the Nibelung. Alberich puts a curse on the ring. Fasolt is killed when the giants fight over it. Now the gods can enter Valhalla.

In *Die Walküre* (The Valkyries), the second opera, first performed in Munich in German in 1870, the weaponless Siegmund takes refuge in the hut of Hunding and his wife, Sieglinde. Siegmund and Sieglinde fall in love, though they realize that they are the Wälsungs, twin children of Wotan. Siegmund wrenches free the great sword, Nothung (Needful), that Wotan had thrust into a tree for him to retrieve, and the two rush away.

Wotan commands his favorite daughter, Brünnhilde, to protect Siegmund in his coming fight with Hunding. But Fricka demands that Siegmund be punished for breaking the marriage laws. Wotan reverses his instructions, but Brünnhilde disobeys. Wotan intervenes, and with his spear breaks Siegmund's sword. Hunding kills Siegmund and is himself killed by Wotan. Brünnhilde gathers up Siegmund's broken sword. After her sister Valkyries refuse to help her, she sends Sieglinde away to bear Siegmund's child. Wotan pities Brünnhilde, but she must be punished. Deprived of her godhood, she will be protected by a circle of flame. The first man who penetrates the fire and awakens her will become her husband. Wotan places Brünnhilde on a rock and orders Loge to surround her with flames.

Siegfried, the third opera, was first performed in Bayreuth in German in 1876. It tells the story of Siegfried, the son of Sieglinde and Siegmund. Sieglinde died when Siegfried was born, and he has been raised by Mime.

Mime tries vainly to mend the sword that Sieglinde had left for her son. Siegfried demands information from Mime about his origin. Mime tells him of Sieglinde and Siegmund and shows him the broken sword, an invincible weapon if it can be mended. Wotan, as the Wanderer, appears and tells Mime that only a man without fear can forge Nothung. Siegfried forges Nothung.

The Wanderer has told Alberich that Siegfried will capture the ring. He urges the dwarf to convince Fafner, now a dragon who guards the Nibelung treasure, to give it up before he is killed. Siegfried, led by Mime, appears and slays Fafner with Nothung. A drop of Fafner's blood enables Siegfried to understand the language of the forest bird. On its advice, he takes possession of the ring and Tarnhelm. He kills Mime when the dwarf tries to poison him.

The bird sings of a beautiful maiden asleep on a rock, waiting to be wakened by a hero. Siegfried encounters the Wanderer on the way and breaks his spear with Nothung. He passes through the flames that ring the rock and bends over Brünnhilde. She awakens at his kiss and greets the hero ecstatically.

In *Götterdämmerung* (The Twilight of the Gods), first performed in Bayreuth in German in 1876, the rope of destiny breaks as the Norns weave it, foretelling the downfall of Valhalla and the end of the gods. Siegfried and Brünnhilde emerge from their cave. He gives her the ring, and she gives him her horse, Grane. In the hall of the Gibichungs, Hagen, son of Alberich, tells his half brother, Gunther, that he must marry Brünnhilde and that Gutrune, his half sister, must marry Siegfried. Siegfried arrives. Hagen brews a potion to destroy his memory of women. Gutrune gives it to Siegfried. He has no recollection of Brünnhilde and woos Gutrune.

Siegfried assumes the guise of Gunther, overpowers Brünnhilde, and forces the ring from her finger. Brünnhilde realizes that Siegfried has betrayed her and plots revenge with Gunther and Hagen.

By the Rhine the maidens beg Siegfried to return the ring, warning him of its curse. Hagen gives him another potion, restoring his memory. Siegfried tells of his life and his marriage to Brünnhilde. Hagen plunges a spear into his back and he dies, singing a farewell to Brünnhilde. Gutrune accuses Gunther of Siegfried's murder. He denies it and accuses Hagen, who admits it and demands the ring on Siegfried's finger. Gunther says the ring is his, and Hagen kills him. The arm of Siegfried rises as if in warning.

Brünnhilde commands that a funeral pyre be built. The Rhine maidens have told her of Hagen's treachery and Siegfried's innocence. She mounts Grane and rides into the flames. The hall collapses, and the Rhine overflows. The Rhine maidens recover their ring from Brünnhilde's dead hand and drag Hagen to his death when he tries to seize it. In the distance Valhalla is in flames. It is the end of the gods.

Der Rosenkavalier (The Cavalier of the Rose), by Richard Strauss, was first performed in Dresden in German in 1911. It takes place in Vienna in the 18th century, during the reign of Maria Theresa. Young Octavian, Count Rofrano, is telling the Marschallin, the Princess von Werdenberg, how much he loves her, when the Marschallin's cousin, Baron Ochs von Lerchenau, arrives. Octavian hides. Ochs has decided to marry Sophie, daughter of the newly rich Herr von Faninal, and seeks a cavalier to present the traditional silver rose. The Marschallin suggests Octavian, who has meanwhile disguised himself as her maid, Mariandel, and reappeared. The Baron tries to arrange a meeting with Mariandel.

The Marschallin receives callers and petitioners. She muses on her lost youth and sends Octavian away. Octavian presents the silver rose to Sophie. She is disgusted by the vulgar Ochs and flatly refuses to marry him. Ochs gets a note from Mariandel suggesting a rendezvous. They meet at a disreputable inn, where Ochs is harassed by a series of pranks. The police, Faninal, and Sophie are summoned. Octavian removes his disguise. The Marschallin arrives. She forces Ochs to give up Sophie, and lamenting that her vow to yield Octavian must be kept so soon, unites Sophie and Octavian, to their great joy.

Salome, by Richard Strauss, was first performed in Dresden in German in 1905. It is based on a play by Oscar Wilde. The story takes place on the terrace of Herod's palace about A.D. 30.

Jokanaan (John the Baptist) is a prisoner in the dungeon. Salome, daughter of Herodias, pleads with the captain of the guard to let her see the prisoner. She is fascinated by Jokanaan, but the prophet cries out that she is cursed and returns to his dungeon.

Herod and Herodias, his wife, appear. When Herod asks Salome to dance, she says she will if he will swear to grant her anything she desires. She performs her Dance of the Seven Veils and then asks for Jokanaan's head on a silver platter. As she exults over the head, Herod, horrified by her behavior, commands his soldiers to kill her.

Samson et Dalila, by Camille Saint-Saëns, was first performed in Weimar in French in 1877. It is based on a Biblical story and takes place at Gaza in Palestine about 1150 B.C.

Samson, mighty leader of the Israelites, who are in bondage to the Philistines, comforts his people by predicting early victory. When Abimelech, the satrap, or ruler, of Gaza, threatens them, Samson slays him. The Philistines flee when the victorious Israelites intone a hymn of praise.

The high priest commands Dalila to deliver Samson to the Philistines. Samson falls in love with her and confesses that the secret of his strength is his hair. Dalila lulls him to sleep and cuts off his hair. She turns the now powerless hero over to the Philistines, who blind him.

The remorseful Samson is chained like an animal to a millstone and forced to turn it. A child leads him to the temple for the Philistines' victory celebration. He prays for a return of his former strength. His prayer is answered. Grasping the pillars, he brings the temple down on himself and the Philistines.

The Tales of Hoffmann, by Jacques Offenbach, was first performed in Paris in French in 1881. It takes place in Nuremberg, Venice, and Munich in the 19th century.

At Luther's Tavern, Lindorf, a rival of the poet Hoffmann, intercepts a note from Stella, an opera singer, inviting Hoffmann to meet her after the performance. Hoffmann, accompanied by his friend Nicklausse, enters and tells the story of his three loves.

The first was Olympia, a mechanical doll created by the scientist Spalanzani and the magician Coppelius. When Coppelius smashed her, Hoffmann found that he had been in love with clockwork.

The second was Giulietta, a courtesan in the power of the magician Dapertutto. Giulietta had a lover, but Hoffmann killed him in a duel. Giulietta then ran off with another man.

The third was Antonia, a singer who had consumption. Urged on by Dr. Miracle, she fell dead while singing.

Stella arrives at the tavern, finds Hoffmann drunk, throws him a flower, and goes off with Lindorf, Hoffmann's enemy.

The roles of Lindorf, Coppelius, Dapertutto, and Dr. Miracle are played by the same person.

Tannhäuser, by Richard Wagner, was first performed in Dresden in German in 1845. It takes place in Venusberg and in and around Wartburg Castle, Thuringia, Germany, in the early 13th century. The minstrel-knight Tannhäuser has tired of his life with Venus and begs the goddess to allow him to return to his own world. He will trust in the Virgin Mary for his salvation. At the mention of this name, Venus and her realm disappear. Tannhäuser finds himself near Wartburg Castle, listening to the singing of pilgrims on their way to Rome.

Wolfram and other knights appear and welcome Tannhäuser after his year's mysterious absence. Princess Elisabeth, in seclusion since his disappearance, greets Tannhäuser joyfully.

A song contest begins. Wolfram sings a hymn to unselfish love, but Tannhäuser bursts into wild song, praising Venus and life in the Venusberg. Elisabeth protects Tannhäuser from the horrified assembly, and he is allowed to join the pilgrims and seek the pope's forgiveness.

Elisabeth awaits the returning pilgrims. Tannhäuser is not among them. He comes later and tells Wolfram that the pope refused him absolution. He will go again to Venusberg.

Elisabeth has died of her grief. Tannhäuser sinks down before her bier and dies, redeemed at last. A group of pilgrims comes, bearing the pope's staff. It has blossomed with new leaves, a sign of God's forgiveness.

Tosca, by Giacomo Puccini, was first performed in Rome in Italian in 1900. It takes place in Rome in 1800. Angelotti, an escaped political prisoner, takes refuge in the church where Mario Cavaradossi is working on a painting of Mary Magdalen. Mario discovers Angelotti, an old friend, and arranges for him to hide at his villa. They are interrupted by Mario's love, Floria Tosca, a singer, who is jealous of the painting because Mario has used another woman as his model. Later, after Angelotti has left, Baron Scarpia, the chief of police, arouses Tosca's suspicions by a fan he discovers.

Mario, suspected of aiding Angelotti, is taken into custody and tortured while Tosca listens. She cannot bear his suffering and reveals Angelotti's hiding place, to Mario's fury. Scarpia condemns him to be executed.

Scarpia avows his passion for Tosca and promises freedom for Mario when she yields. But after Scarpia gives an order for a mock execution and writes out a safe-conduct pass, Tosca stabs him. She then escapes.

Mario is writing a farewell letter to Tosca when she arrives and tells him of the mock execution. But the execution turns out to be real. Mario lies dead. As Scarpia's men come to arrest her, Tosca jumps over the parapet to her death.

La Traviata (The Wayward One), by Giuseppe Verdi, was first performed in Venice in Italian in 1853. It is based on the famous play *La Dame aux Camélias,* by Alexandre Dumas *fils.* It takes place in Paris. The frail Violetta Valery meets Alfredo Germont and for love of him abandons her questionable life. They lead an idyllic existence in the country until Alfredo learns by accident that Violetta has been selling her possessions to support them. He rushes off to Paris to raise the money to pay their debts.

His father arrives and tells Violetta that the future of Alfredo and the fortunes of his sister will be destroyed by his connection with her. With growing remorse she heeds the elder Germont and leaves Alfredo, giving as explanation a desire for her former gay existence.

Grief-stricken, Violetta plunges back into her old life. When she meets Alfredo at a party, he insults her and quarrels with Baron Douphol, her admirer.

Violetta is now seriously ill. The elder Germont, moved by compassion and realizing that Violetta's love for Alfredo is sincere, consents to their union. Alfredo hastens to her, understanding at last that Violetta has sacrificed herself for his sake. He begs her forgiveness, but it is too late, and she dies in his arms.

Tristan und Isolde, by Richard Wagner, was first performed in Munich in German in 1865. It is based on a medieval legend and takes place aboard ship, in Cornwall, and in Brittany in legendary times. The knight Tristan has been sent to bring Isolde, intended bride of King Mark, from Ireland to Cornwall. Isolde falls in love with Tristan, though she recognizes him as the knight whose life she had spared after he had killed her fiancé, Morold. When Tristan spurns her, Isolde directs Brangäne, her lady-in-waiting, to prepare a death potion. But Brangäne substitutes a love potion. Tristan and Isolde both drink of it and fall helplessly in love.

In Cornwall, Isolde, now married to King Mark, continues to meet Tristan. The King is suspicious and returns from a hunting trip to find them together. Tristan is seriously wounded by Melot, one of the King's courtiers. Kurvenal, Tristan's henchman, takes him to his castle in Brittany. Isolde joins him there, and he dies in her arms. King Mark has also followed, intending to forgive the pair. But Kurvenal, not knowing this, intervenes and is killed by Melot. Isolde bids her lover farewell and falls dead on his body.

Il Trovatore (The Troubadour), by Giuseppe Verdi, was first performed in Rome in Italian in 1853. It takes place in Aragon and Biscay, Spain, in the mid-15th century. Leonóra, lady-in-waiting to the Queen, is wooed by two men, Count di Luna and Manrico, a troubadour, believed to be the son of the gypsy Azucena. Azucena has vowed vengeance against Count di Luna because his father, believing that Azucena's mother had bewitched his younger son, had her burned. Azucena had kidnapped the child, intending to kill him, but as she tells Manrico, she hurled her own child into the fire by mistake.

On learning that Leonora loves Manrico, the Count challenges him to a duel. Manrico overcomes the Count but spares his life. Both intercept Leonora as she enters a convent, and Manrico escapes with her. Di Luna captures Azucena and orders her burned at the stake. Manrico rushes to her rescue and is captured. Leonora decides to buy his freedom by supposedly yielding to the Count. She has taken poison and dies in Manrico's arms. The Count orders Manrico to the scaffold, but the final triumph is Azucena's. The Count has killed his own brother.

Turandot, by Giacomo Puccini (completed by Franco Alfano), was first performed in Milan in Italian in 1926. It takes place in Peking, China, in legendary times. The beautiful Princess Turandot has made it known that she will wed any nobleman who can answer three riddles. Failure will be punished by death. Many unlucky wooers have already been put to death by the cruel Princess before Calaf, a Tartar prince, arrives and guesses all three answers correctly. Turandot begs to be released from her promise, but Calaf refuses unless she can uncover his true identity before the next morning.

Calaf's father, Timur, an exiled Tartar king, and a loving handmaiden, Liù, come seeking him. They are tortured at the Princess' command, but the faithful Liù kills herself rather than reveal Calaf's name. Calaf's wooing finally melts the ice in Turandot's heart, and she surrenders to him, announcing that his name is Love.

Wozzeck, by Alban Berg, was first performed in Berlin in German in 1925. It takes place in a town in Germany about 1820.

Wozzeck, a poor soldier, works for extra money for his mistress, Marie, and their child. He barbers his captain and serves as guinea pig for a mad doctor, whose strange diet gives Wozzeck hallucinations.

Marie takes up with a handsome drum major. She defies Wozzeck, who sees her dancing with the drum major. Later, in the barracks, the drum major taunts Wozzeck about Marie and beats him.

Marie repents of her unfaithfulness and seeks comfort from the Bible. She goes for a walk with Wozzeck. He kills her with a knife.

Returning to the scene, Wozzeck searches for the knife, finds it, and throws it into a pond. He wades out to recover it and drowns. The captain and the doctor hear his cries for help, pause momentarily, then hurry away. Some children tell Marie's son of her death, but he does not understand. He rides after them on his hobbyhorse.

HELEN GAUNTLETT
Editor, *Newsletter,* Boosey and Hawkes, Inc.

A scene from *The Bat* (*Die Fledermaus*), a popular operetta composed by Johann Strauss, Jr.

OPERETTA

Operetta, a form of light musical theater, is sentimental drama set to music. The setting is usually some make-believe world or exotic place that lends itself to colorful scenery and costuming. The characters are generally princes and princesses, gaily costumed officers, and ladies in elegant dress. The stories usually involve these characters in plots in which the good people triumph, the evildoers are punished, and the lovers are united. Sentimental romance is always the basis of the story.

The operetta was born in German-speaking countries toward the end of the 19th century. Its ancestors, the older German forms of popular theater, included the 18th-century Singspiel and the light operas of the early 19th century. The Singspiel was basically a German musical comedy that pleased the taste of the masses. Two early 19th-century light operas were *The Merry Wives of Windsor,* by Otto Nicolai (1810–49), and *Czar and Carpenter,* by Albert Lortzing (1801–51). Their music, often derived from folk sources, was light and readily understandable.

If any one person can be called the creator of the operetta, he is Franz von Suppé (1819–95), the composer of *Beautiful Galatea, Boccaccio,* and *Fatinitza.* Von Suppé emphasized romance and sentiment and played down comedy. He was one of the first composers to give the waltz an important part in the musical score. After Von Suppé most operettas included a big waltz scene, which often served as the central point of the plot.

▶ **VIENNESE OPERETTA**

Von Suppé established and popularized some of the main characteristics of operetta. But it was Johann Strauss, Jr., Vienna's "waltz king," who captured the hearts and imaginations of the world's theatergoers. His operettas are filled with gaiety, sparkle, and glamour. Strauss's *The Bat* (*Fledermaus*) is probably the most famous operetta ever written. Certainly it has been the most successful, and it is still revived in many parts of the world. His *Gypsy Baron* is almost as popular as *The Bat.*

Taking their start from Johann Strauss, Jr., an entire generation of German and Austrian operetta composers began producing works in the style of *The Bat.* The most significant of Strauss's successors was Franz Lehár (1870– 1948). Lehár's *Merry Widow* is perhaps second in popularity only to *The Bat. The Count of Luxembourg, Frasquita,* and *The Land of Smiles* are three other Lehár operettas that have gained worldwide recognition.

Other significant successors of Johann Strauss, Jr., include: Oscar Straus (1870– 1954), composer of *The Chocolate Soldier* and *A Waltz Dream;* Emmerich Kálmán (1882–1953), composer of *Countess Maritza* and *Gypsy Princess;* Leo Fall (1873–1925), composer of *The Dollar Princess;* Ralph Benatzky (1884–1957), composer of *The White Horse Inn;* and Robert Stolz (1882–1975), composer of *Two Hearts in Three-Quarter Time.*

▶ OPERETTA IN THE UNITED STATES

In the 1880's and early 1890's Viennese operetta became popular in the United States. A Johann Strauss operetta, *The Queen's Lace Handkerchief,* was the first presentation of the Casino Theater in New York City, on October 22, 1882. This theater was the leading home for light musical productions in the United States for the next 20 years. There was an interest in operetta throughout the country. In one season alone, 1894–95, 14 operetta companies toured the United States.

The earliest productions by American composers were comic operas rather than operettas. Buffoonery and comedy prevailed over romance and sentimentality. These productions were influenced more by the comic operas of Gilbert and Sullivan than by the operettas of Von Suppé or Johann Strauss. The first successful comic opera by an American was *The Little Tycoon,* by Willard Spenser (1852–1933). It opened in Philadelphia in 1887 and received 500 performances there before it was produced in New York.

Another successful comic opera, *The Begum,* by Reginald de Koven (1859–1920), was produced in 1888. However, De Koven's best-known work, *Robin Hood* (1890), which contains the famous song "Oh, Promise Me," was more an operetta than a comic opera. *Robin Hood* paved the way for the operettas of Victor Herbert (1859–1924).

Victor Herbert was America's first great composer for the musical theater. Many of the songs from his operettas are as popular today as they were when they were first heard. His first operetta, *Prince Ananias* (1894), is now forgotten. But he went on to write the scores for such immortal works as *The Fortune Teller* (1898), *Babes in Toyland* (1903), *Mlle. Modiste* (1905), *The Red Mill* (1906), and *Naughty Marietta* (1910). These productions mark the beginning of the golden age of American operetta.

The golden age continued with composers Rudolf Friml (1879–1972) and Sigmund Romberg (1887–1951). Friml's very first operetta, *The Firefly* (1912), was a great success. It established him as an operetta composer of the first importance. His other popular works include *Rose Marie* (1924), *The Vagabond King* (1925), and *The Three Musketeers* (1928).

Sigmund Romberg wrote music for musical comedies for a number of years before writing Viennese-type operettas. His first operetta was *The Blue Paradise* (1915). Its setting was Vienna, and its principal musical number was *Auf Wiedersehen* ("Good-bye"), the first of Romberg's celebrated waltzes. For years Romberg divided his talent between musical comedies and revues, on the one hand, and operettas, on the other. But the triumphs by which he is remembered are operettas. They include *Maytime* (1917), *Blossom Time* (1921), *The Student Prince* (1924), and *The Desert Song* (1928).

In 1928 Romberg wrote his last great operetta, *The New Moon.* American operetta was then a dying art form. Broadway audiences had grown tired of storybook characters in make-believe settings, of simple love affairs set to lilting waltz tunes. After 1934 Romberg returned to the writing of musical comedies, which had taken the place of operettas in the American theater.

Though dying, operetta was not altogether dead. Revivals of the old masterworks keep the tradition alive. People like to see the old operettas, some out of nostalgia, some because of the wonderful tunes. Occasionally, too, attempts are made to write new musicals in the style of the operetta. Most of them are failures, but a few have had enough charm to succeed. One of the latter was *Song of Norway* (1944), an operetta based on the life and music of the composer Edvard Grieg. Another was *Kismet* (1953), with music derived from the works of the Russian composer Alexander Borodin.

▶ PLOTS OF SOME WELL-KNOWN OPERETTAS

The Bat, by Johann Strauss, Jr., is set in 18th-century Vienna. Baron von Eisenstein, convicted of a minor offense, takes leave of his wife, Rosalinde. She, thinking he has gone to jail, receives a visit from her admirer, Alfred. The Baron, however, has gone instead to a masked ball. The police arrive and arrest Alfred by mistake. At the ball the Baron flirts with all the women. Rosalinde, disguised, arrives, and not recognizing her, the Baron flirts with her, too. The Baron learns that Alfred is his wife's admirer and becomes furious with her. Rosalinde reveals that she is the countess he flirted with. He has to forgive her, and they are reconciled before he goes to jail.

The Gypsy Baron, by Johann Strauss, Jr., is set in a castle inhabited by gypsies. Sandor inherits the castle and becomes baron of the gypsies. Czipra, one of the gypsies, tells Sandor that there is a treasure, which Sandor will find only with a faithful wife. Sandor and Saffi, Czipra's daughter, find the treasure. Then Sandor goes off to war. He returns a hero and is made a real baron. Czipra reveals that Saffi is a princess in disguise, and Sandor and Saffi are married.

The Merry Widow, by Franz Lehár. Sonia, a beautiful and wealthy young widow from the mythical kingdom of Marsovia, is on her first visit to Paris. Prince Danilo, a fellow Marsovian, is given the job of seeing that she does not marry a foreigner and take her money out of the country. Danilo and Sonia fall in love, but he does not want to appear to be a fortune hunter and he refuses to propose to her. She then tells him she will lose her money if she remarries. Danilo proposes. Sonia accepts and adds that she will lose the money because by Marsovian law it will go to her new husband.

Naughty Marietta, by Victor Herbert, takes place in New Orleans about 1750. Marietta has come to America with a group of girls sent by the king of France to marry settlers. Captain Dick Warrington has been sent to New Orleans to capture the pirate Bras Pique. Marietta persuades Dick to get her a boy's disguise, and Rodolfo, a marionette showman, passes her off as his son. But Marietta will not pull the marionette wires properly, and neither Rodolfo nor Dick can make her behave. All the town goes to a ball. At the ball Étienne, who is really Bras Pique, sells his slave girl, Adah, so that he can marry Marietta. When Dick buys Adah to set her free, Marietta becomes jealous and decides to marry Étienne. But Adah tells Dick that Étienne is Bras Pique. Étienne is not arrested, because he is the Lieutenant Governor's son, and Marietta and Dick decide they really are in love.

The Red Mill, by Victor Herbert, takes place in the Netherlands. Two Americans, Con Kidder and Kid Conner, are unable to pay their bill at the inn The Sign of the Red Mill. The innkeeper agrees to let them pay the bill by working for him. The innkeeper's daughter, Gretchen, is in love with Captain van Damm, but she is supposed to marry the governor. Con and Kid promise to help her, but her father overhears the plot and locks her up in the windmill. Con and Kid rescue her by riding on the wings of the mill. The guests assemble, and all is in readiness for the marriage; but the bride has disappeared. Con and Kid arrive at the marriage hall and they distract the guests by disguising themselves first as Italian organ-grinders and then as Sherlock Holmes and Dr. Watson. It is then discovered that Captain van Damm is heir to a large fortune, and the innkeeper agrees to let him marry Gretchen.

Rose Marie, by Rudolf Friml, is a simple love story set in Canada. The heroine, Rose Marie, is in love with Jim Kenyon. Jim is falsely accused of murder, but the Canadian Mounted Police, headed by Sergeant Malone, come to the rescue. They are able to catch the real murderer, and Rose Marie and Jim are happily united.

The Student Prince, by Sigmund Romberg, is one operetta that does not end happily. Prince Karl Franz comes to the old German university town of Heidelberg with his tutor, Dr. Engel. The prince falls in love with Kathie, a waitress at The Golden Apple inn. She returns his love, but he is soon called home to be king. He cannot marry Kathie because he must marry a princess.

The Vagabond King, by Rudolf Friml, tells the story of the 15th-century French vagabond poet François Villon. Louis XI makes him king for a day on the condition that Villon make love to the haughty Katherine de Vaucelles. Villon makes love to Katherine. In addition, with the help of the vagabonds, he saves Paris and the French throne from the Burgundians. In the battle with the Burgundians, Huguette, Villon's peasant sweetheart, gives up her life to save his. Villon is consoled by Lady Anne, who is made his wife by royal decree.

DAVID EWEN
Author, *Complete Book of the American Musical Theater, The Book of European Light Opera*

See also GILBERT AND SULLIVAN OPERETTAS; MUSICAL THEATER.

OPINION POLLS

An opinion poll or survey is a way to learn about a very large group of people by studying a small group, or sample, of the large group. If you want to find out something about all Americans, you could not talk to the millions of Americans counted in the United States census. But you could survey a smaller group that represents all Americans.

Even less ambitious surveys present problems. Suppose you wanted to learn what 10-year-old girls and boys in the United States considered their best birthday present. You decide to interview tomorrow everyone who became 10 years old today, asking just one question: "Of the gifts you received yesterday, which one is your favorite?"

This may seem like a simpler endeavor, but about 11,000 people are having their tenth birthday today. It would take 400 interviewers a full day to poll 11,000 youngsters, after someone had compiled a list of the names and telephone numbers of everyone who was having a tenth birthday today, and assuming they were all at home when they were called. Obviously a smaller group—a sample—would be easier to work with.

There are other things to consider, too. Suppose, for example, that today is in the middle of January. The favorite present might turn out to be skis or ice skates. But if it is June, it might be baseball bats or rollerblades.

How can you find a good sample and assure accurate answers to your questions? Before discussing how opinion polls are done, let us look at some of the reasons why they are done.

▶ MARKETING RESEARCH

Marketing studies are usually done by or for companies that make products or provide services, or that advertise those products or services. Manufacturers may want to know, for example, what people do not like about an existing product so they can change or fix it. TV broadcasters may wish to know why more people watch their station than a competing station. Then they can tell advertisers why their commercials should be placed with their TV station. A breakfast cereal company may need to know whether children prefer cereals in the form of flakes, circles, loops, or nuggets.

▶ PUBLIC AFFAIRS AND PUBLIC OPINION POLLS

These kinds of polls are usually done by or for television networks, newspapers, government agencies, political candidates or parties, or other organizations that have an interest in a particular public issue. Probably the best-known surveys of this type are political candidate preference polls. A typical question might be, "If the election for president (or governor or senator) were being held today, who do you think you would vote for, the Democrat Dan Dunn or the Republican Ray Rogers?"

Public opinion polls can also ask questions about the environment, unemployment, schools, the best place to live, or other subjects. Sometimes the questions and subjects are serious and are intended to provide people with important information. Sometimes they are designed primarily to interest or amuse readers and viewers.

▶ HOW IS AN OPINION POLL DONE?

How can a poll be done so that the information gained is accurate and reliable?

Data Collection and Interviewing. In the 1930's, when opinion surveys began, information was collected mainly by knocking on people's doors and talking to them in their homes or by mailing out questionnaires. Later, as more people had telephones in their homes and the demand for getting fast results from surveys grew, more surveys began to be done by phone.

There are other ways surveys are taken that are less accurate. A television program dealing with an election race may invite you to cast your vote by phoning a 900 number, at a cost of fifty cents a call. Some people may vote three or four times. Poorer people, who cannot spare the fifty cents, may not vote at all. Most important, the people who decide to vote are not selected by the polling organization. They select themselves.

The best data-collection methods are those in which the polling organization selects the people to be polled. If an interviewer knocks on your door or phones you, you are more apt to answer the poll questions than you would be to fill out and mail back a questionnaire or pay to make a call yourself.

The Sample. A good sample must be large enough to give stable results, and it must be representative.

Suppose you ask one person, "What is your favorite color?" and that person gives pink as an answer. Would it be reasonable to conclude that everyone's favorite color is pink, based on this sample of one? If you asked a second person, that individual's favorite color might be blue. A third person may choose red. With a sample of one, pink got 100 percent of the vote. With a sample of two, pink got just 50 percent of the vote. With a sample of three, pink got only $33\frac{1}{3}$ percent of the vote. Every time you interviewed one more person, the results changed a lot. You can, however, keep adding people until the results do not change much. By the time you have interviewed 100 individuals, the results will change only a little. By the time you reach 1,000, they will change hardly at all.

Does that mean 1,000 is a big enough sample to get a stable result? Yes, if you only want to determine what everyone's favorite color is, and if being within a few percentage points of the exact number is accurate enough for your needs. But 1,000 is not enough if you also need to know the favorite color of 16-year-old females. There are probably only about eight 16-year-old females in your sample of 1,000, not enough to get a stable result.

A sample of 1,000 is definitely not large enough if you are trying to find out who will win what appears to be a very close presidential election. With a sample of 1,000, Dan Dunn may lead Ray Rogers by half a percentage point. With a sample of 1,500, Rogers may lead Dunn by a third of a percentage point. Such a small difference could change the winner in an election poll.

The second requirement for a good sample is that it be representative of the total population from which it is selected. This means, for example, that you must have a proper mix of males and females; people from big cities and from rural areas; people who live in different regions of the country; people who are rich, middle class, or poor; people who are white, African American, Hispanic, Asian American, or members of other ethnic groups. All groups must be included in their proper proportions. If 9 percent of Americans are Hispanic, then 9 percent of the people in the sample should be Hispanic.

The Questionnaire. In most surveys, the single most important factor is the questionnaire. It does not matter how good the sample is if the questionnaire is biased or uses words that many people will not understand. In a presidential election poll, suppose the following questions were asked: "What do you like about President Dan Dunn? What do you not like about his opponent, Ray Rogers? Who do you think you will vote for, Dan Dunn or Ray Rogers?" Questions like these force people to think of only good things about Dunn and bad things about Rogers. They bias your thinking.

Sometimes two different polls that seem to be asking about the same issue or candidate produce very different results. This may be the result of timing. One poll may have been taken before a certain crucial event took place, and the other after the event. Or it could be that the sample was not the same in each case.

Other factors might explain the different results, but in most cases they are due to the questions that were asked. Before you accept the results of a poll, therefore, you should examine the questions. Reputable polling organizations make their wording available.

Tabulating and Analysis. Finally, there is the matter of data processing, or adding up the answers to the poll, and then analyzing and reporting the results. It used to be done manually. Today it is usually accomplished by computer. One increasingly popular method of interviewing individuals and tabulating results simultaneously is the use of computer-assisted telephone interviews, or CATI (pronounced "KAY-tee"). With this system, answers to one question may be related to answers to other questions by using numbers to identify all questions and answers. Moreover, pollsters can easily learn not only how any question was answered by the total sample, but also how men or young people or southerners answered it. Gender, age, geographic area, and other classifications are entered into the computer with identifying numbers just like the opinion questions. All this information is then studied and analyzed, and the results are written up in a report.

There are many more details to a valid survey or poll, but you now know the main factors involved in why, how, and by whom opinion polls are done.

BURNS W. ROPER
Roper Starch Worldwide Inc.

OPOSSUMS

The opossum is the only marsupial in the United States. Marsupials are mammals that, like kangaroos, raise their young in a pouch. The opossum family has more than 60 species. Some species also live in Mexico, Central America, and South America. They all have pointed snouts, short fur, and ratlike tails.

Opossums are unusual in a number of ways. They can hang by their tails like monkeys, and they have clawless "thumbs" on their hind feet that make them excellent climbers. They also have more teeth (50) than any other North American land mammal. Their teeth are specialized for slashing and tearing like those of dogs and cats.

The opossums that are found in the United States are known as Virginia opossums. They weigh, on average, from 4 to 9 pounds (2 to 4 kilograms) and are from 15 to 25 inches (38 to 64 centimeters) long. Virginia opossums live in an area that extends from southern Canada to Central America. They live in fields, forests, mountains, and almost every other kind of habitat except deserts. They especially prefer open woodlands along streams.

One of the reasons opossums can live almost anywhere is that they can eat almost anything. Their diet includes grass, mushrooms, and bird eggs as well as insects, chickens, and even poisonous snakes. (Opossums are immune to rattlesnake venom.)

Life Cycle

Female opossums carry their young inside them for only 12½ days, but these young spend about 3 months in the pouch. Smaller than honey bees, opossum young are born deaf, blind, and hairless. They are not able to use their hind legs. At birth they must locate their mother's pouch, pull themselves into it using claws on their front feet, and attach themselves to a nipple inside the pouch. This complex birth process is difficult for the babies, and not all of them survive it. The 5 to 9 young who do reach the pouch, out of as many as 25, eventually grow too large to all fit inside. At that time they ride anywhere on their mother they can grasp, usually her back.

The young opossums leave their mother when they are 3 months old and are completely on their own. In another 3 to 5 months, they reach adulthood. Opossums grow throughout

Five baby opossums cling to their mother's body for transportation and safety. Like all marsupials, they spent their first weeks of life in the mother's pouch.

their lives, so that a very big opossum is also a very old one. However, old ones are rare. Opossums usually live less than two years in the wild—a very short life for an animal of their size.

Opossums have many natural enemies, including owls, foxes, coyotes, dogs, raccoons, and humans. This explains why they live such a short life. People, especially in the southeastern United States, eat opossums as food. Opossum fur is also used to trim clothing.

Playing 'Possum

Opossums are probably best known for their trick of playing dead when threatened. They fall over suddenly and lie perfectly still with their eyes and mouth half-open. Most biologists think that this behavior helps opossums fool predators into leaving them alone.

Although not as well known for "playing 'possum," other animals such as some snakes, lizards, birds, and spiders do the same thing. It is not advisable to approach wild opossums, though. More often than playing dead, they attempt to escape by biting.

STEVEN N. AUSTAD
University of New Mexico

OPPENHEIMER, J. ROBERT. See NEW YORK CITY (Famous People).

OPTICAL FIBERS. See FIBER OPTICS.

OPTICAL ILLUSIONS

Sometimes what you see differs from what really exists. The line you see as curved may really be straight. A colored object may really be white. These are illusions, or mistaken ideas, about the things around you. They are called optical illusions because they involve your sense of sight.

Optical illusions are mistakes made within the body by the organs with which you see— your eyes and your brain. Your eyes receive information about the things around you and send this information to the brain. The brain puts it together into something that has meaning for you.

▶ SIMPLE ILLUSIONS

Many illusions are based on the fact that you have two eyes. For example, roll up a piece of paper to make a tube. Hold this tube in front of your right eye, pointing the tube slightly to the left. Hold the palm of your left hand close to your left eye, almost touching the tube. Then spread your fingers apart. With both eyes open, look through the tube and

your fingers at some distant object. Your left hand will appear to have a hole in it. This illusion is the result of your having two eyes. Each eye reports what it sees to the brain. The brain combines the two reports, and what you see is a hole in the palm of your hand.

The movements of your eyes can also cause illusions. For example, your eyes do not move up and down as easily as they move from side

When our eyes show us something that our brain knows is not possible, we are experiencing an optical illusion. For example, which way does the book fold? The gnome's shadow and the pages of the book give conflicting clues to the eye. The brain knows that both clues cannot be true.

to side. Because of this, you see the upright line in Figure 1 as the longer one. The two lines are in fact the same length. Short, heavy people take advantage of this illusion by wearing clothes with long, thin stripes. This makes their bodies seem taller and thinner.

FIG. 1

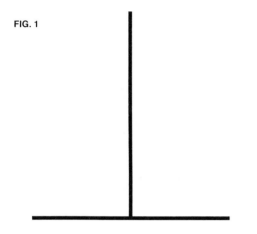

Illusions often occur when your eyes are distracted, or drawn away, by lines or objects within or close to the line or object you are viewing. In Figure 2 you cannot correctly judge the distance from A to B because of the many lines drawn within this space. In moving from A to B, your eyes pause at many places along the way. Therefore this distance seems greater than the distance BC, which lacks these lines.

FIG. 2

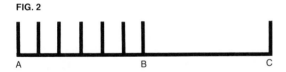

In Figure 3, AB seems longer than BC, although both are the same length. The short lines at the end of AB extend outward. Your eyes follow these lines, and this part of the figure seems longer. Line BC, however, is closed in at the ends by arrows and therefore seems shorter.

FIG. 3

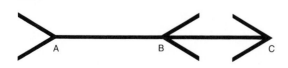

Surroundings Cause Illusions

An object's surroundings may cause illusions about its shape or its size. For example, the circle in Figure 4 makes the straight sides of the square appear curved. In Figure 5, curved lines make the sides of the square seem to bulge. The perfect square in Figure 6 seems out of shape because of the lines. And the parallel lines in Figure 7 seem curved because of the crossing lines.

FIG. 4

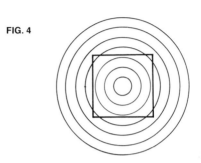

FIG. 5

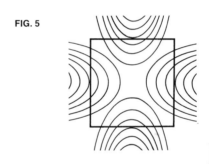

FIG. 6

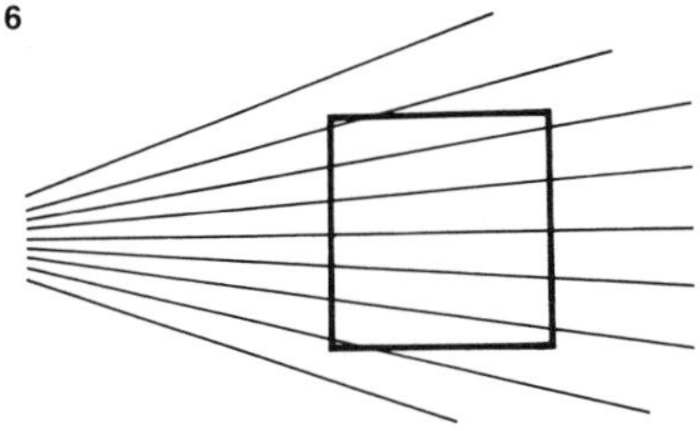

FIG. 7

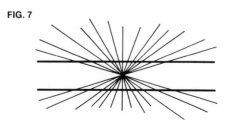

The center circle in Figure 8, surrounded by small circles, seems larger than the center circle in Figure 9, surrounded by larger circles, although the two circles are the same size.

FIG. 8

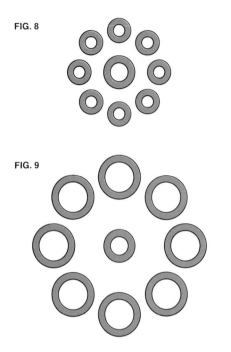

FIG. 9

Background is an important part of an object's surroundings. This is shown in Figure 10. The gray square on the white background seems darker than the gray square on the black background, even though they are the same shade of gray.

FIG. 10

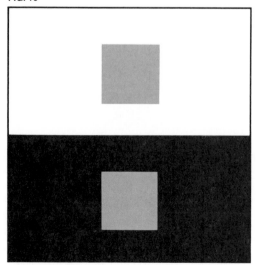

Figure 11 illustrates a similar illusion, based on the contrast between the darkness of the black squares and the brightness of the surrounding area. Look at a black square. Out of the corner of your eye you will see gray dots in the white area. Stare at one of the dots and it will vanish.

FIG. 11

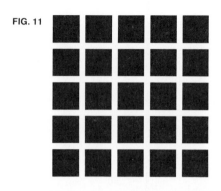

The nature of the background and surroundings is especially important to some animals. Many animals blend with their surroundings so well that they cannot be seen. They give the illusion of being part of their surroundings. Such illusion is called camouflage. Desert animals, brownish in color, seem to be part of the sand itself. Forest creatures have stripes, spots, and other markings on their bodies. They blend into the shadows, leaves, and branches around them. The outlines of their bodies seem to disappear. All of these animals are protected in their natural surroundings. They remain hidden from enemies who would otherwise find them easy prey.

Camouflage is a kind of illusion that makes an object seem to blend into its background. Camouflage helps animals survive in the wilderness. In its summer coat (*opposite page*) this longtail weasel is the color of the grass and rocks. In winter (*below*) the weasel's coat turns as white as the snow surrounding it.

Distant Things Seem Small

Illusions are often the result of things you have learned. For example, suppose someone is walking toward you. As he comes closer to you he seems to grow in size. You know that he does not. You know that his increase in size simply means that he is coming closer to you. Early in your life you learned that distant things seem smaller than those that are close. This is one of the clues you use in judging distance.

Artists use perspective to show distance and to make things appear closer or farther away. In Figure 12, the three men are all the same height, but the lines make them appear to be different.

FIG. 12

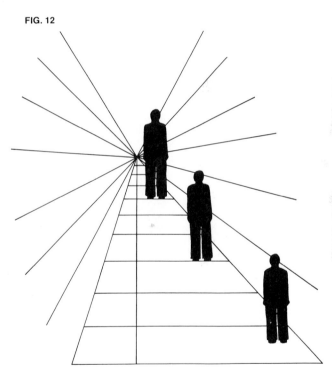

▶ILLUSIONS OF COLOR

Many illusions are the result of the way we see colors. When you look from one color to another, your eyes take a few steps to adjust to the change. Sometimes an afterimage remains from one of the steps and you see a color you did not expect.

For example, look at the bright-blue square in Figure 13 for a while. Then look at a white square of the same size. The white square turns yellow. You can do this with other colors, too. Look at a green square, then at a white one. The white square turns red.

FIG. 13

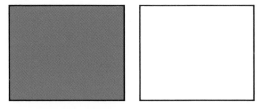

Look at the black, yellow, and green American flag in Figure 14. Look at it steadily under a good light. After a few moments look at a piece of white paper. You will see the familiar red, white, and blue of the American flag. (You may have to try this several times before it will work.)

FIG. 14

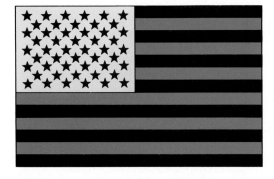

FIG. 15

▶ILLUSIONS OF MOTION

In a movie the actors seem to be moving about much as the people you see all around you do. A movie is really a series of separate pictures, each slightly different from the last. If you saw each picture separately, you would not be able to tell the difference between one and the next. When these pictures are put on film and flashed quickly before your eyes, one after the other, your eyes retain one image for a split second, so that the next image comes along before the first has faded away, giving the illusion of smooth, continuous movement.

A set of flip cards illustrates this illusion of motion. You can make a set by following the instructions in Figure 15 below. You can make other flip cards that show a dog running or a flower growing or a ship sailing across the ocean. Try making them on a pad of paper or in a small notebook so that you can just flip the pages.

You can use an optical illusion to make your own miniature movie. Trace the 8 figures below, being sure to trace the boxes around them. Cut the boxes apart. Paste each box on a separate index card so that the top and left-hand cutting lines are placed along the top and left-hand edges of each index card. Arrange the cards from 1 to 8 with 1 on top. Hold the cards together along the right edge and flip through them by releasing one card at a time along the left edge. The boy will "jump" over the barrier. If you reverse the order of the cards, he will jump backward. To make your own set of flip cards, draw each figure the same—that is, it should have the same length, size, and so on. The parts of the figure that move must differ slightly in each of your boxes. If the central figure is moving forward or backward or up or down, change the position of the figure on the card ever so slightly at each step.

▶ILLUSIONS ARE USEFUL

Illusions can be useful. They can be used to improve the appearance of things. Long ago Greek architects used illusions to improve the appearance of their buildings. They knew that a tall column (Figure 16) built perfectly straight would look pinched in at the middle. So they made it a little larger at this point. This made the column look straight.

Optical illusions are not simply tricks. They occur in the very process of seeing. This means that if you want to be accurate, you cannot depend on your eyes alone. Scientists know this very well. In their work they must always check what they see.

Reviewed by SERGE A. KORFF
New York University

See also LIGHT; MIRAGE.

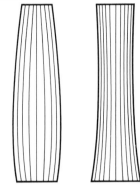
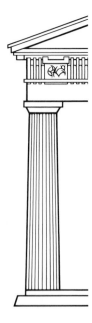

Greek columns are built with a bulge in the middle (*left*) so that to the eye they look straight (*right*). Without the bulge (*center*) they would look pinched.

In the woodcut below, the artist M.C. Escher creates many optical illusions with a playful use of perspective. For example, look at the two men walking left to right side by side on the upper staircase—yet one is climbing up and the other down.

◄ Early optical instruments included the cross-staff (being used by the standing sailor) to measure angles in the sky and the astrolabe (in hands of the seated sailor) used to determine a ship's latitude. Both were important to navigators in the 15th and 16th centuries.

Young scientists explore the ► world around them with the help of optical instruments. Microscopes (*left*) provide close-up views of small objects. A magnifying glass (*right*) makes tiny features easier to see.

OPTICAL INSTRUMENTS

Optics is the science of light and vision. An optical instrument is a device that uses the principles of optics to help us see or analyze the world around us.

The greatest optical instrument in the world is the human eye. In combination with the brain, it can see in three dimensions. It works in the dim of night and in direct sunlight. It can distinguish the finest shades of color. But there are many things that the eye cannot see or do well without help from other optical instruments. We need magnifiers to see very small objects and telescopes to see over long distances. Periscopes enable us to see objects that are not directly in our line of sight. For exact color measurements we require instruments called spectrophotometers. Each of these instruments as well as many others falls into the category of optical instruments.

▶DEVELOPMENT OF OPTICAL INSTRUMENTS

The history of optical instruments goes back to ancient times. It begins with simple aids to the human eye. Archaeologists have found in Egypt a magnifying lens made of rock crystal. It was made about 3000 B.C., which means that magnifiers have been in use for at least 5,000 years. The ancient Greeks and Romans also used lenses as magnifiers and as "burning glasses" to start wood fires. None of these ancient people, however, understood what made lenses work.

The first known optical scientist was an Arabian mathematician named Alhazen who lived around A.D. 1000. He studied the human eye and discovered what each of its parts does. Before Alhazen's time, people thought that the eye saw by sending out light to the object being seen. Alhazen showed that the opposite is true—that light comes to the eye by being reflected off the object. His studies also showed how light is bent, or **refracted,** when it passes from one substance into another. This happens, for example, when light passes from air into glass or from glass back into air. These discoveries helped later scientists understand how lenses and other optical devices work.

Spectacles, or eyeglasses, were the next important optical device to be developed. They were invented in the 1200's, probably in Italy. Several hundred years later, in the 1600's, the telescope and the microscope were invented. No one is sure who made the first telescope, but the first person to realize its usefulness was the Italian scientist Galileo. Using telescopes he built himself, Galileo made many discoveries in astronomy. He was the first to see mountains on the moon, stars in the Milky

Way, and moons revolving around the planet Jupiter.

The inventor of the microscope is also unknown. The first person to make important discoveries with a microscope is the Dutch scientist Anton van Leeuwenhoek. He is usually credited with first developing this important device.

Since the 1600's many new instruments have been invented, and many old ones have been improved. For example, in 1784, Benjamin Franklin made an improvement on spectacles. He was annoyed by having to change back and forth between two pairs of glasses—one for near vision and one for far vision. He cut both pairs of lenses in half and combined the lower half of his near vision spectacles with the upper half of the ones he used for far vision. Spectacles of this type—now made out of a single lens—are called bifocals.

▶ INSTRUMENTS TO HELP US SEE

Some of the first optical instruments—magnifiers, telescopes, and microscopes—helped people see things that were difficult or impossible to see with the unaided eye. Though developed several hundred years ago, telescopes and microscopes are still among the most widely used and important scientific instruments of today.

Magnifiers

The magnifying glass is among the simplest of optical instruments. It is sometimes called the simple microscope. A magnifying lens is a convex lens—one that is thicker at the center than at the edges. The lens bends together the rays of light reflected from an object. This makes the object seem bigger. What we see through the magnifier is called a magnified **image.** The more steeply the lens is curved, the larger the image will be. The amount by which a lens magnifies an object is called the **power** of the lens. A lens that magnifies an object ten times, for example, is called a ten-power lens. In general, magnifiers of more than 25 power are not practical. They cannot give to the eye an image that is sufficiently free of distortion. You can read more about magnifiers and other kinds of lenses in the Lenses article in Volume L.

Microscope

For a magnification of more than 25 power, a compound microscope is used. "Compound microscope" is the proper name of the instrument that is usually simply called a microscope. It has two lenses—or sets of lenses—instead of only one. One lens, near the object, is called the **objective.** The other, near the eye, is called the **eyepiece,** or **ocular.** The magnifi-

Binoculars

Eyepiece

Lenses

Reflecting prisms

Objective lens

Light path

Binoculars are made up of two small terrestrial telescopes. The image is magnified by the lenses and turned right side up by the two prisms.

cation takes place in two steps. The objective lens forms a magnified image of the object, just as a magnifier does. Then the eyepiece forms a magnified image of that image. The power of a compound microscope is found by multiplying the power of the objective lens by the power of the eyepiece.

Compound microscopes can give useful magnifications of up to 1,500 times. Greater magnification is possible, but it serves no useful purpose because it does not increase resolving power. This means that under ordinary conditions smaller details cannot be made visible.

Scientists and engineers are constantly finding ways to improve the microscope. For example, **zoom optics** enables the observer to change magnification smoothly—by either large or small amounts—by simply turning a knob. In ordinary microscopes only three or four fixed magnifications are possible, and a different lens must be moved into place for each.

Another type of microscope that is very useful in industry is the **stereomicroscope.** This instrument is made up of two compound microscopes, one for each eye. This provides stereoscopic vision (seeing in depth), which is not possible with the single eyepiece of a regular microscope. (You can test this principle by closing one eye and holding two pencils in front of you, one slightly closer to you than the other. You will not be able to distinguish which pencil is the closer one.)

Seeing in depth is especially important if precise and detailed work must be done on the objects being viewed. For example, in the manufacture of microcircuits, a tiny weld must be made. It would be almost impossible to make such a weld without a stereomicroscope. You can read about several other kinds of microscopes in the MICROSCOPES article in Volume M.

Telescope

The telescope, like the microscope, has an objective and an eyepiece. As in the microscope, the eyepiece enlarges the image formed by the objective. The difference is that telescopes are used to look at objects that are far away. The objectives of small telescopes are generally lenses, just as they are in microscopes. These telescopes are called **refracting telescopes,** or **refractors.** It is difficult and expensive to make lenses that are more than 1 foot (30 centimeters) in diameter. But a large curved mirror can do the same work as an objective lens, and it is easier to make. The instruments in which such mirrors are used are called **reflecting telescopes,** or **reflectors.**

Enormous telescopes do essentially the same job as small laboratory microscopes—magnify objects so that they are more easily visible to the human eye.

A telescope is called an **astronomical telescope** if it is designed for looking out into space. If it is designed for looking at faraway objects on earth, it is called a **terrestrial telescope.** Because they cost less, terrestrial telescopes are often used by amateur astronomers to look into space.

As in the case of the stereomicroscope, two terrestrial telescopes may be fastened together, so that the user may see a three-dimensional image. Such instruments are the well-known optical devices called **binoculars.**

Periscope

The simplest sort of periscope is a tube with a mirror at each end, tilted so that light from an object strikes the first mirror, is reflected down the tube, strikes the second mirror, and is reflected to the eye. This type of periscope may be used, for example, to see over the heads of a crowd. A simple periscope cannot be made very long, however, because looking down a long, narrow tube allows you to see only a small angle of view. Long periscopes, therefore, must have an eye piece and a lens system that relays the image from one lens to the next. Periscopes of this type are used in submarines so that accurate observations can be made while the submarine is still submerged. Periscopes are also used by scientists to observe dangerous experiments from a safe distance.

Fiberscope

A fiberscope is a type of periscope. But instead of using lens systems to relay images through a tube, it uses tiny bundles of glass or plastic fibers. Fiberscopes are flexible, so they can be used for seeing around curves and corners. They are especially useful for looking into places that are normally inaccessible. For example, doctors use them to examine the inside of the stomach, heart, and other organs, Nuclear technicians use them to examine parts of a nuclear reactor from a safe distance. And engineers use them to inspect aircraft engines without having to take the engines apart.

Fiberscopes are possible because of a technology known as **fiber optics.** Scientists have long known that light can be transmitted through a hollow tube. Light entering one end of the tube is reflected again and again from the inner walls. But each time the light rays are reflected, some light is lost. To overcome

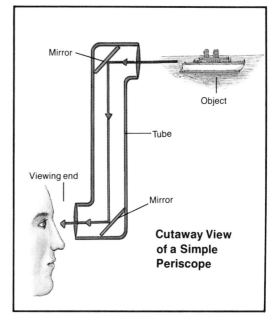

A simple periscope contains two mirrors. One mirror receives light from an object and reflects it to the other mirror, which reflects it to an observer's eye.

this problem, scientists created a special tube out of a hair-thin fiber. Each fiber has two parts, an inner core and an outer coating, or cladding, which protects the inner core. The cladding also reflects the light back onto its path, so there is virtually no loss of light. Even if light were to travel through an optical fiber several miles long, it would still be visible.

Such fibers can transmit laser pulses at very high frequencies. As a result they can transmit television and telephone signals with great efficiency.

▶INSTRUMENTS TO EXAMINE OUR EYES

Spectacles, or eyeglasses, are among the most common optical instruments. When the lenses of our eyes are not shaped properly, we use an extra set of lenses, or spectacles, to make up for the imperfection. The correct lenses are chosen by an optometrist or ophthalmologist. An **optometrist** is a specialist who is licensed to examine eyes and fit glasses. An **ophthalmologist** is a doctor of medicine who specializes in the treatment of diseases of the eye. Spectacles are made by a third specialist, called an **optician.** An optician makes spectacles or other optical parts but is not trained to examine eyes.

The branch of medicine that is concerned with the care of the eye is **ophthalmology.** Instruments used in this study are called ophthalmic instruments.

Ophthalmoscope

The simplest and most common ophthalmic instrument is the ophthalmoscope. It contains a light source and tiny mirror or prism to reflect the light into the patient's eye. It also has several lenses of different powers through which the examiner sees the inside of the patient's eye. By rotating the different lenses into position, the examiner gets enlarged views of the screenlike retina at the back of the eye. The blood vessels at the back are also clearly seen. This is the only place in the human body where this is possible. Sometimes the appearance of these vessels gives warning of disease in other parts of the body.

Refractor

The most useful instrument for finding what power of eyeglass is needed is the refractor. It is a set of lenses mounted so that they can be placed, one after another, in front of the patient's eye. By trying different lenses and noting their effects, the examiner can quickly find the best power of lens for that eye.

▶MEASURING INSTRUMENTS

The simplest method of measuring distance is with a ruler or tape measure. Sometimes this is not possible. In such cases, optical instruments can be used instead.

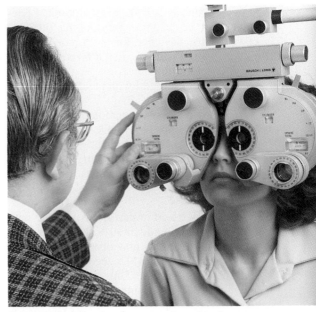

Optometrists determine the power of eyeglass lenses required by testing out a variety of lenses on the patient. This is done with an instrument called a refractor.

A wide river can be measured with the help of angle-measuring optical instruments. When angles *A* and *B* and distance *d* are known, surveyors can easily calculate distance *x*, the width of the river.

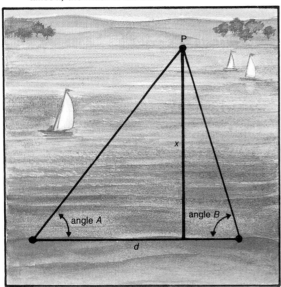

The simplest method of measuring distances with optical instruments is called **triangulation.** By using this method it is possible to find distances that would be difficult to measure directly.

Suppose, for example, that surveyors need to measure the width of a wide river (see diagram). The surveyors choose any convenient point, *P*, on the other side of the river. By measuring the angles *A* and *B* and the distance *d*, they can figure out the width of the river, *x*. The line *x* is at right angles to the direction in which the river flows.

Angle-Measuring Instruments

To measure distance by triangulation, one must be able to measure angles. Several optical instruments are used to measure angles.

Transit. The transit is the instrument most used by surveyors to measure angles. It is a type of terrestrial telescope containing cross hairs and mounted on a special stand.

Cross hairs are used to point the transit accurately. They are a pair of crossed wires or hairs inside the telescope that look like thin lines to the person using the instrument. By moving the telescope so the hairs cross at a particular point in the distance, the telescope can be aimed very accurately at that point. (A telescopic gunsight works the same way. It is a telescope with cross hairs that is attached to the barrel of a gun.)

The stand that the transit is mounted on contains graduated circles. A graduated circle is a metal or glass disk or ring with degrees of a circle marked along its edge. It is read somewhat like the protractors used in school to measure angles. A transit has one circle for measuring horizontal angles and usually a second for measuring vertical angles.

Astronomers measure the distances from the earth to other bodies in the solar system by using their telescopes in much the same way that a surveyor uses a transit. Astronomers use two telescopes on different parts of the earth to measure the two necessary angles.

Sextant. The sextant is an instrument used by navigators, primarily those at sea, to locate their latitude. It is made up of a small telescope, mirrors, and a precisely marked scale on a metal frame. The sextant measures the angle of the sun above the horizon. This information, along with exact time and reference data from an almanac, allows the calculation to be made.

To ''shoot the sun,'' as using the sextant is called, the navigator looks at the horizon through the telescope and a clear glass in front of the telescope. The top of this glass has a mirrored coating and reflects an image of the sun to the navigator. The sextant is adjusted until the reflection of the sun seems to touch the horizon. The scale on the sextant then shows the height of the sun. (If conditions are good enough at night to allow stars to be sighted, longitude calculations can be made as well.) You can read more about how the sextant is used in the NAVIGATION article in Volume N.

Photogrammetry

One way that optical instruments are used to measure distance is in photogrammetry, the science of measuring by photography. Its greatest use is in making maps from aerial photographs. Maps used to be made very slowly, using measurements made by surveyors with transits and tape measures. Nowadays, airplanes or satellites fly over the territory to be mapped and take a series of overlapping photographs of the ground. These are printed in special printers that remove any distortion in the original negative. Then mea-

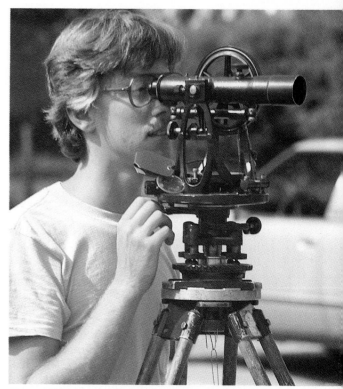

The transit (*top*) is a terrestrial telescope mounted on a special stand. It is used to measure angles such as those in the triangulation problem on the opposite page. The sextant (*bottom*) is used by navigators to determine latitude. It came into use in the 18th century and is still an important navigational tool.

surements are made on the photographs between certain points. The actual distance between these points is measured on the ground by surveyors. In this way the relationship between distances on the photograph and the actual distances on the ground can be found. With just a few measurements by surveyors, the rest of the map can be made from aerial photographs.

One of the most interesting parts of map-making by photogrammetry is the finding of elevation, so that the map can show the heights of various hills and other objects of interest. Two photographs of the same area are taken along the path of flight the airplane used. The mapmaker puts these photographs in projectors and projects both pictures onto the same screen. A red filter is used in one projector, and a blue filter in the other. Then the mapmaker puts on special spectacles fitted with a red filter on one side, and a blue filter on the other. The left eye sees one photograph, and the right eye sees the other photograph. The pictures resemble what a giant would see, looking down. It is as if the distance the airplane flew between the taking of the first and second photographs were the distance between the giant's eyes. Wearing the special spectacles, the mapmaker sees a three-dimensional picture. Valleys appear low, and hills appear high. The mapmaker carefully traces what is seen and marks the objects with their proper heights. With modern instruments, much of this work is automated, thanks in part to computers.

Comparator

Optical comparators, or contour projectors, are used in industry to check the dimensions of small parts. These instruments can be thought of as projection microscopes. Lenses are used to project a greatly enlarged image of the part onto a screen. Distances on the screen can be measured with an ordinary ruler.

Sometimes the outline of a perfect part is drawn on the screen. Then places where the part being examined are not accurate will show up because the image will not match the drawing in those places.

▶INSTRUMENTS THAT ANALYZE MATTER

A great deal can be learned about matter by examining the light that comes from it or passes through it.

Spectroscope

The heart of a spectroscope is a prism or a diffraction grating, both of which separate light into the different wavelengths that make it up. White light, for example, can be separated into all the colors of the rainbow. This separation of colors is called the **spectrum.** The spectrum may be observed visually or recorded electronically or photographically.

Spectroscopes are especially useful for studying chemical compounds. When chemical substances are heated in an electric arc or a flame, they give off light. This light has different wavelengths, depending on the elements that are being heated. For example, the sodium in salt gives a yellow color when salt is thrown into a fire. Each element gives a set of wavelengths that is different from that of any other element. Because of this a spectroscope can be used to identify chemical elements. A mixture of elements will cause patterns of each element to appear. An expert called a spectrographer can pick out the pattern of each element and identify it.

Spectrophotometer

The spectrophotometer is similar to the spectrograph except that it identifies chemicals by passing a beam of light through a material, rather than by burning it. Different materials will absorb different amounts of light depending on the wavelengths of the light. The spectrophotometer makes a graph of the percentage of light that passes through a substance as the wavelength is changed. It has its own source of white or ultraviolet light, and like the spectrograph, it has a prism or diffraction grating to separate the colors. An electronic detector is used to measure the light.

Refractometer

The refractometer measures the refractive index of a material. When light passes from one transparent material into another, it is refracted, or bent. How greatly it is bent depends on the speed with which light travels through the material. The higher the refractive index, the more the light is slowed by the material. The refractive index of a vacuum is 1.00. Any material—solid, liquid, or gas—has a higher index. Water has a refractive index of about 1.3, and glass a refractive index of 1.5 to 1.8. Diamond has a very high refractive index, 2.4.

Chemicals can be analyzed with an optical instrument called a spectrophotometer. A beam of light is passed through a solution. The elements in the solution can be determined by how much light is transmitted.

One of the most important uses of refractometers is in determining the concentration of solutions. The index of refraction of a solution changes with its concentration. A refractometer can be used, for example, to tell when enough water has been boiled out of the soup in a canning plant or when grape-juice concentrate is ready to be bottled.

There are many special versions of refractometers and other optical instruments used to analyze matter. For example, colorimeters are used to measure color, and saccharimeters to measure the amount of sugar in a liquid. Opacimeters measure the amount of light that will show through writing paper. Pyrometers are used for measuring the temperatures of furnaces and flames from a safe distance.

▶ MAKING OPTICAL GLASS

The first and often the most important material needed to manufacture optical instruments is optical glass. Ordinary glass, such as that used for bottles and windows, is not nearly good enough. Special glass must be used. The main ingredient of glass is sand. A very pure grade of beautiful white sand is used for optical glass.

The first step in the manufacture of an optical part is to prepare, by molding or cutting, a blank—a piece of glass just slightly larger than the finished part. After the blank is prepared, it is ready for grinding. It is fastened onto a wheel, and one surface is covered with an abrasive, such as emery. This surface is held up against another wheel. One of the wheels is set spinning, and the abrasive grinds the glass. After the first grinding the abrasive is replaced with a finer abrasive. This removes the larger scratches from the glass and gives it a smoother surface. This is continued, using finer and finer abrasives. Then the glass must be polished.

Polishing is similar to grinding except that the abrasive does not cut away the surface of the glass, as in grinding. Instead it causes the glass to flow, filling in the tiny scratches. A material called rouge is used for this.

In most optical instruments it is important for as much light to be transmitted as possible. To bring this about, the glass surfaces are given a special treatment called anti-reflective coating, usually with the chemical magnesium fluoride. Sometimes several other chemicals are used, in separate layers.

By controlling the number and thickness of these coating layers, unusual effects can be produced. For example, color filters can be made as well as mirrors that reflect one color and transmit another. Reflectors in the bulbs of slide and movie projectors are coated so that they reflect visible light but transmit infrared, or heat, rays to the rear. This allows the film to be illuminated without burning it up.

CORWIN H. BRUMLEY
Bausch & Lomb, Inc.
ERWIN G. LOEWEN
Fellow, Optical Society of America

See also LASERS; LENSES; LIGHT; MICROSCOPES; SURVEYING; TELESCOPES.

ORANGE (VALENCIA)

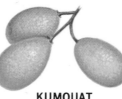

KUMQUAT

**MANDARIN
(DANCY TANGERINE)**

GRAPEFRUIT (MARSH)

TANGELO (MINNEOLA)

ORANGE AND GRAPEFRUIT

Oranges have been grown since ancient times, but the grapefruit was not discovered until about 200 years ago. Both fruits belong to the citrus family, along with mandarins, tangelos, kumquats, lemons, and limes. Citrus fruits have a thick rind. The fruit is divided into segments filled with juicy pulp. The fruits grow on evergreen trees that were once native to southeastern Asia.

▶ ORANGE

There are two kinds of orange tree, the sweet and the sour. For many years people thought that the sweet orange (which includes all varieties of commercial orange) and the sour orange were originally the same tree. Experts now believe that the trees have always been entirely separate and that they are equally old. Early Chinese records indicate that the orange was known at least 4,000 years ago.

Sour Orange. The sour orange was the first orange grown in Europe. It was introduced by the Moors, North African Muslims, who invaded southern Spain and Sicily around the 9th century. By the 11th century the Moors had a strong foothold in the conquered countries, and they planted sour orange and other trees. Sour oranges were widely grown in southern Europe until the 15th century, when increased trade with the Orient brought sweet oranges to Europe. Although some sour oranges are still grown and eaten, they are now used mainly as rootstocks for sweet oranges.

Sweet Orange. Sweet oranges were at first a luxury only the wealthiest could afford. Kings and nobles paid great prices for the exotic trees, which they proudly showed off in their gardens. Since in the colder countries the delicate trees would be killed during a cold winter, special greenhouses called orangeries came into fashion. The orange trees were planted in tubs. During the summer they were moved outside, but in winter they were safely behind glass in the orangerie, where they could bloom in spite of the cold wind outside.

When Christopher Columbus sailed for the New World, he carried seeds of oranges and many other citrus fruits with him. The seeds were planted on the island of Hispaniola. Citrus trees flourished in the tropical climate of the West Indies and what is now Florida. Indians spread citrus trees beyond the Spanish plantations by dropping seeds from the fruit they were eating. Soon there were groves of wild citrus trees.

Today the United States is the largest citrus-producing area in the world. Florida has the greatest number of orange trees and produces more sweet oranges than any other state or country. Spain, Italy, and Japan also are important citrus producers. Brazil and Cuba have extensive plantings.

Varieties of Sweet Orange. It is hard to classify oranges into groups, since many varieties have characteristics in common. But in general, oranges are grouped as **blood**, **navel**, and **Spanish**, or **Mediterranean**, oranges.

Varieties of the blood orange are very popular in Europe. These oranges are well named, because the fruit pulp is red.

Navel oranges are also easily recognized, because a second, very tiny orange with a navel-like pit can be seen at one end. The earliest description of the navel orange is in a book (1646) by Giovanni Battista, an Italian monk. In his book Battista listed and illustrated various fruits known in his time. But the navel orange was never widely grown in Europe, and it has not thrived in Florida's soil and climate. However, these oranges have been very successful in California and are the most important variety of orange grown there. The most popular varieties of the navel orange have no seeds.

The most popular variety in the United States is the **Valencia**, a Mediterranean orange. This orange has an excellent flavor and is often used in making frozen orange juice.

Another way to divide orange varieties is to classify them according to when they ripen—as early, midseason, and late. Some varieties ripen in October, and others in December, while varieties such as the Valencia ripen from March to June. In most commercial orchards, oranges from all three groups are planted. In this way the harvesting season lasts from autumn into the following summer.

Growing Orange and Other Citrus

Oranges and other citrus fruits are commonly called subtropical fruits. The trees are injured by heavy frosts and freezing temperatures, although some cool weather is necessary to develop highly colored, tasty fruits.

The growing of young citrus trees is a specialized business handled by nurserymen. Although orange trees that bear fruit can be grown from seed, they will not grow true to type. The seed from one kind of orange will not produce oranges of the same variety as the parent tree. All commercial varieties are budded, or grafted, onto citrus seedlings called the **rootstock**. Rough lemon and sour orange are most often used as rootstocks.

The seed to be used for the rootstock is planted in the nursery. It grows there for about 2 years before it is grafted with a bud of the desired orange variety. The bud, called the **scion**, will grow into the new orange tree. Thus it is important that the buds are selected carefully. They must be the correct orange variety, and they must be completely free from any virus diseases.

The bud is inserted into the side of the rootstock seedling and wrapped with budding tape. The wrap is removed when the bud and rootstock have grown together. The top of the rootstock seedling is cut away so that the new bud will have room to grow into a small tree. After about one year, the trees are large and strong enough to be sold. The buyers transplant the young trees in their orchards. Usually five more years must pass before the orange tree is able to produce fruit.

The orange tree never stops growing. By the time it is 20, it may be 4.5 meters (15 feet) high and producing more than 1,000 oranges yearly. There are a few trees over 100 years old that still produce oranges.

Citrus growers must protect their trees against freezing temperatures, which sometimes occur even in warm citrus-growing regions. For this they use either heaters that burn fuel oil or large wind machines. The wind machines have airplane-type propellers that mix the air and help prevent frost.

Citrus trees are called evergreen because they have leaves in all seasons. Actually the old leaves fall to the ground and new ones are continually being produced. The tree puts out new leaves, commonly called **flushes**, usually three times a year.

The fragrant white blossoms on the orange tree appear each year in the spring. Oranges developing from these blossoms may take 7 to 15 months to ripen, depending on whether the trees are early- or late-season varieties. Sometimes orange blossoms and ripe fruit can be seen at the same time on a tree that bears fruit in the late season.

When the fruit is picked, it may be sold as fresh fruit or it may be sent to a factory to be made into juice. Oranges are not picked until they contain the desired amount of sugar and acidity. Fruitgrowers take samples and test them chemically. Ripeness, contrary to popular opinion, cannot be measured by the color of the orange. A few late-season varieties may be partially green in color and still be sweet and of good quality.

Preparing the Fruit for Market

Oranges that will be sold fresh are sent to a packinghouse. The fruit is usually unloaded automatically. Belts carry the oranges into the packinghouse, where they are washed and treated with decay-controlling chemicals. For further protection the oranges are coated with a wax material. Then they are transported to the sizers and graders, where they are separated into lots of the same size and quality before they are packed in boxes or cartons for shipment to market. Harmless orange dyes are sometimes added to the rind of the orange to make the fruit look better.

Frozen orange concentrate is made in processing plants with automatic equipment. Orange concentrate is made by removing the water from the orange juice. Orange concentrate has become very popular because the consumer does not have to squeeze the juice from oranges. Just by adding water, a drink can be made that tastes almost like freshly squeezed orange juice. The first step in making orange concentrate is to squeeze out the juice mechanically. Then most of the water is removed by boiling the juice in a high vacuum at 15°C (59°F). The concentrated juice is transferred to refrigerated blending tanks, where a small quantity of fresh juice is added. Adding fresh juice is known as **cutback**. It helps restore any flavor that might have been lost during evaporation. The concentrated orange juice is cooled, poured into cans, and quickly frozen to −23°C (−10°F). This process was first developed in 1945. Most of the orange crop in Florida is now made into frozen orange concentrate.

Nothing is wasted at the processing plant. The peel, pulp, and seeds are turned into useful products. One of the main uses of citrus peel and pulp has been in the production of cattle feed. The moisture and oil are removed by pressure. The material is dried in huge rotary driers. The dried citrus pulp is placed in bags and sold to beef and dairy farmers.

The oils from citrus peels are highly prized for flavoring. After they are pressed from the peel, they are refined by special processes. The peel itself is also used in marmalades and jellies. Citrus waste juices are used in industrial alcohol. The by-products have been used in making dyes and even paint. New uses are still being found.

▶ MANDARIN, KUMQUAT, AND TANGELO

Several kinds of citrus fruit that many people think of as oranges actually are not oranges at all. They are separate plants that, except for recently developed hybrids, have been grown for hundreds of years in Asia.

The **mandarin** was brought to England in the early 19th century. It has been nicknamed the kid-glove orange because the skin fits rather loosely and can easily be peeled by hand. Also, the sections of the fruit are easily separated. The Japanese grow large quantities of a mandarin known as the **satsuma.** The most important mandarin grown in Florida is the **Dancy tangerine,** though new complex hybrids are becoming increasingly popular. The largest market for tangerines is the fresh-fruit trade. Tangerines often are thought of as Christmas fruit because they ripen only once a year—during December and January.

The **kumquat** also was introduced to the West in the 19th century. Its name means "gold orange." Preserved kumquats in a sweet syrup are a Chinese specialty. The combination of the spicy rind and sour pulp gives a pleasing, unusual taste. Kumquat trees are very hardy and make attractive garden plants.

The **tangelo** is another orangelike fruit that has been gaining in popularity. The first part of the name "tangelo" comes from "tangerine." The tangelo is a hybrid (offspring of two different parents) between a tangerine and a grapefruit. The two main varieties are the **Orlando** and the **Minneola.** The tangelo is a very juicy fruit and has a strong flavor somewhat like that of the tangerine.

▶ GRAPEFRUIT

The grapefruit is an important citrus that probably originated in Jamaica. There is no record or description of the grapefruit before 1750. As far as authorities can tell, the grapefruit is a mutation (an offspring different from the parent) of the pummelo. Pummelos, also known as shaddocks, have been grown in Europe since the 12th century. How the pummelo came to North America and when the grapefruit first appeared are unknown. The unusual name "grapefruit" originated either because of the grapelike flavor of the fruit or because they grow in bunches like grapes.

The grapefruit has been grown commercially for more than 100 years. Citrus growers began to ship the fruit to northern markets about 1880. Before that, a few people in Florida ate grapefruit, but most of the crop rotted on the ground. The young industry had barely started when it was almost completely destroyed by a severe freeze in 1894–95. The grapefruit industry did not recover for many years. After 1920 new plantings of grapefruit on rough-lemon stock flourished and brought about a new growth in the grapefruit industry.

Grapefruits and oranges are grown in the same way. As with oranges, the varieties of grapefruit are divided into several groups. Some varieties, such as the **Marsh,** do not have any seeds. Other varieties, such as the **Duncan,** have many seeds. The Duncan is one of the hardiest grapefruits. There are also pink grapefruits, such as the **Ruby.** The fruit pulp of pink grapefruits is a deep-pink or red color. The Rio Grande Valley of Texas has been an important area for the production of pink grapefruit. In the United States, the main grapefruit-producing area is Florida, followed by Texas, California, and Arizona. The United States produces about half of the world's grapefruit crop. China, Cuba, and Israel are the next largest producers.

The main use of grapefruit is as a fresh fruit or a canned product served at the breakfast table. Canned grapefruit juice and frozen grapefruit concentrate are not as popular as frozen orange concentrate, but their use has helped to stabilize the grapefruit industry.

HARRY W. FORD
Agricultural Research and Education Center
University of Florida

See also FRUITGROWING; LEMON AND LIME.

ORATORY

Oratory is a kind of public speaking that expresses important thought in artistic, forceful language. Usually its aim is to persuade large audiences. It might ask them to go to war, to seek freedom, or to follow the teachings of a religion. The speakers of oratory are called orators and their speeches orations. When the thoughts and ideas in oratory are worked out with skill and the language is used with beauty, oratory becomes eloquent. It is thought of as spoken literature. Abraham Lincoln's Gettysburg Address, for example, is one of the most eloquent short orations ever spoken. It is also one of the noblest pieces of American prose.

Oratory has been best in those countries where people decide public matters in open meetings and free elections. Speeches seem to be necessary then; certainly they were in ancient Athens and in the ancient Roman republic. Oratory also thrives when masses of people seek a new way of life. Great Britain and the United States produced their greatest orators when people in each country struggled for their beliefs.

Oratory in Ancient Greece and Rome

Oratory as both a useful art and a fine art was first taught and practiced in ancient Greece, beginning about 400 or 500 years before the birth of Christ. In Greece oratory became especially important to the general public. There were no professional lawyers. Citizens had to plead their own cases in the law courts, although professional speech writers could help them in advance. Particularly in Athens, the citizens took an active part in debating new laws and other questions in the assembly. Also, the ancient Athenians, perhaps more than any other people since, enjoyed the beauty of fine language well used.

As a result, the systematic teaching of oratory began in Greece about 450 B.C. The teachers were called **sophists** and **rhetors**, and the study of speaking and writing well was called **rhetoric**. Some of the teachers were themselves excellent orators. The sophist Gorgias (485?–380? B.C.) was especially noted for his colorful style.

The ancient book on rhetoric that has been most famous through the years was not written by a rhetor or a sophist but by the philosopher Aristotle. He observed and described three kinds of orations. The first was the **deliberative**, in which political matters were debated in the assembly. The second was the **forensic**, in which cases at law were argued. The third was the **epideictic**, or ceremonial—an oration for a funeral or some other special event.

Aristotle told how to make these three kinds of speeches most persuasive: (1) The argument should be strong and logical. (2) The speaker should be likable and believable. (3) The speaker should win the audience's sympathy. Aristotle also taught the best ways of finding arguments, putting a speech together, and making the language strong and beautiful.

Many later writers, both Greek and Roman, further developed the fine art of rhetoric. They taught, for example, that the perfect oration should have six parts. These are: (1) introduction, (2) narration leading to the main idea, (3) statement of the idea, or proposition, (4) argument, (5) refutation, or answering the arguments on the other side, and (6) peroration, or conclusion.

By the power of his oratory Pericles led Athens at the height of its glory during the 5th century B.C. None of his speeches have come to us, but we know about them through the writing of the historian Thucydides.

The most famous Greek orator was Demosthenes (385?–322 B.C.). Fortunately many of his orations have been preserved as he wrote them. With his oratory he urged the Athenian people to resist the invading conqueror Philip II of Macedon, father of Alexander the Great. Because of the force of his speeches against Philip, similar speeches have since been called **philippics**. Later Demosthenes defended his political work against the orator Aeschines (389–314 B.C.) in the long oration *On the Crown*. It is one of the three or four most famous orations ever given. Other notable Greek orators were Lysias (450–380? B.C.) and Isocrates (436–338 B.C.).

Among Roman orators Marcus Tullius Cicero ranks first. He, like Demosthenes, wrote out speeches that passed down to later generations. An important leader in the last days of the Roman republic, Cicero delivered some of his most famous orations against men who were trying to destroy the republic. Among these were the conspirator Catiline and the ambitious politician Marcus Antonius (Mark Antony). Cicero's oratory later became the ideal of Western Europe. He wrote one of the two most important Roman books on rhetoric. Quintilian, a teacher, wrote the other.

Among other notable orators in Rome were Cato the Elder (234–149 B.C.); Gaius Julius Caesar, Rome's greatest general; and Cato the Younger (95–46 B.C.), who supported Cicero against Catiline.

Oratory in Religion and Politics

After the days of Cicero and until A.D. 1600 and later, the best oratory was produced mostly by men of religion. Saint Augustine, an early Father of the Church, excelled as an orator. Almost 1,000 years later, during the latter half of the 15th century, one of the most powerful orators of all time preached in Florence, Italy. He was the monk Savonarola (1452–98). Outstanding orators of the Protestant Reformation were Martin Luther, John Calvin, and John Knox. In 17th-century France, Bishop Bossuet preached moving funeral orations. They are considered noble examples of French prose.

In the same century English people could hear the stirring eloquence of John Donne, Dean of St. Paul's Cathedral in London, and the clear, reasonable preaching of John Tillotson (1630–94). A little later, colonial Americans were inspired and instructed by such Puritan orators as Cotton Mather and Jonathan Edwards and by the popular Methodist preacher George Whitefield (1714–70). In England John Wesley, the founder of Methodism, was probably the most important pulpit orator of the 18th century.

During the 19th and 20th centuries the United States had many fine pulpit orators, among them Henry Ward Beecher (1813–87) and the evangelists Dwight L. Moody (1837–99) and Billy Graham (1918–   ); Harry Emerson Fosdick (1878–1969); Rabbi Stephen S. Wise (1874–1949); and Bishop Fulton Sheen (1895–1979). One of the best-known orations of the 20th century was *I Have a Dream* by Martin Luther King, Jr. In England, Cardinal Manning (1802–92) and Charles

Spurgeon (1834–92) were among the greatest orators.

In the modern world the oratory of politics and the law courts has flourished best in the British Isles and the United States. British oratory reached its peak during the time of the American and French revolutions. William Pitt, a masterful orator and prime minister of England at the age of 23, inspired the people of his country during the wars with Revolutionary France and Napoleon. Pitt's father, the Earl of Chatham, made the superb oration *On Peace with America* in 1777. Two years earlier, Edmund Burke (1729–97) had given his *On Conciliation with the Colonies.*

In the 19th century, oratory in England became less distinguished. Still, the two great political opponents Benjamin Disraeli and William E. Gladstone were excellent orators. Britain's last great orator of the old school, Sir Winston Churchill, led the United Kingdom and inspired the Allied nations during and after World War II.

In the early history of the United States, too, political oratory prospered. Patrick Henry and Alexander Hamilton shone as orators during the making of the nation. In the first half of the 19th century, brilliant oratory came from Henry Clay, Daniel Webster, John C. Calhoun, Stephen A. Douglas, and Abraham Lincoln.

Oratory after the Civil War can be well represented by such eloquent men as William Jennings Bryan and the lawyer and lecturer Robert G. Ingersoll (1833–99). Bryan, "The Boy Orator of the Platte," became one of the most popular leaders of the West. His Cross of Gold speech in 1896 made him the Democratic nominee for United States president.

Radio, television, and other modern means of communication seem to demand a less formal kind of speaking than oratory. To most people oratory now means the great speaking of the past or, sometimes, speaking that sounds fancy and old-fashioned. For the most part we refer to speeches and talks instead of orations and oratory. In some schools, however, certain speaking contests and events are still called oratory.

DONALD C. BRYANT
Professor of Speech
University of Iowa

See also PUBLIC SPEAKING.

ORCHESTRA

An orchestra is a large group of musicians playing many kinds of instruments. The standard orchestra usually has from about 75 to over 100 players. Of these, more than half play stringed instruments. An orchestra of this size is capable of playing the symphonic music of the great composers and is therefore

is made up of only the stringed instruments of the symphony orchestra.

Jazz or dance bands are sometimes called orchestras, but the proper term for such groups is "band." A military or concert band may be as large as an orchestra, but it does not use stringed instruments.

To most musicians, the term "orchestra" means the symphony orchestra. When all the

A symphony orchestra performs in a large concert hall. The conductor, in front, leads the four main sections of instruments: strings, woodwinds, brass, and percussion.

called a **symphony orchestra**. Because of its size, it typically performs in large concert halls.

Although the term "orchestra" usually refers to a large ensemble of musicians, it is also used to describe musical groups of other sizes. A group of about 15 to 30 players is called a **chamber orchestra**. It has been given this name because it is small enough to play in a small hall, or chamber. A **string orchestra**

instruments in a symphony orchestra are played together, they can create a glorious and energetic wave of musical sound.

▶ THE SYMPHONY ORCHESTRA

The modern symphony orchestra consists of four main sections, or families, of instruments: strings, woodwinds, brass, and percussion. Two important instruments, the piano and the harp, are often placed in their own category. The entire orchestra is directed by a conductor.

Stringed Instruments

The largest family of instruments in a symphony orchestra is the strings. It includes the violin, viola, cello, and double bass—instruments that are all shaped alike but differ in size. Each is

played with a bow of horsehair and wood, which is drawn across the strings.

The violins, to the conductor's left, form the largest group of strings. There are usually 30 or more, divided into two sections—the first and second violins. Most of the time, all the first violins play one part while all the second violins play another. In the center, or just to the right, are the violas, which are slightly larger than violins. The violin and viola are held in a similar fashion, resting between the musician's chin and shoulder.

To the conductor's right are the larger strings—the cellos and the double basses. While the cellists sit with their cellos resting in front of their bodies, the double bass players typically stand or sit on tall stools to accommodate the instrument's height.

The size of the instrument is one factor in determining its sound. The violins, the smallest of the strings, are the sopranos—they are often called upon to go soaring to great heights. At the other extreme are the double basses, the largest of the strings, with their rumbling low voices.

Because the instruments in the string family are similar in construction and style, they produce a unified sound. They often perform alone, as a string orchestra. While the strings usually play together, it is not uncommon for the principal player in the string section—the player designated to play in the lead chair—to play a solo.

Woodwind Instruments

The woodwinds are usually found near the center and back of the orchestra, often positioned directly in line with the conductor. They are generally small and quiet wind instruments. The instrument with the highest range is the tiny piccolo. A smaller relative of the flute, the piccolo has a thin, piercing tone, while the flute has a pure, sweet one.

Lower in pitch than the flute are the oboe, the English horn, and the clarinet. These instruments sound very different but look somewhat alike. Each is a straight pipe; however, the oboe and the English horn produce their sounds by the vibration of a double wooden reed. The English horn is similar to the oboe, though it is a bit larger and has a distinctive bulb-shaped end. The clarinet has a single reed attached to a mouthpiece. The bass clarinet has a lower range than an ordinary clarinet. And, as it is much longer, it has an endpin that slides out of the bottom of the instrument to help prop it up on the floor.

The saxophone is another woodwind with a single-reed structure. This brass instrument

Above: The woodwind section of the orchestra includes flutes, oboes, clarinets, and sometimes saxophones. *Right:* The brass section includes trombones and French horns.

The trombones and the tuba—the bass of the brass section—dominate the lower brass register. A musician plays a trombone by moving a slide to various positions; each position represents a different tone. The tuba, like the trumpet, involves the musician pushing down valves to create alternate pitches.

is the only woodwind that was never made of wood.

The bassoons, with their deep and mellow sound, can produce the lowest sounds of the woodwinds and some of the lowest sounds in the entire orchestra. Their double reed structure is similar to that of the oboe, but larger. The contrabassoon, with a lower pitch than the bassoon, is the lowest wind instrument in the orchestra.

A symphony orchestra usually has two flutes, two oboes, two clarinets, and two bassoons. Sometimes the number of each is doubled. The piccolo, English horn, bass clarinet, and contrabassoon add their tones when needed. Saxophones sometimes play in symphony orchestras but are more at home in jazz and dance bands.

Brass Instruments

Usually located in the back and center of the orchestra, the brass section includes the horns, trumpets, trombones, and tuba. In order to produce tones, musicians blow air into the mouthpieces of brass instruments—basically long metal tubes that flare at the far end. These tubes have been bent and folded into compact shapes so they are easier for musicians to play.

The trumpets and horns play the higher brass parts. These instruments have a velvety tone and fill in the middle range. While the musicians in the horn section play a variety of instruments, they most typically play the French horn.

Most symphony orchestras have four horns, three trumpets, three trombones, and a tuba. You will spot these instruments gleaming at the back of the stage. Together they can play more loudly than the rest of the orchestra combined.

Percussion Instruments

Every once in a while, a crash, boom, or rattle makes you aware of an unusual collection of instruments spanning the rear of the orchestra. This is the percussion section. Percussion instruments include just about anything you can hit, rattle, thump, scratch, or shake. Many percussion instruments are played with the hands, but sometimes wooden mallets, metal bars, and other musical tools are used.

The most basic and common instruments in this family are the drums: the kettledrums, or **timpani**; the snare drum; and the bass drum. In the symphony orchestra, timpani are used more often than other percussion instruments; they come in several sizes and can play recognizable pitches. Most other drums, from the bongo to the big bass drum, produce a sound, not an exact pitch.

Other members of the percussion group make a variety of sounds. Cymbals are metal plates that are clashed together or struck with a drumstick. Composers sometimes include even more unique percussion instruments in their music, such as the gong, triangle, tambourine, woodblocks, and rattles.

In addition to the timpani, there are a variety of bells and chimes that can produce definite pitches. The glockenspiel has small metal bars, which produce a bell-like sound when tapped with a stick. The bars of a celesta are struck with hammers operated by a keyboard, much like a piano. The xylophone is similar to the glockenspiel, but the bars are made of wood and produce a dry, clattering sound.

A percussionist strikes kettledrums (timpani) during an orchestral performance.

The Piano and the Harp

The piano and the harp are important instruments in the symphony orchestra. Some argue that the piano and harp belong to the string family because they both have strings. However, they are often placed in the percussion family of instruments because in order to create sound, their strings must be either plucked (harp) or struck (piano).

The Conductor

Standing on a podium in front of the symphony orchestra, the conductor leads all the musicians through the classical music compositions. The conductor expresses ideas with hand movements and facial expressions. Conductors are often like actors in that they must communicate feelings, thoughts, and ideas in a way that others can understand.

Conductors usually use a wooden stick called a baton to help clearly signal beats, rhythms, entrances, endings, and expression. But if the piece is slow or expressive, conductors will often use only their hands.

While men have played a prominent role in the world of conducting since the early 1800's, an increasing number of women are leading symphony orchestras and being recognized for their outstanding talents and musical abilities. You can read more about the role of the conductor in the article ORCHESTRA CONDUCTING in this volume.

▶ HISTORY OF THE ORCHESTRA

In ancient Greece and Rome, "orchestra" was the term for the ground level of an outdoor theater. Later it came to mean the area in front of the stage and, eventually, the preferred place for instrumentalists to sit during a performance. About 1670, the term began to be used throughout Europe to refer to the musicians themselves.

The modern orchestra is the result of centuries of development, experiment, and change. Composers have played a vital role in shaping the orchestra. **Orchestration**, the art of writing music for the orchestra, became increasingly important in expanding the sound of the symphony orchestra as composers found ways to combine the various sounds of the instruments in musically effective ways.

The first great pioneer in writing for the orchestra was the Italian composer Claudio Monteverdi. He was also the first great composer of opera. In his *Orfeo* (1607), Monteverdi used an orchestra of 35 musicians, playing violas, guitars, harpsichords, organs, trumpets, trombones, and flutes. He used these instruments in new and interesting combinations.

With the perfection of the violin in the 1600's, the strings became the leading instruments of the orchestra and have remained so to this day. Important composers who helped develop the orchestra during this period were Arcangelo Corelli and Antonio Vivaldi. They wrote many works for an orchestra of strings with a contrasting small group of solo strings or woodwinds. Such a composition is called a

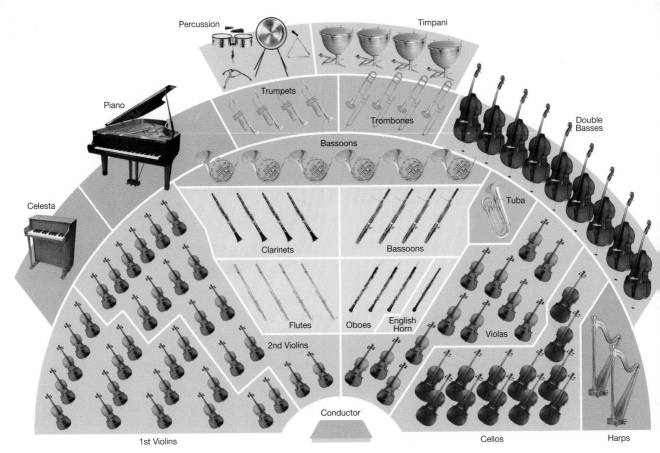

PHILADELPHIA ORCHESTRA SEATING PLAN

concerto grosso. George Frederick Handel and Johann Sebastian Bach wrote many concertos of this kind. Bach used imaginative combinations of instruments in his *Brandenburg* concertos, completed in 1721.

The French opera composer Jean-Philippe Rameau wrote many books about harmony and was an important innovator in handling the orchestra. He was one of the first composers to use clarinets in the orchestra. He also used bassoons and horns regularly.

The Classical Orchestra

The classical orchestra, in all its essentials, was the basis of the modern orchestra. It developed in the late 1700's, during the so-called classical period in music. The symphony became the most important form of orchestral composition. The strings were firmly fixed as the basic orchestral group. But following the example of Rameau and others, composers began using more woodwinds.

The development of the classical orchestra owed much to the work of Johann Stamitz.

Stamitz was famous for the orchestra he trained and conducted at the Mannheim court in Germany. This orchestra was celebrated throughout Europe for its amazing virtuosity.

Turkish bands traveling in Europe introduced several new percussion instruments. These included the bass drum, triangle, cymbals, and others of this family.

The greatest composers in the development of the symphony were Joseph Haydn, Wolfgang Amadeus Mozart, and Ludwig van Beethoven. Haydn wrote for an orchestra of no more than 25 players. Mozart's orchestra was sometimes larger, and Beethoven's orchestra was larger still. Beethoven's symphonies, particularly the glorious Ninth Symphony (1822–24), are some of the most beloved works in all of classical music.

The Orchestra in the 1800's

The generation of composers following Beethoven sought further variety of tones in their writing. The greater demands made by

A handwritten orchestral score by Hector Berlioz. Each instrumental section is indicated on a score, and the conductor must direct the musicians accordingly.

their music developed the players' techniques. The modern orchestra conductor began to appear toward the end of the 1700's.

The men who established the modern style of conducting were also composers. The most famous were Carl Maria von Weber, Ludwig Spohr, Felix Mendelssohn, Hector Berlioz, and Richard Wagner. The conducting techniques of Berlioz and Wagner had great influence on the development of the orchestra. Berlioz created in his music a new world of orchestral sound by highlighting the various unique sounds of the instruments.

Richard Wagner, Anton Bruckner, Richard Strauss, Claude Debussy, and many Russian composers continued to enlarge the orchestra. Gustav Mahler wrote huge symphonies calling for great numbers of usual and unusual instruments. This trend continued into the 1900's.

As the role of the conductor became more prominent, many musicians began to specialize in conducting as a career. Louis Spohr is believed to have introduced the baton at a concert in London in 1820—the first sign of the growing importance of the conductor.

While many musicians can be credited with the increased status of the conductor, it was Felix Mendelssohn who is known to have brought great seriousness and importance to the role. History remembers him as a composer, but he was a passionate conductor. He was known for his facial expressions and intense eye contact with his musicians.

The Orchestra As an Institution

The 1800's saw the growth of orchestras as independent, self-governing organizations. Many of today's famous European orchestras were outgrowths of court orchestras. Others were formed by combining various small theater and opera orchestras. For example, the Berlin Philharmonic, which is considered one of the world's greatest orchestras, grew out of the Royal Opera and theater orchestras. Many orchestras are now professional, with musicians creating music as their full-time occupation, a governing board, administrative staff, and hundreds of concerts and activities each season.

Orchestras Today

Superb orchestras exist all around the world. In Europe, the most famous include the Vienna Philharmonic Orchestra, the Berlin Philharmonic Orchestra, the London Symphony Orchestra, and the Czech Philharmonic Orchestra. There are also world-class orchestras throughout Asia, in places such as Japan, China, South Korea, and Taiwan.

Today the Philadelphia Orchestra, the Chicago Symphony, the New York Philharmonic, and the Boston Symphony are considered among the great American orchestras. However, hundreds of professional and amateur orchestras exist across the United States.

Many orchestras offer concerts for families and schoolchildren. Not only are they enjoyable and informative, but they also begin a process of understanding and appreciation of classical music.

EUGENE ORMANDY
Conductor Laureate, The Philadelphia Orchestra
Reviewed by GARY ALAN WOOD
Director of Education and Community Partnerships
The Philadelphia Orchestra

See also BANDS AND BAND MUSIC; MUSICAL INSTRUMENTS; ORCHESTRA CONDUCTING.

ORCHESTRA CONDUCTING

People constantly ask, "Why are conductors necessary? Aren't orchestras, after all, groups of highly trained musicians? Why do they need someone to beat time for them? And what's so glamorous about beating time? Can't anybody do it?"

Conducting as we know it today is actually only about 200 years old. Before that, a member of the orchestra, the so-called violin conductor, started and stopped the orchestra and kept the flow of the music going. This was fine as long as orchestras were small. But around the time of Ludwig van Beethoven, orchestras began getting larger and larger. It soon became apparent that someone was needed to keep the players together.

The first real conductor in our sense of the word was the composer Felix Mendelssohn. He founded a tradition of conducting based on the idea of precision, as symbolized in the wooden stick we call the baton. But there soon arrived a great dissenter named Richard Wagner, another composer, who declared that everything Mendelssohn was doing was wrong. He said that conductors should color the music they conduct with their own emotions and their own creative impulses. And so, out of the clash of these two points of view, the modern conductor was born. Both attitudes are necessary, and neither one is completely satisfactory without the other.

The ideal modern conductor should have a combination of the two attitudes, but this combination is rarely achieved. Almost any musician can be a conductor, even a pretty good one. But only a rare musician can be a great conductor. A conductor's "instrument" is 100 individual musicians, who must play with a single will. A conductor must have great authority in dealing with this large group—and this is just the beginning. Now let us find out what the functions of the ideal conductor really are.

▶ BEATING TIME

Let us start with the mechanics. And let us pretend that you are the conductor. The very first mechanical thing you must master is the beat. Beating time is easy. Anyone can do it. All you have to know is that music exists in time and that time is divided into measures, or bars. Each measure is further divided into equal subdivisions, called beats, which go at a certain rate of speed. The main thing is to know how to beat one, two, three, or four beats per bar.

But as a conductor, you must beat at a certain rate of speed—in what is called a tempo. According to Wagner, finding the true tempo is the most important part of conducting. But what is the true tempo? If you listen to six different conductors interpret the same piece of music, you are likely to hear six different tempos. The main thing is that whatever tempo you take, you must keep it steady. This is not as easy as it sounds.

Sometimes you may wish not to keep a steady beat but to have a free flow instead of a mechanical one. Musicians call this *rubato*. The Italian word *rubato* means "robbed." You steal a little time by shortening one beat or

measure and give it back by lengthening another. In so doing, you can create a kind of liberty, or free play, among the beats.

▶ STUDYING THE SCORE

After all that, you are still at the beginning of the conductor's job. Now you are faced with the prospect of a sea of knowledge that must be yours—and so deeply yours that it is automatic. This knowledge begins with being able to read the score.

An orchestral score is highly complicated. A singer has to learn only one line of music, one note at a time. A pianist has to learn many more notes at a time. But a conductor has to learn, and know thoroughly, an astonishing number of notes and parts all at once. Take the opening page of Johannes Brahms's First Symphony, for instance. There are 55 notes in the first bar alone, being played by 100 instruments. As a conductor, you must know them all. And this is only one bar out of 1,260 in this symphony.

What do you do when faced with a score like this for the first time? You should begin by reading it through more or less quickly, somewhat like racing through a detective story. You are filled with suspense and the desire to discover how it will all turn out. And you hear the score in your head as you look at it. People are amazed to discover that conductors can do this.

In this first reading, you must form your own opinion of how the work fits into music history. Here an entirely different kind of knowledge comes into play—a knowledge of

Brahms's period, the goals he set for himself in his work, and the atmosphere of his life and of his country. It also includes a knowledge of the influence of other composers and artists on him. In other words, a conductor must be not only a musician but also a kind of music historian.

After you have examined the score of Brahms's First Symphony swiftly, from cover to cover, the real work begins. You must take it apart and study all aspects of it. You must find the melody and distinguish it from the instrumental parts that are of secondary importance only. This is the other function that Wagner declared to be especially required of a conductor—the ability to find the melody in a mass of notes.

Finding the Right Tempo and Dynamics

Now you must decide how fast this all goes. The tempo mark by Brahms is *un poco sostenuto*. This is Italian for "a little sustained." But can you measure a rate of speed by these words? You cannot. There is such a thing as a metronome—a mechanical instrument that clicks off any tempo you want, at the rate of so many beats per minute. But Brahms did not give us a metronome marking, or number, and neither did many other composers. So we are stuck with three Italian words—*un poco sostenuto*. Well, at least we know it must be sustained and therefore not fast. But why, then, didn't he just say "slow"? What Brahms is getting at is a kind of steady tread that must be solemn and ominous and yet not so slow as to hurt the flow of the music. All this considered, it is up to the conductor to find the true tempo.

Now, perhaps, you are ready to conduct page 1 of the Brahms First Symphony. No—wait. You still have not considered the letter *f* that appears at the beginning of each part. The *f* stands for *forte*, Italian for "loud." Even here you are faced with a decision—how loud? If Brahms had wanted it very loud, he would have written two *f*'s or three. But he wrote only one *f*—just plain loud. And then there are those little words *legato*, "connected" or "smoothly"; *espressivo*, "expressively"; *pesante*, "heavy on the bass notes."

Balancing the Orchestra

Are you at last ready to conduct this page? I am afraid not, for now we come to the

Leonard Bernstein (1918–90), famous orchestra conductor—and author of this article—is pictured at left. The pictures show his skillful use of gesture and facial expression to communicate with the orchestra.

Bernstein, born in Lawrence, Massachusetts, was the first American-born music director (1958–69) of the New York Philharmonic. An impassioned conductor and a prolific composer, he helped define a generation of American music. His compositions include symphonies, ballets, choral works, and Broadway musicals, including *West Side Story* (1957). He brought classical and popular music to millions through his live and televised concerts.

More profiles of well-known orchestra conductors can be found in this article.

Arthur Fiedler

More information about the following conductors can be found in this encyclopedia:
Louis-Hector Berlioz, Aaron Copland, Franz Liszt, Felix Mendelssohn, Sergei Rachmaninoff, Johann Strauss, Jr., Arturo Toscanini, and Richard Wagner.

Arthur Fiedler (1894–1979), born in Boston, Massachusetts, was one of America's most beloved conductors and a true ambassador of classical music. His concerts were well known for their splendor and creativity. Fiedler was given his first piano lessons by his mother, a gifted musician. For nearly 50 years, beginning in 1930, he was music director of the Boston Pops, a unique orchestra that performed both light classical and popular music. Boston Pops recordings sold over 50 million copies during his lifetime.

Herbert von Karajan (1908–89), born in Salzburg, Austria, studied at the city's Mozartteum Conservatory and the Vienna Academy of Music and Performing Arts. In 1929 he became chief conductor at the Stadttheater in Ulm, Germany, and made his debut there. He made his debut at the Vienna State Opera in 1937 and at the Berlin State Opera in 1938. In 1955, he became music director for the world-renowned Berlin Philharmonic, while also serving as the music director of the Vienna State Opera and the Salzburg Festival. He made over 800 recordings and was one of the first conductors to record concerts on video.

Herbert von Karajan

Otto Klemperer (1885–1973), born in Breslau, Germany, was widely regarded as one of the greatest conductors of the 1900's. He is remembered for his recordings of music by German composers, of which he often led serious and grand performances. Klemperer first studied music in Frankfurt. His tall stature made him a dominating figure on the conductor's podium, and his interpretations of classical music were influential. He made many recordings, full of imagination and energy, and conducted orchestras worldwide.

Sir Neville Marriner (1924–) was born in Lincoln, England. He studied at the Royal College of Music in London and at the Paris Conservatory and began his career as a violinist. In 1959, while playing as a principal violinist in the London

problem of balancing the orchestra. The conductor must realize that for the music to have real balance, the horns are going to have to start playing in a slightly reduced version of that one *f—forte*. Then the horns can increase their volume to match the rest of the orchestra. This is only one of the many fine points that are the conductor's responsibility, since Brahms indicated nothing in the score about varying the volume.

Naturally, the ability to balance an orchestra depends also on the conductor's knowledge of the instruments—their capacities, weaknesses, and tone colors. You must know what shades of sound you want (that is, the shades you imagine the composer wanted) and then know how to ask the players to produce these sounds. There are thousands of other details, too. The study of a score is endless, and a conductor is always a student.

So, in a way, you will never be completely ready to conduct page 1 of the Brahms First Symphony. But let us assume that you are reasonably ready now. You still have 165 more pages to go, and they are even more complex. When you have gone through all these matters of balance, dynamics, tempo, expression, style, concept, and cultural background, you are then ready to conduct a good routine performance of the Brahms First.

▶ **QUALITIES OF THE GREAT CONDUCTOR**

The qualities that distinguish great conductors lie far beyond what we have spoken of. We now begin to deal with the mystery of relationships—conductor and orchestra bound together by the tiny but powerful split second. It is difficult to describe the magic of the moment before beginning a piece of music. There is only one possible fraction of a second that feels exactly right for starting. There is a wait while the orchestra readies itself. You concentrate your whole will and force on the work at hand. The audience quiets down, and the last cough has died away. The instruments are poised and—bang! That's it. One second later it is too late, and the magic has vanished.

This psychological timing is constantly in play. If you are a great conductor, you have great sensitivity to the flow of time. You make one note move to the next in exactly the right way and at the right instant. The conductor is a kind of sculptor, whose medium is time instead of marble. To sculpt it, you must have a superior sense of proportion and relationship.

These are the intangibles of conducting—the mysteries that no conductor can learn or acquire. If you have a natural faculty for deep perception, it will increase and deepen as you mature. If you have not, you will always remain just a pretty good conductor.

Symphony Orchestra, Marriner founded the Academy of St. Martin-in-the-Fields, a chamber orchestra. He served as the orchestra's musical director and also as conductor, leading concert tours and making many recordings. Marriner was also guest conductor at a number of orchestras around the world. He was made a Commander of the Order of the British Empire in 1979 and was knighted in 1985.

Eugene Ormandy (Eugene Ormandy Blau) (1899–1985), born in Budapest, Hungary, conducted the Philadelphia Orchestra for more than forty years (1938–80). Trained as a violinist, he immigrated to the United States in 1921 and became a U.S. citizen in 1927. He led the Minneapolis Symphony (1931–36), then moved to Philadelphia where he served as associate conductor (1936–38) under the great Leopold Stokowski, whom he succeeded as music director and principal conductor in 1938. Ormandy remains one of the most recognized names in the history of symphony orchestra recording.

Sir Georg Solti   Leopold Stokowski

Sir Georg Solti (1912–97) was born in Budapest, Hungary. His early years were spent at the piano, and he began his conducting career in his 20's. In the 1960's he became music director of the Royal Opera in London, England, and is credited for turning this orchestra into one of the most respected in the world. As music director of the Chicago Symphony from 1969 to 1991, Solti led unforgettable performances and worked with some of the world's greatest musicians.

Leopold Stokowski (1882–1977), born in London, England, is considered one of the greatest conductors of all time. He started his musical career as an organist. Known for his flamboyant conducting style, Stokowski gained a following in the United States and Europe. After conducting the Cincinnati Symphony (1909–11), he began his tenure with the Philadelphia Orchestra, developing it into one of the world's greatest orchestras from 1912 to 1936. He is popularly known as conductor for Walt Disney's animated film *Fantasia* (1940).

Bruno Walter (1876–1962), born in Berlin, Germany, is considered one of the leading conductors of the first half of the 20th century. Walter's early studies were in piano, and he turned to conducting in 1891. His career flourished, and he made appearances in Vienna, London, and Rome. After settling in the United States in 1939, he conducted orchestras across the country, including the Chicago Symphony, the Los Angeles Philharmonic, the NBC Symphony Orchestra, and the New York Philharmonic.

▶ **COMMUNICATION WITH THE ORCHESTRA**

Even if you are only a pretty good conductor, you must have one more characteristic in your personality. Without it, all the mechanics and knowledge and perception are useless. This characteristic is the power to communicate all your knowledge and perception to your orchestra—through your arms, face, eyes, and fingers. Baton or no baton, your gestures—your tiniest movement—must always be meaningful in terms of the music.

Communication with the orchestra requires a technique that is physical. As you know, certain emotions produce physical reflexes. If you are pleased, certain muscles around the mouth move involuntarily, and you smile. It is the same in conducting. The feelings called forth by the music cause certain muscular reactions. And these reactions—given back to the orchestra through conducting—can call forth those feelings in the players. Of course, there must also be some discussion at a rehearsal to explain things that gestures alone cannot.

The chief element in the conductor's technique of communication is the preparation. Everything must be shown to the orchestra before it happens. Once the player is playing the note, it is too late. So, as the conductor, you must always be at least a beat or two ahead of the orchestra. And you must hear two things at the same time—what the players are doing at any moment and what they are about to do a moment later. Therefore, the basic trick is the preparatory upbeat. If you are back again on page 1 of the Brahms First, you must show in your silent upbeat the character of the music that is about to sound. The players are able to respond as you wish only if you give them such clues.

But you must do more than make your musicians play. You must make them want to play. You must exalt them, lift them—through cajoling or demanding or raging. However you do it, you must make the orchestra love the music as you love it. Only then will 100 people share your feelings and respond as one.

Well, there is our ideal conductor—one who is humble before the composer and who never comes between the music and the audience. All the conductor's efforts should be made in the service of the composer's meaning—the music itself. The music, after all, is the whole reason for the conductor's existence.

LEONARD BERNSTEIN
Former Conductor Laureate
New York Philharmonic Orchestra

Reviewed by GARY ALAN WOOD
The Philadelphia Orchestra

OREGON

No one knows what the name "Oregon" means or how it originated, but it has been used for hundreds of years. It was first spelled the modern way in 1778 by Jonathan Carver, a British fur trader in the Great Lakes region. He wrote of a great river Oregon, far to the west, spoken of by Native Americans. In 1792, the American trader Robert Gray sailed along the Pacific Coast to the mouth of this river. He named it after his ship, the Columbia. *But the lands around the river were still called the Oregon country.*

Oregon is officially nicknamed the Beaver State, for the animal whose valuable pelt drew fur traders to the region in the 1800's. Unofficially, Oregon is sometimes called the Webfoot State. The state gets so much rain, it is claimed, that people must paddle about like web-footed ducks. In fact, western and southern areas do receive heavy rainfall, but eastern Oregon is quite dry. Oregon has great variety—ocean beaches, mountains, fertile farmlands, lush forests, sagebrush plains.

Oregon is part of the area generally known as the Pacific Northwest. The state's population is growing rapidly. Many people have moved to Oregon to work in its expanding industries, especially in high-technology fields. Others, drawn by the state's natural beauty, have come to retire. Most of Oregon's people live in the Willamette River valley, in the western part of the state. That is where the major industries and the largest cities—Portland, Eugene, and Salem—are located. Southern Oregon has farming and retirement communities. Many people in central and eastern areas are farmers and ranchers or work in the tourist industry.

Oregon's citizens pride themselves on their colorful history. The fur traders of the early 1800's were followed by missionaries and pioneers. In the 1840's and 1850's, thousands of families journeyed west on the Oregon Trail to farm in the Willamette Valley. In the early 1900's, the state became famous for the Oregon System, a set of political reforms that allowed citizens to take part more directly in government. More recently, Oregon has sought to balance economic growth with preservation of the environment, leading the way in measures to protect air and water quality.

State flag

▶ **LAND**

The towering peaks of the Cascade Range are Oregon's most notable feature. Fertile valleys and more mountains lie between the Cascades and the Pacific Ocean. About two-thirds of Oregon is east of the Cascades. Most of the eastern region lies within the Columbia Plateau.

Oregon's coast runs less than 300 miles (480 kilometers) north to south. But with all its bays, inlets, and islands, the shoreline measures 1,410 miles (2,270 kilometers). Along the coast are rain forests, sand dunes, and dramatic headlands of basalt, a hard rock that resists erosion.

Land Regions

Oregon can be divided into six distinct land regions.

The Coast Range is a narrow strip of mountains that runs parallel to most of Oregon's coastline. The range begins near Coos Bay and extends northward. Scattered mountains called monadnocks rise from a rough, forested plateau. Marys Peak, near Corvallis, is the highest monadnock—4,097 feet (1,249 meters).

The Klamath Mountains. To the south of the Coast Range lie the rugged Klamath Mountains. Sometimes called the Siskiyous, these

Opposite page, clockwise from left: **Windsurfers race through the Columbia River Gorge. The Pacific Ocean breaks against the cliffs at Cape Kiwanda. Snowcapped Mount Hood, Oregon's tallest peak, towers over the Hood River valley.**

State flower:
Oregon grape

State tree:
Douglas fir

FACTS AND FIGURES

Location: Northwestern United States; bordered on the north by Washington, on the east by Idaho, on the south by Nevada and California, and on the west by the Pacific Ocean.

Area: 97,132 sq mi (251,571 km²); rank, 10th.

Population: 3,421,399 (2000 census); rank, 28th.

Elevation: *Highest*—11,239 ft (3,426 m), at Mount Hood; *lowest*—sea level, along the Pacific Ocean.

Capital: Salem.

Statehood: February 14, 1859; 33rd state.

State Motto: *She Flies with Her Own Wings.*

State Song: "Oregon, My Oregon."

Nickname: Beaver State.

Abbreviations: OR; Oreg.

State bird:
Western meadowlark

mountains vary in elevation from about 2,000 feet (610 meters) near the coast to more than 7,000 feet (2,130 meters) inland.

The Willamette Valley. The Willamette Valley is a lush, fertile region sandwiched between the Coast and Cascade ranges. The Willamette River follows a winding course through the valley as it flows northward to the Columbia River. The valley has some of the best farmland in the state.

The Cascade Range. The Cascades are a string of volcanic mountains extending from northern California to Canada. In Oregon, the largest of these towering cones is Mount Hood, east of Portland. Other notable peaks include Mount Jefferson and the Three Sisters. In the north, the Columbia River has cut a scenic gorge through the mountains.

The Columbia Plateau. This area of central and northeastern Oregon extends from the Cascades east to the Wallowa Mountains and the Snake River. The central area, often called the High Desert, is a wide, high, flat upland punctuated by spectacular cliffs, volcanic cinder cones, and ancient lava flows. Much of this area is dry and desolate. Streams and springs in deep canyons are the main sources of water.

Northeastern Oregon is a land of rugged mountains, deep canyons, and deserts. The Blue Mountains include several ranges, among them the Elkhorn and Greenhorn

Wildflowers bloom in the rugged country around Hells Canyon, in northeastern Oregon. The canyon is the deepest gorge in North America.

ranges, that reach elevations of over 9,000 feet (2,740 meters). In the Wallowa Mountains, 17 jagged granite peaks reach that height. Hells Canyon, through which the Snake River flows, is up to 7,900 feet (2,400 meters) deep, the deepest gorge in North America.

The Basin and Range Region. Part of the Basin and Range Region, one of the largest physical regions in the western United States, extends into Oregon from the south. This is a harsh, dry land, with hot springs, lava caves, and several mountain ranges.

Rivers, Lakes, and Coastal Waters

The Columbia River is the most important river in the Pacific Northwest. It rises in the Canadian Rockies, flows south through Washington, and turns west to form about three-fourths of the boundary between Oregon and Washington. The river empties into the

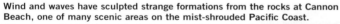

Wind and waves have sculpted strange formations from the rocks at Cannon Beach, one of many scenic areas on the mist-shrouded Pacific Coast.

Pacific near Astoria, and its mouth forms a wide deepwater harbor.

The Columbia and its tributaries drain most of Oregon. Major tributaries include the Willamette, the Deschutes, and the John Day rivers. The Snake River, the largest tributary of the Columbia, forms much of the boundary with Idaho. Eastern Oregon is drained by tributaries of the Snake—the Powder, the Malheur, the Owyhee, and others. The largest rivers of southwestern Oregon are the Umpqua and the Rogue, which flow into the Pacific Ocean.

The south central and southeastern parts of Oregon have little exterior drainage. In these areas, water collects in shallow, brackish (partly salty) lakes called playa lakes. Some of the largest are Harney Lake, Summer Lake, and Lake Abert.

Upper Klamath Lake, in southern Oregon, is the largest natural freshwater lake. Crater Lake, high in the Cascades, is the deepest lake in the United States. It lies in the bowl, or caldera, of an enormous volcano that blew apart in prehistoric times.

Many large artificial lakes have been created behind dams along the major rivers, especially along the Columbia.

Tall basalt cliffs line the Columbia River from The Dalles to Troutdale. They form one of Oregon's great scenic attractions—the Columbia River Gorge.

Climate

Oregon has a varied climate. West of the Cascades, moist Pacific air keeps tempera-

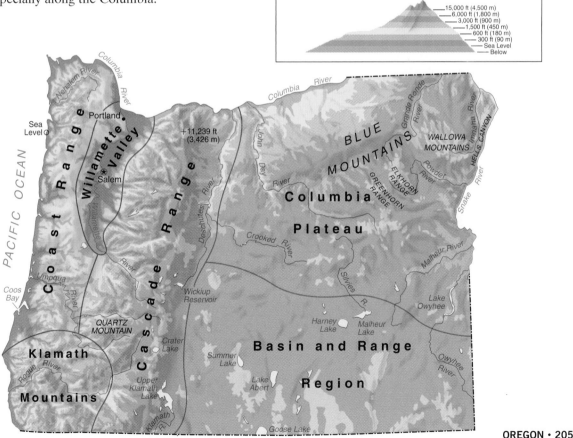

Above: Pioneer Courthouse Square is the heart of Portland. With its mild climate, Portland is among the most pleasant U.S. cities. *Right:* A bronco rider competes at the annual Tygh Valley All-Indian Rodeo, near Pendleton in the northeastern part of the state.

most of the state and 74°F (23°C) along the eastern border.

Oregon's growing season averages about 250 days along the coast, 200 days in inland western valleys, and 100 to 200 days east of the Cascades.

Plant and Animal Life

Oregon has larger stands of virgin timber than any other state. Forests cover large areas in the mountain and coastal areas. The western slopes of the Cascade, Klamath, and Coast ranges are heavily forested with Douglas fir, the most valuable commercial tree. East of the Cascades there are great stands of ponderosa and lodgepole pine. Other softwoods include hemlock, spruce, and cedar. Among the hardwoods are alder, maple, and oak. Ferns, mosses, and rhododendrons thrive in moist western regions. Sagebrush and juniper grow in central and eastern Oregon.

The Columbia has long been known as one of the world's great salmon rivers. Chinook and coho, or silver, salmon make up most of

tures moderate and winters rainy. East of the Cascade Range, however, winters are cold, and summers are generally quite hot and dry.

Annual rainfall ranges from 8 inches (200 millimeters) in the eastern plateau regions to more than 130 millimeters along the crest of the Coast Range. Snowfall is heaviest in the Cascades, ranging from 300 to 550 inches (760 to 1,400 centimeters) yearly. January temperatures average 29°F (-2°C) east of the Cascades, 36°F (2°C) in the inland western valleys, and about 45°F (7°C) along the coast. July temperatures average 65°F (18°C) in

the commercial catch. Sturgeon, smelt, bass, shad, and several varieties of trout also are found in the state.

Large animals include mule deer, black-tailed deer, elk, antelope, black bears, bobcats, and coyotes. Cougars are found in the east. Gophers, beavers, raccoons, lizards, and rattlesnakes are among the many smaller animals that inhabit Oregon.

Natural Resources

Oregon's natural resources include fertile soils, minerals, and an abundant water supply.

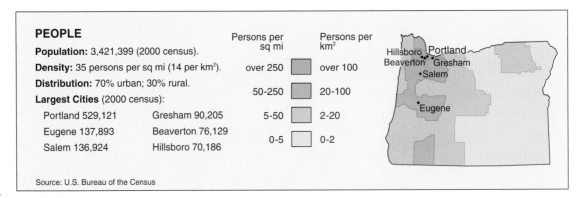

PEOPLE

Population: 3,421,399 (2000 census).

Density: 35 persons per sq mi (14 per km²).

Distribution: 70% urban; 30% rural.

Largest Cities (2000 census):

		Persons per sq mi		Persons per km²
Portland 529,121	Gresham 90,205	over 250		over 100
Eugene 137,893	Beaverton 76,129	50-250		20-100
Salem 136,924	Hillsboro 70,186	5-50		2-20
		0-5		0-2

Source: U.S. Bureau of the Census

Right: Hatfield Library at Willamette University in Salem. *Inset:* An Oregon State University botany student works on plant specimens.

Oregon has a range of soil types. The most fertile are the soils of the Willamette Valley, which developed from alluvial materials (materials left by flowing water). Elsewhere, more than half the total area of the state is range and pasture.

Many of Oregon's mineral resources have yet to be developed. The southwestern part of the state has extensive reserves of nickel, chromite, coal, quartz, and silica sand. The Cascades contain deposits of pumice and perlite. Bauxite, iron ores, shale, limestone, and silica sand are found in the northwest. The northeast has large reserves of marble, while gold, silver, copper, zinc, and gemstones are found in various places.

Most of Oregon has an abundant supply of pure, soft water. The Coast Range and the Cascade Range serve as huge watersheds for hundreds of mountain streams and rivers. The Pacific Northwest produces a large amount of hydroelectric power. Oregon's largest dams—McNary, John Day, The Dalles, and Bonneville—are on the Columbia River.

In recent times Oregon has led in conserving natural resources and protecting the environment. Statewide land-use planning and pollution-control laws have been adopted.

▶ **PEOPLE**

About 70 percent of Oregonians live in urban areas—cities, suburbs, and towns. The most populous areas are Portland and its surrounding towns and the cities of the middle Willamette Valley. About 87 percent of the population is white, mostly of European ancestry. About 3 percent is Asian American. African Americans and Native Americans together make up about 3 percent. Native American groups include the Burns-Paiute, Klamath, and Coquille tribes and the confederated tribes of Grand Ronde, Warm Springs, and Umatilla reservations. Hispanic Americans, a cultural rather than a racial group, make up about 8 percent of the total.

Education

The state's first public school opened in Oregon City in 1843. It was for primary grades only, and pupils were required to pay a small yearly tuition. Free public elementary schools began after 1854, and free public high schools after 1901.

The Oregon State System of Higher Education was organized in 1932. The six universities in the system are Eastern Oregon State University in La Grande, Oregon State University in Corvallis, the University of Oregon in Eugene, Portland State University in Portland, Southern Oregon State University in Ashland, and Western Oregon State University in Monmouth. The Oregon Health Sciences University is in Portland. The Oregon Institute of Technology is in Klamath Falls. The Division of Continuing Education has branches in several cities. The Oregon Board of Education oversees 13 community (two-year) colleges.

Private universities and colleges include Pacific University in Forest Grove, George Fox University in Newberg, Northwest Christian College in Eugene, the University of Portland in Portland, Willamette University

Manufacturing: Lumber and wood products; processed foods; paper and related products; scientific instruments; nonelectrical machinery; computers and computer components; electrical equipment; transportation equipment; fabricated metal products; primary metals; products of printing and publishing; stone, clay, and glass products; chemicals and related products.

Agriculture: Cattle and calves, wheat, milk, hay, greenhouse and nursery products, hazelnuts, berries, cherries, plums, pears, apples, mint, green peas, potatoes, onions.

Minerals: Stone, sand and gravel, lime, diatomite, nickel, pumice, talc, soapstone, clays, gemstones, gold, silver.

Services: Wholesale and retail trade; finance, insurance, and real estate; business, social, and personal services; transportation, communication, and utilities; government.

*Gross state product is the total value of goods and services produced in a year.

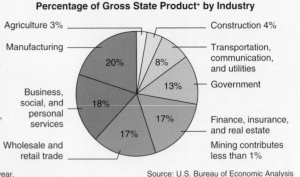

Percentage of Gross State Product* by Industry

Agriculture 3%
Construction 4%
Manufacturing — 20%
Transportation, communication, and utilities 8%
Government 13%
Business, social, and personal services 18%
Finance, insurance, and real estate 17%
Wholesale and retail trade 17%
Mining contributes less than 1%

Source: U.S. Bureau of Economic Analysis

and Western Baptist College in Salem, and Linfield College in McMinnville. Lewis and Clark College, Multnomah School of the Bible, and Reed College are all in Portland.

Libraries, Museums, and the Arts

There are more than 180 free public libraries in the cities and towns of Oregon, and about half the counties have county libraries. The oldest library is the State Library in Salem, which developed from the Territorial Library established in 1848. The Oregon Historical Society in Portland maintains a collection of rare books, pictures, and other items pertaining to the history of Oregon and the region. Other historical collections are maintained by Oregon State University in Corvallis, the University of Oregon in Eugene, and various local historical societies.

The Oregon Museum of Science and Industry in Portland has a planetarium and scientific and industrial exhibits. The major art museums in the state are the Portland Art Museum in Portland and the University of Oregon Museum of Art in Eugene. The Salem Art Association in Salem maintains an art museum and historic Bush House.

Portland is the center for many of the state's performing arts institutions—the Oregon Symphony Association, the Oregon Ballet Theater, and the Portland Opera, Repertory Theater, and Youth Philharmonic. The Oregon Shakespeare Festival performs plays in Ashland.

▶ ECONOMY

In Oregon's early days, the people made their living fishing, trapping, farming, logging, and mining. These occupations are still followed. But today, service and manufacturing industries are the leading employers.

Services

Tourism is the most important service industry in Oregon, making up the third largest sector of the state's economy. The 1980's and 1990's brought growth in advertising, data processing, and many other services as well. Banking, real estate, and retail, wholesale, and import-export trade are also important. Government employment has shrunk since Oregon set limits on property taxes in the 1990's.

Manufacturing

Manufacturing is concentrated mainly west of the Cascades, especially in and around

Portland and other Willamette Valley cities. Oregon long has led in the manufacture of lumber, wood products, paper, and related goods. But other kinds of manufacturing have grown, especially in high-technology fields. Today, factories turn out computer components and other electronic equipment, precision instruments, transportation equipment, machinery, chemicals, and bricks and tiles.

Processed foods, mostly from Oregon's farms and orchards, rank second in value to products of Oregon's forests. Millions of cases of fruit and vegetables are canned or quick-frozen each year, especially in Salem and other cities in the Willamette Valley. Portland is the chief meat-packing center. Fish and shellfish are processed in Astoria.

Agriculture

Oregon's farms produce an amazing variety of products. East of the Cascades, many large farms and ranches grow wheat and raise beef cattle. West of the Cascades, farms tend to be small, and agriculture is specialized.

Pears, peaches, and apples are grown in the southwest. The greatest variety of crops is found in the Willamette Valley, where fruits, vegetables, nuts, and many specialty crops are grown. Portland is the center of a huge greenhouse and nursery industry. Yamhill County is noted for vineyards.

Sheep, poultry, and horses are raised in several parts of the state. The northern coastal area is known for dairy farms.

Mining and Construction

Oregon's most important minerals are those used in the construction industries—stone, sand and gravel, cement, lime, and clays. All the counties quarry stone, and nearly all produce sand and gravel. Clays for brick and tile come from northern parts of the state and from Klamath County.

The major metallic mineral is nickel, mined from open pits near Riddle. Other minerals include pumice, gemstones, gold, and silver. Major oil companies are exploring for petroleum and natural gas.

The state's increasing population has meant growth for the construction industry. Construction projects include new houses, industrial and commercial buildings, and resorts and hotels.

Transportation and Communication

Oregon's rugged Cascade Range long stood as a barrier to transportation. But the valley of the Columbia River provides a nat-

Opposite page: Loggers fell a tree in the Willamette National Forest, and an inspector with the U.S. Forest Service examines tree growth. *Above:* Flowers, such as these tulips, are an important Oregon crop. *Right:* At Portland's busy port, grain is loaded onto a ship for export.

Places of Interest

Crater Lake

Multnomah Falls

Fort Clatsop National Memorial

John Day Fossil Beds National Monument

The Astor Column is a 125-foot (38-meter) monument in Astoria. Made of reinforced concrete, it is covered with carvings in a spiral frieze, or band, that tell the story of the exploration of the Columbia River and the founding of Astoria. A climb up its 166 steps rewards visitors with a spectacular view.

Crater Lake National Park is located high in the Cascades, northwest of Klamath Falls. It contains famous Crater Lake, the deepest lake in the United States with a depth of nearly 2,000 feet (600 meters). Because of its depth, the water appears incredibly blue. The park covers more than 250 square miles (650 square kilometers) of forested land. It abounds in wildlife and wildflowers.

Fort Clatsop National Memorial, near Astoria, preserves the site of the winter encampment of the Lewis and Clark expedition, which reached the Pacific Coast in November 1805. Members of the expedition named the fort for a friendly Indian tribe and wintered there before beginning the return trip the fol-

lowing year. The memorial includes a replica of the fort.

High Desert Museum, near Bend, has displays and re-enactments of early Native American and pioneer life. Trails provide glimpses of native plants and animals.

John Day Fossil Beds National Monument, west of Canyon City, contains fossil beds estimated to be up to 60 million years old. The fossil beds were discovered in 1862. They were named for John Day, a pioneer hunter.

Kam Wah Chung & Company, in John Day, offers a fascinating look into the mining towns of the 1800's and the lives of the many Chinese who lived in them. Built in 1866 as a trading post, the compound served as the office of a Chinese herb doctor, a store, an assay office (for analyzing ores), a Taoist shrine, and a social center.

Malheur National Wildlife Refuge covers 180,850 acres (72,340 hectares) south of Burns. Several hundred different species of birds have been sighted

in this preserve, including trumpeter swans and eagles. The refuge was founded in 1908 by Theodore Roosevelt.

Mount Hood is the site of one of 13 national forests in the state. It is known for skiing, mountain climbing, pack trips, and other sports. Timberline Lodge, a year-round resort on the mountain, was built by local artisans in the 1930's. It is a national historic landmark.

Multnomah Falls, west of Bonneville, descends in a series of cascades and plunges over a cliff beside the Columbia River Highway. The total height of the falls is 850 feet (259 meters).

Oregon Caves National Monument includes a series of spectacular caverns in Elijah Mountain, in the southwest. Water has carved the limestone into formations of great variety and beauty.

State Areas. The state maintains more than 200 recreational areas. For information, contact the Tourism Division, Economic Development Department, 775 Summer Street, NE, Salem, Oregon 97310.

ural water and land route through the Cascades. The Columbia and its tributaries form an excellent inland waterway system. Oceangoing ships navigate the Columbia and the Willamette rivers to Portland. St. Helens and Astoria are other important river ports. Smaller vessels travel on the Columbia River into Washington. Barges ply the Columbia and the Snake rivers as far inland as Lewiston, Idaho.

An extensive network of highways links all parts of the state. Interstate 5 is the major north-south route, running from California through the Willamette Valley and on to Washington. Interstate 80N runs east from Portland along the Columbia River.

Portland International Airport is the chief center for national and international air traffic. Several major railroads serve the state, using more than 3,000 miles (4,800 kilometers) of track.

The Oregon Spectator, published in Oregon City in 1846, was the first newspaper west of the Rocky Mountains. Today approximately 135 newspapers are published in Oregon. More than 20 of them are dailies. The *Portland Oregonian* has the largest circulation. There are more than 100 radio stations and about a dozen television stations, including a state-owned educational radio and television system.

▶ CITIES

Oregon's chief centers of population are on the Willamette River. The three largest are the Portland, Eugene-Springfield, and Salem metropolitan areas.

A narrow band of park land stretches for 20 blocks along the Willamette River in Portland. It is one of more than 160 parks in the city.

Salem, the state capital, is in the center of the Willamette Valley. It was founded by the Methodist missionary Jason Lee in 1840. Salem became the capital of the Oregon Territory in 1851 and the state capital in 1859. The modern capitol building, completed in 1939, is noted for its murals depicting historic events of Oregon. State government is Salem's largest employer.

Portland, Oregon's largest city, is located near the junction of the Willamette and Columbia rivers. See the article PORTLAND in Volume P.

Eugene, near the source of the Willamette River, is Oregon's second largest city. It is a major sawmilling, plywood, and pulp center. The city was laid out in 1852 and incorporated ten years later. It was named for Eugene F. Skinner, one of its founders.

▶ GOVERNMENT

Oregon is governed under a constitution drawn up in 1857 and amendments adopted since that time. The state legislature, the Legislative Assembly, is composed of a senate and a house of representatives. The executive branch of gov-

Eugene, home of the University of Oregon, is a city of trees. Trails for running, hiking, and biking run through the town.

INDEX TO OREGON MAP

ernment administers state agencies and enforces state laws. It is headed by the governor and other elected officials.

The highest court is the state supreme court, with seven justices. Other courts are the court of appeals, tax court, and district and circuit courts.

The legislature has the authority to make laws, but the voters of the state also may take a direct part in lawmaking. They are able to do so through processes known as the initiative and the referendum, which were adopted by an amendment to the Oregon state constitution in 1902. The initiative gives voters the right to propose laws to the legislature or to submit laws to popular vote without first proposing them to the legislature. The referendum gives voters the right to approve or disapprove laws that the legislature has proposed or passed.

Oregon's state capitol building, in Salem, was completed in 1939. It contains murals that depict the history of the state.

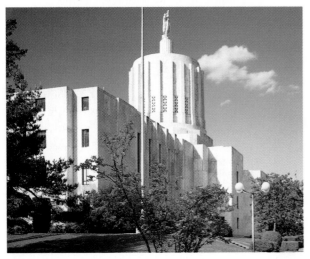

In 1904 Oregon became the first state to use direct primary elections. In a direct primary the candidates of each party are chosen by the voters instead of by conventions. In 1908 Oregon's constitution was amended to provide for another process, known as recall. Through recall a public official may be removed from office by a vote of the people.

All these features of government have come to be known as the Oregon System. Use of the initiative, referendum, and recall did not begin in Oregon, but the Oregon System furnished a model that has been fol-

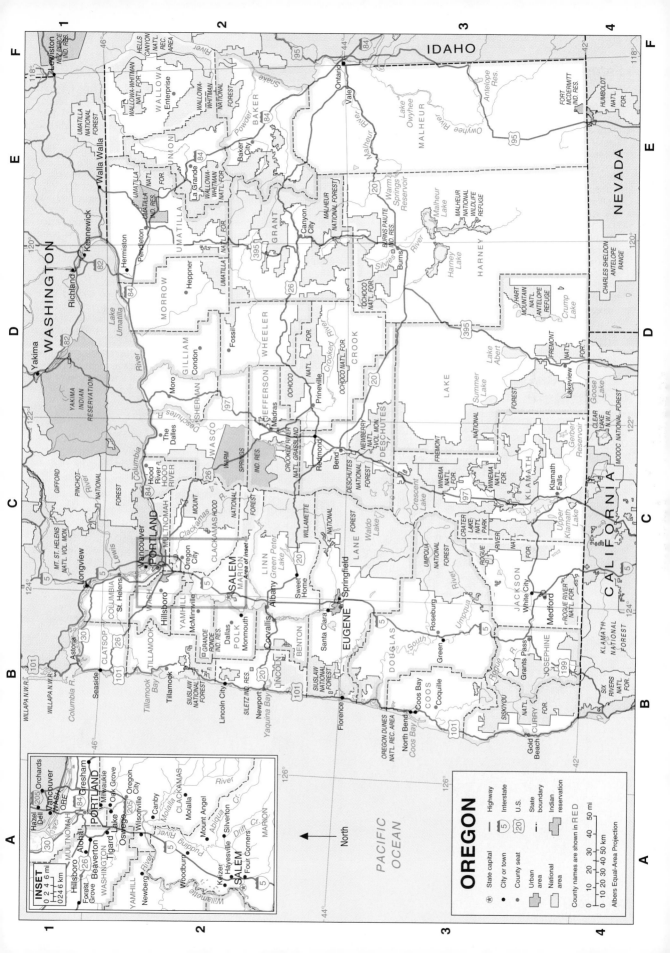

Famous People

Consult the Index to find more information in *The New Book of Knowledge* about the following people who were born in Oregon or are otherwise associated with the state: fur merchant John Jacob Astor (1763–1848), children's book author Beverly Cleary (1916–   ), Nez Percé leader Chief Joseph (1840–1904), and chemist Linus Pauling (1901–94).

Simon Benson (1851–1942), a Norwegian immigrant, was one of the Northwest's most successful lumbermen. He donated large amounts of money earmarked for improvements in Oregon. To preserve the natural beauty of Multnomah Falls and Wakeena Falls, Benson purchased land around the falls and donated it to the state. He also funded the installation of 20 public drinking fountains in Portland, including one with a low bowl for dogs.

Abigail Scott Duniway

Beatrice Cannady (1880–1974) was active in journalism and civil rights. She was Oregon's first African American lawyer, founded chapters of the National Association for the Advancement of Colored People, and worked for school desegregation. As assistant editor of the *Advocate*, a black-owned newspaper, Cannady often wrote on issues of racial justice and equality.

James DePreist (1936–   ), born in Philadelphia, Pennsylvania, became music director and conductor of the Oregon Symphony in 1980, one of the first African Americans to direct a symphony orchestra. He has been a guest conductor of leading orchestras in the United States and abroad and has made numerous recordings. He is also a poet.

Abigail Scott Duniway (1834–1915), born in Tazewell County, Illinois, came over the Oregon Trail in 1852. She became a leader in the woman suffrage movement. Duniway owned the *New Northwest*, a Portland newspaper that advocated women's rights. When Oregon granted women the right to vote in 1912, she was the first to cast a ballot.

Jason Lee (1803–45), missionary and pioneer, was born in Quebec, Canada, near the Vermont border. He preached in that area until 1834, when he went west to establish an Indian mission in the Willamette Valley near present-day Salem. When the pioneers began to arrive, Lee devoted much of his time to the new settlements. He helped form Oregon's provisional government in 1843. He also helped to establish Oregon Institute (later Willamette University) in 1842.

Ursula K. Le Guin (1929–   ), born in Berkeley, California, moved to Portland in 1959. A well-known writer of science fiction, she is the author of more

lowed by other states. The leader of the movement that resulted in this system was William U'Ren, who was elected to the Legislative Assembly in the late 1800's.

▶ HISTORY

Sometime between 12,000 and 15,000 years ago, ancestors of the American Indians crossed from Siberia to the Pacific Northwest. They were the first people in the land we know as Oregon. In southeastern Oregon, archaeologists have found artifacts, including sagebrush sandals, more than 9,000 years old. But we know little of these ancient people.

White explorers did not glimpse the Oregon coast until 1542. By that time, Native

An 1878 engraving depicts pioneers traveling the Oregon Trail. Beginning in the 1840's, "Oregon fever" sent thousands of families west by wagon train.

than 30 books for adults and young people, among them the *Earthsea Trilogy* and *The Farthest Shore*.

Edwin Markham (1852–1940), poet and lecturer, was born in Oregon City. His mother was Elizabeth Winchell Markham, one of the earliest woman writers in the Oregon country. He is best known for the poems "The Man with the Hoe" and "Lincoln, Man of the People." In 1923 Markham was named poet laureate of Oregon.

Thomas Lawson McCall (1913–83), born in Prineville, was governor of Oregon from 1967 to 1975. A former journalist, he sponsored anti-pollution laws and other environmental legislation.

John McLoughlin (1784–1857), known as the Father of Oregon, was born in Canada. In 1824 he became the chief agent of the Hudson's Bay Company in the Oregon country. From his

John Reed

Minoru Yasui

base at Fort Vancouver in present-day Washington, McLoughlin monopolized the fur trade for his company. By helping missionaries and pioneers, he opened the way to the settlement of the Oregon country. Farms, gristmills, and sawmills that he started were the beginnings of agriculture and the lumber industry. The house he built in Oregon City is a national historic site.

John Silas Reed (1887–1920), born into a leading Portland family, was a journalist and political radical. He rode with Pancho Villa to cover the Mexican civil war. A socialist, he was jailed several times for supporting labor strikes. Reed was in Russia when the Bolsheviks seized power in 1917, and he wrote an eyewitness account, *Ten Days that Shook the World*. Returning to the United States, he founded the Communist Labor Party. Reed was charged with sedition (trying to overthrow the government) and fled to Russia, where he died.

Minoru Yasui (1916–86), born in Hood River, was an attorney known for his work on behalf of Japanese American civil rights. He worked to redress the wrongs done to Japanese Americans forced to relocate to camps in World War II. The first Japanese American admitted to the Oregon bar association, he helped pave the way for passage of the federal Civil Liberties Act of 1988.

Americans in the region had a rich and varied culture. There were four main cultural groups. One group lived on the coast and the lower Columbia River. The ocean and the river provided food, as well as a means of communication and trade. Another group, living on the Columbia Plateau, obtained food by hunting, fishing, and gathering. These groups met and traded goods at places along the river. The other groups lived in the south central area and in the Basin and Range region. They depended on hunting, gathering, and fishing in their rugged homelands.

Discovery and Exploration

The first known visitors to the Pacific Northwest coast were the Spanish. Bartolomé Ferrelo sailed north along the coast in 1542–43 and probably saw Oregon's southwestern shore. The English explorer Francis Drake may have reached the coast in 1579. A Spanish expedition may have reached the mouth of the Umpqua River in 1603. Many of the early explorers were searching for the Northwest Passage, a fabled route between Europe and Asia. None landed on the Oregon shore.

In the 1770's Spain sent expeditions. One of these was led by Bruno Heceta, who sighted and mapped the mouth of the Columbia River. But Great Britain and the United States established the most important claims to the area. Captain James Cook passed along the coast in 1778. Ten years later another Englishman, John Meares, entered the wide mouth of the present Columbia River. When he found that it was not the Northwest Passage, he named it Deception Bay. He named the cape on the north Cape Disappointment.

In 1788, Robert Gray—an American sea captain, fur trader, and explorer—became the first American to land in Oregon, at Tillamook Bay. He returned in 1792 and became the first white person to cross the bar of the Columbia River. Later that year Lieutenant William R. Broughton explored the river. He was a member of a British expedition under Captain George Vancouver.

Americans again reached Oregon in 1805, this time from across the land. Meriwether Lewis, William Clark, and members of their expedition reached the Pacific Coast in November of that year and wintered at Fort Clatsop. They carried home news of the land and its people. Soon fur trappers and traders invaded the wilderness.

The Fur Trade

In 1811, John Jacob Astor's Pacific Fur Company established Fort Astoria as a trading post at the mouth of the Columbia River. But when the War of 1812 broke out, Astor's partners feared the fort would be seized by the British. To prevent the loss, they sold it to a British fur company based in Canada. Later the site of the fort was returned to the United States. In 1818 the United States and Great Britain agreed to occupy the Oregon country together. In the early 1820's, John McLoughlin, chief agent of the Hudson's Bay Company in Oregon, became, in effect, the ruler of the area.

Early Settlement

Missionaries contributed greatly to the settlement of Oregon. Jason Lee, the first to arrive, established a mission in the Willamette Valley in 1834. Many more missionaries followed, and with them came the first trickle of American settlers, especially to the Willamette Valley. Word of opportunities in Oregon spread rapidly. By about 1840, "Oregon fever" was sweeping the Mississippi Valley, and settlers were heading west in covered wagons. The most famous of the wagon trains made the journey in 1843, with about 1,000 men, women, and children. Their safe arrival proved that wagons could carry families and provisions all the way to the Columbia River.

Serious trouble with the Indians developed as pioneers pushed into southern Oregon and the ranchlands east of the mountains. By the 1850's, the number of Indians was decreasing. Many died of diseases brought by white settlers. Conflict continued until the late 1870's, when the Nez Percé were forced out of the Wallowa Valley. Their resistance, led by Chief Joseph, marked the last major Indian conflict in the Northwest.

Provisional Government to Statehood

Settlers in the Willamette Valley were eager to have Oregon become a territory. They sent several petitions to Congress. Until 1846 the petitions were ignored because the northern boundary had not been established. In that year the United States and Great Britain agreed that the 49th parallel of latitude would be the border between their lands in the Northwest. But creation of the territory was delayed by the issue of slavery—

Southern legislators opposed the creation of a new nonslave territory. Finally, in 1848, Congress created the territory of Oregon. The area to the north of the Columbia River became the territory of Washington in 1853. Oregon City was the capital of Oregon Territory until 1851.

A movement for statehood began almost as soon as the territory was organized. A state constitution was approved in 1857. Two years later, on February 14, 1859, President James Buchanan signed the statehood bill.

Development

After gold was discovered in California in 1848, thousands of people rushed to the West. Later, gold strikes throughout the Rocky Mountains brought more people. The growing population created a market for Oregon's products. Steamboats carried goods and people on the Columbia and the Willamette rivers, and many roads were built. By the 1880's Oregon was linked to the transcontinental railroad systems, which helped the state's agriculture and trade expand.

In the 1930's Bonneville Dam was built on the Columbia River. This dam and other dams and reservoirs supplied needed hydroelectric power, flood control, and water for irrigation. During World War II large shipbuilding, chemical, and metal-processing plants were established in Oregon.

Since the 1940's, the state has seen the expansion of high-technology industries. But its growing population and industry have threatened the natural environment. Beginning in the 1960's, Oregon passed pioneering environmental protection laws. In the 1990's, the state received national attention for an experimental program to control the cost of providing health care to the poor.

The Future

Oregon has a diversified economy, based on a combination of agriculture, industry, and tourism. Its agreeable climate is attractive to new residents. Oregonians are experiencing the benefits and the problems of growth. Their concern for the environment is helping to preserve the state's natural beauty.

GORDON B. DODDS
CATHLEEN CROGHAN ALZNER
Portland State University

OREGON TRAIL. See OVERLAND TRAILS.

ORES

Ores are rocks and minerals from which useful metals can be mined profitably. Many rocks and minerals contain tiny amounts of valuable metals, but only those containing enough metal to yield a profit when sold are called ores.

Various factors determine whether mining an ore will be worthwhile. These include the value of the metal in the ore, the size of the ore deposit, and the type of mine needed to reach the ore. Even factors such as climate, transportation, and environmental concerns influence whether an ore will be mined.

Before any ore can be mined, it must be found. Ore minerals are found scattered throughout rock, in layers, called **beds**, or in thin strands, called **veins**. Although most ores are found underground, rocks on the surface may contain ores, too. Sometimes bits of metal in the ore are worn away by erosion and deposited into streambeds. These are called **placer deposits**. The miners in the American West who panned for gold were trying to separate gold grains from sand and gravel in placer deposits.

The most important deposit of the bright red mineral cinnabar, which provides the world's supply of mercury, is found in Almadén, Spain.

Most metals found in ores are combined chemically with other substances, such as carbon, oxygen, or sulfur. These are called **compound ores**. For example, lead commonly is combined with sulfur in lead ores.

Metals are usually obtained from more than just one ore. Iron is obtained from ores known as hematite, magnetite, and limonite. Nickel ores include pentlandite and pyrrhotite.

▶ TYPES OF ORES

Sometimes a valuable metal is found in an almost pure state. This is called a **native ore**. Native ores are rare but usually are easy to recognize. You may be lucky and find flakes of native gold in gold-bearing quartz.

Gold (shown in crystal form, *left*) and copper (shown in copper ore, *right*) were the first metals that ancient civilizations learned to use.

▶ PROCESSING AND USING ORES

Metals must be extracted from ores to have any value. Some metals can be removed by simply crushing the ore and separating out the un-

Glowing with heat, molten iron streams from the blast furnace. In the furnace, high temperatures were used to free the iron from ore.

wanted rock, which is called **gangue**. Smelting involves melting the ore to free the metals. Pig iron, a material used to make steel, is obtained by smelting iron ore in a blast furnace.

Flotation involves putting crushed ore in a special liquid and forcing air through the mixture. The air bubbles carry metal particles to the surface where they are collected. Leaching uses strong liquids to dissolve the metal in an ore. In electrolysis, an electric current is passed through melted, purified ore to extract the metal.

Reviewed by JEFF STEINER
Earth Sciences
City University of New York

See also EARTH; EARTH, HISTORY OF; GEOLOGY; IRON AND STEEL; METALS AND METALLURGY; MINERALS; ROCKS.

ORGAN

The organ is a musical instrument played with a keyboard. The **pipe organ** is the largest and most complex of all musical instruments. A wind instrument, it produces sound when air is blown through pipes of varying sizes. Often called the king of instruments, the pipe organ can produce an almost unlimited number of different sounds. It is the oldest key-

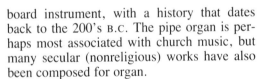

Above: The console of an organ contains the keyboards, foot pedals, and stop controls with which the organ is played. *Right:* An organ may have hundreds or even thousands of pipes, arranged in ranks, or rows.

board instrument, with a history that dates back to the 200's B.C. The pipe organ is perhaps most associated with church music, but many secular (nonreligious) works have also been composed for organ.

Another kind of organ, the **electronic organ**, was invented in the 1900's. The electronic organ is not a wind instrument. It produces sound by means of electronic devices called oscillators, which create variations in an electric current to produce different tones. (You can read more about electronic instruments in the article ELECTRONIC MUSIC in Volume E.) Small electronic organs cannot produce the variety of sounds that pipe organs can, but they are well suited for home use and are also frequently used in popular music. Larger electronic organs capable of producing a wide range of sounds are often found in churches and concert halls.

▶**CONSTRUCTION OF PIPE ORGANS**

The pipe organ consists of three main sections: the pipes themselves; the **console**, which contains the keyboards, pedals, and stop controls with which the organ is played; and the **action**, a system linking the pipes to the console and to a wind supply.

Organ pipes may vary in length from several inches to more than 30 feet (9 meters). There are two basic types of pipes: the **flue** pipe, which works like a tin whistle, and the **reed** pipe, which has a thin metal tongue, or reed, at its base. The type of pipe, as well as its size and shape, determines what kind of sound it produces. The pipes are arranged in **ranks**, or rows. All the pipes in a given rank have the same tone quality.

Most organs have two to four keyboards; some have as many as seven. Each keyboard controls one or more ranks of pipes. In addition to hand keyboards, called **manuals**, an organ usually has a foot keyboard, a set of wooden pedals played with the feet. The main manual is called the great organ; other manuals include the swell organ and the choir organ. The foot keyboard is called the pedal organ. Near the manuals are knobs called **stops**. The stops move **sliders**, thin strips that can open or close entire ranks of pipes. By pulling the stops, the organist determines which ranks of pipes will be used.

The ranks of pipes are set on a box called the **wind chest**. Air is pushed into the wind chest, usually by an electric blower. When the organist presses a key, valves in the wind chest open to let the air into certain pipes, and sound is produced.

▶ **HISTORY**

The organ probably developed from the ancient panpipes, a row of small pipes tied together and played like a harmonica. The first instrument to resemble the modern organ was the **hydraulus**, or water organ, invented by the Greeks about 250 B.C. It consisted of one or more rows of pipes played by a system of keylike levers. The air was forced into the pipes through the use of water power. The hydraulus was used by the ancient Romans at feasts and gladiator contests.

By the A.D. 300's, organs were made and used in the Eastern Roman (Byzantine) Empire. These organs were the first to pump air with a bellows. Organs were first played in Christian churches in the 700's and 800's. Because these organs did not have stops, all the pipes of a certain note sounded when the key belonging to that note was pressed down. Later, stops were added so that individual pipes or ranks of pipes could be used. By the 1200's, organs had keyboards that looked and worked like those of today. The pedal keyboard was added a century later.

By the 1600's the organ had become very much as it is today. Many experts believe that the finest organs were built in the 1600's and 1700's. These organs are as beautiful to look at as they are to listen to. Two famous German organ builders of this period were Arp Schnitger and Gottfried Silberman. The type of organ they built remained the ideal for many years.

The 1600's and 1700's also were a golden age of organ music. The two greatest composers of the age—Johann Sebastian Bach and George Frederick Handel—were also great organists. The organ compositions of Bach, in particular, remain unsurpassed. Organ music decreased in importance after 1750, although notable organ compositions were written by Felix Mendelssohn, Franz Liszt, and Johannes Brahms.

In the late 1800's many solo stops were added that imitated the sounds of the orchestra. In fact, the organs built at this time often

The 1600's and 1700's were a golden age of organ music. One of the greatest composers of the period, Johann Sebastian Bach, was also a master organist. He composed many outstanding works for the instrument.

were not equipped to play the older organ music properly. Organs were made larger than ever before, with as many as one hundred stops. The wind pressure was increased. Different types of action were invented, using wind, electricity, or a combination of both.

The development of electrical power also made possible the invention of electronic organs, which were first sold in the United States in 1935. In addition, the 1900's have seen a revival of older music. As a result of this interest, modern organ builders have worked to develop organs capable of producing the sounds of masterpieces of organ music from the age of Bach and Handel.

BARBARA J. OWEN
Organ Historical Society
Reviewed by MARGARET R. TUCKER
Minister of Music
First Congregational Church, Houston

ORGANIZATION FOR ECONOMIC COOPERATION AND DEVELOPMENT (OECD)

The Organization for Economic Cooperation and Development (OECD) is an international organization whose members meet to discuss domestic and international policies. Often referred to as a "rich man's club," the OECD is made up of the world's most prosperous nations, which together produce two-thirds of the world's goods and services. It currently has 30 member countries. Headquarters are located in Paris, France.

The OECD's stated mission is to help build strong economies, improve efficiency in market systems, and expand free trade. To further that mission, the organization collects what may be the world's largest and most reliable sources of data on a wide range of subjects relating to governmental policies—economics, trade, social policy, the environment, agriculture, science and technology, and energy. For example, the OECD collected information on how much money European Union (EU) countries spend for farm subsidies (public funds given to support agricultural output)—information that later helped the EU negotiate lower payments to farmers.

The OECD was established after World War II (1939–45) as the Organization for European Economic Cooperation. It was created to administer the financial aid that was given by Americans and Canadians under the Marshall Plan for the reconstruction of war-torn Europe. It acquired its current name in 1961 and has since expanded its membership beyond North America and western Europe to include Asian and eastern European countries. To pay for its activities, the OECD operates on a budget of about $200 million a year, which is funded by its members. Contributions are based on a formula related to the size of each member's economy. The largest contributor is the United States, which provides 25 percent of the budget, followed by Japan and Germany.

Unlike many international organizations, the OECD has no formal requirements for membership other than being committed to democratic institutions and free-market (capitalist) economic systems. Member countries decide which other countries may be invited to join the OECD and on what conditions.

MEMBER STATES OF THE OECD

Australia	Korea, South
Austria	Luxembourg
Belgium	Mexico
Canada	Netherlands
Czech Republic	New Zealand
Denmark	Norway
Finland	Poland
France	Portugal
Germany	Slovakia
Greece	Spain
Hungary	Sweden
Iceland	Switzerland
Ireland	Turkey
Italy	United Kingdom
Japan	United States

The OECD occasionally produces binding (legal) agreements, such as codes for the free flow of capital. It is also known for "soft law"—unofficial agreements that offer guidelines for addressing such controversial issues as standards of behavior for the leaders of multinational corporations. Nonmembers are invited to join OECD agreements and treaties. Unlike the International Monetary Fund (IMF) and the World Bank (formally known as the International Bank for Reconstruction and Development), however, the OECD does not dispense or loan money.

In the early 1990's, the OECD began reaching out to emerging market economies. It provided assistance to the many countries that were formed when the Soviet Union broke apart in 1991. Such help was needed especially as these former Communist nations made the transition from centrally planned (state-run) economies to capitalist free-market systems. More recently the OECD has expanded its statistical data to include 70 nonmember countries, including such large economies as Brazil, China, and Russia, as well as less-developed countries in Africa, South America, and Asia.

The OECD's outreach effort has grown along with the globalization of the world's economy. Globalization—characterized by free trade and the free flow of capital—is a controversial issue. Economically, it tends to favor rich nations. On the other hand, globalization has benefited less-developed countries by making it easier for them to sell their goods and services throughout the world, especially in wealthy OECD markets. But it has also threatened their ability to maintain independent cultures and economic policies.

MARY H. COOPER
"The CQ Researcher,"
Congressional Quarterly

ORGANIZATION OF AFRICAN UNITY (OAU)

The Organization of African Unity (OAU) was an association of nearly all the countries of Africa. Its purpose was to unite the peoples of Africa so that they might work toward common goals of freedom, justice, equality, and economic development.

The OAU was founded in Addis Ababa, Ethiopia, in 1963. It could not force the member countries to follow its policies but worked to achieve its goals through diplomatic and other means. The OAU helped African countries win their independence, but it was against moves to redraw national boundaries. It encouraged the building of communication and transportation networks to link all parts of the continent and sought to create an all-Africa defense force and an African declaration of human rights. In general, it contributed to the continent's stability.

The OAU was governed by three bodies. The Assembly of Heads of State and Government set the OAU's policies. It met once a year in the country of the head of state who had been chosen presiding officer for that year. The Council of Ministers met twice a year to discuss the budget and prepare the list of topics for discussion by the Assembly. The General Secretariat, headed by an elected secretary-general, carried out the decisions of the Assembly. The OAU was replaced by the African Union in 2002.

> MARGARET A. NOVICKI
> African-American Institute

See also AFRICAN UNION.

MEMBER STATES OF THE OAU	
Algeria	Libya
Angola	Madagascar
Benin	Malawi
Botswana	Mali
Burkina Faso	Mauritania
Burundi	Mauritius
Cameroon	Mozambique
Cape Verde	Namibia
Central African Republic	Niger
Chad	Nigeria
Comoros	Rwanda
Congo	São Tomé and Príncipe
Democratic Republic of Congo	Senegal
Djibouti	Seychelles
Egypt	Sierra Leone
Equatorial Guinea	Somalia
Eritrea	South Africa
Ethiopia	Sudan
Gabon	Swaziland
Gambia, The	Tanzania
Ghana	Togo
Guinea	Tunisia
Guinea-Bissau	Uganda
Ivory Coast (Côte d'Ivoire)	Western Sahara*
Kenya	Zambia
Lesotho	Zimbabwe
Liberia	

*Not recognized as a sovereign state and claimed by Morocco.

ORGANIZATION OF AMERICAN STATES (OAS)

The Organization of American States (OAS) is the oldest international regional organization. In 1890 the International Union of American Republics was formed. It adopted an official charter and its present name in 1948.

The main goals of the OAS are to promote peace, security, mutual understanding, and cooperation in the Americas. The member countries have pledged to defend one another against outside attacks. OAS members may also bring their own disputes to the OAS for settlement. In addition, the OAS helps its members with loans for economic projects, which are made through the Inter-American Development Bank, founded by OAS members in 1959. The OAS also concerns itself with problems of human rights. The policies of the OAS are determined in annual meetings of the General Assembly, where each member nation has one vote. The day-to-day affairs of the organization are carried out by the General Secretariat in Washington, D.C., which is headed by an elected secretary-general.

> Reviewed by ALEJANDRO ORFILA
> Former Secretary-General
> Organization of American States

MEMBER STATES OF THE OAS	
Antigua and Barbuda	Guyana
Argentina	Haiti
Bahamas	Honduras
Barbados	Jamaica
Belize	Mexico
Bolivia	Nicaragua
Brazil	Panama
Canada	Paraguay
Chile	Peru
Colombia	Saint Kitts and Nevis
Costa Rica	Saint Lucia
Cuba*	Saint Vincent and the
Dominica	Grenadines
Dominican Republic	Suriname
Ecuador	Trinidad and Tobago
El Salvador	United States
Grenada	Uruguay
Guatemala	Venezuela

*Excluded from participation in the OAS since 1962.

ORGANIZATION OF PETROLEUM EXPORTING COUNTRIES (OPEC)

In 1960 the oil-producing countries of Iran, Iraq, Kuwait, Saudi Arabia, and Venezuela created the Organization of Petroleum Exporting Countries (OPEC). Their aim was to work together to ensure they received what they considered a fair price for their oil exports. By 1971, Algeria, Ecuador, Gabon, Indonesia, Libya, Nigeria, Qatar, and the United Arab Emirates had joined the group. Ecuador left OPEC in 1992 and Gabon in 1995.

OPEC countries control nearly 80 percent of the world's proven crude oil reserves and produce about 31 million barrels of oil per day, or 39 percent of world output.

Growth of OPEC. In the 1960's, OPEC had almost no influence on the price it charged oil companies for its oil, because the demand for oil was much lower than the supply. In the early 1970's, however, demand grew rapidly at the same time as oil output in some countries, such as the United States, leveled off. OPEC was thus able to negotiate higher prices for its oil. Between 1970 and 1973, the average cost of OPEC oil rose from $1.80 to $3.01 per barrel. (A 42-gallon barrel is the standard measurement.)

During the 1973 Arab-Israeli war, several Arab countries refused to sell oil to the United States and other nations friendly to Israel. In the world oil crisis that followed, prices rose nearly four times—from about $3 a barrel in 1972 to over $12 a barrel in 1974. From 1974 to 1978, oil prices ranged from just over $12 to $13.55 a barrel. But prices took off again, reaching $35 a barrel in 1981, as output fell in the wake of the Iranian Revolution and Iraq's invasion of Iran in 1980.

OPEC's Oil Wealth. The great increase in oil prices brought tremendous wealth to the OPEC countries. Many put their oil income (often referred to as petrodollars) into their economies, expanding manufacturing and improving agriculture.

Falling Prices. In the 1980's, OPEC's control over world oil prices weakened. Conservation and higher oil production created an oil surplus. OPEC set a target price for oil of $18 a barrel and tried to control supply by establishing quotas, which fixed the amount of oil each member country could produce. But

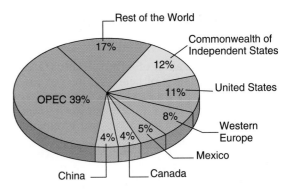

World Petroleum Production

Rest of the World 17%
Commonwealth of Independent States 12%
United States 11%
Western Europe 8%
Mexico 5%
Canada 4%
China 4%
OPEC 39%

Source: Energy Information Administration

OPEC members frequently ignored the quotas, and oil production continued to exceed demand. As a result, prices tumbled, sinking close to $10 per barrel in mid-1986.

New Highs. The price of oil hit an unexpected high of $40 a barrel in 1990, as market turmoil and a fall in output followed Iraq's invasion of Kuwait in August of that year. After the Persian Gulf War (1990–91), which drove Iraq from Kuwait, prices soon stabilized at about $22 per barrel. In the late 1990's the price of oil once again fell to close to $10 a barrel, as Asian demand for oil fell.

Looking for greater price stability, in 2000, OPEC set a target of $22 to $28 a barrel, and prices stayed mostly within that band until 2003. That year, a U.S.-led invasion of Iraq disrupted that country's already low oil exports. The ensuing war and other factors, including a drop in Venezuela's oil output, helped push up oil prices.

The price of oil reached $50 a barrel in 2004, fueled by strong demand and fears of oil shortages. A record high of over $60 a barrel occurred in June 2005, reflecting continued fighting in Iraq and strong demand for oil by the United States and China, the second largest consumer of oil after the United States. OPEC foresees a rise in its production of oil in response to strong increases in demand in the years ahead, particularly from China and India. In those countries a major part of the increase in demand for oil will come from new car owners.

MARY H. COOPER
"The CQ Researcher,"
Congressional Quarterly

See also ENERGY SUPPLY; PERSIAN GULF WAR; PETROLEUM AND PETROLEUM REFINING.

ORGANIZED CRIME

Throughout history, people have formed organized groups for the purpose of committing crime. Those involved in organized crime engage in a variety of illegal activities—up to and including murder—to make money and gain power.

Organized crime groups engage in fraud, robbery, kidnapping, and hijacking. They may run protection rackets (demanding money to protect people from violence, usually by the group itself). They may also provide illegal goods—drugs and stolen guns, for example—and illegal services such as gambling and loansharking (loaning money at excessively high interest rates).

Although organized crime groups generally operate in big cities and metropolitan areas, they affect the day-to-day lives of many, even those who live in rural areas and small towns. According to the FBI, organized crime has a significant impact on labor unions, political institutions, financial markets, and major industries. The profits it generates from its illegal activities (close to $1 trillion per year worldwide) create financial losses that are passed along to the consumer.

▶ ORGANIZED CRIME GROUPS

All organized crime groups share certain characteristics. Organization is hierarchical (divided into ranks), and members have clearly defined duties according to their rank. Those at the top possess the most power and receive the largest share of the profits. Membership is restricted, and violence and the threat of it are used to attain goals.

In the United States and Canada, the best-known and most powerful organized crime group is the **Mafia**, or the "Mob." North American law enforcement officials often label it Traditional Organized Crime. Its members—men of Italian heritage—call their organization *Cosa Nostra*, Italian for "Our Thing."

Like the Mafia, many other organized crime groups are based on ethnicity and originated in immigrant communities. These communities are often home to both the criminals and their victims, who usually share the same language and customs. From Jamaican communities, for example, the Jamaican Posse has emerged. Vietnamese communities have produced the organized crime group known as Born to Kill.

Other groups have emerged from a common environment or situation. Examples of these include motorcycle gangs such as Hell's Angels and Outlaws and prison gangs such as the Aryan Brotherhood. The latter began in California state prisons and now exists throughout the U.S. federal prison system.

Organized crime groups in other countries include the Hong Kong-based Triads; the Japan-based Yakuza; the United Bamboo in Taiwan; the Camorra, the Sicilian Mafia, and N'Drangheta in Italy;

Law enforcement officials pack money seized in a drug bust. The sale of illegal drugs is often linked to organized crime.

Charles "Lucky" Luciano (1897–1962) was considered the father of today's Mafia. First arrested at age 10 (for shoplifting), he later joined the famous Five Points gang. In the 1920's he headed the crime family of Joe "the Boss" Masseria. In the 1930's, after ordering the murder of two older crime bosses, Luciano became New York's organized crime leader. In 1936 he was convicted of heading a prostitution ring and sentenced to 30 to 50 years in prison. During World War II the U.S. Navy sought the imprisoned mobster's help to eliminate possible sabotage by enemy forces on ships using the New York docks. Luciano was released from prison in 1946 and deported to Italy.

Vito Genovese (1897–1969) was born in Italy and came to the United States at age 15. He began as a small-time thief and later took over the Luciano crime family after "Lucky" Luciano was deported to Italy. In 1937 Genovese went to Italy to escape murder charges but was returned to the United States to stand trial. He was released after the prosecution's main witness was murdered. Genovese eventually became one of the most powerful Mafia bosses in the United States. In 1959 he was sentenced to the Atlanta Penitentiary on a federal narcotics charge. He died in the prison hospital.

Alphonse (Al) Capone (1899–1947), born in Brooklyn, N.Y., was the prohibition era's most famous mobster. He was nicknamed Scarface for a razor slash on his face. Capone moved to Chicago and achieved dominance as a crime boss by killing his rivals. In the Saint Valentine's Day Massacre of 1929, Capone's gunmen killed seven members of the "Bugs" Moran gang. Unable to prove him guilty of violent crimes, federal authorities arrested Capone in 1931 on charges of income tax evasion. He was sentenced to eleven years in prison but was released in 1939 with a terminal illness and died several years later in Florida.

Dutch Schultz (1901–35) was born Arthur Flegenheimer on Manhattan's East Side. During prohibition he became known as

Al Capone

the Booze Baron of the Bronx. He was arrested several times for murder, but there was never enough evidence to convict him. After prohibition, Schultz took over illegal gambling operations in Harlem and was labeled Public Enemy Number One in the East. Schultz reportedly wanted to kill prosecutor Thomas E. Dewey (who later became governor of New York). Fearful of the problems this would cause for their organization, Mafia leaders ordered Schultz' death. He was killed in a Newark, New Jersey, restaurant.

Albert Anastasia (1902–57) was born Umberto Anastasio in Italy and came to the United States about 1917. He became a leader of the longshoremen's union and helped solidify Mafia control of the New York docks. Anastasia was known for his violent temper and in his 20's strangled a fellow dockworker. Although sentenced to death, he was allowed a new trial and was freed after several witnesses disappeared. He became known as a short-

---

Police destroy bootleg liquor during prohibition. Most of the liquor was produced and distributed by the Mafia.

Colombian drug cartels; and so-called Russian gangsters from eastern Europe.

▶ HISTORY OF ORGANIZED CRIME

Although organized crime existed in the United States and Canada before the 1920's, it was fairly limited and associated with gambling, prostitution, local politics, and police corruption. During prohibition (1920–33), however, when it was illegal to manufacture, transport, or sell liquor in the United States, organized crime grew tremendously. Despite the government's ban on alcohol, people still wanted liquor. And organized criminals were willing to provide bootleg (illegal) liquor—at a high price. As a result, they profited immensely.

Weeks before prohibition began, armed hoods began stealing stored liquor from warehouses. When this supply was gone, Mafia bosses around the country began making their own, either at existing facilities that had been reopened, new permanent plants, or homemade distilling operations that were small enough to be periodically moved.

The Mafia also operated thousands of speakeasies (illegal bars and nightclubs), which were usually jammed with customers. Because corruption among law-enforcement officials was widespread, many of them accepted bribes to allow the speakeasies to remain open.

tempered gangster responsible for scores of killings in the 1930's, 1940's, and 1950's. Anastasia was shot and killed in New York while receiving a shave in a barber chair.

Carlo Gambino (1902–76) was born in Italy and came to New York at age 21. He worked during prohibition transporting liquor and as a strong-arm man. During the last 20 years of his life he headed New York's most powerful crime family and was supposedly one of the models for the title character of Mario Puzo's book *The Godfather*. After prohibition, Gambino continued selling alcohol, but did not

Carlo Gambino

pay taxes. He was arrested and charged with tax evasion, but the charges were dropped. Gambino died on Long Island.

Meyer Lansky (1902–83) was born in present-day Poland to Jewish parents. He came to the United States in 1911. Lansky combined ruthless instincts and brilliant business tactics to reportedly make a personal fortune of about $300 million. During prohibition he ran bootleg businesses with other mobsters and later established gambling operations in Florida, New Orleans, and Cuba. In 1970 he fled to Israel to avoid prosecution for income tax evasion, but he was arrested and returned to the United States. In 1973 he was acquitted. He died in Florida.

Benjamin "Bugsy" Siegel (1906–47), born in Brooklyn, N.Y., began his life of crime on New York's Lower East Side. His quick temper, or tendency to "go bugs" when angered, earned him the nickname Bugsy. By the 1920's, he and Meyer Lansky had formed a criminal partnership and organized an assassination-for-hire syndicate. Siegel later became involved in Mob activities on the West Coast, including a nationwide bookmaking (betting) service. In the 1940's, Siegel built Las Vegas' first casino, the Flamingo, using Mafia funds. He was shot and killed in Beverly Hills, California, after it failed to make a profit.

Benjamin "Bugsy" Siegel

John Gotti

John Gotti (1940–2002) was a former truck hijacker from New York. He captured public attention after orchestrating the assassination of Paul Castellano, head of the Gambino crime family, in 1985. Following Castellano's death, Gotti took control of the family. During the 1980's he earned the name Teflon Don because authorities were unable to obtain convictions all three times they brought charges against him. In 1992, however, authorities successfully prosecuted Gotti for racketeering and five murders. Gotti served ten years of his sentence, then died in the Springfield, Missouri, prison hospital.

Handling this vast amount of liquor and beer required considerable manpower. So did fighting off other bootleggers. Despite the thousands of prohibition-era killings, Mafia "families" grew in size. The Mafia also grew stronger as contact among its families increased. Bootleg liquor, often exported from Canada, was constantly on the move, and Italian organized crime groups worked together. While they sometimes did business with other ethnic gangs, primarily Jewish and Irish hoodlums, they usually dealt with each other.

Although prohibition-related activities made up much of its business, the Mafia also engaged in labor racketeering schemes. Among other things, members of crime families would gradually gain control of various labor unions and then demand money from employers to prevent workers from going on strike or otherwise disrupting normal business routines. Mafia involvement in these areas raised the cost of many goods and services.

▶ **ORGANIZED CRIME TODAY**

Since the 1980's, federal prosecutors in the United States, working closely with other federal, state, and local police agencies, have severely reduced the Mafia's power and influence. This has been largely due to the effective use by federal prosecutors of the Racketeer-Influenced and Corrupt Organizations (RICO) Act, which imposed harsher penalties for certain crimes (such as gambling and mail fraud) when it could be proved that they were committed as part of a criminal enterprise. Many Mafia bosses have been sent to jail for life, and some smaller Mafia families have been completely eliminated. Many Mafia members have been removed from the larger labor unions. The Mafia still clings to life, however, and poses a greater threat to the economic well being of North Americans than any other organized crime group.

At the same time, emerging ethnic organized crime groups are beginning to gain greater status and influence. In response, both U.S. and Canadian law enforcement officials have begun to establish special squads to focus on these groups and prevent their further expansion.

JERRY CAPECI
John Jay College of Criminal Justice

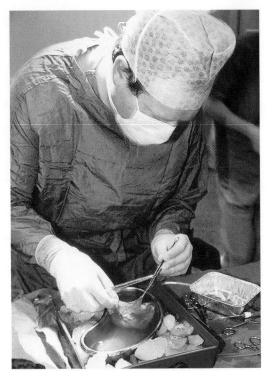

A surgeon prepares a kidney for transplant. Other organs that can be transplanted include the heart, lungs, pancreas, liver, and intestines.

ORGAN TRANSPLANTS

An organ transplant is the process of transferring a usable organ from one person's body to another. These organs are usually taken from people who have died suddenly but have healthy organs, and they are given to people with diseased or damaged organs that need replacing. Transplantable organs include the heart, kidneys, lungs, pancreas, liver, and intestines. Currently, more than 22,000 organ transplants are performed in the United States each year. Body tissues such as corneas, skin, tendons, and bone can also be transplanted.

Many organ transplants are performed to prolong the life of someone who would otherwise die; doctors recommend them only after other treatment options, such as medications, have been unsuccessful. Other kinds of transplants may be performed for different reasons. Corneas, for example, are transplanted to restore a person's sight.

▶ THE TRANSPLANT PROCESS

To receive an organ transplant in the United States, a patient must be evaluated at a transplant center. There, specialists determine whether the patient is sick enough to need the new organ but healthy enough to survive the surgery. Mental and emotional health are also considered; a patient must be able to follow instructions for maintaining the transplanted organ after the surgery.

If these conditions are met, the patient's name and medical information are added to a national waiting list administered by the United Network for Organ Sharing (UNOS), a private nonprofit organization. When a donor organ becomes available from someone who has just died (after doctors certify that the brain has completely stopped functioning), organizations that handle their distribution consult the list for a potential recipient.

Adults who want to donate organs after they die should indicate this on their driver's license, carry an organ donor card, and discuss their wishes with family members and loved ones. People under 18 can donate organs with a parent's or guardian's consent.

Because the demand for organs far exceeds the supply, several factors determine which person on the waiting list should receive the organ. These include geographical location, the size of the organ needed, blood type, length of time on the waiting list, and the person's health status. In some cases, the degree of medical urgency is also considered.

It is also essential to match the donor-recipient tissue as closely as possible. This process is called **tissue typing**. Tissues are matched by comparing certain proteins found on the surface of cells. These proteins are special types of antigens—part of the immune system that helps the body fight against potentially harmful agents such as viruses and cancers. If the donor and recipient do not match closely, the recipient's immune system will perceive the transplanted organ as foreign and can reject it.

For this reason, drugs called immunosuppressants are used to limit the immune system's response to transplanted organs. The goal of immunosuppressive therapy is to block the activity of cells that could destroy a transplanted organ but not of those that the body needs to fight infections. The progress in controlling rejection has allowed the great majority of patients to successfully undergo organ transplantation.

OTHER TRANSPLANT OPTIONS

The shortage of organs from dead bodies, or cadavers, has led doctors and patients to also use living donors. These donors—usually healthy family members or friends—can donate certain organs under certain circumstances. For example, a person may donate a single kidney, since the body has two and only one is needed to survive. Partial liver transplants are possible from a living donor because the liver can regenerate itself.

Another potential transplant option is **xenotransplantation**—the transfer of cells, tissues, or organs from one species to another. Although some applications of this technology have worked, many have not. Animal tissues, such as pig heart valves, have been used successfully in humans since 1971. However, attempts to transplant entire organs (from pigs and other animals) have all eventually failed. Some experts believe that new developments, such as genetically modified pigs, may allow living animal cells and organs to be transplanted in the future. But many questions on this issue still remain.

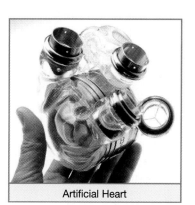

Artificial Heart

A less controversial option is the use of artificial organs. Advances in artificial organ development are most promising with organs that function mechanically, such as the heart and lungs. Devices designed to help the natural heart pump, called ventricular-assist devices, are already being used. Self-contained artificial hearts have been less successful, although scientists continue working to improve them. By 2003, eleven patients had received the AbioCor, the first totally implantable artificial heart. However, all but one died within a few months.

HISTORY OF ORGAN TRANSPLANTS

Research in transplant surgery began during the early 1900's, when French surgeon Alexis Carrel perfected a method for connecting large blood vessels end-to-end. The first recorded attempt to replace a failing human organ was that of Russian surgeon Yu Yu Voronoy in 1933. Although these developments proved that organ transplants were technically possible, the body's rejection of the transplanted organ remained a problem.

Following advances in immunology, methods were developed to suppress the body's immune system so that organs could be successfully transplanted from one person to another. Among these methods were the development of immune suppression drugs in the 1950's by Gertrude Elion and George Hitchings.

The first successful human organ transplant operation took place in 1954. A Harvard University team, led by Joseph Murray, removed a kidney from a healthy man and transplanted it into the donor's identical twin, whose kidneys had failed. The operation was a great success because there was little danger of rejection; the donor-recipient tissue matched exactly because the twins had identical genes. The transplanted kidney began working almost instantly, and both brothers remained healthy. Soon after that, doctors began perfecting the techniques for transplanting skin, hearts, pancreases, livers, and intestines.

FUTURE OF ORGAN TRANSPLANTS

Despite greater public awareness of the need for organ donation, the demand for donor organs will always exceed the supply. Currently, more than 80,000 Americans are on the UNOS waiting list, and many people die while waiting for a donor organ. The only way to address this shortage is to develop artificial organs or use organs from animals. Other future developments may include cell transplantation, which would involve replacing faulty cells with normal cells to cure certain conditions. Currently, the most common procedure of this kind is bone marrow transplantation, which is often used to treat cancers of the bone marrow. It is also possible that tissue created from human stem cells (those that can develop into many other types of cells) may someday be used to grow human organs.

JOHN J. FUNG, M.D.
Thomas Starzl Professor of Surgery
University of Pittsburgh

ORIENTAL EXCLUSION ACTS

Oriental Exclusion Acts were acts approved by the U.S. government that excluded or limited the number of Asians allowed to immigrate to the United States. Large numbers of Chinese first immigrated to the United States in 1848, attracted by the discovery of gold in California. In 1865, thousands more came to help build the transcontinental railroad. After its completion in 1869, there was a surplus of labor. Many American workers considered the Chinese workers a threat because they worked for lower wages. This led to outbreaks of violence. As a result, Congress passed the Chinese Exclusion Act of 1882, which barred all Chinese immigration for ten years.

Japanese immigrants filled the demand for labor, arriving in Hawaii to work on sugar plantations and in the western United States to work on farms. They, too, soon faced hostility from white workers. In 1907, the U.S. government and Japan reached an unwritten understanding, or "gentleman's agreement," wherein Japan agreed to stop workers from emigrating to the United States and the United States agreed to discourage discriminatory immigration laws against the Japanese.

The Immigration Act of 1917 created the Asiatic Barred Zone, restricting immigration from a region including India, Southeast Asia, and the Pacific Islands. Further restrictions on Asian immigration came into effect with the passage of the 1924 Immigration Act. This act established a national origins quota system for immigration that favored northern and western Europeans.

During World War II (1939–45), immigration was permitted for some Asians. In 1943, as a sign of goodwill toward China, an ally, the United States repealed the Chinese Exclusion Act, allowing foreign-born Chinese to be eligible for citizenship rights. In 1946, Asian Indians and Filipinos were also offered citizenship rights.

The Immigration and Nationality Act of 1952 granted citizenship rights to Japanese and Korean immigrants. However, the national origins quotas were still in effect. In 1965, the quota system was removed, and the Asian American population grew tremendously.

JUDY SOO HOO
UCLA Asian American Studies Center

ORIGAMI

Origami is the art of folding paper into decorative objects. The name "origami" comes from the Japanese words *oru* (to fold) and *kami* (paper). All you need is the proper paper and a hard surface to work on. With a few folds, a square piece of paper can be transformed into one of many creative designs.

Traditional origami is always done without cutting or pasting. In creative origami, which is a more recently developed art, scissors and even paste can be used to help form more complicated designs.

▶ **HISTORY**

The Chinese invented paper almost 2,000 years ago, and origami is just as old. Origami may have developed from the ancient custom of making paper houses, furniture, and money as part of Chinese funeral rites, so the deceased could live in earthly comfort in the next life. Colored paper symbols are still burned at Buddhist funerals.

Paper folding was brought to Japan in the A.D. 600's. The Japanese developed many of China's arts and crafts into their own forms of expression. They found new methods of folding paper into pretty forms and images and made origami a highly creative art. From simple folds, the Japanese make things of great beauty and realism. Some are used as religious symbols to decorate shrines and temples.

Others are good-luck symbols, such as the crane, tortoise, and lobster, which are used as ornaments (*Noshi*) fastened to gifts or as festive decorations.

It was Japanese magicians who introduced some of the charms of paper folding to the Western world. The magicians were so expert that with a few quick movements, they could make a bird, animal, or insect to surprise and delight the audience.

▸ **GETTING STARTED**

To get started in origami, you will need paper that is thin and crisp enough to hold the folds and creases well, yet strong enough to give body to the models so they will stand. Use inexpensive paper, such as photocopy paper, to practice with. Once you gain confidence, you may want to use colored paper, which makes more interesting models. Thin Japanese paper, called *washi*, is usually brightly colored on one side and plain on the other. The paper for your model must be a perfect square. Start practicing with one that measures 8 inches (20 centimeters) square.

Find a hard, flat surface on which to work, such as a table or a solid book. Directions and diagrams should be placed so you can easily read them while you fold.

Now you are ready to begin. Here are some tips and suggestions that will help you.

• Start simple. Practice the basic, traditional forms. The more experience you have

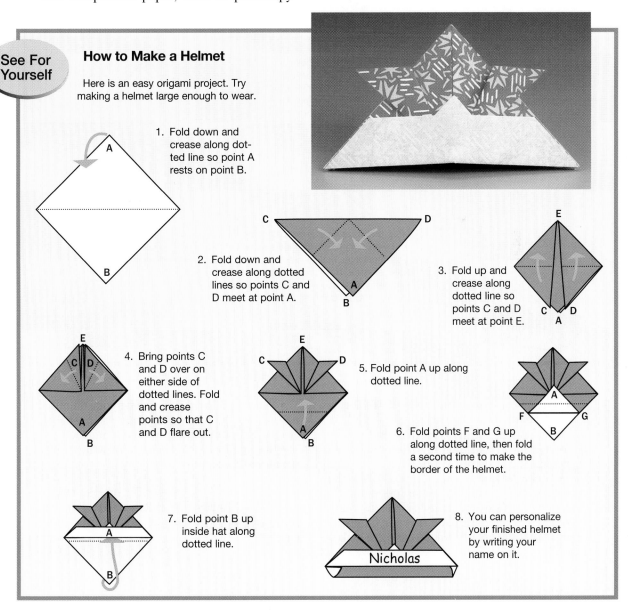

See For Yourself

How to Make a Helmet

Here is an easy origami project. Try making a helmet large enough to wear.

1. Fold down and crease along dotted line so point A rests on point B.

2. Fold down and crease along dotted lines so points C and D meet at point A.

3. Fold up and crease along dotted line so points C and D meet at point E.

4. Bring points C and D over on either side of dotted lines. Fold and crease points so that C and D flare out.

5. Fold point A up along dotted line.

6. Fold points F and G up along dotted line, then fold a second time to make the border of the helmet.

7. Fold point B up inside hat along dotted line.

8. You can personalize your finished helmet by writing your name on it.

Nicholas

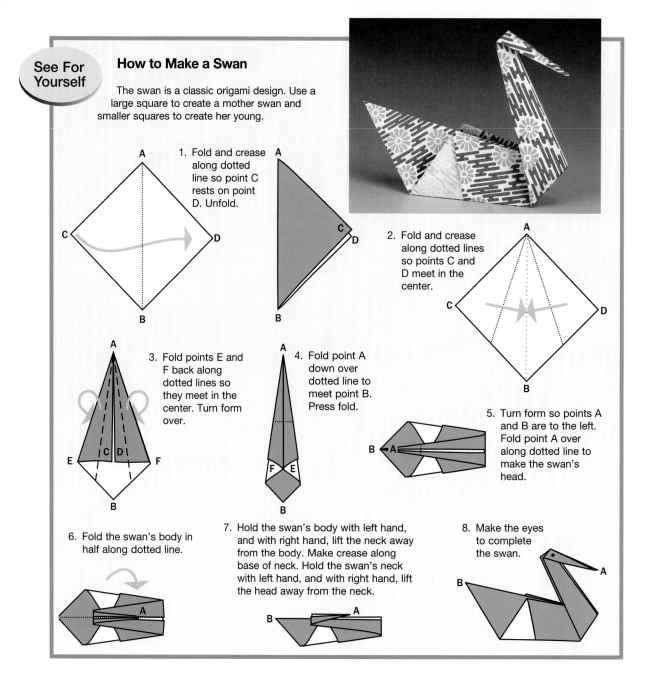

How to Make a Swan

The swan is a classic origami design. Use a large square to create a mother swan and smaller squares to create her young.

1. Fold and crease along dotted line so point C rests on point D. Unfold.

2. Fold and crease along dotted lines so points C and D meet in the center.

3. Fold points E and F back along dotted lines so they meet in the center. Turn form over.

4. Fold point A down over dotted line to meet point B. Press fold.

5. Turn form so points A and B are to the left. Fold point A over along dotted line to make the swan's head.

6. Fold the swan's body in half along dotted line.

7. Hold the swan's body with left hand, and with right hand, lift the neck away from the body. Make crease along base of neck. Hold the swan's neck with left hand, and with right hand, lift the head away from the neck.

8. Make the eyes to complete the swan.

perfecting the basics, the easier it will be to expand upon these designs.

• Be patient. At first you may find the instructions a little difficult to follow, but do not give up.

• Make accurate folds. Correct folds and creases are very important, so follow the directions carefully and do not skip steps. Mark your own paper with the given symbols so your folds and creases will be easier to make.

• Make firm folds. By pressing your thumbnail along the fold, you will get a sharp crease, and this will keep your fold in place.

• Be creative. Make a hat and write your name on it, or draw designs that you can paint or color.

RACHEL CARR
Author, *The Picture Story of Japan*

ORMANDY, EUGENE. See ORCHESTRA CONDUCTING (Profiles).

OROZCO, JOSÉ (1883–1949)

José Orozco was a Mexican artist who painted dramatic murals of mythological and historical subjects. Orozco was part of a movement of Mexican muralists who strove to portray the native culture of Mexico, which they believed had been overlooked during 400 years of European domination.

José Clemente Orozco was born on November 23, 1883, in Zapotlán, Mexico. As a young man, he studied at the Academy of San Carlos, a noted art school in Mexico City, and drew political cartoons in support of the Mexican Revolution of 1910. His paintings, with their strong lines and expressive gestures, reflect this early interest in cartooning.

Orozco's first murals, completed in 1923 on the walls of the National Preparatory School in Mexico City, portray revolutionary themes.

In 1927 he was invited to paint in the United States. His murals there include a huge image of Prometheus, the Greek god of fire, at Pomona College, Claremont, California (1930–31), and a series of paintings depicting the history of the Americas at Dartmouth College, Hanover, New Hampshire (1932–34).

Orozco returned to Mexico in 1934. Between 1936 and 1939, he painted some of his greatest murals, at the Hospicio Cabañas in Guadalajara. He covered the walls of this building with images showing the harsh and cruel lives of the ancient Aztecs and their Spanish conquerors.

Orozco died in Mexico City on September 7, 1949. His works provided inspiration for abstract expressionists in the 1950's and political muralists in the 1960's.

LINDA BANK DOWNS
Director, Davenport (Iowa) Museum of Art

ORTEGA, DANIEL (1945–   )

Daniel José Ortega Saavedra, leader of the Sandinista National Liberation Front (FSLN), was president of Nicaragua from 1985 to 1990. The FSLN, a guerrilla force, had come to power after overthrowing dictator Anastasio Somoza Debayle in 1979.

Ortega was born on November 11, 1945, in La Libertad, Nicaragua. Like his parents, he strongly opposed Somoza's dictatorial rule, and he was only 15 when he was first arrested for political activities. By 1967, Ortega had taken charge of one of the Sandinista guerrilla units, but he was captured that same year by Somoza's National Guard. After being released from prison in 1974, Ortega went to Cuba, where he met Fidel Castro, who had led a successful revolution in 1959. Ortega then returned to Nicaragua to help lead the fight against the Somoza government. When the Sandinista forces defeated Somoza in 1979, Ortega became head of the ruling junta (revolutionary governing committee). In 1984, he was elected president for his left-wing policies. He took office the following year.

Ortega and the Sandinistas faced many problems. The war had ruined the economy, and poverty was widespread. Ortega's administration launched agricultural, social, and educational reforms, including a campaign to increase literacy. But in the late 1980's, the Sandinistas became involved in a war against the contras, a mixed force of landless peasants and supporters of the deposed Somoza who were being helped by the United States. Tens of thousands of people were killed in the fighting. (For more information, see IRAN-CONTRA AFFAIR in Volume I.)

Peace negotiations led to new national elections in 1990. Ortega and the Sandinistas lost to the United Opposition (UNO), a group of 14 political parties led by Violeta Barrios de Chamorro. Ortega again ran for the presidency in 1996 and 2001 but was defeated on both occasions.

MARION MORRISON
Author, *Nicaragua*

Orthodontic treatment results in straight teeth and a healthy "bite" for many teenagers. That is something to smile about!

ORTHODONTICS

A gleaming smile can be a person's most striking feature. But for millions of young people, a smile means a gleam of metal because they are wearing braces to straighten their teeth.

Human teeth are engineered for cutting, tearing, and grinding food. They work best when they are evenly spaced and the upper teeth mesh smoothly with the lower ones. When teeth are crowded or out of line, or when the upper and lower teeth do not fit together properly, the result is a "bad bite," called **malocclusion.** Malocclusion may lead to inefficient chewing. The teeth are also more easily injured and more likely to decay.

An **orthodontist** is a dental specialist who straightens teeth, bringing them into line to form an attractive and effective bite. The tools, or "hardware," used by the orthodontist include a variety of wires and elastics, commonly called **braces.** These are attached to the teeth to make the teeth move in a very slow, controlled way.

▶WHAT CAUSES MALOCCLUSION?

The main cause of bad bites seems to be heredity. In the modern world, marriages between people of very different heritages are common, and the children inherit traits from each parent. If you inherit large teeth from one parent and a small jaw from the other, you may have dental problems: your teeth may be too large to fit comfortably in your jaw and may be crowded and out of line.

If you have missing teeth, the neighboring teeth move into the gap, forcing the whole bite out of line. Malocclusion can also be caused by habits like thumb sucking and tongue thrusting (a forward movement of the tongue during swallowing).

▶DIAGNOSING THE PROBLEM

Usually a family dentist first spots the need for orthodontic treatment. The dentist may find crowded or crooked teeth, a crossbite (when upper teeth fit inside the lower ones instead of fitting over them), or a jaw that protrudes (sticks out) far beyond the other jaw. A protruding upper jaw, producing "buck teeth," is the most common orthodontic problem.

The orthodontist uses a variety of diagnostic tools, including a panoramic X ray that shows all the teeth in the jaws on one film, X rays of the skull, and plaster models of the teeth and jaws. The orthodontist's aim is to bring the teeth into an efficient arrangement and to produce a pleasing appearance of the teeth, jaws, and face.

▶ORTHODONTIC TREATMENTS

Generally, orthodontic treatment starts when the patient is 12 or 13 years old. Teenagers may complain about having to wear braces at a time when they are adjusting to so many other changes and are also concerned about their appearance. But the treatment works best if it is done while the jaws are still growing. Although the majority of braces are worn by teenagers, many adults have orthodontic treatment to correct malocclusions and to improve their appearance.

Most of the work of moving the teeth is done by braces. Braces are brackets attached to the teeth with wires and rubber bands that exert carefully controlled pressure. Sometimes the brackets are fastened to metal bands that clamp around the tooth, but today high-strength adhesives are often used to bond the brackets directly to the tooth.

Teeth are anchored sturdily in the jawbone by their roots, but under the steady pull of the wires and bands, the teeth and roots slide slowly. When the teeth reach their new, straightened positions, the jawbone fills in solidly around the roots, anchoring teeth and roots firmly in place.

While that anchoring is going on, the patient wears a removable **retainer** made of wire and plastic or a **positioner**—a plastic mold into which the teeth fit. If the upper jaw protrudes, the orthodontist may prescribe wearing **headgear** to hold back the upper jaw while the lower jaw grows into line.

The whole process of straightening the teeth takes an average of about two years. In adults, bone does not repair itself as rapidly as in young people, so orthodontic treatment usually takes longer.

People who wear braces need to be especially careful about keeping the teeth clean. Food particles tend to get caught on the brackets and bands and may cause decay if they are not removed promptly. Often people who wear braces have to give up chewing gum and eating some favorite foods, like corn on the cob, that might damage the wires or brackets.

▶ **ORTHODONTICS IN PRACTICE**

Attempts to straighten teeth date back to ancient Greece. But orthodontics did not become a real science until the late 1800's, in the United States. In the 1880's, Dr. J. N. Farrar made the first scientific study of how forces actually move teeth. Another important pioneer was Edward Angle, who developed a classification of kinds of malocclusion, which orthodontists still use.

Today orthodontists are highly trained specialists. In the United States, for example, orthodontists have five to eight years of training in college and dental school. They have two or three more years of specialized study in orthodontics and may have a year of training in a hospital as well.

Research in orthodontics includes a focus on the use of new materials and techniques to make braces more effective, less noticeable, and easier to wear. Developments such as removable appliances made of wire and plastic and braces that are fastened to the backs of teeth are appealing alternatives to the all-metal braces that stay fixed to teeth for years. Researchers are studying the use of tiny electric currents to stimulate the bone and speed up the tooth-moving process.

ALVIN SILVERSTEIN
VIRGINIA SILVERSTEIN
Co-authors, *So You're Getting Braces*

See also DENTISTRY; TEETH.

ORTHODOX CHURCHES. See EASTERN ORTHODOX CHURCHES.

ORTHODONTIC DEVICES

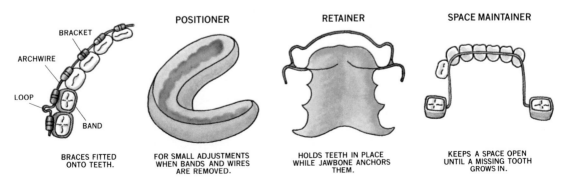

BRACKET
ARCHWIRE
LOOP
BAND

BRACES FITTED ONTO TEETH.

POSITIONER

FOR SMALL ADJUSTMENTS WHEN BANDS AND WIRES ARE REMOVED.

RETAINER

HOLDS TEETH IN PLACE WHILE JAWBONE ANCHORS THEM.

SPACE MAINTAINER

KEEPS A SPACE OPEN UNTIL A MISSING TOOTH GROWS IN.

ORWELL, GEORGE (1903–50)

George Orwell is the pen name of the English writer Eric Arthur Blair. He is best known for his novel *Nineteen Eighty-Four*, a savage portrait of a society of the future in which speech, thought, and behavior are strictly controlled.

Eric Arthur Blair was born in Motihari, Bengal, India, on June 25, 1903. His father was an official in the Indian Civil Service. By the age of 5 or 6, the boy knew he wanted to be a writer. He was sent to St. Cyprian's, a boarding school in England. There he was made to feel inferior because he did not come from a wealthy family.

From 1917 to 1921, Eric attended Eton, the famous boys' school, on a scholarship. At age 19, he joined the Indian Imperial Police in Burma. But after five years he resigned, disillusioned with Britain's dominance over the countries within its vast empire. He decided to live among the poor, taking odd jobs and barely earning enough money to survive. His first book, *Down and Out in Paris and London* (1933), published under the name George Orwell, describes this experience.

Three novels followed *Down and Out,* but Orwell was still not able to earn a living solely from his writing. He became better known with the publication of *The Road to Wigan Pier* (1937), a report on the lives and working conditions of miners in northern England.

George Orwell wrote two famous political satires, *Animal Farm* and *Nineteen Eighty-Four.* He is also admired for his nonfiction, which includes a firsthand account of life among the poor and working-class people of Europe.

With this book, he established himself as a socialist who believed in government policies to help poor and working-class people. *Homage to Catalonia* (1938) recounts Orwell's experiences in the Spanish Civil War (1936–39), in which he fought with the Loyalists to save the Spanish republic.

Orwell's two best-known novels have political themes. *Animal Farm* (1945), a fable about an uprising of farm animals, describes the betrayal of a revolution by its leaders. It is a satire on the Russian Revolution and its aftermath. *Nineteen Eighty-Four* (1949) warns against the dangers of an all-powerful government. The two books brought Orwell fame and financial success at last. He died of tuberculosis in London on January 21, 1950.

Reviewed by FREDERICK R. KARL
Author, *The Contemporary English Novel*

Rebellious farm animals stage an uprising in *Animal Farm*, only to be betrayed by their own leaders. The fable is a satire on the Russian Revolution and its aftermath.

OSAKA

Osaka, a bustling international port city on the Inland Sea, is Japan's third most populous city, after Tokyo and Yokohama. It is centrally located on Honshū, the largest island in the Japanese archipelago. More than 2.6 million people live within its 86-square-mile (222-square-kilometer) area.

The City. Osaka means "big slope" in Japanese, a name that accurately describes the local terrain. The city slopes gradually downward in a westerly direction on a flood plain, where several rivers, including the mighty Yodogawa, flow into Osaka Bay.

Osaka is highly built up and heavily congested. Residents are crowded into neighborhoods with an average population density of nearly 4,630 people per square mile (12,000 people per square kilometer). At the center of the city is a checkerboard grid of streets and avenues that were laid out more than 400 years ago. Today these thoroughfares are lined with banks, corporate headquarters, department stores, theaters, boutiques, hotels, restaurants, and other business enterprises.

Every day, more than 1 million commuters stream into and out of Osaka. Many travel by rail—on the Shinkansen (Japan's bullet trains), the national Japan Rail (JR) network, or private suburban railway lines. Within the city people ride buses, the subway, and an elevated railway that loops around Osaka. The city is also served by two major airports. Osaka Airport mainly supports travel to other destinations in Japan, while Kansai International Airport (KIA) is a hub of global travel. KIA, which opened in 1995, is

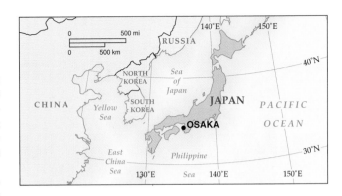

situated on its own artificial island in the middle of Osaka Bay.

The city's most prominent historical symbol is Osaka Castle. The building itself is a modern replica of the original castle, which was built in the 1500's. However, it is surrounded by the massive walls and deep moats of the original fortification. Other important historical sites include Tekijuku Academy, Central Town Hall, and two ancient places of worship—Shitennoji Temple (Buddhist) and Sumiyoshi Shrine (Shinto).

Visitors flock to Osaka's many and diverse cultural attractions. These include the National Bunrakuza Theatre, the old theater district of Dotonbori, the covered shopping arcade of Shinsaibashi, the shopping and entertainment district of Umeda, the zoo and art museum at Tennoji Park, the Osaka Kaiyukan Aquarium, and the Universal Studios Japan theme park. Osaka is also home to major educational institutions, including Osaka University, Osaka City University, and Kansai University.

Economic Activity. Osaka has thrived on maritime trade since the late 1500's. Today

Osaka Castle, the city's most historical symbol, stands in marked contrast to Osaka's modern skyscrapers. It is a replica of the original castle, which was built in the late 1500's when the city was formally established.

The streets of Osaka are crowded with shops and restaurants. This bustling metropolis is Japan's third most populous city, after Tokyo and Yokohama.

vessels from all over the world unload cargo at Osaka Port's massive wharfing facilities, and truckers from across Japan carry goods to its many loading docks. Many of these same ships and trucks are then loaded with products made in Osaka's factories and workshops. Machinery leads the list of the city's manufactures, followed by chemicals, metal products, printed materials, iron and steel, processed foods, plastics, paper, clothing, and textiles.

Osaka has a lively commercial sector, led by international trading companies. It also possesses one of the largest stock exchanges in the world, the Osaka Securities Exchange, and serves as headquarters for twenty of the world's wealthiest companies.

History. The city of Osaka was founded in 1583 by Hideyoshi Toyotomi, a great samurai lord who helped reunify Japan after a century of fighting. A thousand years earlier, the Japanese emperor Nintoku had claimed the site for his court. Called Naniwa, it served as his capital until he died. Officials and traders from Korea and China continued to use

Naniwa as a Japanese port of entry until the Yodogawa River delta silted up in the 800's and blocked the harbor.

The area sprang to life again in the late 1400's when militant Buddhist monks from the Ikko sect erected a fortress there and formed a religious community. But the following century, the great lord Nobunaga Oda destroyed them both.

Following Oda's death in 1582, Hideyoshi Toyotomi rose to national authority and decided to create a great castle town on the site. He forced thousands of laborers to build walls, moats, and fortifications and had surveyors lay out streets. Then he pressed merchants from neighboring port towns to relocate there. By the time of Toyotomi's death in 1598, Osaka had become a thriving port and castle town.

Toyotomi's young son retained control of Osaka until he was defeated by another lord, Ieyasu Tokugawa, in 1615. He and his successors, the Tokugawa shoguns (national lords), made Osaka the center of domestic trade for the western part of Japan. This was especially important because the shoguns had stopped almost all trade from outside the country.

By the late 1600's, because of the wide array of foodstuffs and other goods that filled the city's warehouses, Osaka became widely known as the Pantry of Japan. Enterprising merchants traded in rice and numerous other products, set up guilds for businesses, dug canals for transport, and constructed hundreds of bridges over the city's waterways. They also contributed to the rise of a townspeople's culture that was soon dramatized in Kabuki stage plays, Bunraku puppet theater, and serialized popular literature.

In the late 1800's, civic leaders deepened the port for oceangoing foreign trade, local entrepreneurs set up mills and factories, and gradually Osaka was transformed into an industrial metropolis. From the mid-1920's to the mid-1930's, Osaka surpassed the capital of Tokyo as Japan's most populous and prosperous city. Osaka was almost completely destroyed by the Allied fire bombings at the end of World War II (1939–45). After the war, the city was rebuilt and modernized. But in the postwar years, it steadily lost ground to the rapid expansion of Tokyo and Yokohama.

JEFFREY HANES
University of Oregon

OSBORNE, JOHN (1929–1994)

The playwright John Osborne helped revolutionize modern British drama. He was foremost among a group of British writers who became known as the "angry young men." Departing from the refined stories of upper-middle-class life that were typical of British plays of the time, Osborne introduced dramas that were bitterly critical of British society and politics in the decade after World War II.

John James Osborne was born on December 12, 1929, in London, England, the son of a commercial artist and a barmaid. After working briefly as a journalist he became an actor. In 1950, he collaborated with Stella Linden on his first play, *The Devil Inside Him*. He continued to act as he collaborated with Anthony Creighton on another play, *Personal Enemy* (1955).

In 1956, Osborne's play *Look Back in Anger* began a new era of social awareness in Britain. The play's leading character, Jimmy Porter, is a rebellious working-class youth frustrated with the values of his society. He came to symbolize not only Osborne and his fellow "angry young men" but also all the bright young people who were disillusioned with the postwar world.

Among Osborne's other dramas were *The Entertainer* (1957), *Luther* (1961), *Inadmissible Evidence* (1964), and *A Patriot for Me* (1965). He also wrote for television, and he won an Academy Award in 1963 for his screenplay of the motion picture *Tom Jones*.

Osborne modified his social criticism as he grew older, and his later works were increasingly psychological and personal. His final play, *Déjà Vu* (1992), depicted Jimmy Porter as an old man, still disillusioned with the world but rich and more conservative in his views. Osborne died on December 24, 1994, in Shrewsbury, England.

KIMBALL KING
Author, *Twenty Modern British Playwrights*

OSCEOLA (1800?–1838)

Osceola was a Seminole Indian who led his people in their fight against United States settlement in Florida. Although he was never a chief, he became one of the most respected members of his tribe.

Little is known about Osceola's early life. It is believed that he was born among the Creek Indians of Georgia or Alabama in the early 1800's. When he was a boy, he and his mother joined the Seminole tribes of Florida after being displaced by the Creek War (1813–14). During this war, the Creeks were forced to give up their land to the United States.

In 1832, some of the Seminole chiefs signed the Treaty of Payne's Landing, which gave the United States their land in Florida. The treaty called for the relocation of the Seminoles to reservations west of the Mississippi River (in present-day Oklahoma). Osceola was strongly opposed to the treaty. He gathered followers to fight resettlement in what became known as the Second Seminole War (1835–42).

Although the Seminoles fought fiercely, they were greatly outnumbered. Some

200,000 U.S. troops poured into Florida, while the Seminoles had fewer than 5,000 men. In 1837, bearing the white flag of truce, Osceola met to negotiate with U.S. troops under General Thomas Jesup. In a move that was to anger many Americans, Jesup violated the flag of truce and ordered Osceola's capture. Osceola was imprisoned at St. Augustine, Florida. Later he was sent to Fort Moultrie, South Carolina, where his health declined. He died there on January 30, 1838.

Reviewed by DANIEL JACOBSON
Montclair State College

OSLER, SIR WILLIAM (1849–1919)

Sir William Osler was a Canadian physician and a famous medical educator. He pioneered new teaching methods, as well as ideas in preventive medicine that promoted sanitation and other public-health measures. Osler was also well known for his expertise in diagnosing diseases related to the heart, lungs, and blood.

Osler was born in Bond Head, Ontario, Canada, on July 12, 1849, the eighth of nine children. When he was 8, the family moved to Dundas, also in Ontario, where he began school. At the age of 18, Osler entered Trinity College in Toronto and planned to become a minister. But within a year he decided that he wanted to be a physician and began to study medicine at the University of Toronto. He later transferred to McGill University in Montreal, graduating with a medical degree in 1872. The following year, Osler discovered the existence of tiny particles in the bloodstream, now known as platelets, that play a key role in clotting.

After studying further in Europe, Osler returned to McGill University in 1875 where, at the age of 25, he became a professor of medicine. He taught medicine, conducted medical research, and practiced as a physician at Montreal General Hospital. By the time he was 35, Osler was well known for his medical research. In 1884, he moved to Philadelphia after accepting a position as the professor of clinical medicine at the University of Pennsylvania. In 1889 he was appointed the first professor of medicine and physician in chief at the newly founded Johns Hopkins University in Baltimore.

Osler's methods of instruction emphasized direct observation and included teaching students at patients' bedsides. His ideas were widely adopted, and his publication, *The Principles and Practice of Medicine* (1892), became a standard medical text.

In 1892, Osler married an American woman, Grace Revere Gross, and they had two children. In 1905 he moved to England after accepting a professorship of medicine at Oxford University. Here he lectured and wrote about medical history. Osler was made a baronet in 1911. He died on December 29, 1919.

DUANE H. D. ROLLER
The University of Oklahoma

OSLO

Oslo is the capital and largest city of Norway. It is the country's chief port and one of its most important cultural, economic, and educational centers. Greater Oslo, which includes the city and its suburbs, wraps around the north end of the Oslo Fjord, which is linked to the North Sea by a channel, the Skagerrak. The city's population is about 513,000. Greater Oslo has a population of about 1 million.

The City. The heart of Oslo lies in an arc at the head of the fjord, near Akershus Castle, a medieval fortress built in the 1300's. Oslo's main street, Karl Johans Gate, runs from Central Station, the main railroad hub, to the Royal Palace. Nearby are many important buildings, including the Storting (parliament) Building, the National Gallery, the National Theater, the Rådhus (City Hall), and the city's cathedral, which dates from the late 1600's. The University of Oslo is Norway's oldest and largest university. Other sites include the World War II Resistance Museum, the Viking

Ship Museum, and the Edvard Munch Museum. Holmenkollen, a famous ski jump and site of the 1952 Winter Olympic Games, overlooks the city. Frogner Park, with its collection of works by noted sculptor Gustav Vigeland, draws many visitors.

Tram, bus, and ferry systems help people get into and around Oslo easily. However, many of the city's main attractions are relatively close together and can be reached easily on foot. Norwegians love the outdoors, and many people enjoy walking and cross-country skiing

Oslo's main street, Karl Johans Gate, runs through the central part of the city to the Royal Palace.

through Oslo's extensive park system and paths.

Economic Activity. Greater Oslo is Norway's most rapidly changing economic region. Over its history, Oslo has been a center of trade, shipping, shipbuilding, and manufacturing. Today the metropolitan area is increasingly developing into the center of Norway's services, technology, education, and research and development sectors—as well as a popular tourist destination.

History. According to legend, Oslo was founded by King Harald III about 1050 on the site of a small trading town. It grew as a commercial, government, and religious center during the Middle Ages and was an important administrative center during the period of Norway's union with Denmark (1380–1814). A fire destroyed most of the city in 1624. Christian IV of Denmark rebuilt the new city closer to the royal fort, Akershus, and it was renamed Christiania, after its founder. The city became Norway's capital in 1814, when the country entered into a union with Sweden. It remained the capital after Norway became independent in 1905. The original name, Oslo, was restored in 1925.

Until the 1900's, Oslo was a relatively small city. Its population grew from about 10,000 residents in 1800 to over 220,000 by 1900. In recent decades, Oslo has become increasingly multicultural due to immigration, adding diversity to the city.

BYRON J. NORDSTROM
Gustavus Adolphus College

OSMOSIS

Osmosis is the process by which liquids and substances dissolved in them pass through a membrane—a kind of skin. Osmosis takes place in all living things. Plants get the water they need to live by absorbing it through their roots, which are made up of many living cells. All cells have a membrane surrounding a liquid interior. Water passes in and out of the cell through the cell membrane by osmosis.

Osmosis also occurs in your body. Your blood carries digested food, nutrients, and oxygen as it flows through your body. By osmosis, these things pass through the cell walls of small blood vessels called capillaries to nourish the cells of your body.

To understand osmosis, you must first know something about diffusion.

▶ **DIFFUSION**

To "diffuse" means to spread out. When you put a drop of ink in a glass of water, the molecules that make up the ink diffuse, eventually coloring all the water evenly. This happens even without stirring. If you open a bottle of household ammonia, a person a few feet away will soon smell it. The ammonia molecules have diffused through the air.

Diffusion takes place because the molecules of a substance are always in motion and naturally tend to move to where there are fewer molecules of the same kind. But if you place a tightly closed bottle of ink in a jar of water, diffusion does not occur. The bottle is a barrier that keeps the ink and water molecules separated.

▶OSMOSIS IS A KIND OF DIFFUSION

If you pour water into a cloth bag, the water goes through the cloth. The cloth is not a barrier to diffusion. Cloth is **permeable** to water and most other liquids; that is, it allows them to pass through. But water will not go through the walls of a rubber balloon. Rubber is a barrier to diffusion. It is **impermeable** to water and most other liquids.

However, if you fill the balloon with helium, the atoms of helium slowly move through the walls of the balloon. The helium atoms are small enough to move between the molecules that make up the walls of the rubber balloon. This is why a helium-filled balloon deflates if it sits around for awhile.

Thin walls such as cloth and rubber are membranes. Some membranes are impermeable to some substances but permeable to others, just as the balloon is impermeable to water but permeable to helium. These membranes are called **semipermeable**, or selectively permeable, membranes. The cell walls of plant roots, blood vessels, and the intestines of animals are examples of semipermeable membranes.

Osmosis is diffusion through a semipermeable membrane. This process can take place in living or nonliving things whenever two liquids are separated by a semipermeable membrane. Often the two liquids are the same but have different substances, or different amounts of the same substance, dissolved in them. The two solutions must have different total concentrations for osmosis to occur.

Let us imagine a system in which a semipermeable membrane separates two liquids. Both liquids are solutions of salt dissolved in water. But one is a more concentrated solution—it has more dissolved salt than the other solution.

In our system, the membrane will allow water to pass but not salt. The water will tend to move through the semipermeable membrane from the side with less salt to the side with the greater concentration of dissolved salt. If we start with equal volumes of the two solutions, the volume of the less concentrated side will decrease and the volume of the more concentrated side will increase. The volumes will stop changing when the concentrations of the two solutions are equal. At that point, osmosis stops. The water will continue to move back and forth across the membrane, but the amount of water moving in one direction will be the same as the amount moving the other way.

▶OSMOTIC PRESSURE AND REVERSE OSMOSIS

The volume of the side with the more concentrated solution can be kept from increasing by applying pressure to that side. If we apply enough pressure, the volumes will not change at all. If the less concentrated side of the solution is made of pure water—water with no salt dissolved in it—the amount of pressure we need to apply to keep the volume from changing is known as the **osmotic pressure** of the solution.

If we apply more pressure than the osmotic pressure, we can force the water to mi-

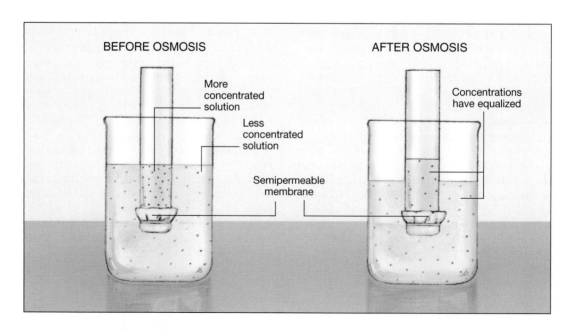

BEFORE OSMOSIS

More concentrated solution

Less concentrated solution

Semipermeable membrane

AFTER OSMOSIS

Concentrations have equalized

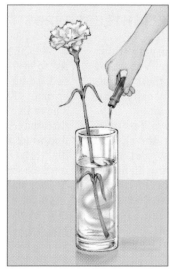

See For Yourself

How Osmosis Works

Here are two easy ways to observe osmosis in plants.

Place a white carnation in a glass of water. Without stirring, add a couple of drops of food coloring to the water. Let the carnation stand undisturbed for a few days. What happens?

Carrots are roots. Leave a carrot out in the open for a day or so. It will begin to shrivel up. Now place the carrot in a glass of water. What happens? What does osmosis have to do with the changes you observed?

---

grate from the more concentrated solution to the less concentrated one. This is the process known as **reverse osmosis**. Reverse osmosis is used to convert saltwater into pure water. Removing salt from seawater by osmosis is also called desalination.

▶ OSMOSIS IN LIVING THINGS

Living organisms are made of cells. Each cell is made of a thick solution called **protoplasm** surrounded by a semipermeable cell membrane. The protoplasm is made of many different dissolved substances. If a fluid surrounds the outside of the cell, osmosis may take place through the cell membrane. The cell membrane allows water and some of the dissolved substances to pass into the cell and allows others to leave. In this way, food and other nutrients are supplied to living cells and waste materials are removed.

Osmosis in Plants

Plants need minerals that are found dissolved in soil water. This solution surrounds and passes through the cell membranes of their roots. The mineral solution passes from the roots to the rest of the plant by osmosis between cells.

Sugar is made in the green leaves of plants. It dissolves in water inside the leaves' cells. By osmosis, this solution is transported through the cell membranes to all other parts of the plant, where it is used for energy and growth.

Osmosis in the Human Body

Many body processes depend on osmosis. For example, your blood uses osmosis to do its many jobs. Blood is made of red blood cells suspended in a clear liquid called **plasma**. Plasma continually passes between the blood vessels and the various cells of the body by osmosis. The red blood cells, however, cannot move through cell walls and must remain in the blood vessels.

Digested food and other nutrients get into the plasma by osmosis through the capillaries in the walls of the small intestine. When plasma reaches the other cells of the body, osmosis carries the food and nutrients into the cells. The plasma returns to the capillaries, carrying with it waste products from the cells. In the kidneys, osmosis transports the waste products from the plasma into the bladder, where they are excreted from the body.

Osmosis also allows your cells to get the oxygen they need to live. Oxygen in the air we breathe gets into our blood through capillaries in the lining of the lungs. Much of the oxygen in the blood is carried by osmosis into the red blood cells, where it is stored and transported throughout the body. The blood cells release the oxygen where it is needed. The carbon dioxide that is produced is passed through the cell membranes and capillary walls into the blood. The blood carries it back to the lungs, where it is breathed out.

KENTON H. WHITMIRE
Rice University

OSTRICHES AND OTHER FLIGHTLESS BIRDS

When we think of birds, we usually think of creatures that fly and sing. Yet some birds cannot fly, and most of these flightless birds do not sing. They usually hiss, snort, roar, boom, whistle, or grunt.

Of course, most birds can fly. They depend on flying to get food, to travel, and to flee when they sense danger. But some kinds of birds—a few dozen—are flightless. Some, like penguins and ostriches, have very heavy bodies with wings that are too small to support their weight in the air. A few parrots, ducks, and other birds in families of normally powerful fliers are also flightless.

Scientists believe that all the flightless birds living today are descended from birds that could fly. The reason for this belief is that the wing bones of flightless birds have the same structure as those of flying birds. But the wings of these birds are no longer used for flight.

Why should some birds have lost their ability to fly? The flightless parrots and ducks and some nearly flightless pigeons give us a clue. These birds have no need to fly. They live in places where they are not threatened by enemies, and they can easily find food by walking or swimming. The larger flightless birds, such as ostriches, also live in places where they have few or no enemies, or they can run fast enough to escape.

Once a bird no longer needs to fly, it may evolve into a form so large that it cannot fly. The ostrich, for example, feeds on plant material that requires a very long intestine for digestion. The intestine of an ostrich measures 14 meters (46 feet). If the ostrich had to fly, its body could not contain such a long and heavy intestine. Then, perhaps, it would not be able to eat the food that grows in some of the very dry areas where it lives.

Ostrich chicks are about 30 centimeters (1 foot) tall when they hatch. They are carefully guarded by their fathers at all times. When they are only a month old, the young birds can run about 55 kilometers (35 miles) an hour for short distances. Adult ostriches can run at speeds of almost 100 kilometers (60 miles) an hour. They can also give a powerful kick to protect themselves or their young. Ostriches have very keen eyesight. If they spot danger, they may crouch down—with their necks stretched out—and disappear from view. People who saw ostriches acting in this way once believed, mistakenly, that the huge birds were burying their heads in the sand.

The best known group of flightless birds is made up of ostriches, rheas, emus, cassowaries, and kiwis. All live in the Southern Hemisphere. They are known as ratites, from the Latin word for raft (a boat without a keel). Ratites have a flat breastbone without the keel-like structure to which flight muscles are attached in flying birds.

Scientists cannot decide whether all the ratite families are truly related or whether they merely seem similar because they lead similar lives. But most ratite families share one form of behavior that is very unusual. The males build the nests, incubate the eggs (warm them by sitting on them until they hatch), and care for the young birds. The females usually lay their eggs, which are very large, in the nests that have been prepared for them. Then they leave and lay eggs in the nest of another male. If the females had to stay on the nests, they might not be able to look for the large amount of food that they need to produce more eggs.

OSTRICHES

The ostrich is the largest living bird. It may be as much as 2.5 meters (8 feet) tall and weigh about 135 kilograms (300 pounds). It has long, bare legs; only two toes on each foot (fewer than any other bird); and a long, pink, featherless neck. Males are black with white wing and tail feathers. Females are grayish brown. Both have thick eyelashes of fine feathers.

Today ostriches are found in the wild only in the grasslands and semi-desert areas of eastern and southern Africa. They usually live in groups of one male and three to five females. But sometimes as many as 40 to 50 birds may be found together. Ostriches eat grasses, leaves, and fruits, as well as insects and lizards. They also swallow large amounts of sand and small pebbles to help digest their food. Ostriches make a loud, hissing sound. In the breeding season, the male produces a booming roar. In east central Africa these huge birds often gather with herds of zebras, antelope, and giraffes.

During the breeding season, several female ostriches lay eggs in the nest made by a male. The eggs are huge and creamy white in color. Each female lays about six to eight eggs, usually one every three days. Unlike

HUMMINGBIRD EGG

LARGE HEN EGG

OSTRICH EGG

Ostriches produce the largest eggs of any living bird. One egg may weigh about 1,500 grams (53 ounces) and have the same volume as 26 hen eggs. The shell is very thick. Here you can see how an ostrich egg compares in size with a large hen egg and with a hummingbird egg, the smallest of all bird eggs.

other ratites, male and female ostriches share the incubation. The male sits on the nest at night, and the females take turns by day.

The long feathers of ostrich wings have been used as ornaments since ancient times. In the 1890's the feathers were often used to decorate women's hats. The establishment of ostrich farms, mainly in South Africa, reduced the killing of the wild birds. Today ostriches are still raised on farms for their feathers as well as their hides, which are made into leather. But the demand for these products is not so great as in the past. On ostrich farms the feathers are clipped off the wings without hurting the birds. New feathers grow in later.

Ostriches have one of the longest life spans of any land animal. Some ostriches, especially those raised in captivity, may live to be 70 years old.

RHEAS

Rheas are found only in South America. They are sometimes called South American

RHEA

CASSOWARY

EMU

KIWI

ostriches, or pampas ostriches. There are two kinds of rheas. The common rhea of Argentina and southern Brazil is about 1.5 meters (5 feet) tall. It may weigh more than 25 kilograms (55 pounds). The Darwin's rhea is somewhat smaller. It is found on the plains of western Argentina and high in the Andes mountains. Both the common rhea and the Darwin's rhea are brown in color. Unlike ostriches, rheas have feathers covering their heads and necks, as well as their bodies.

Rheas live in flocks of 20 or 30 and sometimes more. At times they mix with herds of deer or cattle. They eat leaves, roots, and seeds, as well as insects and lizards. When they run, rheas hold their necks stretched out in front of them. Often they make sudden twists and turns. Their calls are whistling noises and a deep booming sound.

This scale shows how members of the ratite group compare in height with a human being. To the right of the human figure are two extinct ratites. The elephant bird of Madagascar stood as high as 3 meters (10 feet) and weighed 450 kilograms (1,000 pounds). The moa of New Zealand was as much as 3.5 meters (12 feet) tall and weighed 235 kilograms (520 pounds). Both of these gigantic birds have been extinct for centuries.

3.5 METERS
(12 FEET)

3 METERS
(10 FEET)

2.5 METERS
(8 FEET)

1.8 METERS
(6 FEET)

1.5 METERS
(5 FEET)

0.5 METER
(1¾ FEET)
LONG

KIWI   RHEA   CASSOWARY   EMU   OSTRICH   ELEPHANT BIRD   MOA

The shells of rhea eggs change color. When they are laid, the eggs are green. During incubation they become yellow, then blue. Finally, when the chicks hatch, the eggs are white. As the newly hatched birds begin to search for food, they and their father whistle to keep in contact.

Rheas are no longer hunted for sport as much as in the past. But their numbers continue to decrease for another reason. Fences have been built to enclose cattle on ranches. These fences limit the areas where the rheas can find the food they need to survive.

▶ EMUS

The tallest ratite after the ostrich is the emu, which lives in Australia. It may be as much as 1.8 meters (6 feet) tall and weigh up to 55 kilograms (120 pounds). Its hairlike feathers are brown or blackish brown. Like ostriches and rheas, emus live in open country. They feed on a wide variety of fruits and other plant material. They also eat insects. Emus make hissing, grunting, and booming sounds, and the females lay eight to ten dark green eggs.

The emu is sometimes considered a pest because it knocks down fences and tramples crops. At one time, bounties (payments) were offered for shooting these birds. But today specially designed fences are used to keep the emus from entering the fields. Emus are raised in some countries for their meat and the oil obtained from their fat.

▶ CASSOWARIES

Cassowaries live in thick forests. Their feathers are black and shaggy. The long, white quills that stick out from the ends of their wing feathers are thought to show that the wings were used for flight long ago. Their heads and necks are bare of feathers and are brightly colored. The top of a cassowary's head has a casque, or bony helmet. The casque is thought to protect the bird as it runs at great speed, head first, through dense forest. Cassowaries may be more than 1.5 meters (5 feet) tall and weigh about 55 kilograms (121 pounds). The female cassowary is larger than the male and lays between three and five pale green eggs.

The one-wattled cassowary and the Bennett's cassowary are found in New Guinea and on some of the nearby islands. The Australian cassowary lives in coastal forests in northeastern Australia.

Cassowaries usually live singly or in pairs. They are active day and night, feeding mainly on berries and fruit. Their calls sound like snorting, grunting, and bellowing.

Cassowaries are hunted for use as food. They are also valued for their feathers, which are used in headdresses. But these birds are difficult to hunt, and they can be very dangerous. Cassowaries will charge at people, feet first, often killing or badly wounding their victims with the long, sharp claws of their inner toes.

For hundreds of years the people of New Guinea have used cassowaries as a form of money. The government of Papua New Guinea has begun raising cassowaries on farms and selling them to the villagers so that more of them will be left in the wild.

▶ KIWIS

Kiwis are very small ratites. A kiwi is the size of a domestic hen and weighs between 1.5 and 4 kilograms (about 3 and 9 pounds). Kiwis are tailless and have short legs and short necks. This gives the body a rounded or hunched appearance. The tiny wings cannot be seen through the shaggy, brown feathers. A kiwi has a very sharp sense of smell, which most birds lack. Its bill is long, slender, and flexible. And unlike the bills of other birds, a kiwi's bill has the nostrils at the tip. Female kiwis are larger than males

There are three kinds of kiwis—the common, or brown, kiwi; the great spotted, or large gray, kiwi; and the little spotted, or little gray, kiwi. All are found in New Zealand and on its offshore islands.

A kiwi egg is white. It is 180 millimeters (7 inches) long. This is an extremely large egg for the size of the bird.

Kiwis live in burrows in thick forests. They hide by day but come out at night to feed on earthworms and insects. Their calls are shrill whistles or screams. To the Maori, the first people to live in New Zealand, the calls sounded like "kee-wee." At this time there is no threat to the survival of these shy birds because they are strictly protected by law in New Zealand.

ROGER F. PASQUIER
Author, *Watching Birds:
An Introduction to Ornithology*

See also PENGUINS.

OSWALD, LEE HARVEY (1939–1963)

On November 22, 1963, Lee Harvey Oswald was arrested in Dallas, Texas, for the assassination of President John F. Kennedy. Oswald, who declared his innocence, was  murdered two days later while in police custody. As a result, Oswald's guilt or innocence—and whether he acted alone or was part of a conspiracy— was never determined at trial. In 1964, the government commissioned the Warren Report, which concluded that Oswald had been the sole assassin.

Oswald was born in New Orleans, Louisiana, on October 18, 1939. A troubled youth, he dropped out of high school at age 16 and joined the U.S. Marines. Sympathetic to Communism, he obtained an early release and in 1959 moved to the Soviet Union, where he married a Russian woman. Oswald soon became disenchanted with life in the Soviet Union, and in 1962 he returned to the United States with his wife and baby daughter.

In 1963, Oswald went back to New Orleans and became part of an organization that supported the regime of Cuba's Communist dictator Fidel Castro. He later moved to Dallas and took a job at the Texas School Book Depository in Dealey Plaza.

At about 12:30 P.M. on November 22, an open-car motorcade carrying President Kennedy, his wife Jacqueline, and Texas governor John Connally passed by the Texas School Book Depository. According to the Warren Commission, Oswald, using a rifle and telescopic sight, fired three shots from a sixth-floor window, killing Kennedy and seriously wounding Connally. Less than an hour later, Oswald killed a police officer, J. D. Tippit, who was trying to arrest him. Oswald was taken into custody at about 1:50 P.M.

On November 24, as he was being moved to another jail, Oswald was shot and killed by Jack Ruby, a local nightclub owner. This murder, along with Ruby's own death in prison in 1967, only fueled the conspiracy theories surrounding the assassination.

Reviewed by JOHN McADAMS
Marquette University

See also WARREN REPORT.

OTIS, JAMES (1725–1783)

James Otis, a leading American patriot, was born in West Barnstable, Massachusetts, on February 5, 1725. After graduating from Harvard in 1743, he became a lawyer.

In 1750 he moved to Boston and was appointed to represent the British Crown in the vice-admiralty court, which handled matters related to commerce and shipping. However, he resigned in protest in 1760. The court wanted him to defend writs of assistance. These were search warrants that allowed government agents to enter any residence to look for smuggled goods. In 1761, Otis argued against these writs in court, saying they violated a citizen's right to privacy. John Adams said that American independence was born when Otis spoke out against the writs.

Otis argued for the rights of the American colonists as English people, and he opposed independence for some time. Later, however, he took a major part in the events leading to the Revolutionary War.

As a member of the Massachusetts legislature (1761–69), Otis continued to shape colonial opinion. In response to taxes levied by the British Parliament, Otis argued that taxation without representation was tyranny. At his suggestion, colonial leaders met in New York in 1765 to plan their opposition to the Stamp Act. They drew up a set of grievances, which were presented to Parliament. The Stamp Act was repealed the next year.

The Crown criticized Otis for his actions, and British customs agents in Boston accused him of treason. In 1769 he quarreled violently with one of them and received a severe head wound. Otis spent the rest of his life in retirement. On May 23, 1783, he was killed by a bolt of lightning in Andover, Massachusetts.

JOHN J. WATERS
Author, *The Otis Family in Provincial and Revolutionary Massachusetts*

OTTAWA

Ottawa is the national capital of Canada. It is situated on the southern bank of the Ottawa River, on Ontario's eastern boundary, about 125 miles (200 kilometers) west of Montreal. The Rideau Canal divides the city into upper and lower sections. The name "Ottawa" comes from the Algonkian word "adawe," which means "to trade."

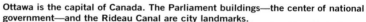

▶ HISTORY

Fur-trading posts were established along the Ottawa River before the 1800's, as it became an important route for the Montreal fur trade. But the first permanent settlement in the Ottawa River valley was Wright's Town, now the city of Hull, Quebec. It was begun in 1800 on the north shore of the river. Then in 1826, activity shifted to a point on the south shore opposite Wright's Town. This was the site chosen as the place to begin the Rideau Canal, which would link the river to Lake Ontario. Two men were responsible for the choice: Lord Dalhousie, the British governor of Upper and Lower Canada, and Lieutenant Colonel John By, of the Royal Engineers.

John By supervised the design, construction, and operation of the Rideau Canal. More than 7,000 people worked on the canal at the height of the project. Upon completion, it cost the British government about $5 million, making it Britain's most expensive military construction project up to that time. The canal was intended to ferry troops and supplies from Montreal to Kingston, on Lake Ontario, in case of war with the United States. It also became a trade route.

Ottawa is the capital of Canada. The Parliament buildings—the center of national government—and the Rideau Canal are city landmarks.

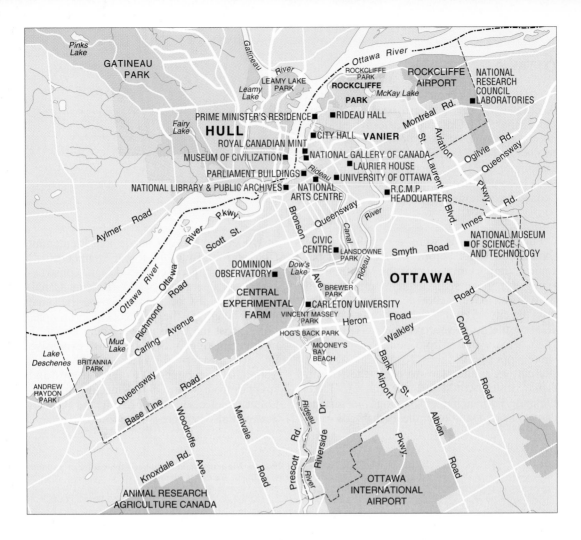

John By stayed on until 1832, when the 125-mile (200-kilometer) canal was completed. He established a military garrison (post), and he designed and organized a town. At first, the town had no name. Then it was called Bytown, named after By.

The canal set the social character of the town as its route separated it into two parts. Upper Town, west of the canal, was reserved mainly for the gentility, who were mostly British Protestants. Lower Town, east of the canal, was the commercial district. The homes of tradespeople and workers—mainly Roman Catholic French Canadians and Irish—were also there.

After completion of the Rideau Canal in 1832, Bytown grew to be the largest lumber center on the river. By the 1850's, a lumber industry had also developed. Large mills sprang up at Rideau Falls and Chaudière Falls. In 1855, Bytown was incorporated as a

city, and its name was changed to Ottawa. By 1860, it was the main center of British North America's lumber industry.

Ottawa's role as capital resulted from rivalry among the cities of the Province of Canada. The Province of Canada was formed in 1841 by the union of Upper Canada and Lower Canada. However, no one could agree on a site for a capital. For twenty years, the role of capital passed, in turn, among Kingston, Montreal, Toronto, and Quebec City. To end the argument, Queen Victoria of England was asked to pick a permanent site. In 1857, she chose Ottawa, the most central city, as a compromise between a French Canadian and an English Canadian location.

The arrival of government had important effects on the city. It brought new people and new business opportunities. Government's impact was perhaps greatest on Upper Town, which benefited most from nearby Parlia-

Skating on the frozen Rideau Canal is a popular winter activity in Ottawa. The canal, completed in 1832, divides the city into two sections.

ment Hill. Since the 1860's, this area has become the major shopping center and office area of the city.

The construction of Parliament buildings—Center Block, East and West Blocks, and Library—began in 1859. The Center Block was styled similarly to Britain's new Houses of Parliament at Westminster. The buildings were officially opened in 1866, in time for only one legislative session of the Province of Canada. In 1867, Ottawa became the capital of the Dominion of Canada.

The Parliament buildings are now the centerpiece of a network of dozens of government buildings. The Center Block burned down in 1916 but was soon rebuilt on an enlarged scale. It is home to the House of Commons and the Senate. The Center Block faces a large parade ground that is the site of many colorful ceremonies, including, in summer, the changing of the guard.

▶ THE CITY TODAY

Ottawa is the heart of the national capital region, which includes Hull and nearby towns on both sides of the Ottawa River. Almost 324,000 people live within the city limits. The metropolitan population, including towns in both Ontario and Quebec, is more than 1 million.

Ottawa's inhabitants are mostly of British origin. Other ethnic groups are French and Irish. Ottawa's people are largely bilingual because federal government employees are required to know both English and French.

Today, there is still much evidence of Ottawa's lumber era—including a layer of sawdust more than 20 feet (6 meters) deep at the bottom of the Ottawa River. The lands from which timber was cut have been reforested, and many areas have become parks. But the great homes of the lumber barons are perhaps their greatest legacy to the city. One of these homes, Earnscliffe, became the residence of John A. Macdonald, Canada's first prime minister. It is now the home of the British High Commissioner. Another is the mansion at 24 Sussex Drive, the official residence of the Canadian prime minister.

Parts of the two town sections remain, especially in Lower Town. The Mile of History, on Sussex Street, is a strip of restored commercial buildings from the 1800's. Nearby is the Byward Market, an open-air farmers' and artisans' market. Artisans' cottages dating from the 1800's can be found on the backstreets. And Lower Town's Roman Catholic roots can be seen in such institutions as the Basilica of Notre Dame, with its beautiful wood carvings.

Economy and Transportation. The federal government has a major influence on Ottawa's economy. The government owns about one-third of the land in the city and, since 1940, has been the largest employer. The tourism and convention industry is the second largest employer. Although manufacturing has declined since the beginning of the 1900's, a major computer technology industry has developed.

The growth of government and government's decisions about the location of buildings and jobs have made great changes in the region. Much activity has shifted out of Ottawa's center, and suburbs have grown. This trend led the province of Ontario to create a regional government for Ottawa and its suburbs. (Quebec has set up a similar government for the Hull area.)

City government is headquartered in Ottawa's modern City Hall, which stands on an island at the mouth of the Rideau River. The city and regional governments confer with the National Capital Commission in planning the future of the capital region.

Ottawa is an important transportation center. It has one of the busiest airports in Canada, largely because of its location as a hub on the Montreal-Toronto-Ottawa air triangle. Ottawa's excellent OC Transpo provides bus transportation within the Ottawa-Carleton county region.

Culture and Education. Much of Ottawa's cultural life and most of its facilities are dominated by the federal government. There is a network of national museums with collections covering military history, technology and science, anthropology, natural history, air transportation, and postage. The National Gallery displays Canadian art and art from other countries. (An article on the National Gallery of Canada appears in Volume N.) The Canadian Museum of Civilization contains the re-creation of a West Coast Native village, as well as a town square and shipyard from the 1800's. Also in Ottawa are the National Library, the National Archives Building, and the Royal Canadian Mint. The National Arts Center also attracts international and North American performers.

The National Gallery of Canada is one of Ottawa's many outstanding museums. It houses the world's most complete collection of Canadian art.

The University of Ottawa is Canada's oldest and largest bilingual university. Carleton University, founded after World War II (1939–45), serves a mainly English-speaking community.

Sports and Recreation. Outdoor sports are very popular in Ottawa. The Rideau Canal and Gatineau Park, in nearby Hull, Quebec, provide many opportunities for recreation. The canal is flanked by bicycle paths and parks. In summer, the canal is filled with boats. In winter, it becomes a skating rink very popular during Winterlude, Ottawa's February festival.

Gatineau Park is crisscrossed with bicycle paths, hiking trails, and cross-country ski routes. In the midst of the park, visitors have access to Kingsmere, the estate created by William Lyon Mackenzie King, Canada's longest-serving prime minister, and bequeathed to the nation he led for almost 22 years.

JOHN H. TAYLOR
Carleton University
Reviewed by PETER BISCHOFF
University of Ottawa

See also KING, WILLIAM LYON MACKENZIE.

OTTERS AND OTHER MUSTELIDS

Otters, skunks, weasels, badgers, and related animals belong to a group of mammals called mustelids, from a Latin word meaning "weasel." They are short-legged animals that usually have long, slender bodies covered with thick fur. They range in size from about 9 inches (23 centimeters) to more than 6 feet (2 meters) in length and weigh from a few ounces to up to 100 pounds (45 kilograms). All are meat eaters, and most have sharp teeth for tearing food.

Otters make up one group of mustelids. Skunks have been considered a second group, although many scientists now classify them as mephitids, a group separate from the mustelids. Badgers are a third group, and a fourth group includes weasels and similar animals.

▶ OTTERS

The water-dwelling otters are among the largest of the mustelids. Their webbed feet, dense fur, and streamlined bodies make them well suited for life in the water. Two species of otters live exclusively in the ocean. All other otters usually live in fresh water, although a few species (including the Canadian otter, Eurasian otter, and clawless otter of South Africa) are sometimes found in saltwater environments.

Freshwater Otters

Freshwater otters live in and around rivers, lakes, and streams on every continent except Australia. They are sometimes known as river otters.

The North American otter ranges from Mexico to Alaska, with the largest numbers in Canada. The North American otter is constantly on the move. A male sometimes covers a distance of about 60 miles (97 kilometers) during the winter. This otter sometimes lives in areas where people also live, but it is rarely seen. The otter's home may be a hollow log or an abandoned beaver lodge, but it usually digs a hole into the bank of a stream or lake. The hole leads to a leaf-lined den where two to four young are born in late winter or early spring. Before they can swim, the mother sometimes carries them about on her back in the water. But they quickly learn to swim by themselves, and their parents teach them to dive and catch fish. Soon the young are able to stay underwater for as long as four minutes. The dark brown coat of the North American otter is a valued fur for clothing.

The Eurasian otter is similar to the North American otter in habits and appearance. It was once found in great numbers along the waterways of Europe, North Africa, and much of Asia. It has disappeared from many regions because of habitat destruction and

The freshwater, or river, otter is a large mustelid skilled at catching fish. Freshwater otters live on every continent except Australia.

pollution of the rivers and lakes where it lived.

There are many other species of river otters. The clawless otter of Africa has no claws on its small front feet. On the hind feet, the middle toes have tiny claws. The endangered giant otter, also known as the saro, lives in South America. Its tail is broad and flattened at the tip. Large specimens sometimes measure 6½ feet (2 meters) or more. The hairy-nosed otter of Asia and Sumatra is named for its nose, which is covered with fine hair.

River otters are playful creatures, even when full grown. A favorite pastime is sliding

The sea otter often places a rock on its belly and cracks the shells of clams and other sea creatures against it to get at the animal inside.

down banks of mud or snow to splash into the water below. Such playfulness is rare among adult wild animals. In parts of India, people tame otters and teach them to drive fish into fishing nets.

Marine Otters

There are two species of marine otter, the North Pacific sea otter and the South American marine otter.

The North Pacific sea otter is one of the largest mustelids. Males can grow to almost 5 feet (1.5 meters) in length and weigh up to 100 pounds (45 kilograms). Females are slightly smaller. This otter has thick fur that is dark brown, sometimes almost black, with white hairs blended in. It has white whiskers on its face.

When not in a hurry, North Pacific sea otters often swim on their backs. They float that way, too, while using their bellies for tables. Sea otters eat crabs, sea urchins, mollusks, and other sea creatures. Often, they use their broad teeth to crack the hard shells of their prey. But sometimes a sea otter will bring a flat rock up from the ocean floor, lay the rock on its belly, and break the shells by pounding them against the rock.

North Pacific sea otters are found in kelp (seaweed) beds off the western coast of North America, from California to Alaska and the Aleutian Islands. They also live along the coast and the offshore islands of northeastern Russia. Females give birth to one offspring in the water. The mother will sometimes float on her back to cuddle the offspring on her belly.

Except for killer whales, bald eagles, and human hunters, North Pacific sea otters have few enemies. In the past, they were widely hunted for their valuable fur. They were almost extinct until they were finally protected by an international treaty in 1911. After hunting ended, their numbers increased rapidly in many areas. But in the late 1900's populations declined again in southwest Alaska because killer whales were eating an increased amount of sea otters.

The South American marine otter, one of the smallest otters, does not spend all of its time in the water. It lives onshore and only goes into the ocean to feed.

▶ SKUNKS

Skunks are found only in North, Central, and South America. They live in hollow logs or in burrows in the ground and come out at night to search for insects, rodents, birds' eggs, and other small animals to eat. Because they eat insects that are harmful to crops, skunks are protected by law in many areas. Skunks produce between one and ten young a year.

Above: The spotted skunk of North and Central America is the smallest species of skunk.
Right: A North American striped skunk prepares to defend itself by spraying a foul-smelling liquid.

try in North America and Central America. Skunks are sometimes incorrectly called polecats, which are actually a kind of weasel. For more information, see the article SKUNKS in Volume S.

▶ **BADGERS**

Badgers have broad, heavy bodies; short, thick legs; and flattened heads with long snouts. They are excellent diggers, using their long sharp claws to dig rodents from burrows and to rip apart logs and soil in search of insects and other creatures to eat. Markings on the face form a kind of "badge," from which the badger gets its name. Before synthetic materials were common, badger fur was used for shaving brushes.

Badgers are found throughout much of Europe, Asia, and North America, and they vary in appearance and habits. The Eurasian badger is found from England to Japan. Its face is white, with two black stripes that start at the nose and run up each side, over the eyes and ears. The coarse fur on the back is grayish brown. Males grow to about 35 inches (90 centimeters) in length and weigh about 27 pounds (12 kilograms). It lives in clearings or wooded areas and travels at night, searching for eggs, worms, mice, and rats to eat.

Although many mustelids have scent glands at the base of their tails, skunks are especially known for their use of these glands to defend themselves. When threatened, they may shoot out a foul-smelling liquid from the glands, aiming for the head of their enemy. In addition to its odor, the spray can cause temporary blindness. Because of this, few animals will attack a skunk.

The most common North American skunk is the striped skunk, found from Canada to Mexico. It is black, usually with two white stripes running down its back. The hooded skunk, a close relative, lives in dry regions from the southwestern United States to Central America. The hog-nosed skunk has a long snout somewhat like a pig's. It lives in open or wooded areas from the southwestern United States to South America. Spotted skunks are the smallest skunks, measuring from 7 to 14 inches (18 to 36 centimeters) long and weighing about 2 pounds (0.9 kilogram). They are good tree climbers and can be found in deserts, plains, and brushy coun-

The American badger is smaller than the Eurasian. Its dark brown or blackish face is marked by a narrow white stripe down the center. The stripe continues down the animal's back. There are white markings below the eyes and in front of the ears. Each hair in the American badger's soft, silky coat has three different colors. It is gray at the base, gray-white near the middle, and black with a silver tip on top. This is what gives this badger its grizzled (sprinkled with gray) appearance.

American badgers live on the plains and prairie regions from Canada to Mexico. They were once quite numerous. But as people settled these areas, the badgers became far fewer in number. This has been a great loss, because badgers feed on rodents and insects that destroy crops.

Other kinds of badgers live in Southeast Asia. Ferret badgers are the smallest badgers, and unlike other species, they have long, slender bodies. Some are tree climbers. The hognosed badger has a snout like a pig's and a rather long white tail. The teledu, or Malayan stink badger, of Borneo, Sumatra, and Java is a small brown-black badger with

Right: The Eurasian badger is active at night, when it searches for eggs, worms, and small rodents to eat. *Below:* As its name implies, the stink badger of Southeast Asia can, like skunks, spray a smelly liquid in self defense.

a white stripe down its back. Like skunks and some other mustelids, this animal can spray a foul-smelling liquid a long distance.

Badgers fight fiercely to protect themselves. At one time in Europe, some people engaged in a sport called badger baiting. A badger was placed in a barrel or a pit, and dogs were set upon it. Bets would be placed on the outcome of the contest. Badger baiting has long since been outlawed. But the word "badger" is still used to mean "to tease or annoy persistently."

▶ WEASELS AND RELATED ANIMALS

There are more than 30 different kinds of weasels, most of which live in Europe, Asia, and North America. They hunt and kill small animals such as mice, rats, and young birds, but often kill more than they can eat. As they hunt, weasels are sometimes attacked by owls and eagles. But they often escape because they are small and swift. A weasel can move its long, slender body through any space that is big enough for its head. Weasels often live in burrows made by other animals, and they may line their nests with the fur of animals they have eaten. Weasels and similar animals produce from two to ten young each year. Like other mustelids, weasels give off a foul-smelling liquid that keeps away many enemies.

The European weasel, known as the stoat, changes color twice a year. During the summer, it has a brownish coat with a white belly. In autumn, stoats that live in cold places begin to shed their brown fur. White fur grows in its place, except for a large black patch on the tail. In spring, the color change is reversed. During the white stage, the animal is called an ermine. Its fur is very valuable.

Three kinds of weasels live in North America: the least weasel (the smallest mustelid), the short-tailed weasel (which is the same animal as the stoat), and the long-tailed weasel.

The coats of weasels in northern areas also change to white in winter. During the white stage, these weasels are also referred to as ermines.

Polecats and Ferrets

Polecats live in open areas of Europe, Asia, and northern Africa. The European species are the European polecat and the Steppe polecat. Their fur is a mix of colors, with a shiny blackish topcoat covering a buff-colored undercoat. Polecats are usually active at night. During the day they sleep in holes they have dug or in burrows deserted by other animals. They feed mainly on mice, rats, and other small rodents. People in many parts of Europe hunt polecats because they kill chickens and game birds. In the fur industry, a polecat pelt is known as fitch.

A close relative of the European polecat is the black-footed ferret, which ranges from southern Canada to Texas. It has pale yellow-brown fur, black feet, a black-tipped tail, and eyes covered by a black mask. Now one of the world's rarest mammals, it lives in prairie dog tunnels and feeds on prairie dogs and other burrowing animals.

The domestic ferret, often kept as a pet, is a relative of the European polecat. It has pale yellow to almost white fur, pink eyes, and a pink nose. Its long, slender body allows it to follow rats and rabbits into their burrows.

During the winter, the coats of weasels living in northern areas turn white. While they are in this white stage, the animals are called ermines.

People have used domestic ferrets to help catch these animals since ancient times.

Mink

Mink are slender-bodied animals with rather bushy tails. They are found throughout the northern parts of the world. They inhabit wooded areas near streams and live in burrows or under tree roots. Their partly webbed hind feet make them good swimmers. Mink catch fish, mice, rats, and birds and are especially fond of muskrat. The fur of the wild mink varies from light brown to a deep blackish brown. This fur is highly prized. Today the number of wild mink trapped for fur has declined. More than half the mink used in

Mink live in northern wooded areas throughout the world. Their fur has long been highly valued.

the fur industry are raised on mink ranches. Through selective breeding, many different shades of fur have been developed.

Martens

Martens inhabit forests in the northern parts of the world. They are very agile in moving through trees. They hunt at night, preying on squirrels, birds, frogs, and other small animals. They also eat eggs and berries. Martens like to keep their dark brown coats dry, so they avoid rain.

The beech, or stone, marten of Europe and central Asia lives in rocky places but is also found around stables, barns, and woodpiles. The yellow-throated marten, which lives in eastern Asia, gets its name from its yellow-orange chin and throat. It is fond of honey. The pine marten, found in Europe and Asia, has a patch of golden fur on its chest. Its fur is highly val-

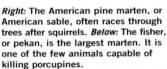

Right: The American pine marten, or American sable, often races through trees after squirrels. *Below:* The fisher, or pekan, is the largest marten. It is one of the few animals capable of killing porcupines.

ued. Other marten species include the Japanese marten and the Nilgiri marten of southern India.

The American pine marten, often called the American sable, is usually dark brown with a white or orange patch on its throat. An active hunter, it moves quickly through trees to catch squirrels. It is found in evergreen forests of the northeastern and western United States and in Canada and Alaska.

The marten called the Siberian or Russian sable is often considered the most valuable furbearing mustelid. This animal lives in forests from eastern Russia through Siberia to Japan. It is hunted for its beautiful and durable fur, which is usually dark brown to

almost black. A spot on the throat may be white, buff, or orange. Sable are rare, even though laws now regulate trapping them.

Another rare marten is the fisher, or pekan. The largest marten, it sometimes measures more than 3 feet (1 meter) in length. The fisher hunts rabbits, squirrels, and other small game on the ground. It sometimes hunts in treetops, and it is one of the few animals that kills and eats porcupines. The fisher inhabits forest regions of the northern United States and Canada. The fur of the female is especially valuable.

Wolverines

The wolverine is a large and powerful mustelid, measuring more than 30 inches (76 centimeters) and weighing up to 60 pounds

Ratel

Although it is not a true badger, the ratel is often called the honey badger because of its fondness for honey. A bird called the honeyguide helps the ratel find honey. When the honeyguide finds a beehive, it emits a shrill call that attracts the ratel. The ratel then tears apart the hive to fill up on bees and honey. The animal's very thick hide and dense fur protect it against stings.

The pattern of the ratel's coat is unusual. It is gray and white on the back and black on the belly. Most furbearing animals have dark backs and light bellies. The ratel, about the size of a true badger, lives in burrows or hollow trees during the day. At night it searches for small animals, honey, and fruit to eat. The ratel is also a powerful fighter. It is found in southern Asia and in Africa south of the Sahara desert.

(27 kilograms). It has a heavy body and strong claws and teeth. Its dark fur is marked with a pale band that runs along each side of the body, from the neck to the upper part of the bushy tail. In the winter a wolverine can kill animals much larger than itself, such as elk and caribou, by overtaking them in deep snow. The wolverine jumps on the animal's back and sinks its sharp teeth into its neck.

The wolverine is found in the evergreen forests and mountainous areas of northern North America, Asia, and Europe. Its fur does not retain moisture, which makes it especially valuable to people in the Arctic. They use it to trim the hoods of their parkas.

Reviewed by JAMES A. ESTES
University of California, Santa Cruz

OTTO

Otto is a Germanic name that means "prosperous." Four kings of Germany and Holy Roman emperors and one king of Greece reigned (r.) under this name.

▶ **KINGS OF GERMANY AND HOLY ROMAN EMPERORS**

Otto I (the Great) (912–73), king of Germany (r. 936–61) and Holy Roman emperor (r. 962–73), was born in Quedlinburg, Saxony, to the future king Henry I (the Fowler). One of the most important rulers and warriors of the early Middle Ages, Otto earned his reputation by stabilizing Germany and Italy, a feat he accomplished by installing family members as dukes and bishops throughout his realm. For example, he made his brother Bruno archbishop of Cologne.

Otto's most spectacular military victory came in 955 when he defeated the Magyars (Hungarians) at Lechfeld (near Augsburg). It was one of the most decisive battles of the Middle Ages as it was crucial to ending attacks of the so-called barbarians from the east. Otto then turned his attentions to Italy, where he met opposition from local nobles and from the Byzantine Empire.

In 962 he was crowned Holy Roman emperor by Pope John XII, which revived the empire begun by Charlemagne in 800. Otto deposed the pope in 963 and replaced him with his own candidates, first Leo VIII and, after Leo's death in 965, John XIII.

Otto II (955–83), king of Germany (r. 961–83) and Holy Roman emperor (r. 973–83), was born in Saxony, the son of Otto I (with whom he had ruled as co-emperor from 967). In 974 Otto II put down a rebellion in Bavaria led by his distant cousin. He later fought a war with France and won the province of Lorraine. But in 982 he was defeated at Crotone in southern Italy by a combined Arab and Byzantine force. He died in Rome the following year.

Otto III (980–1002), king of Germany (r. 983–1002) and Holy Roman emperor (r. 996–1002), came to the throne at an early age on the death of his father, Otto II. In Otto's youth the kingdom was ruled by his mother, Theophano, and his paternal grandmother, Adelaide.

When he became old enough to rule, Otto expanded German influence to the east by campaigning against the Wends (a group of Slavic tribes) in 997, forming an alliance with Poland, and establishing diplomatic links with Russia.

A patron of the arts and learning, Otto was a central figure in what is known as the Ottonian Renaissance. He left no descendants and was succeeded by a cousin, Henry III.

Otto IV (1174–1218), king of Germany (r. 1198–1218) and Holy Roman emperor (r. 1209–18), was the son of Henry the Lion, Duke of Bavaria and Saxony. Otto IV, also known as Otto of Brunswick, was elected emperor after his rival, Philip of Swabia, was assassinated in 1208.

In 1212 Otto was excommunicated (excluded from the Church) by Pope Innocent III. Two years later, he was defeated by King Philip Augustus of France at the Battle of Bouvines. Otto, greatly weakened in the fighting, retired to his Duchy of Brunswick in 1215. He was succeeded as emperor by Frederick II, whose candidacy was supported by Innocent III.

▶ **KING OF GREECE**

Otto I (or Otho) (1815–67), the first king of Greece (r. 1832–62), was born in Austria, the second son of a German prince, Louis I of Bavaria. After Greece won its independence from the Ottoman Empire in 1829, a conference of European powers elected Otto to rule as the first king of modern Greece. His reign was unpopular, however, and in 1843 he was forced to accept a constitutional monarchy. He was deposed (removed from the throne) in 1862. He was succeeded by a Danish prince, who became George I.

JEREMY BLACK
University of Exeter

Otto I (the Great) was one of the most influential rulers of the early Middle Ages. He is credited with firmly establishing the Holy Roman Empire, an alliance of central and western European kingdoms that lasted nearly 1,000 years.

OTTOMAN EMPIRE

For more than six centuries, from about 1290 until 1922, the Ottoman Empire was one of the world's great powers. The center of the empire was located in Anatolia, in the region of modern-day Turkey. At the height of its influence in the 1500's, it was the world's mightiest empire. It nearly surrounded the Mediterranean Sea, covering much of southeastern Europe, northern Africa, and the Arab Middle East.

▶ ORIGINS

The Ottoman Turks were descendants of Turkoman nomads from central Asia, who entered Anatolia in the 1000's. In the late 1200's, Osman I (?–1326) became sultan (king) of a small principality in northwestern Anatolia, which bordered the Byzantine Empire. His dynasty was called Osmanli, meaning "the sons of Osman." The English word "Ottoman" comes from this.

▶ THE EMPIRE EXPANDS

In little more than a century, the Ottoman Turks became a powerful imperial force. The Turks, who were Muslims, conquered nearby lands ruled by Christian princes. The Ottoman lords allowed their subjects to remain Christian in exchange for payment.

The expansion of the empire was disrupted in 1402 when the Ottoman sultan Bayezid I was captured by Tamerlane, a conqueror from central Asia. But the sultans who followed reunited the empire, and in 1453, Mehmed II conquered Constantinople (modern-day Istanbul), the seat of the Byzantine Empire. Christians were fearful that the Ottomans would soon conquer all of Europe.

From the late 1300's, the sultans began to develop the *devshirme* system, under which some Christians were forced to convert to Islam (the Muslim religion) and serve in the Ottoman army. These Christian slaves were organized into the elite infantry corps called the **Janissaries**.

▶ THE HEIGHT OF POWER

The Ottoman Empire reached the height of its power in the 1500's. Sultan Selim I, who reigned from 1512 to 1520, conquered Egypt and Syria and gained control of the Arabian Peninsula. His successor, Suleiman I, was

In 1453, the Ottoman sultan Mehmed II conquered Constantinople, the seat of the Byzantine Empire, and established Muslim rule in southeastern Europe.

known as the Lawgiver or the Magnificent. Suleiman ruled from 1520 until 1566. During his reign he conquered the regions of modern-day Iraq, Hungary, and Albania.

Suleiman I placed great emphasis on naval power and sought to control the Mediterranean Sea. His fleet, commanded by fierce pirates called corsairs, managed to defeat the combined forces of Europe's greatest seafaring powers.

The most famous of the Ottoman corsairs was Khayr ad-Din, whom the Europeans called Barbarossa (the Italian word for "redbeard"). Between 1518 and 1544, Barbarossa repeatedly ravaged the coasts of Spain, Greece, and Italy and added Tunis, Algiers, and Oran to the Ottoman holdings in northern Africa.

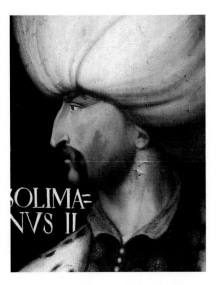

The conquests of Suleiman I (the Magnificent) brought the Ottoman Empire to the height of its power in the mid-1500's. ·

In addition to territorial conquests, Suleiman I reorganized the legal system in his empire and instituted political reforms. During his reign, literature, architecture, and art flourished. Suleiman I also established trade agreements with European nations. When he died in 1566, he left to his successors the most powerful empire in the world.

▶ **THE DECLINE OF THE EMPIRE**

After Suleiman I died, the empire began a slow, centuries-long decline. The gradual loss of power and prestige was due to many factors. First, there was no standard procedure for the orderly transition of power. The death of each sultan sometimes led to a bloodbath between his sons and other male relatives who would try to gain control. Corruption in the form of bribery was widespread. In addition, rebellions and civil wars within several provinces helped weaken the empire, as did the fact that most sultans following Suleiman I were not able rulers.

Also at this time, several nations in Europe were growing stronger in economic and military power. In 1571, Pope Pius V organized a Holy League of Christian princes (which included Genoa, Venice, Spain, Austria, and the Papal States) with the purpose of challenging Ottoman power. In that year, the fleet of the Holy League defeated the Ottoman Navy at the Battle of Lepanto, off the coast of Greece. The European alliance sank 80 Ottoman ships and captured 130 others. More important, the victory did much to dispel the myth that the Turks were invincible.

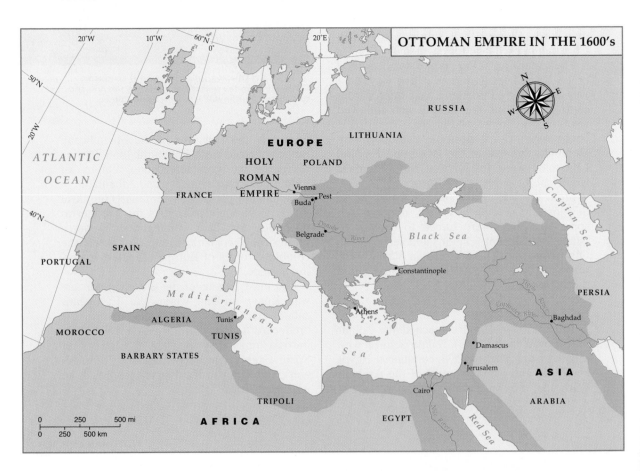

OTTOMAN EMPIRE IN THE 1600's

Although the Ottomans reconquered part of Iraq in 1638 and captured Crete from the Venetians in 1669, they failed to take Vienna in 1683 during an invasion of central Europe. After this defeat, the Ottoman Army became increasingly disorganized and major Ottoman territories were lost to the Europeans.

During the 1700's a series of wars with Russia and Austria accelerated the empire's decline and loss of territory. At the same time, the sultans lost much of their influence, even in the territories they still controlled. Russia sought to incorporate Ottoman lands into the Russian Empire. Other European nations were opposed to this plan, and disagreements over this issue eventually sparked the Crimean War (1853–56). France and Great Britain allied themselves with the Ottoman Empire and succeeded in preventing Russian expansion into Ottoman territory.

However, the empire failed to regain any strength and became known as the Sick Man of Europe. And the problem called the Eastern Question—which revolved around who would take control over the Ottoman territories when the empire disintegrated—was a persistent issue in European politics.

In addition, several of Europe's major powers interfered with the empire's internal affairs to make sure that the "Sick Man" would not recover.

▶ **THE FOUNDING OF MODERN TURKEY**

World War I (1914–18) dealt the final blow to the Ottoman Empire. Allied with Germany and the other Central Powers, it succeeded in holding on to Constantinople and the Dardanelles, a strategically important waterway. However, when the Central Powers lost the war, the Ottomans were forced to give up the remnants of their empire.

The continued attempt of the victorious Allied Powers to take control of Anatolia from the Turks led to the Turkish war for independence (1918–22). Under the leadership of Kemal Atatürk, the Turkish nationalists expelled the foreigners and established the Republic of Turkey, which was recognized by the Treaty of Lausanne, in 1923.

CASS R. SANDAK
Author, *Explorers and Discovery*
Reviewed by WILLIAM OCHSENWALD
Virginia Polytechnic Institute and State University

OURAY. See COLORADO (Famous People).

Mehmed II

SULTANS OF THE OTTOMAN EMPIRE

NAME	RULED
Osman I	1290–1326
Orhan	1326–60
Murad I	1360–89
Bayezid I	1389–1402
Interregnum	*1402–13*
Mehmed I	1413–21
Murad II	1421–44
Mehmed II	1444–46
Murad II (restored)	1446–51
Mehmed II (restored)	1451–81
Bayezid II	1481–1512
Selim I	1512–20
Suleiman I	1520–66
Selim II	1566–74
Murad III	1574–95
Mehmed III	1595–1603
Ahmed I	1603–17
Mustafa I	1617–18
Osman II	1618–22
Mustafa I (restored)	1622–23
Murad IV	1623–40
Ibrahim	1640–48
Mehmed IV	1648–87
Suleiman II	1687–91
Ahmed II	1691–95
Mustafa II	1695–1703
Ahmed III	1703–30
Mahmud I	1730–54
Osman III	1754–57
Mustafa III	1757–74
Abdulhamid I	1774–89
Selim III	1789–1807
Mustafa IV	1807–08
Mahmud II	1808–39
Abdulmecid	1839–61
Abdulaziz	1861–76
Murad V	1876
Abdulhamid II	1876–1909
Mehmed V	1909–18
Mehmed VI	1918–22

OUTDOOR COOKING AND PICNICS

Almost everybody loves a cookout or a picnic. With good company and a pleasant setting, even the simplest foods seem tastier.

▶ OUTDOOR COOKING

Most people use grills to cook outdoors. Grills come in many shapes and sizes. The most common types are gas, electric, and charcoal. You can also burn wood in a charcoal grill.

Gas and electric grills are usually used at home, on a patio or deck. Charcoal grills are more portable and can be used anywhere. Picnic and camping areas often provide grills, and picnickers need only bring charcoal.

In addition to a grill, other supplies needed for outdoor cooking include fireproof mitts, long-handled barbecue tools (forks, tongs, and a spatula), trays to hold meat and other supplies, and a pastry brush or large plastic baster for applying barbecue sauces or marinades. A carving knife and carving board, metal or bamboo skewers, and aluminum foil may also be useful.

If you are using a gas or electric grill, you must wait until it reaches the proper temperature (usually about 10 to 15 minutes) before beginning to cook; many of these grills are equipped with thermometers. If you are using a charcoal grill, you will know that the coals have reached the right temperature when the flames have died down and the coals are red and glowing.

Before placing the grill rack over the heat, be sure it is clean. Next, moisten it with cooking oil, using a small brush, cloth, or paper towel. This will keep the food from sticking. Later, after removing the cooked food from the grill, leave the grill rack in place so the fire will burn off any food residue.

Many foods are suitable for grilling, including steaks, hamburgers, hot dogs, chops, chicken, fish, and many vegetables. Some people even grill fruits such as bananas, peaches, and plums.

Most foods should be turned several times during cooking. You may also want to move food around on the grill so that it cooks evenly. To do this, use long-handled tongs or a spatula. Do not use a fork because it will puncture the food and release the juices.

When you are grilling (or anytime you are cooking), be sure to keep raw meat and poultry—and anything it has come into contact with—separate from ready-to-eat foods. This helps avoid the transmission of bacteria that can cause food poisoning. For example, you should never put cooked chicken on the same plate that held raw chicken, unless it has been washed in hot, soapy water.

▶ PICNICS

It is also important to consider food safety when planning a picnic. Since picnics are most popular during warm weather, special care must be taken to prevent food spoilage. The best way to avoid this is to select foods that do not spoil easily. These include many baked goods, canned or ready-to-eat packaged foods, peanut butter and jelly sandwiches, pickles, chips, and fruit.

However, if your picnic includes foods that may spoil, you must keep them at the proper temperature until you are ready to eat. To keep food hot, store in a thermos or other insulated container. To keep food cold, chill well first, then pack in an insulated container or cooler with plenty of ice or cold packs.

You can also keep food cold by freezing it ahead of time; it will defrost on the way to the picnic. Foods that freeze well include meats such as chicken and ribs (either cooked or uncooked) and cheese and meat sandwiches. If you are planning to grill hamburgers, it is easier if you make the patties in advance, then wrap and freeze. Before wrapping, place a small square of waxed paper between each burger so you can easily separate them later.

Beverages, such as those that come in individual packages and bottles, can also be frozen ahead of time. These can help keep other foods cold.

When you are eating outdoors, try to keep food covered whenever possible. This will protect it from insects, birds, and pets.

In addition to food, your picnic basket should include plastic cups, dishes (or paper plates), napkins, and utensils. You may also want to include bottle and can openers, a picnic tablecloth, a cutting board, trash bags, plastic bags or containers for leftovers, insect repellent, and hand wipes.

SYLVIA ROSENTHAL
Author, *Live High on Low Fat*

Masked outlaws cut a fence to steal cattle from a Nebraska ranch. Lawlessness was common on the frontier during the early days of the American West.

OUTLAWS

Throughout history, the outlaw has been portrayed as a victim of circumstance—one who has been driven by unjust laws or unfair treatment to perform illegal acts. Unlike other kinds of criminals, however, the outlaw has been romanticized as a criminal of honor; his or her crimes are seen as being directed against those who oppress or exploit others, rather than the innocent. One of the best-known examples of this is Robin Hood, the legendary hero of medieval England. He and his followers robbed from the rich and gave to the poor, often risking their own lives.

Not all outlaws fit this description, however. Although an outlaw does not fall into the same category as, for instance, a serial killer, some have killed many people. Others have been driven more by a desire for money, prestige, and power than a wish to help the less fortunate.

Regardless of the reasons for their crimes, many outlaws have become folk heroes simply because they defied authority. To those who feel restricted or oppressed by social or political forces, the outlaw's behavior represents freedom.

Although outlaws have existed for as long as there have been laws, some times and places have produced more than others. During the early days of the American West, for example, lawlessness was common because circumstances permitted more crime. The frequent transport of unprotected goods, money, and people over vast distances led to numerous stagecoach and train robberies among those seeking quick and easy wealth. Law enforcement officials were unable to police such a huge area and, as a result, outlaws could easily escape. In time, however, they were brought under control. And when law enforcement was slow or ineffective, groups of citizens called **vigilantes** would sometimes band together to capture and punish the outlaws themselves.

Outlaws also thrived during prohibition (1920–33) and the Great Depression of the 1930's. In recent times, people who committed Internet crimes such as computer hacking and file sharing have been viewed as outlaws. They claimed their crimes were not meant to cause harm, however, but to challenge unjust laws and regulations.

Reviewed by GEORGE CANTOR
Author, *Bad Guys in American History*

See also JAMES, JESSE; ORGANIZED CRIME; ROBIN HOOD.

Profiles of famous outlaws appear on the following page.

Rob Roy (1671–1734), born Robert MacGregor in Scotland, has been called the Scottish Robin Hood. As a young man he raised cattle for the English market on land inherited from his father, then became a cattle thief who sold his neighbors protection against other cattle thieves.

Rob Roy

After his land was seized by the Duke of Montrose over a bad debt, he was financially ruined and declared a fraud. He fled to the Highlands with a group of armed clansmen and waged war against Montrose. He spent the next decade engaged in robbery and extortion, then surrendered to authorities. He was imprisoned, but eventually pardoned. He died at his home in Balquhidder. MacGregor was the hero of Sir Walter Scott's novel *Rob Roy*.

William Clarke Quantrill (1837–65), born in Canal Dover, Ohio, was a Confederate guerrilla leader during the U.S. Civil War. As a young man, he was a farmer, gambler, and a schoolteacher. When the Civil War began, Quantrill organized a band of guerrilla troops and led raids against Union sympathizers. His men burned and looted Union strongholds in Kansas and Missouri, diverting thousands of Union troops. Quantrill's band was mustered into Confederate service in 1862, but continued to operate independently. On August 21, 1863, they pillaged Lawrence, Kansas, killing more than 150 civilians. Quantrill died in prison in Louisville, Kentucky, after being wounded by Union troops.

Belle Starr

Belle Starr (1848–89) was born Myra Mayelle Shirley in Carthage, Missouri, and educated at the Carthage Female Academy. During the U.S. Civil War, she provided the Confederates with information about Union troops. She later joined the outlaw gang of William Quantrill and married another gang member, Jim Reed. After Reed was killed she married Sam Starr, who was part Cherokee, and moved to Indian Territory in present-day Oklahoma. Their home became a haven for outlaws. An expert rider and crack shot, Belle was accused of various crimes over the years. These included arson, robbery, horse theft, and the illegal sale of liquor. She was shot and killed near Eufaula, Oklahoma, by an unknown assailant.

Ned Kelly

Ned Kelly (1854–80), Australia's most famous outlaw, was born to a poor Irish pig farmer in Beveridge, Victoria. He was arrested and imprisoned at age 16 for receiving a stolen horse. After shooting a police officer who was arresting his brother, he fled with his brother and two friends into the bush. The group then began robbing banks. However, by robbing only the rich and sparing lives—and publicizing his mistreatment by police—Kelly became a folk hero. Several months later, during a battle with police, Kelly killed three constables. He escaped, but police eventually cornered him and his companions. During the ensuing battle, Kelly's companions were killed and he was arrested. He was hanged several months later in a Melbourne jail.

Pancho Villa

Francisco "Pancho" Villa (1878–1923) was born to sharecropper parents in the Mexican state of Durango. After killing a man to defend his sister, he hid out in the mountains and became a thief, robbing trains, looting banks, and raiding mines. He later led revolts against Mexican president Porfirio Díaz and dictator Victoriano Huerta. He also led a guerilla raid into the United States to retaliate against U.S. recognition of conservative leader Venustiano Carranza. In response, U.S. president Woodrow Wilson dispatched a cavalry force against Villa. After Carranza was killed in 1920, Villa was given amnesty in return for laying down his arms. He was assassinated three years later at Hidalgo del Parral, Chihuahua.

Bonnie and Clyde

Clyde Barrow (1909–34) and **Bonnie Parker** (1910–34) were partners during the Great Depression. Barrow, born in Tellice, Texas, met Parker in January 1930, shortly before he was jailed for theft. Parker, born in Rowena, Texas, was working as a waitress in a Dallas cafe. Although she was married, her husband, Roy Thornton, was serving a 99-year prison sentence for murder. Several months after Barrow was imprisoned, he and his cellmate escaped after Parker smuggled a pistol into their cell. Parker and Barrow then formed a stickup team with Ray Hamilton and began robbing grocery stores, gas stations, and small banks in the Southwest. They killed twelve people before they were caught and killed in a police ambush in Black Lake, Louisiana, in May 1934. Barrow and Parker were the subject of the 1967 movie *Bonnie and Clyde*.

Kevin Mitnick

Kevin Mitnick (1963–), born in Van Nuys, California, became the world's most wanted computer hacker in the 1990's. Mitnick first learned how to bypass computer security systems in his teens. His goal, he said, was to understand how computer and telecommunication systems worked. He later hacked (broke into) some of the largest and best-protected computer systems in the world. In 1995, Mitnick was arrested by federal authorities and charged with breaking into the networks of software and phone companies. He and his supporters claimed his hacking had not caused any harm, but he was sentenced to five years in prison. Mitnick was released in January 2000 and placed on parole for three years. He now operates a computer security company.

OUTLINES

Have you ever seen a tree outlined against the sky or a person outlined against a bright light? What did you learn from these outlines? You discovered certain general characteristics, or main features. You saw that the tree was tall or short, wide or narrow, leafy or bare. You were able to tell that the person was an adult or a child, tall or short, heavy or thin.

In much the same way, a written outline provides a general description, or overview, of a subject. An outline is a plan that organizes material to show its main ideas and their relative importance. You can use outlines to help you understand and remember material you have read. You can also use them to organize your own ideas for oral or written reports and compositions.

▶ **OUTLINE STRUCTURE**

There are two kinds of outlines. When ideas are written down in single words or phrases, the outline is called a **topic** outline. When ideas are written down in complete sentences, the outline is called a **sentence** outline. Do not mix the two kinds within the same outline.

In either case, the outline must have an organized structure, with the material divided into topics and subtopics. These are ordered using a system of numbers and letters. Items that have equal importance are assigned comparable numbers or letters. That is, an item labeled A should be equal to those labeled B and C, while an item labeled 1 should equal those labeled 2 and 3, and so on. For example, if you are outlining material you have read on the westward movement, your outline might be written in the following way:

The Westward Movement
A. Routes
  1. Overland
  2. Isthmus of Panama
  3. Cape Horn
B. Life of settlers
  1. Indian troubles

  2. Communication problems
C. Ways of living
  1. In a mission
  2. On a farm
    a. Women's work
    b. Men's work
  3. In a mining town

This same outline could be presented using a number of other forms. For example, Roman numerals could be used for the top level of topics, capital letters for the next level, and Arabic numerals for the third. Whatever form is chosen, it should be used throughout the entire outline.

Notice how the information is organized in the outline above. Related ideas are grouped together. And within each group a general topic is followed by more specific subtopics. Each subdivision has at least two parts: An A is always followed by a B, and number 1 is always followed by number 2. Notice also that a straight vertical line can be drawn from one main topic to any other main topic or from one subtopic to any other subtopic; that a period is put after every letter and every number; and that the first word in each item is capitalized.

▶ **OUTLINING MATERIAL YOU HAVE READ**

Outlining material you have read is easier than outlining your own ideas. The author's organization helps you recognize main topics and subtopics and provides the sequence in which to list them.

For example, a student read a chapter in a book on the South before the Civil War. He took the following notes:

Was agricultural society
Developed large plantations
Needed many field-workers
Raised tobacco and cotton
Used slave labor
Life of slave very hard
Planter's life easy
Different opinions about slavery

When asked to submit an outline of the chapter, the student organized his notes as follows:

The South Before Civil War

A. Physical factors
    1. Climate
    2. Natural resources
    3. Dependence on agriculture
    4. Crops—tobacco, cotton
B. Social factors
    1. Class distinctions
    2. Plantation life
    3. Slave labor—1619
C. Differing views
    1. North
    2. South
    3. Abolitionists—Garrison, Stowe

Another student decided to write a report on penguins. She gathered information from several books and magazine articles, taking the following notes as she read:

Have black backs, white breasts
Swim better than they walk
Can stay underwater 45 seconds
Can't fly—wings are short flippers
Live in Antarctic
Look like fat men in dress suits
Oily feathers keep them warm
Nest on rocks and ice

She made the following sentence outline from her notes:

Penguins

I. Penguins are strange-looking birds that look like little fat men in dress suits.
    A. They have black backs and white breasts.
    B. They are about 3 feet tall, with short legs and wings.
II. Penguins live on the land and in the water.
    A. On the land the penguin stands up straight on his short legs and walks with a clumsy waddle.

    B. In the water the penguin can swim fast and stay underwater for as long as 45 seconds.
    C. Penguins cannot fly.
        1. Their wings are short flippers.
        2. The flippers are used in swimming.
III. Penguins live in the Antarctic region.
    A. They build nests on rocky and icy cliffs.
    B. They are kept from getting cold by oily feathers.

Using the same notes, the student could have made a topic outline.

Penguins

I. Strange-looking birds
    A. Look like short fat men in dress suits
    B. Black backs and white breasts
    C. Short legs and wings
II. Live on land and water
    A. Walk with a clumsy waddle
    B. Swim fast
    C. Can stay underwater for 45 seconds
    D. Cannot fly
III. Live in the Antarctic
    A. Build nests on rocks and ice
    B. Kept warm by oily feathers

▶ OUTLINING YOUR OWN IDEAS

When you are asked to give a talk or write a composition, you may be tempted to skip outlining your ideas and plunge into the writing. You will find, however, that though outlines take time, they greatly improve the quality and effectiveness of your work.

Your experience outlining the ideas of others will help you organize and outline your own material. In beginning to prepare your outline, it is helpful to follow the key steps listed below.

Determine Your Purpose. Think about the purpose of your talk or composition. Are you trying to prove a point? Resolve a dispute? Answer a question? Once you have determined your purpose, try to express it in a single sentence. This is called a topic sentence, or

thesis statement, and it is a very helpful first step in preparing your outline.

Gather Ideas. Think of as many ideas as you can about your topic and jot them down. If you have chosen your own topic, you will probably have no problem thinking of ideas. If you are assigned a topic, however, you may have to do some reading on the subject or question people who may have useful information.

Organize Your Thoughts. Once you have listed your ideas, group together those that are related to each other. For example, if you are describing the care of a dog, you might group items related to feeding, to training, to bathing, and so on. If you are reporting on famous people of our day, you might group them by occupation—as political leaders, astronauts, scientists, athletes, and so on.

Order the Outline. Evaluate the items within each group and order them according to their relative importance. Pick out the main ideas in your list; they will be your topics. Divide each topic into a series of related subtopics.

Remember to present your ideas in a logical order or sequence—from general to specific, for example. You can also use a chronological, or time, order. Or you can follow the steps that might be taken to make something, do something, or go somewhere.

▶ **PREPARING A TALK OR COMPOSITION**

Suppose you are asked to prepare material on a subject of very common concern to students: taking an after-school job. You might try the following approach.

First, think about the topic before you begin to write. When a particularly important idea comes to mind, jot it down as a possible thesis statement. A good thesis statement for this particular topic might be "There are advantages and disadvantages to taking a job after school."

Make two columns, headed **Advantages** and **Disadvantages**. Put down ideas in either column as they occur to you.

Advantages	Disadvantages
Money for family	Long day
Money for myself	Less time for homework
Good experience	No after-school sports
Feeling of independence	
Make new friends	
Please Mom and Dad	

After introducing your topic, discuss the advantages and disadvantages. Your outline might look something like this:

An After-School Job

A. Why I need a job
   1. Need money for Christmas gifts
   2. Need to chip in on car insurance
B. Advantages
   1. Extra spending money
   2. Please Mom and Dad
   3. Feel independent
C. Disadvantages
   1. Less time for homework
   2. No after-school sports
   3. Long day

Check the completed outline, looking particularly for items that are out of place. Make sure that your topics and subtopics are properly ordered and that items of equal importance have been given comparable numbers or letters.

Begin to write your composition. Feel free to add any new ideas that occur to you as you write. If you have to hand in the outline, be sure it includes the new ideas.

Outlining is a skill you will find useful throughout your life. In school, at work, and in many other areas, you will find that an organized approach to thinking and writing can be a great help in making decisions and resolving problems.

ROSEMARY E. WAGNER
Bureau of Curriculum Research, New York City

OVERLAND TRAILS

"Old America seems to be breaking up and moving westward," a British traveler wrote in the early 1800's. Thousands of Americans would have agreed with him. To many farmers of that time, the grass always seemed greener just over a western hill.

The mass migration into the West that began late in the 1700's, after the Revolutionary War, was greater than any previous movement like it in history. When the migration started, the American colonies were all on the eastern coast of North America. When it ended, less than 100 years later, pioneers had settled across the continent, a distance of nearly 3,000 miles (4,800 kilometers) from east to west.

The charters of seven of the American colonies granted territories from sea to sea. But in the 1600's and 1700's, when these charters were drawn up, no one knew how far it was to the western sea (Pacific Ocean) or how much of the land was free for the colonies to claim. Native American Indians roamed the Far West, and parts of it were explored and claimed by France and Spain. Early in the 1700's, France held the region from the Appalachian Mountains to the Mississippi River. England won this section after the French and Indian War (1754–63), and after the Revolutionary War (1775–83) it became part of the United States. However, even before the region belonged to the United States, Americans were settling into it.

▶ THE FIRST TRAILS

The westward movement followed a pattern. Pioneers hungry for land and freedom pushed toward the wilderness, but barriers such as mountains stood in the way. Advance scouts found trails through the mountains. More and more settlers followed the trails until the land was filled. Then scouts found paths past the next barrier, which might be another mountain range or a vast forest or desert. Since migration was often blocked by the Indians who held the land, moving into the West meant fighting as well as trail blazing. But one by one the barriers came down.

The trails were as simple as nature would allow. The first trailbreakers were buffalo, deer, and antelope. Their trails led to low divides and shallow fords across rivers. The Indians followed these animal trails, beating them down and widening them. Later scouts—mostly hunters, trappers, and traders—followed the Indian trails.

Most animal and Indian trails were short, but trappers linked them together into routes leading from one part of the country to another. Where possible, the routes followed rivers, since river travel was easier than overland travel, especially where rivers cut through the mountain ranges.

In the 1700's, scouts from the backwoods of the eastern colonies roamed into Kentucky or Tennessee in pursuit of deer and other

In his painting *Traders Descending the Missouri* (1845), American frontier artist George Caleb Bingham captured the serenity of a time when rivers were common routes of transportation.

▶ THE APPALACHIAN WALL

By 1740 the eastern coast of North America from Maine to Georgia held a rapidly growing population. Plantations in Virginia spread into the hills and stopped before the barrier of the Blue Ridge Mountains, a chief range of the southern Appalachian Mountains. In the middle colonies German and Scotch-Irish newcomers pushed south along the Shenandoah Valley and northwest up the Susquehanna River. They settled the valleys between the Appalachian ridges. They, too, faced a mighty Appalachian barrier—the Great Allegheny Front, rising 1,000 feet (300 meters) or more above the valley. Pioneers had come up against a stone wall.

Beyond the mountains, according to traders, lay a vast saucer-shaped lowland. They knew that it stretched at least as far as the Mississippi River, but no one knew how much farther it might reach. The land was level and fertile. Through this fertile land ran a mighty network of rivers—the Mississippi and its tributaries—providing a water highway from the Appalachians to the Gulf of Mexico. Dreamers hoped that there were rivers that ran all the way to the western sea.

Two natural routes led past the mountain walls to this rich land. There was a northern route, through the Mohawk Valley, and also a southern route, around the mountains. However, the Mohawk Valley was inhabited by unfriendly Iroquois Indians, and the southern route was blocked by Cherokee Indians. Beyond the mountains lay fortified

animals whose hides they could sell. They found that a man could live on the land with only his ax and his gun. Some hunters built lonely huts far beyond the edge of the settled colonies. There were also fur trappers who sought beaver pelts, which were much in demand. When they had trapped most of the beaver in the Appalachian hunting grounds, they moved farther west. Early in the 1800's, beaver trappers went up the Missouri River and into the Rocky Mountains. In their search for beaver they eventually explored much of the North American continent. They found the mountain passes and marked the paths that wagon trains would follow later.

Traders followed the trails the trappers had blazed and traded with the Indians for furs. Traders brought back news of beautiful lands and new trails. Government explorers also went into the wilderness. Unlike the trappers, these men published reports about their discoveries and made maps of the wilderness. Speculators saw a chance to buy land cheaply from the government and make a fortune selling it to settlers hungry for farmland. They

While hunting for furs, mountain men explored the western wilderness and found the best routes across the mountains.

promoted the land and nurtured among easterners a growing enthusiasm to go west along the trails that trappers, traders, and explorers were opening.

French trading posts. In the mid-1700's, the Appalachian Mountains, the French, and the Indians all stood like a dam, holding back the flood of Americans eager to reach the new lands.

Gist's Trace

Between 1740 and 1750 brisk trading went on between the British and the Shawnee and Delaware tribes near present-day Pittsburgh, Pennsylvania. However, the trails blazed by traders were not wide enough or smooth enough for wagons. Christopher Gist (1706?–59) blazed the first wagon road in 1753. The road started in Maryland, near Fort Cumberland on the Potomac River, and followed Indian trails to the Monongahela River, which joins the Ohio River. Gist's Trace, as the road was called, was too rough to accommodate the migration of large numbers of people, but

known as the Cumberland, or National, Road. In 1758, General John Forbes, a British officer who captured Fort Duquesne from the French and renamed it Fort Pitt, carved another road—Forbes Road—through the Pennsylvania Alleghenies, from Fort Loudon to Fort Pitt. These early roads soon became the first of many heavily used overland trails.

After the war the French were gone, and the Treaty of Fort Stanwix (1768) opened the country south and east of the Ohio River for settlement. Pittsburgh, at the western end of the military roads, was the jumping-off place for settlers bound for Ohio. The town was filled with excitement every spring. Families poured in along the trails—about 50,000 settlers by 1774. Covered wagons and flatboats

The Cumberland Road was the first national highway. Begun in Cumberland, Maryland, in 1811, it eventually led to Vandalia, an early capital of Illinois.

it was the first wagon road to connect the East with the Mississippi waterways.

The Cumberland (National) Road

The French and Indians resisted the invasion of traders from British colonies, and these conflicts led to the outbreak of the French and Indian War in 1754. However, in order to move their troops and supplies, armies needed roads. The British general Edward Braddock cut a road that ran near Gist's Trace, from Fort Cumberland to Fort Duquesne (now Pittsburgh) at the fork of the Ohio River. In the early 1800's, this road was extended to Vandalia, Illinois, and became

crowded the banks of the Monongahela River, waiting for the spring thaw to break the ice on the Ohio River. Then there was high water and clear sailing to Kentucky and new farm homes along the rich river valleys.

Boone's Wilderness Road and the Cumberland Gap

From his home in North Carolina, Daniel Boone went hunting far into the Blue Ridge Mountains. Like other frontiersmen, he knew the hunters' tales of a paradise west of the Shenandoah Valley, a place where deer crowded the grasslands and turkeys got so fat they broke the branches of trees when they perched on them. But the forbidding Allegheny wall blocked the way. People said there was a break in the wall, but no one knew where it was.

In 1769, Boone entertained a peddler, John Finley. As a captive of the Indians, Finley had seen the bluegrass meadows alive with game. He had heard that this land lay near the rumored mountain pass, and he thought he could find it. He offered to guide Boone. The men set out, and in time they came to a giant V in the ridge, beneath a 1,500-foot (457-meter) cliff. This was what they had sought—the Cumberland Gap, gateway to Kentucky.

Turning north, Finley and Boone followed the Warriors' Path (an Indian path) and hunters' trails. After many adventures, Boone came out of the mountains and looked for the first time upon the fabled bluegrass land. In 1775, with 30 men, he cut a wagon road along this route they called the Wilderness Road. At its western end, near the Kentucky River, the men built a frontier stockade and named it Boonesborough. The Wilderness Road, the most difficult trail through the mountains, never became an improved highway. But it was an important migration route during the Revolutionary War period. Between 1775 and 1790, about 70,000 people traveled the route to settle in Kentucky. They paid a high price, however, as many lost their lives to Indian attacks. With good reason this country became known as the Dark and Bloody Ground.

▶ **FROM THE APPALACHIAN MOUNTAINS TO THE MISSISSIPPI RIVER**

Between 1790 and 1840, settlers filled the plains between the Appalachians and the Mississippi River. During the War of 1812 almost the last of the hostile Indian tribes was defeated. The Mississippi basin set up no barriers. Its river system provided a highway along which settlers could float their families and household goods on flatboats. Towns sprang up rapidly along the riverbanks. By 1825 the frontier had reached St. Louis.

The land of the Mississippi basin seemed to be the heaven that the pioneers had been trying for so long to find. Its soil was rich and black, and its rivers gave farmers a way to market their goods downstream as far as New Orleans. Traders often returned on horseback, following the road called the

From 1804 to 1806, Lewis and Clark headed an expedition to find an overland route to the Pacific Ocean. They were guided on their journey by Sacagawea, a Shoshoni Indian woman.

Natchez Trace from Natchez, Mississippi, to Nashville, Tennessee.

Until about 1840 the Middle West supplied enough land for pioneers. Therefore the settlers' frontier paused along the Mississippi and the Missouri rivers. Beyond the rivers, a sea of grass stretched as far west as the eye could see. Farmers assumed that because there were no trees the soil must be poor. Stephen Long, a government explorer, had visited the Southwest in 1820 and called the Great Plains the "Great American Desert." Few pioneers wanted to venture beyond the rivers. But the advance scouts went on, finding new paths and trails that would carry the next wave of wagons west when the time came.

▶ **SCOUTING THE FAR WEST**

Meriwether Lewis and William Clark led the most famous exploring party of pioneer days, the Lewis and Clark expedition (1804–06). They struggled through the northern Rockies, where only Indians had gone before, and reached the Pacific Ocean. Returning from Oregon, they tested new routes. They brought back the first accurate information about the Far West. The news that Rocky Mountain streams teemed with beaver aroused great excitement in the East.

Fur traders hurried in the wake of Lewis and Clark. In 1811 and 1812, traders sent west by John Jacob Astor (1763–1848) crossed the continent to Oregon and returned east. Coming back, they traced part of the route that became the Oregon Trail. They crossed the Rockies at South Pass, the main gateway through the mountains. The pass was forgotten but was rediscovered twelve years later by a great American explorer, a trapper named Jedediah Smith (1799–1831). Then, in 1826, Smith led the first explorers to reach California overland from the United States.

By the 1820's traders and trappers were already exploring the Rockies. And the earliest of the Far Western overland wagon trails was open—the road to Santa Fe.

▶ THE SANTA FE TRAIL

The Santa Fe Trail was a traders' path. Never an actual road, it was a broad route following rivers and wagon ruts, passing known landmarks. It led from the Missouri River to Santa Fe, New Mexico.

For some time American traders had been eyeing the riches of Santa Fe. The people of that lonely Mexican mission town wanted to trade with Americans, for Missouri was nearer than Mexico City. But Mexico's Spanish rulers forbade trade and jailed American traders. When Mexico rebelled against Spain in 1820, however, Santa Fe was opened wide to the expanding American trade.

Traders Blaze the Trail

The first man to reach Santa Fe after trade opened was William Becknell (1790?–1832), who is called the Father of the Santa Fe Trail. He was on a western trading trip in 1821 when he heard that Mexico had declared its independence from Spain. He immediately turned his caravan to Santa Fe, where he traded his goods for Mexican dollars, then worth five times what the goods had cost. On the return trip, winter snow clogged the

northern trail through the Raton Pass, pioneered by explorer Zebulon Pike (1779–1813). Becknell took a shortcut across the Cimarron Desert. This Cimarron Cutoff became part of the Santa Fe Trail. When Becknell returned to his home in Franklin, Missouri, in January 1822, he poured out his silver dollars onto the sidewalks, to the amazement of his neighbors. A new era had begun. By May, Becknell had organized a trading party. They planned to take wagons where wagons had never gone before.

Becknell and his 21 men had three heavily laden Conestoga wagons, each carrying more than 2 tons of goods. They crossed the Missouri, struck out across the Great Plains to the Arkansas River, and followed its course. Often they had to float or drag wagons across the river, to avoid steep cliffs.

At Cimarron, west of Dodge City, they turned south across the parched plains. Wagons could never travel the steep Raton Pass, so they would have to journey through the Cimarron Cutoff. That meant crossing 50 miles (80 kilometers) of dry, hot wasteland without a landmark to help them find their way or a sign of life. They struggled on, bitter dust stinging their throats and blinding them. At times they feared they would die of thirst.

Finally they reached the Cimarron River and crossed it. They were safely past the desert. But another 300 miles (480 kilometers) of rough travel through foothills lay ahead before they would reach Santa Fe. Nevertheless, they had proved men could

American traders celebrated their arrival in Santa Fe, New Mexico, after an arduous 780-mile (1,260-kilometer) journey from Independence, Missouri.

After Mexico gained its independence from Spain in 1821, Santa Fe became Mexico's primary center of trade with the United States.

take wagons over the trail. When they returned and showed their rich profits, others flocked to the trade. From 1822 to 1843, caravans headed west each spring over the Santa Fe Trail.

The First Wagon Trains

The wagons started from Franklin, and later from Independence, Missouri. At Council Grove, Kansas, 145 miles (230 kilometers) southwest of Independence, traders camped and waited for other wagons to arrive, so they could organize into one big wagon train.

Trail life had taught people that a lonely wagon was an easy target for Indians. They had to cooperate or die. So Santa Fe traders invented the wagon train, copied by all later pioneers. They organized the train like an army, electing a captain and his aides. The captain was trail boss, and his word was law. All wagons got in line and stayed together, usually in single file but sometimes, in dangerous country, in rows of two or four. A team of eight to twelve mules or oxen pulled each wagon. Mule skinners had to catch the mules, harness them, and crack whips and shout to drive them. Spare animals were herded along. Men rode horses beside the wagons, watching for trouble, or ranged far out as scouts and hunters.

The traders learned other lessons that saved lives during later migrations. They learned to post guards at night, each man taking his turn. They learned to form their wagons into a circle or square when they camped, to make a temporary fort with animals inside. In many ways they set the pattern for trail travel.

Every inch of the wagons was crammed with trading goods. Traders could carry little for their own use. For the first 270 miles (430 kilometers), till they passed the Great Bend of the Arkansas River, they lived on bacon, bread, and bitter coffee. Then they entered buffalo country and could shoot buffalo for fresh meat. They also tied strips of meat to ropes strung along wagons, to dry for future meals.

They passed Pawnee Rock, where they stopped to carve their names, and went on, crossing many streams that joined the Arkansas River. Some riverbanks were cliffs, where wagons had to be lowered with ropes. When they crossed the Arkansas, a half mile wide, some wagons struck boulders and turned over in midstream. Others got stuck in quicksand.

Danger was always around them. Indians attacked. Rattlesnakes hid in the bed blankets. Mules ran away and left wagons stranded. If someone got hurt or fell ill, there were no doctors. Sudden flash floods turned sandy flats into roaring torrents. Most of all, they dreaded crossing the desert, where there were no landmarks to guide them.

Once across the Cimarron Desert, they could follow the Cimarron River for 85 miles (137 kilometers). Then they had to climb 200 miles (322 kilometers) through rocky foothills to reach the village of Las Vegas, New Mexico. The trail rose steeply to the Apache Canyon. It was a perfect spot for an ambush. Thanks to watchful guards, few died on the trail at the hands of Indians. But one of the few was Jedediah Smith, who was killed in 1831.

Near Santa Fe, traders would stop to wash and put on clean shirts. Then they whooped into town, cracking their long whips. The people would swarm out, cheering. Santa Fe had a permanent population of about 3,000, but Mexicans came from all around to trade with the Americans.

The caravan's arrival was the big event of the year and called for celebration. Then trading would begin. The Americans brought tools, cutlery, materials, and dresses. The Mexicans paid in mules, furs, buffalo skins, silver, gold, and Mexican silver dollars.

Protecting the Trail

The Santa Fe trade was a great adventure and also a source of profit. During the twenty years it lasted, Americans made almost $3 million. Some traders made a 300 percent profit. But it was a rough and dangerous trip. To cut their losses in suffering and lives, traders asked the government for surveyors to mark the trail and for soldiers to act as guards. The government granted their requests, but the surveyors marked a longer road, which the traders refused to use. The traders also had bad luck with soldiers. In 1829, Captain Bennett Riley and a troop of foot soldiers guarded the wagons as far as the Mexican border (at the Cimarron Crossing) and stopped. One trader said this was like running a ferry to the middle of a river.

When Indians attacked the traders in the desert, the troops rushed to their defense and went on with them for two more days. The soldiers returned to the border and camped until the wagons came back. The Indians then attacked the soldiers. The army learned that without horses, soldiers were helpless in the West. Mounted soldiers guarded later wagon trains.

Territorial disputes with Mexico stopped the trade in 1843, and in 1846 the United States went to war against Mexico. When the war ended in 1848, Santa Fe belonged to the United States, and the Santa Fe Trail began serving California gold seekers. In the 1860's dust clouds thickened as traffic increased. But in the 1870's, increased use of the railroad lessened traffic on the Santa Fe Trail.

▶ THE GILA TRAIL AND THE OLD SPANISH TRAIL

Some traders wanted to trade between Santa Fe and California. In 1827 James Pattie (1804–50) and his father blazed a trail from Santa Fe along the Gila River through Arizona to the Colorado River. The Gila Trail ran through southern California.

In 1829 other groups blazed the Old Spanish Trail. Men under a Mexican trader, Antonio Armijo, and trappers led by Ewing Young (?–1841) took a route that swung north to bypass the worst deserts and the Grand Canyon. The routes from Santa Fe to California saw much use in this period. Both routes served prospectors during the California gold rush.

▶ THE GREAT MIGRATION ALONG THE OREGON TRAIL

Unlike the Santa Fe Trail, the Oregon Trail was a settlers' road. Trappers and traders blazed it, missionaries traveled it, and in the 1840's farmers poured along it by the thousands. This migration differed from any before it. Earlier pioneers had pushed perhaps 100 miles (160 kilometers) west and settled. But the pioneers of the 1840's thought the land across the Missouri was useless. So they passed by prairies, deserts, and mountains, going 2,000 miles (3,220 kilometers) to the

---

THE GREAT MIGRATION

The following is an estimate of the number of people who traveled through Nebraska along the Oregon Trail each year between 1841 and 1866:

Year	Number
1841	100
1842	200
1843	1,000
1844	2,000
1845	5,000
1846	1,000
1847	2,000
1848	4,000
1849	30,000
1850	55,000
1851	10,000
1852	50,000
1853	20,000
1854	10,000
1855	5,000
1856	5,000
1857	5,000
1858	10,000
1859	30,000
1860	15,000
1861	5,000
1862	5,000
1863	10,000
1864	20,000
1865	25,000
1866	25,000
Total	**350,300**

More than 150 years after the first wave of pioneers traveled west along the Oregon Trail, ruts carved by their wagon wheels can still be seen.

Fort Laramie, in Wyoming, was founded by fur traders in 1834. It later served as a supply station on the Oregon Trail.

Clark, the fur trappers, and the fur traders. But no one had tied the pieces together into a continuous route. The eastern part of the trail was the traders' path to their meeting place in the Rockies and was well known by 1832. In that year Captain B. L. E. de Bonneville (1796–1878) took twenty wagons through South Pass and across the Green River, proving that wagons could go at least halfway to the Pacific. Without wagons, large migrations of settlers were impossible.

The next year a Boston businessman, Nathaniel Wyeth (1803–56), took a caravan the entire length of the trail. In 1834, on his second trip, Wyeth took Protestant ministers with him. Jason Lee (1803–45) and his nephew, going to Oregon to convert the Indians, spearheaded a new movement of Christian missionaries. They were guided by mountain men, who knew the wilderness trails as well as others knew the streets in their hometown.

Trading Posts

Before 1834 there were no trading posts between Missouri and the Hudson's Bay Company post at Fort Walla Walla. In 1834 three of the four Oregon Trail stations went up. Fur traders built Fort Laramie, first called Fort William, on the North Platte River. Wyeth built Fort Hall on the Snake River. British traders built Fort Boise, also on the Snake River, northwest of Fort Hall. Only one post came later—Fort Bridger, completed by the famous scout Jim Bridger (1804–81) in 1843.

Missionaries Lead the Way

The Lees settled in the Willamette Valley. In 1836 the next Protestant missionaries, Dr. Marcus Whitman and Henry Spalding, brought their wives—the first white women to cross the continent. The trappers they met on the journey liked the Whitmans. Narcissa Whitman, charming and lively, lightened the boredom

lush meadows of Oregon. This huge cross-country drive meant traveling four to six months on the trail—and living a life few families had experienced before.

In those days, Oregon Country was a vast territory that stretched from the Rocky Mountains to the Pacific Ocean, from Alaska in the north (claimed by Russia) to California in the South (claimed by Spain and Mexico). Oregon itself was claimed by both the United States and Great Britain.

Migration was spurred by the panic of 1837, which brought hard times to midwestern farmers. Poverty made them listen to missionaries' tales of an earthly paradise in Oregon Country. The Willamette River valley had land for all and a long growing season. The Hudson's Bay Company, a British fur-trading company, dominated the region with their trading post Fort Vancouver, on the Columbia River. But enough American settlers might make it qualify to become American territory.

With more than 40 years experience as a fur trapper, trader, and guide, Jim Bridger was one of the most famous mountain men.

Establishing the Route

The Oregon Trail had already been traveled, one piece at a time, by Lewis and

of trail life. Whitman, a doctor, had won their admiration earlier, when he had successfully removed a 3-inch (8-centimeter) arrowhead from Jim Bridger's shoulder. The trappers were glad to guide his party. But they told him he could not take his wagon to Oregon. No one had ever taken wagons past Fort Hall. Whitman took the wagon on anyway, but at Fort Boise he had to leave it behind.

Marcus Whitman, one of the first pioneers to blaze the trail to Oregon, founded a mission in the Oregon Territory to convert the Indians to Christianity.

Until then the women had sometimes rested in the wagon—a bumpy ride, for it had no springs. From then on for most of the way to Oregon, they rode on horseback, sidesaddle in their long dresses, though Mrs. Spalding was sick and Mrs. Whitman was expecting her first baby. They founded the Whitman Mission in what is now southeastern Washington State.

Oregon Fever

In 1839 the first farmers—13 men from Illinois, led by Thomas Farnham (1804–48)—reached Oregon with packhorses. In 1842, a minister named Elijah White led the first large group—107 pioneers—over the trail. By 1843 the "Oregon fever" had spread among farmers suffering from hard times. They formed Oregon societies to plan the trip. That spring the trickle along the trail became a flood, which came to be known as the Great Migration.

Organizing the Wagon Trains

The Oregon Trail started at Independence, Missouri. From all over the Mississippi River valley, more than 1,000 men, women, and children gathered at Elm Grove, 33 miles (53 kilometers) west of Independence. Farmers were amazed to see only two elm trees there. This was not their idea of a grove. They brought covered wagons, packed with all their worldly goods, and herded over 1,400 cattle and oxen. Though they were inexperienced, mountain men and Marcus Whitman guided them.

They began their great march on May 22, 1843. At first they took the Santa Fe Trail, but 8 miles (13 kilometers) from Elm Grove the trail forked. A sign pointing northwest said "Road to Oregon." A few miles along this fork they came to Big Springs (just east of present-day Topeka, Kansas) where they organized the wagon train. They held a meeting on the plain, voting on rules and electing Peter H. Burnett (1807–95) captain. Candidates for Burnett's aides, the Council of Ten, stood up in front of the others. Then each voter (any man over 16) fell in line behind his choice. The men with the longest "tails" of voters won.

The huge size of the party meant safety from Indians, but it made problems too. Those with no cattle could travel faster. So the pioneers split into two columns, with sixty wagons in each. The "light column," with few animals, went first. The "cow column" came slowly behind. At night the cow column caught up and camped with the rest. Jesse Applegate (1811–88), captain of the cow column, wrote a famous book about the trip.

The Difficult Journey

About 300 miles (480 kilometers) from Independence they reached the Platte River, 6 inches (15 centimeters) deep and 1 mile (1.6 kilometers) wide. Pioneers said it was "too thick to drink and too thin to plow." They followed its south bank for about 100 miles (160 kilometers). The pilot, a mountain man, ranged ahead. Wagons changed places in line, so everyone could have some relief from the choking dust. Men walked beside teams, while wives and children picked wildflowers or napped in the wagons. They made a short midday lunch stop called nooning.

Late in the afternoon they watched for the place the pilot had marked with a big circle on the ground. Men drove their teams along the circle, making a ring of wagons. They turned the oxen free to graze and locked the wagons into a fort. Children gathered buffalo chips (dung) for fuel. When the fire was hot, the women prepared dinner—usually salted meat, bread, and coffee. After dinner people told stories and sang or the council met. Tired out, all went to bed as darkness fell, except the guards, who had to keep watch all night.

At the fork of the Platte River they crossed the South Platte and followed the northern fork toward the Rockies. At Fort Laramie they stopped to rest a few days and wash clothes. Up the North Platte they came to Independence Rock—838 miles (1,349 kilometers) from their starting point—where they carved their names. Now they could see the peaks of the Rockies. Following the Sweetwater River through a canyon (Devil's Gate), they reached South Pass. Here they crossed the backbone of the continent. Beyond this point rivers flowed west. But the "great divide" seemed very tame, as the pass was a smooth stretch 20 miles (32 kilometers) wide.

At the Green River (northern branch of the Colorado) they turned south. Earlier migrants had gone north, but the Great Migration cut a fresh path, to visit Jim Bridger's new post. Then they headed north again, joining the main trail near Soda Springs. They marveled at Steamboat Spring, which spurted hot water.

At Fort Hall they rested. They were 1,288 miles (2,074 kilometers) from Independence, over halfway to their goal, but the worst part lay ahead. Here the Oregon Trail turned into a narrow pack trail. Only once had a wagon—the one belonging to Marcus Whitman seven years earlier in 1836—gone past this point. But Whitman's light wagon had been much smaller than the bulky prairie schooners, and even that he had been forced to abandon at Fort Boise.

The pioneers had babies and household goods. They could not manage without wagons. Whitman promised to get the wagons through—against the advice of mountain men. But the wagons had to be lightened. Already the pioneers had thrown away furniture and precious belongings. Women had to give up extra clothes. At the Snake River they traded party dresses to the Indians for salmon.

Whitman's wagon led the caravan through "a wild, rocky, barren wilderness, of wrecked and ruined Nature; a vast field of volcanic desolation." The burning sun beat down on the weary travelers. On they jolted, over sharp rocks that made oxen's feet bleed, along slopes so steep that men had to hold the wagons up to keep them from turning over. They rested at Fort Boise and again in a beautiful green valley, the Grande Ronde. They followed a creek along a rocky canyon and through snowcapped mountains where wagons had never gone. At last they came to Whitman's mission near the Columbia River. Where the river foams through the Cascades, they turned wagons into boats. Boys drove the cattle over mountain trails, and families

Independence Rock, on the Sweetwater River in Wyoming, was a major landmark on the Oregon Trail. It signaled the end of the journey on the plains and the beginning of the trek over the Rocky Mountains.

floated down the Columbia to the rich meadows of the Willamette Valley. It was October. They marked off their new farms—their reward for five months on the trail.

The 49th Parallel

Every year more settlers came. By 1846 more than 5,000 pioneers had made the journey to the Willamette Valley, making it clear to the British that Americans intended to remain in Oregon. That year Great Britain signed a treaty giving up claims to land south of the present Washington-Canada border, establishing the boundary at 49 degrees north latitude, known as the 49th parallel. Then in 1848, Oregon became a U.S. territory. It covered the present-day states of Washington, Oregon, and Idaho as well as the western portions of Montana and Wyoming.

By the end of the Civil War in 1865, more than 300,000 people had followed the Oregon Trail to settle in the Far West. Some went to California. These people left the main trail at Fort Bridger or Fort Hall and headed south. From there on they had a different trail and a different and more terrible story.

▶ THE CALIFORNIA TRAIL

The California Trail had several branches where it left the Oregon Trail, and again where it entered California. It was unusual in that the pioneers themselves blazed parts of it. Most of the pathfinding was done by mountain men and explorers, particularly John Charles Frémont, Jedediah Smith, Kit Carson, and Joseph Walker (1798–1876). The trail had to cross two forbidding barriers—the desert and the Sierra Nevada mountains. Cliffs faced the eastern side of this range, with few streams cutting through.

Two of the mountain men, Smith and Walker, were the first to challenge these barriers. Walker blazed a trail across the deserts of the Great Basin along the Humboldt River. The river provided water and a handy guide partway across the desert, until it drained into the Humboldt Sink. Though the Ute Indians, who were known to steal horses,

Frontier scout Kit Carson (*left*) guided the explorer John C. Frémont (*above*) on several western expeditions. Together they opened up trails to Utah, California, and Oregon.

lived nearby, this was the only route for this part of the trail.

From the Humboldt Sink the trail crossed 65 miles (105 kilometers) of desert to the mountains. There was no grass, and water holes were few and far between. The explorers found several streams leading to mountain passes. Most passes were rough, narrow, and steep. In 1841 only a few trappers knew where they were. But this was the year that the first pioneers went through unguided.

Stories of California's beauty spread, and people formed California societies, ready to make the trip. Hundreds signed up to go with John Bidwell (1819–1900), known as the Prince of California Pioneers. One group of 69 people met at Sapling Grove, Tennessee, in May 1841. They had little money and less information. Everything was new to them. About the trail, as Bidwell wrote, "We knew only that California lay to the west." Their maps showed rivers running from the Great Salt Lake to the Pacific. They had tools for building canoes to float them along these nonexistent streams. These pioneers would soon travel unaided where none but trappers had dared go before.

They had one piece of good luck. At first Thomas Fitzpatrick (1799–1854), a skilled mountain man, guided them and corrected their worst mistakes. But he was bound for Oregon. At Soda Springs the party split up. About half the party went with Fitzpatrick. Another group of 32, including one woman and her little girl, struck off for California.

Mountain men told them to head straight west for the Humboldt River. If they wandered too far south, they would die in the desert. To the north they would get lost in a wild land of canyons and cliffs.

The First Trail

It was September before they reached the Great Salt Lake. Ahead lay the desert, "glimmering with heat and salt." Wagon wheels sank into the sand. Leaving the wagons, the pioneers packed goods on the animals and floundered on. They struck the Humboldt and followed it west, as Walker had done. Then they hiked south to the Walker River.

Facing the towering cliffs, they almost gave up. It was October. They saw the high peaks hooded with snow, and they feared freezing in the mountains. But if they tried to go back, they would surely starve. So they toiled up the Walker River, along a narrow Indian trail cut in the side of the canyon. They ate some of the mules to keep from starving. At last they found the Stanislaus River, flowing west, and followed it down to the San Joaquin Valley, arriving on November 4, 1841. They were the first settlers to reach California by land.

The Main Route

Others followed. Some, guided by Walker, crossed the mountains at Walker Pass and took the Kern River trail to the valley. But this route took people miles south of the direct line.

In 1844 the Stevens-Murphy party blazed a shorter trail, north of Walker's. Going straight west from the Humboldt, they struck a mountain stream, which they named Truckee, for the Paiute Indian chief who guided them. Truckee led them up the canyon and across the mountains at what became known as Truckee Pass. They followed the American River down to the Sacramento Valley, getting wagons through for the first time. News of the route spread, and it became the main trail.

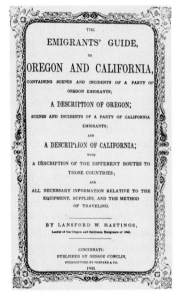

In the 1840's, numerous guidebooks were published to encourage people to go west.

Hastings Cutoff

During the 1840's, California land speculators tried to lure emigrants to California. One of them, Lansford Hastings, planned a shortcut. Instead of making the long northward loop to Fort Hall, wagons should go south to Fort Bridger and from there southwest through the Wasatch Range. They would pass the Great Salt Lake at its south end, instead of its north end as did other trails, and head west across the Great Salt Lake Desert.

This was the terrible Hastings Cutoff. It was shorter and looked fine on the map, but it crossed 80 miles (130 kilometers) of scorching desert, where nothing lived but scorpions, lizards, and snakes. There was no grass or water for oxen. A mountain man who had crossed with Hastings warned people to stay away from it. But Hastings settled down beside the trail to wait for emigrants.

The Harlan-Young party set out in 1846. Hastings guided them through the Wasatch Range to the desert and pointed out the peaks on the other side. He told them it was only 40 miles (65 kilometers), so they took hay and water for that distance. They hoped to cross in a forced march of a day and a night. But it took twice that long. Nearly fainting from heat and exhaustion, the men finally dragged themselves across. They had to leave the wagons, for the oxen had dropped in their tracks. Then they had to haul grass and water 30 miles (50 kilometers) back, to save the animals. Some say their curses against Hastings can be seen in Utah today as a blue haze over the hills. Behind them came the unluckiest pioneers of all, the Donner party. (For more information, see the feature in this article.)

The Gold Rush of 1849

After the Mexican War (1846–48), California became American territory. In 1848 gold was found on the American River. During 1849 about 80,000 gold seekers, known as

THE DONNER PARTY

Of the thousands of pioneers who experienced hardship and tragedy, the Donner party suffered perhaps the greatest misfortune.

In the spring of 1846, George and Jacob Donner led a party of 82 pioneers out of Illinois on an overland journey to California. When they reached Utah, they wasted precious days waiting for their guide, Lansford Hastings, to show them his shortcut to the California Trail. Hastings failed to appear, and the party went on without him, following an untested route through the treacherous Great Salt Lake Desert.

The Donner party reached the Sierra Nevada—the mountain range between Nevada and California—so late in the fall that early snows caught them as they tried to cross by the Truckee Pass. In mid-December, as their precious food supplies dwindled, a group of 15 set out in desperation to try to bring help from California. Only seven survived the journey.

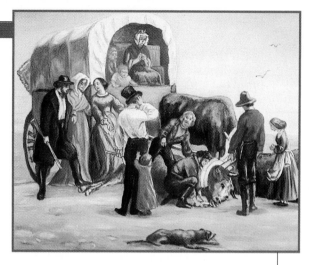

When the rescuers returned in the spring, they found that more than two dozen men, women, and children had already died from starvation and that some of the survivors had been forced to eat the dead to keep themselves alive. Of the original 82 members of the Donner party, only 47 lived to reach California.

forty-niners, plodded along the California Trail or the southern trails. By 1850 the California Trail was the most traveled road of all—well marked with hoofprints, wagon ruts, the bleached bones of thousands of animals, and the graves of pioneers.

▶ THE MORMON TRAIL

When the Mormons left Illinois in 1846 to seek a home in the wilderness, they traveled in stages. Advance parties moved across Iowa, stopping to build cabins and plant crops for the next group. The biggest camp, farthest west, was Winter Quarters, near today's Omaha.

On April 9, 1847, Brigham Young (1801–77) left this camp with 143 men, three women, and two children. They followed the north bank of the Platte, keeping away from other pioneers, who might be hostile to their religious beliefs. They crossed the stream near Fort Laramie, stopping to build boats for a ferry. Some waited behind to ferry the Mormon groups that were following. The

Seeking religious freedom, Mormon leader Brigham Young led a whole community of pioneers to Utah, where they founded Salt Lake City.

band went past South Pass, turned southwest at Fort Bridger, and started along the faint track of the Hastings Cutoff. There was no trail, but scouts went ahead, finding passes and clearing a wagon path with picks and shovels.

On July 24 the band came through a canyon and looked upon the valley of the Great Salt Lake. They saw a curving bowl of sagebrush and cactus, rimmed with mountains. They saw nothing green. In a week came the second group, and within a month, the third. The third band, 1,500 people, saw greenery, for already grass had sprung up in the fields the first Mormons had irrigated.

The Mormon Trail, with its rest stations, was the best-managed trail of all. At the trail's end the Mormons built Salt Lake City.

▶ THE CHISHOLM TRAIL

The Chisholm Trail was the most famous of the cattle trails. Unlike other trails, cattle trails ran north and south, from southern Texas to the railroad towns in Nebraska and Kansas. Cowboys drove herds of cattle along the trails, sometimes for 1,000 miles (1,600 kilometers). This was called the Long Drive.

The Cattle Drives

During the 1860's railroads grew like vines across Kansas. If cattlemen could get their stock to a railroad station, cattle cars could take them east to market. So the idea of the Long Drive was born. The first longhorns left Texas in 1866, heading for the railroad town of Sedalia, Missouri. But the wooded hills scared range cattle, and in Missouri, farmers came out with guns to stop the cattle from trampling their fields. It was not a good trail for the drive.

The next year, an Illinois meat dealer got the Kansas Pacific Railroad to give special freight rates for cattle. He chose Abilene, Kansas, as the town where the Long Drive should end. To get there, cowboys herded stock west of the first trail—through grasslands with streams, few trees, no farms.

This route was the Chisholm Trail. It went straight north from a point near San Antonio, across Texas and the Red River, through Oklahoma, to Kansas. It crossed the Arkansas River and the old Santa Fe Trail and went north to Abilene. It proved to be a fine trail. Between 1868 and 1871, 1.5 million longhorns passed along it.

As railroads pushed west, the trail changed. Its northern end moved west to Ellsworth and to other towns on the newly built Santa Fe line. After 1876 the Western Trail led to Dodge City.

The Long Drive ended in the 1880's. Farmers were moving west, fencing in the land. Indians were charging cowboys ten cents for each head of cattle driven over their property. Kansas farmers feared the ticks carried by longhorns, which spread Texas fever. Some farmers shot cattle. In 1884 Kansas passed a law permitting the drive only in winter. The Chisholm became a ghost trail.

▶ THE BOZEMAN TRAIL

Increasing settlement and the expanding livestock industry caused trouble between the pioneers and the Indians. The Sioux particularly resented the establishment in 1863 of the Bozeman Trail that led from Fort Laramie to the gold fields of Virginia City, Montana. The trail crossed through hunting grounds that the Sioux regarded as theirs by treaty with the United States. The establishment of Fort Phil Kearny in 1866 to protect the Bozeman Trail led to further conflict. In December of that year, Chief Red Cloud and his Sioux warriors fought U.S. troops near the fort, killing 81 soldiers as well as their commanding officer, Lieutenant Colonel William J. Fetterman. Red Cloud's victory led to a peace treaty in 1868, and the Bozeman Trail was closed.

▶ SUMMARY

In less than 100 years the westward tide of settlers that began at the Appalachian Mountains had pushed the American frontier to the Pacific Ocean. Along the trails new cities sprang up. Trade and industry developed. A great nation began to take shape and fill the West.

Some trails faded and died. Others became arteries of commerce. Portions of most Far Western trails are now followed by highways or railroads. But overland trails are not important as ancestors of modern highways. They are important because during the century of migration, they carried a whole people west. The United States grew along its trails until it stretched "from sea to shining sea."

WILLIAM J. RAMPON
West Chester State College (Pennsylvania)

See also FUR TRADE IN NORTH AMERICA; PIONEER LIFE; TERRITORIAL EXPANSION OF THE UNITED STATES; WESTWARD MOVEMENT.

To endure the hardships of life on the cattle trails, cowboys had to be tough, spirited, and independent.

OVID (43 B.C.–A.D. 17?)

The Roman poet Ovid (Publius Ovidius Naso) was born in Sulmo (now Sulmona, in Italy) on March 20, 43 B.C. His father wanted him to have a distinguished career and sent him to Rome to study law.

Ovid was soon known as a brilliant student of public speaking. He practiced law for some time, but he preferred poetry, which he wrote with great ease. As he himself said, "Everything I tried to say came out as verse." When he was 27 or 28, his first book, a collection of love poems, won him immediate success. From then on he was the most popular poet in Rome, with many friends in the highest social circles.

Ovid's success delighted him, but it brought him to ruin. At the height of his career, when he was working on his greatest poem, the *Metamorphoses* ("Transformations"), he was involved in a scandal at the royal court that deeply angered Emperor Augustus. Ovid was sent into exile. What the scandal was, he never dared to reveal. We know, however, that Augustus disapproved of the frivolous tone of Ovid's love poetry.

In one of his most moving poems, Ovid describes his tearful last farewell to his wife and to Rome, in A.D. 8. For the rest of his life he lived in Tomis (now Constanta, Romania), a remote town on the Black Sea.

Ovid wrote many poems on love, exploring all its aspects with great psychological skill. His two collections of poetic letters written in exile, *Tristia* ("Laments") and *Epistulae ex Ponto* ("Letters from the Black Sea"), are sad utterances of misery and despair. But his very best poems are those that retell, with marvelous skill, the wonderful old tales from Greek and Roman mythology: the *Fasti*, a calendar of Roman festivals, and, above all, the *Metamorphoses*.

Vainly hoping to the last that the emperor would relent and allow him to return to Rome, Ovid died in Tomis in A.D. 17 or 18.

Reviewed by GILBERT HIGHET
Formerly, Columbia University

OWEN, ROBERT (1771–1858)

Robert Owen, an influential industrialist and social reformer, was born in Newtown, Wales, on May 14, 1771. After leaving school at age 9 to work, he progressed rapidly, becoming the manager of a large cotton mill in Manchester, England, by the time he was 19. In 1799, Owen and two partners purchased a textile mill in New Lanark, Scotland. Owen was shocked by the poor living conditions of the workers, many of whom were children. He took steps to improve their situation, shortening the workday, providing comfortable housing, and establishing schools.

Owen felt that a person's character is shaped by his or her environment. He expressed this belief in his book *A New View of Society* (1813). And he worked for the passage of laws that would improve conditions for workers and their families.

Owen came to believe that poverty could be eliminated if people lived and worked together in cooperative communities. To promote this idea, he founded an experimental community in New Harmony, Indiana, in 1825. His goal was to create a **utopia** (an

Welsh industrialist Robert Owen influenced social reform movements of the 1800's.

ideal society). In New Harmony, property was owned by the community rather than by individuals. Workers were all paid the same salary, no matter what type of work they did. Schools were free. But the community soon failed due to disagreements among its members.

After returning to England, Owen continued to promote his social theories. He died in Newtown on November 17, 1858. One of his sons, Robert Dale Owen, became a leading social reformer in the United States.

Reviewed by WILLAM E. SHAPIRO
Consultant, children's encyclopedias

OWEN, WILFRED. See WORLD WAR I (Profiles: Allied Powers).

OWENS, JESSE
(1913–1980)

The African American track and field star James Cleveland (Jesse) Owens is considered one of the greatest athletes of all time. His performance at the 1936 Olympic Games made him a legend and dealt a dramatic blow to racism.

Jesse Owens was born on September 12, 1913, in Oakville, Alabama. When he was 7, his family moved to Cleveland, Ohio, where he went to East Technical High School. There he tied the world record in the 100-yard dash.

After high school, Owens entered Ohio State University. During his sophomore year (1935), he gave a remarkable athletic performance. In one afternoon, he set new world records in the 220-yard dash, the long jump, and the 220-yard low hurdles, and he tied the world record in the 100-yard dash.

Owens achieved international fame at the 1936 Olympic Games, held in Berlin, Germany. German dictator Adolf Hitler believed that the Germans belonged to a "master race," superior to other peoples, especially Jews and blacks, and he saw the Games as an opportunity to prove his view to the world. Owens discredited these racist beliefs by winning gold medals in the 100- and 200-meter dashes and the long jump and as a member of the 400-meter relay team. In each event, he set or equaled Olympic records.

Afterward, Owens was hailed as a hero. But opportunities for blacks were severely limited at the time, and for several years he found it difficult to support himself. He eventually became an inspirational speaker and organized sporting events for young people. In 1976, Owens was awarded the Presidential Medal of Freedom, the highest honor available to American civilians. He died in Tucson, Arizona, on March 31, 1980.

MARTY GLICKMAN
Member, U.S. Olympic Track Team, 1936

OWLS

A hunter sits on a tree branch at night—watching, listening, waiting. A mouse scurries along the ground, and the patter of its feet is heard by the hunter. In a second, the hunter swoops silently down, grabs the mouse with its sharp claws, and returns to the branch.

The hunter is a bird of prey called an owl. There are more than 130 different kinds of owls. Most belong to the Strigidae family, which includes the barred owl and the great gray owl. The other family, Tytonidae, is composed of owls with heart-shaped faces, such as the barn owl and grass owl. Owls are found everywhere on Earth except Antarctica, in habitats ranging from open woodlands to towns and cities.

Characteristics of Owls. Owls have large heads and short necks. Their eyes are large and very sensitive and are surrounded by feathers that radiate outward. They are the only birds that blink like humans, by dropping their upper eyelids. But when owls sleep, they close their eyes the way other birds do—by raising the lower lids. An owl cannot move its eyes from side to side. Instead, it turns its head. Some owls can turn their heads more than 270 degrees. An owl can even turn its head upside down.

An owl's feathers range in color from browns and grays to black and white, which helps the owl blend into its surroundings. Snowy owls, which often live in snow-covered regions, are generally white. Owls that live in forests are often dark brown.

The owl's sensitive ears are hidden by feathers. Some owls have long tufts of feathers on their heads that are sometimes referred to as ears or horns. Such species include the great horned owl and the long-eared owl.

The heart-shaped face of this barn owl (*left*) is characteristic of owls in the Tytonidae family. A great horned owl (*above*), a member of the Strigidae family, protects its owlets at a nest. The "horns" are actually tufts of feathers.

An owl has powerful feet and very sharp claws, or talons, for catching prey and for defending itself. Each foot's outer toe can be moved forward, outward, and backward. This makes it easier for the owl to grasp its prey.

Not all owls "hoot." The eastern screech owl of North America makes a whistling whinny, while the barking owl of Australia can sound like a growling dog. Other owl sounds include snores, coughs, hisses, and chirps.

The smallest owls are the pygmy owls of Central and South America and the elf owl of North America. They are about 5 inches (13 centimeters) in length with wingspans as short as 4 inches (10 centimeters). The largest are the eagle owls of Europe, Asia, and Africa. They may reach 30 inches (76 centimeters) in length and have wingspans of up to 60 inches (150 centimeters).

The Life of Owls. Owls usually eat rodents, but their diet may also include other small mammals, reptiles, amphibians, insects, and earthworms. Some hawk owls eat crabs, while the diet of some eagle owls consists mostly of frogs. In Africa and Asia, there are owls that use their claws to scoop fish out of the water.

Owls typically hunt at night, although a few hunt during the day. The larger the owl, the larger the animals on which it can prey. The great hawk owls of Australia can tackle animals as large as rabbits and opossums.

Most owls swallow small prey whole. Digestive juices in the stomach break down the soft parts of the animal. The parts that cannot be digested, such as bones and fur, are regurgitated (brought up) in compact little pellets.

Many owls do not build nests. Some use nests abandoned by other birds, while others lay their eggs in holes in trees or on cliff ledges. The tiny elf owl nests in holes made by woodpeckers in the giant saguaro cactus. The burrowing owl nests underground, usually in a prairie-dog community.

Female owls lay from one to twelve white eggs, which take 21 to 42 days to hatch. The owlets, or nestlings, are born with their eyes closed and are covered with a whitish down. They are cared for by both parents. Owls generally do not live very long in the wild. One study of barn owls indicated that few reach the age of 9 years. In captivity, owls live much longer.

Some species of owls are endangered, primarily due to loss of habitat. The most notable example is the spotted owl of North America's Pacific coast, which has been threatened in recent years because of extensive logging of the forests in which it lives.

Reviewed by ALLISON CHILDS WELLS
Cornell Lab of Ornithology

The gaur of India and Southeast Asia is the largest wild ox. Oxen are related to cattle, goats, and buffalo.

OXEN

To most people, the name "oxen" refers to domestic cattle trained to pull a wagon or plow. To scientists, however, "oxen" refers to a small group of closely related species in the family Bovidae, which also includes cattle, sheep, goats, gazelles, African antelopes, and buffalo.

Five species of oxen have been identified: The extinct aurochs and the yak, gaur, banteng, and kouprey. Musk oxen, despite their name, are not true oxen; they are more closely related to sheep. All but the kouprey have been domesticated, and all are endangered in the wild.

Domesticated oxen have been important to humans throughout history. They are used to carry heavy loads, pull wagons, and plow fields. Oxen are a source of meat, and their milk is used to make butter and cheese. Their hide is made into leather, their hooves are a source of glue and gelatin, and their fat (tallow) is made into candles. Their dung is dried and used as a fertilizer, a fuel, and even a building material.

Characteristics of Oxen. Oxen are large hoofed animals with two toes on each foot. Their heads are crowned with two bony horns, which are larger on males (bulls) than on females (cows). They have long tails and a four-chambered stomach. Their flat teeth are well suited for grinding their food, which consists mostly of grasses. Oxen usually have brown or black coats, and some of the tropical species have light-colored legs. Most oxen live in small herds, although males sometimes live alone. Cows typically give birth to one young (calf) at a time.

Kinds of Oxen. The **aurochs** was a large and fierce black ox that ranged throughout Europe, Asia, and northern Africa. It is thought to be the ancestor of modern domestic cattle. Prehistoric people painted its image on cave walls, and Roman gladiators fought it in contests at the famous Colosseum. But as people destroyed its forest habitats, the animal became rare. The last aurochs died on a preserve in Poland in 1627.

The wild **gaur** is the ancestor of domestic animals called mithan, and it is the largest of the wild oxen. Gaurs have large shoulder humps, thick horns that curve upward, and cream-colored legs. Wild gaurs live in forests and grasslands in India and Southeast Asia.

Both wild and domestic **yaks** live in the high mountain pastures and steppe grasslands of Tibet and Nepal. They are agile climbers. With their thick, shaggy, dark-brown coats, they can survive in temperatures as low as –40° F (–40° C). Yaks are heavily built, with short legs, broad hooves, and a shoulder hump. Domestic yaks are much smaller than wild yaks.

Bantengs resemble gaurs, but they have a white patch on their rump and lack a pronounced shoulder hump. They live in dry open areas of tropical Southeast Asia. Domestic bantengs are known as Bali cattle, for the island of Bali where they were first tamed.

The **kouprey** was identified in 1937. It is one of the world's rarest mammals; the wild population is thought to number fewer than 250 animals. Kouprey have large bodies and long, narrow legs. They live in wet, remote forests in Vietnam and Cambodia.

DAN BRADLEY
Trinity College

See also BUFFALO AND BISON; CATTLE.

OXIDATION AND REDUCTION

At one time, the term "oxidation" was used to mean a reaction in which a substance combined with oxygen. Today, however, scientists use the word more broadly to mean any reaction in which electrons are moved from one atom or molecule to another.

Atoms are made up of electrons and protons. The number of protons an atom has determines what type of atom it is. If an atom has exactly the same number of electrons as it does protons, it is neutral, because protons have a positive charge and electrons have a negative charge. If an atom has lost its electrons, it is positively charged. If it gains electrons, it becomes negatively charged.

When an atom is **oxidized**, it loses electrons. When iron rusts, for example, the iron atoms lose their electrons to oxygen, and iron oxide is formed. The iron has become positive, but the oxygen atoms have become negatively charged. When an atom becomes negatively charged, it is said to be **reduced**. Whenever one thing is oxidized, something else must be reduced. Oxidation cannot happen without reduction. We refer to the substance that does the oxidizing as the **oxidant** or **oxidizing agent** and the substance that is oxidized as the **reductant** or **reducing agent**.

Reactions in which electrons are transferred from one element or compound to another are called **redox reactions**, to emphasize the fact that both oxidation and reduction are taking place at the same time. During a redox reaction, the oxidizing agent is reduced and the reducing agent is oxidized.

Oxidation gets its name from oxygen, an element that has a strong electron pull. It can easily pull electrons from the atoms of other elements. But while oxygen is one of the most important oxidants, it is not the only one. Bleach, hydrogen peroxide, ozone, and chlorine are other examples of good oxidizing agents.

Many reactions you encounter every day are redox reactions. When paper burns, the molecules that contain carbon and hydrogen react with oxygen to produce carbon dioxide and water in a process called **combustion**. An automobile oxidizes gasoline to make the

Corrosion, which appears as rust (*left*), and combustion, or burning (*right*), are two of the most common redox reactions.

engine work. Bleach works by oxidizing the molecules that stain clothing. Chlorine is used to oxidize bacteria and fungi, removing them from drinking water and swimming pools.

Batteries make use of redox reactions to produce an electric current. A flashlight works because the electrons that are transferred from the reductant are made to pass through a lightbulb before they get to the oxidant. A battery runs down when the chemical substances involved in the redox reaction have been used up. In some batteries, it is possible to reverse the redox reaction that took place inside the battery by applying an electric current to it. This process regenerates the oxidant and reductant, making the battery rechargeable.

With so much oxygen in the air, oxidation often occurs where it is not wanted. The redox reaction known as **corrosion**, which appears as rust, causes billions of dollars worth of damage to metal structures every year. Sometimes metal is painted to prevent moist air from touching it. Galvanizing, in which an iron object is coated with zinc, is a more effective method of preventing corrosion. Not only does the zinc help to keep oxygen away from the iron, but it also oxidizes before the iron does. Even if the zinc coating is scratched, exposing the iron underneath, the object will not rust.

KENTON H. WHITMIRE
Rice University

OXYGEN

Oxygen is one of the naturally occurring chemical elements, and it makes up one-fifth of the air around us. It has been given the atomic symbol O, and it has an atomic number of 8 and an atomic mass of 16. Oxygen atoms are so reactive that they rarely survive by themselves. They readily combine in pairs to form oxygen molecules, O_2, the form of oxygen that exists in the air you breathe. Most of the time when people speak of oxygen, they are referring to oxygen molecules rather than oxygen atoms.

▶ THE DISCOVERY OF OXYGEN

Because oxygen is a colorless, odorless gas, it was difficult to discover. In the 1770's, Carl Wilhelm Scheele in Sweden and Joseph Priestley in England, working independently, devised chemical reactions that produced oxygen. But it was the French chemist Antoine Lavoisier who recognized that the gas they had produced was a newly discovered chemical element. He named it oxygen from Greek words *oxys* and *genos*, meaning "acid" and "forming," because he believed incorrectly that all acids contained oxygen. This discovery was important to the development of the modern understanding of atoms.

▶ OXYGEN AND LIFE

Oxygen is necessary for life. When you breathe, oxygen enters your lungs and combines with molecules in the foods you eat to release energy. The carbon dioxide produced is exhaled from the lungs. The process of taking in oxygen and releasing carbon dioxide is known as **respiration**. Plants use sunlight to convert carbon dioxide into carbohydrates and oxygen in a process called **photosynthesis**. Plants in turn are eaten by animals and are used to produce the energy they need to live.

Respiration and photosynthesis are opposite processes. Respiration takes oxygen from the air, and photosynthesis adds oxygen to the air. Huge amounts of oxygen are taken in by animals every day, but the balance of oxygen in the atmosphere remains the same since enormous quantities of oxygen are also returned to the air by plants.

▶ THE CHEMISTRY OF OXYGEN

Oxygen reacts readily with many chemical elements and compounds in a process known as **oxidation**. For this reason, a large amount of oxygen is found in nature combined with metals such as aluminum and iron in the Earth's crust. Many minerals, including rubies, sapphires, turquoise, and topaz, are compounds of various metals and oxygen.

The rusting of iron results from the reaction of iron with oxygen, a process that forms brown iron oxide. This oxide layer does not protect the metal, so it crumbles away, or corrodes. Aluminum also reacts with oxygen, but the aluminum oxide that forms sticks very well to the surface of the aluminum, forming a protective coating. This keeps the aluminum object from oxidizing completely, so it is practical to make some tools, such as ladders, out of aluminum.

The burning, or **combustion**, of gasoline, paper, or wood occurs because oxygen combines with the carbon and hydrogen molecules in these substances. Carbon dioxide and water are the products of combustion.

One of the most important compounds that oxygen forms is water, H_2O. The bonds

OXYGEN CYCLE

Sun

Oxygen

Carbon Dioxide

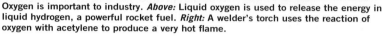
Oxygen is important to industry. *Above:* Liquid oxygen is used to release the energy in liquid hydrogen, a powerful rocket fuel. *Right:* A welder's torch uses the reaction of oxygen with acetylene to produce a very hot flame.

between oxygen and hydrogen are very strong, and a great deal of energy is released when these elements react. Even though the water molecule is very stable, it can be split into hydrogen and oxygen by passing electricity through it. This process is called **electrolysis**. Much research has gone into finding ways to use sunlight to carry out this reaction, but an inexpensive way to do this has not yet been found. If this can be done, then hydrogen will become a cheap and environmentally friendly source of energy.

While Lavoisier was wrong in believing that all acids contain oxygen, many do. Sulfuric acid, nitric acid, and phosphoric acid all contain oxygen. Sulfuric acid is used in the petroleum industry. When coal or gasoline containing sulfur compounds is burned, the sulfur reacts with oxygen to form sulfur trioxide, which combines with water in the atmosphere to produce sulfuric acid. Sulfuric acid formed this way is one cause of acid rain. Nitric acid is used in fertilizers because it is a source of nitrogen for plants. The nitrate ion is highly oxidizing and can be used in explosives. Nitric acid is created when automobiles burn gasoline, and it contributes to acid rain. Phosphoric acid is used in many soft drinks, and the phosphate ion is important for life.

When ultraviolet light strikes oxygen molecules, it can lead to the formation of ozone, O_3, a molecule that plays an important role in protecting the Earth from harmful ultraviolet radiation.

▶ **PRODUCTION OF OXYGEN**

Most of the oxygen used in industry today is obtained by separating the gas directly from nitrogen and the other components of air. Oxygen can be produced by electrolysis of water, but it is more expensive to obtain it this way than from air. The presence of oxygen in the Earth's atmosphere is the result of photosynthesis. Without the photosynthetic production of oxygen, animal life could not exist on Earth.

▶ **OTHER USES**

Oxygen is used to help remove impurities from the molten metal in the manufacture of steel. An acetylene torch uses the reaction of oxygen with acetylene to produce a very hot flame that is capable of melting many metals. This process is known as welding.

If oxygen is cooled below –297.4°F (–183°C), it becomes liquid. Liquid oxygen, also known as LOX, is pale blue in color and must be handled very carefully because it can react explosively with substances that can be oxidized. Because oxygen takes up so much less space as a liquid than as a gas, it is often transported in the liquid form. LOX reacts dramatically with liquid hydrogen, and for this reason the reaction of these liquids is used to propel rockets into space.

KENTON H. WHITMIRE
Rice University

See also ATMOSPHERE; CHEMISTRY; FIRE; NITROGEN; OXIDATION AND REDUCTION; OZONE; PHOTOSYNTHESIS.

OYSTERS, CLAMS, AND OTHER BIVALVES

Oysters, clams, mussels, and scallops are the four most familiar groups of animals known as **bivalves**. Bivalves belong to a larger group of invertebrates (animals with no backbone) called **mollusks**, which also include snails, octopuses, and squids. Most mollusks have a

Clams, oysters, and other bivalves are mollusks that have a single shell divided into two halves, or valves.

hard outer shell. The shell of a bivalve is divided into two halves, or **valves**, that are hinged together.

About 20,000 different species of bivalves live in lakes, rivers, estuaries, and oceans throughout the world. The smallest bivalves measure only a few millimeters. The largest bivalve, the giant white clam, can measure up to 4½ feet (1.4 meters) across and weigh up to 500 pounds (227 kilograms).

▶ CHARACTERISTICS OF BIVALVES

The two halves of a bivalve's shell are held closed with muscles attached to the inside of each valve. The shell opens when the muscles relax. Most bivalves have a pair of muscles, but some, including scallops, have just one large muscle.

Bivalves eat microscopic organisms called plankton, which they strain from the water with gills. Where bivalves are plentiful, they eat enough plankton to keep the water clean and clear. They also use their gills to get oxy-

gen from the water. Tiny hair-like **cilia** on the gills beat back and forth to move water across the gills.

A skin-like tissue called the **mantle** covers the gills and also secretes the material for the shell. Bivalve shells grow outward from the hinge, with new layers of shell added at regular intervals. Counting the growth rings on a shell, like counting the growth rings on a tree, can tell you how old the animal is. The shells' inside surface is usually smooth and shiny and is often called mother-of-pearl. In some bivalves the mantle also forms **siphons**, straw-like structures that suck in and squirt out water. When a clam is buried in mud, its siphon can sometimes be seen sticking up into the water.

Many bivalves are male and female at the same time. A few turn from males into females as they grow. Most bivalves reproduce by releasing gametes (eggs and sperm) into the water, where fertilization occurs. In some species, the males release sperm into the water and females take it in as they filter the water for food. The eggs are fertilized inside the female's shell.

While all bivalves have similar physical characteristics, they do not live the same way. Clams use a flat, muscular foot to burrow into the sand or mud. Mussels and oysters attach themselves to rocks or other hard surfaces. Mussels attach themselves by secreting strong threads of protein, called **byssal threads**, from a special gland. Oysters cement one valve to a hard surface. Scallops are unique among bivalves in their ability to swim. They open their shell to take in water

Did you know that...

some clams and mussels live in complete darkness? These animals live deep in the ocean—so deep, in fact, that sunlight cannot reach them. They gather around underwater hot springs, called hydrothermal vents, that spew intensely hot, mineral-rich fluids into the water. There, the bivalves—and many other unique animals—feed on special kinds of bacteria that receive their energy from the chemicals around the vents instead of from sunlight.

Oysters gather together into large formations called reefs or beds, which provide a vital habitat for many other kinds of animals.

and then quickly snap the halves together, expelling the water and propelling them a short distance.

Look at a bivalve on the beach. The shape of its shell tells you how it lives. The thin and smooth shells of razor clams help them burrow deep and fast into the sand. Cockles, which dig slowly and burrow just under the surface, have thick, round shells.

Some bivalves are parasites for part of their life cycle, living on the bodies of other sea creatures. Other bivalves, commonly called shipworms, bore into hard substances, such as rocks or the wooden hulls of ships.

▶ BIVALVES AND PEOPLE

Bivalves are valued throughout the world as sources of food, for their role in maintaining healthy ecosystems, and for the beauty of their shells. Many bivalves eaten by people are taken from the wild, but others are grown on special "farms" in a practice called **aquaculture**. Some bivalves are valued for their ability to form pearls; the most valuable pearls come from pearl oysters in the tropical South Pacific. Oysters and mussels naturally grow in massive formations called reefs or beds, which, like coral reefs, create an important habitat for fish, shellfish, and other animals. Some bivalves contain chemicals that are used in medicines.

Bivalve shells come in a wide variety of colors and shapes, and collecting them and other mollusk shells is a popular hobby. For more information, see SHELLS in Volume S.

Some bivalves are considered pests. In the Great Lakes, zebra mussels form dense colonies that often clog intake pipes.

A few bivalves are considered pests. Problems often start when a new species of bivalve arrives in a new place accidentally—carried in ship ballast water, for example, or imported for food or bait. Zebra mussels, which are native to the Black Sea in Europe, were first observed in the United States' Great Lakes in 1988. These animals multiply rapidly, forming dense colonies that clog intake pipes for power plants and cover ship hulls. They have also replaced native freshwater mussels, changing the ecology of the lakes.

As bivalves filter food particles from the water, they take in bacteria and viruses along with plankton. Sometimes they take in so many harmful microbes that people who eat them get sick. For this reason, the harvesting of these animals for food is closely monitored.

LOREN D. COEN
Marine Resources Research Institute
South Carolina Department of Natural Resources

DAVID BUSHEK
Haskin Shellfish Research Laboratory
Rutgers University

See also MOLLUSKS; OCTOPUSES, SQUIDS, AND OTHER CEPHALOPODS; SNAILS AND SLUGS.

OZONE

Ozone, O_3, is a form of oxygen that contains three atoms of oxygen rather than two as found in the oxygen you breathe. It has a molecular mass of 48. Like oxygen, ozone is a gas, but it has a sharp, pungent odor; the name "ozone" comes from the Greek word meaning "to smell."

Ozone was first observed by the German chemist Christian Friedrich Schönbein about 1840 during his studies of electrical discharges. When an electrical discharge, such as lightning, passes through oxygen, ozone is produced. You may have noticed it as the "fresh" smell arising after a lightning strike or near high-voltage electrical lines. Ozone is also produced when oxygen molecules interact with ultraviolet light. Ultraviolet light has enough energy to split O_2 molecules into separate O atoms. When some of these atoms combine with other O_2 molecules, ozone is produced.

Harm and Benefits of Ozone. Ozone is both beneficial and harmful to life. In the lower atmosphere, ozone produced by industry is a pollutant that can damage the cells of plants and animals. Some large cities have ozone alerts when the concentration of ozone gets high enough to be a health concern.

But the survival of life on Earth is possible because of the properties of ozone. In the upper atmosphere, or stratosphere, a layer of ozone absorbs harmful ultraviolet radiation from the sun and keeps it from reaching the surface of the Earth, where it can damage living things. In recent years, a hole has developed in the ozone layer over parts of the Southern Hemisphere. This hole is an area where the amount of ozone is much lower than it is normally the rest of the year. The hole is centered over Antarctica and generally lasts from September until December, which is spring in the Southern Hemisphere. Greater exposure to ultraviolet radiation as a result of this thinning of the ozone layer is linked to a rise in illnesses such as cataracts and skin cancer.

A 2002 satellite photo of Earth shows the ozone hole over Antarctica. The hole was smaller than in previous years and had split into two separate lobes.

What Causes the Ozone Hole? Constant bombardment by ultraviolet light normally maintains the proper level of ozone in the stratosphere. But this balance is altered by the presence of certain substances in the atmosphere that speed up the process by which ozone converts back into oxygen. One of these substances is chlorine atoms. Chlorine atoms react with ozone to break it down into ordinary oxygen. In that process, the chlorine atoms are given off again. (A substance that increases the speed of a reaction but that is not used up by the reaction is called a catalyst.) Because the chlorine atoms are not used up, they can cause the destruction of many ozone molecules. This process has caused the thinning of Earth's ozone layer.

Where do these chlorine atoms come from? Many of the chlorine atoms are present in the stratosphere as a result of the use of chlorofluorocarbons, or CFC's. CFC's are molecules made up of chlorine and fluorine atoms attached to carbon. For many years they were industrially produced for use in refrigerators and air conditioners, aerosol sprays, and foam packaging. Released into the lower atmosphere, CFC's eventually reach the stratosphere. There they are destroyed by ultraviolet light, which splits off the chlorine atoms.

In the past few years, many countries have agreed to monitor and reduce these harmful emissions. Other molecules have now been substituted for CFC's, and it appears that the ozone layer is slowly beginning to recover.

KENTON H. WHITMIRE
Chairman, Department of Chemistry
Rice University

See also OXYGEN.

Index

HOW TO USE THE DICTIONARY INDEX

See the beginning of the blue pages in Volume 1.

Obsidian (cont.)
  natural glass **F:**143; **G:**229
  Yellowstone National Park **Y:**355
Obstetrics (medical care of pregnant women) **H:**247
Obstructive jaundice (disease) **L:**269
Obtuse angles (in geometry) **G:**121
  diagram(s) **G:**121
Ocalan, Abdullah (Kurdish leader) **K:**307; **T:**349
"O Canada" (song by Robert Stanley Weir) **N:**20
Ocarinas (wind instruments) **A:**237; **L:**72
O'Casey, Sean (Irish playwright) **D:**305; **I:**322, 327
  picture(s) **I:**322
Occipital lobes (of the brain) **B:**365
Occluded front (in meteorology) **W:**85
Occupation, military
  division of Germany and Berlin after World War II
    G:164–65
Occupational diseases **D:**186; **O:**13; **W:**253
Occupational health and safety **O:**13
  biological clock **B:**194
  cancer prevention **C:**95
  noise control **N:**271
  nursing in industry **N:**419
Occupational Outlook Handbook **V:**376
Occupational Safety and Health Act (United States, 1970) **L:**6;
    O:13
Occupational Safety and Health Administration (OSHA) **C:**95;
    L:2; **O:**13
Occupational therapy **D:**179; **O:**14–15 *see also* Disabilities,
    people with
Occupations *see* Vocations; the people and their work section of
    country, province, and state articles
OCD *see* Obsessive-compulsive disorder
Ocean **O:**16–29 *see also* Oceanography
  Antarctic **A:**292, 293
  Arctic Ocean **A:**378
  Atlantic Ocean **A:**478–79
  cables **T:**51
  climate affected by **C:**363, 364
  continental shelves **E:**18
  corals **C:**555–56
  currents *see* Ocean currents
  desalting of seawater **D:**130
  diamonds discovered in ocean beds **D:**147
  Earth **E:**17–20
  Earth, history of **E:**26, 27
  earthquakes create tsunami waves **E:**41
  fisheries of the world **F:**216
  floor **E:**17–18; **G:**111, 113
  glacial dating from deep-sea sediments **I:**10, 15
  How do we get salt? **S:**22
  icebergs **I:**17–18
  Indian Ocean **I:**160–61
  Is there a new source of energy in the oceans? **O:**42
  lighthouses and lightships **L:**227–29
  mollusks **M:**405–8
  navigation **N:**72–77
  oceanography **O:**34–42
  oceans and seas of the world **O:**43–47
  Pacific Ocean **P:**2
  plankton **P:**283–85
  sea breezes **W:**187
  sonar **R:**40–41
  tides **T:**193–97
  water pollution **E:**302–3; **W:**064, 065, 066, 067
  water pollution threatens seals **S:**108
  water stores the sun's heat **E:**20
  map(s)
    oceans and seas of the world **O:**45
  picture(s)
    sea vents **B:**10
Oceanariums (huge aquariums) **A:**336; **D:**275, 277
Oceanauts *see* Aquanauts
Ocean City (Maryland) **M:**128

Ocean currents **E:**18–20; **O:**18, 19, 20
  Atlantic Ocean **A:**478–79
  climate affected by **C:**363, 364
  El Niño **W:**83
  Gulf Stream **G:**413
  icebergs drift with **I:**18
  Japan Current **J:**34
  Japan Sea **O:**46
  North America, effect on climate of **N:**291
  North American Current **I:**35
  oceanographic research **O:**35, 40
  Oyashio Current **J:**34
  shore currents create lake basins **L:**26
Ocean Drilling Program (ODP) **O:**39
Oceania (Pacific islands) **P:**3–10
Oceanic islands **I:**360
Oceanic ridges *see* Ridges, oceanic
Oceanic zone (habitat zone of the ocean) **O:**23
Ocean Island *see* Banaba
Ocean life *see* Marine biology
Ocean liners (ships) **O:**30–33
  ships and shipping **S:**153
  transportation, importance to **T:**284
  What caused the *Titanic* tragedy? **O:**33
  picture(s) **O:**32
Ocean observatories **O:**40
Oceanography (study of the sea) **O:**34–42 *see also* Deep-sea
    diving; Ocean
  earth science **E:**8
  experiments in earth sciences **E:**392
  geological and geophysical studies **G:**113
  ice age studies **I:**10, 15
  Indian Ocean research **I:**161
  Is there a new source of energy in the oceans? **O:**42
  plankton **P:**283–85
  sonar used in **R:**41
  tides **T:**193–97
  underwater exploration **E:**415–16; **U:**21–27
Ocean State (nickname for Rhode Island) **R:**212
Ocean Thermal Energy Conversion (OTEC) **E:**223
Oceanus (in Greek mythology) **G:**362
Ocellated turkeys (birds) **T:**350
Ocelli (simple eye sets of insects) **A:**319; **I:**235
Ocelots (wildcats) **C:**145
Ocher (Ochre) (mineral) **P:**15, 436
Ochoa, Estevan (American public official) **A:**405 *profile*
  picture(s) **A:**405
Ocho Ríos (Jamaica) **J:**18
Ochre *see* Ocher
Ockeghem, Jean d' (Flemish composer and teacher) **D:**372;
    F:445; **R:**172
Ockenheim, Johannes *see* Ockeghem, Jean d'
"O Come, All Ye Faithful" (carol) *see* Adeste Fideles
O'Connell, Daniel (Irish patriot) **I:**321, 323; **O:**47
O'Connor, Flannery (American writer) **A:**218–19; **G:**145 *profile*
O'Connor, Frank (Irish short-story writer) **I:**328
O'Connor, Sandra Day (American jurist) **S:**508 *profile; **W:**214
  picture(s) **U:**171
Ocotillo (plant)
  picture(s) **L:**114; **T:**125
OCR devices *see* Optical character recognition devices
Octagon (eight-sided geometric figure) **G:**122
Octahedron (eight-faced solid figure) **G:**123
Octane numbers (gasoline classification) **G:**62
Octants (navigation instruments) **N:**75
Octave (first eight lines of a sonnet) **P:**352
Octaves (in music) **M:**534, 537
Octavian (Octavianus) *see* Augustus
Octet rule (in chemistry) **A:**487
October (10th month of the year) **O:**48–49
October (motion picture, 1927) **M:**490
October Manifesto (Russia, 1905) **N:**249
October Revolutions (revolts against czarist regime in Russia,
    1905, 1917) **R:**371; **U:**33, 41
Octopus, The (novel by Frank Norris) **A:**213

Octopuses (mollusks) **M:**405–6, 407; **O:50–51**
 picture(s) **O:**50
Ocular (Eyepiece) (set of lenses in a compound microscope)
 L:147
 diagram(s) **L:**146
Oculists (eye doctors) *see* Ophthalmologists; Optometrists
Oda Nobunaga (Japanese general and statesman) *see* Nobunaga
Odd lots (stocks sold or bought a few at a time) **S:**458
Oddsson, David (prime minister of Iceland) **I:**37
Odd-toed hoofed mammals **F:**81–82; **H:**216, 217–18
 horses **H:**236–44
Odense (Denmark, birthplace of Hans Christian Andersen)
 A:246
Oder River (Europe) **C:**619; **G:**154; **P:**359; **R:**244
Odes (form of lyric poetry) **O:52**
 literature, forms of **L:**259
 poems of noble sentiment **P:**352
 Schiller's "Ode to Joy," in Beethoven's *Ninth Symphony*
 G:186
"Ode to a Nightingale" (poem by John Keats)
 excerpt from **O:**52
"Ode to the West Wind" (poem by Percy Bysshe Shelley)
 excerpt from **O:**52; **P:**352
Odets, Clifford (American playwright) **A:**216
Odin (Norse god) **N:**279, 281
 picture(s) **N:**278
O'Donovan, Michael (Irish short-story writer) *see* O'Connor,
 Frank
Odontocetes (Toothed whales) **W:**149–51
Odo of Cheriton (British preacher and fabulist) **F:**4
Odor
 animal communication **A:**284
 natural gas **N:**59–60
 odors of flowers attract insects **F:**286; **P:**308
 perfumes **P:**150–51
 scents of butterflies and moths **B:**476, 478
Odysseus (in Greek mythology) **G:**369; **O:**53–54; **T:**316
Odyssey (epic poem by Homer) **G:**360; **O:**53–54; **P:**353, 354
 Aeneid compared with **A:**36
 early form of fiction **F:**113–14
 early Greek literature **G:**355
 Greek mythology **G:**369
 Homer **H:**184
 myths overlap with other types of stories **M:**569–70
 oral poetry later put in writing **F:**309
 picture(s)
 adventure with the Sirens **G:**354
OECD *see* Organization for Economic Cooperation and
 Development
Oé-Cusse (East Timor) **T:**207
Oedipus (king of Thebes in Greek mythology) **G:**364; **J:**126
Oedipus Rex (play by Sophocles)
 picture(s) **G:**356
Oehlenschläger, Adam (Danish dramatist and poet) **S:**58h,
 58i
Oelschlagel, Charlotte (American ice skater) **I:**45
Oersted, Hans Christian (Danish physicist) **A:**194f; **E:**133,
 140, 154
 electromagnetism **M:**30; **P:**230
Oerter, Al (American discus thrower) **T:**260 *profile*, 263
 picture(s) **T:**260
Off-Broadway theater **D:**307; **T:**159
Offenbach, Jacques (French composer of operettas) **F:**446;
 M:553; **O:**54, 163–64
"Offensive defense" (military strategy of Jefferson Davis)
 C:496
Offensive missiles **M:**348
Offerings (in religion) **H:**140
Office buildings *see also* Skyscrapers
 central air conditioning **A:**102–3
 heating and ventilating systems **H:**97
 New York City **N:**230
 Sullivan, Louis **S:**486

Office machines **O:55–60**
 computers **C:**480–94
 typewriters **T:**371–74
Office workers
 occupational health **O:**13
Official Languages Act (Canada, 1969) **C:**52
Off-off-Broadway theater **D:**307
Off-road automobile racing **A:**538
Off-road bicycle races **B:**177
Offset press (for printing) **P:**475–76
Offset printing
 communication, history of **C:**464
 duplicating machines **O:**59
 lithography **P:**474–76
 magazines **M:**17
 picture(s)
 web offset press **P:**469
Offshore gas wells **N:**59
Offshore islands *see* Continental islands
Offshore oil drilling **P:**170–71
Of Human Bondage (novel by W. Somerset Maugham) **E:**289
Of Thee I Sing (musical by Gershwin) **M:**554
Ogaden region (Ethiopia) **E:**330, 334
Ogallala Aquifer (underground reservoir in the United States)
 K:178, 180; **N:**86; **U:**84–85; **W:**54
Ogasawara Islands *see* Bonin Islands
Ogden (Utah) **U:**247, 251
Ogden, Peter Skene (Canadian explorer and fur trader) **N:**135
Ogen melons **M:**214
Ogilvie Mountains (Yukon Territory) **Y:**370
Oglethorpe, James (English founder of Georgia) **G:**144; **O:61**;
 T:178
Ogooué River (Gabon) **G:**3
O'Grady, Standish James (Irish writer) **I:**326
Ogre-faced stick spiders
 picture(s) **S:**402
Oh, Sadaharu (Chinese-Japanese baseball player) **B:**85
O'Hare International Airport (Chicago) **A:**568; **C:**219; **I:**69
Oh, Boy! (musical by Kern) **M:**553
O'Higgins, Bernardo (Chilean leader) **C:**255; **O:61**
 picture(s) **C:**254
Ohio **O:62–77**
 Cleveland **C:**356
 Columbus **C:**444
 education, history of **E:**84
 westward movement **W:**141, 142
 map(s) **O:**73
 picture(s)
 barges on Lake Erie **O:**71
 baseball game **O:**68
 Canton **O:**70
 Cincinnati **O:**72
 Cleveland **C:**356; **O:**63, 66, 67, 70
 Columbus **C:**444; **O:**67, 71, 74
 Cuyahoga Valley **O:**65, 70
 Great Serpent Mound **A:**352; **O:**63
 oats farming **O:**69
 Ohio River **O:**64
 steel industry **O:**69
 Till Plains **O:**64
 tool industry **O:**69
Ohio and Erie Canal **C:**356; **O:**72, 75
Ohio Company (Virginia land company) **O:**74; **V:**358
Ohio River (United States) **O:78**
 junction of Allegheny and Monongahela **P:**128, 266
 Kentucky **K:**214, 221
 major river and tributaries in Ohio **O:**64, 69
 West Virginia **W:**128, 133, 135
 westward movement into the Ohio Valley **W:**141–42
 map(s) **O:**78
 picture(s) **O:**64; **W:**128
Ohio State University (Columbus, Ohio) **A:**376; **C:**444; **O:**67,
 68
 picture(s) **O:**67
Ohio University (Athens, Ohio) **O:**67

Oh, Kay! (musical by Gershwin)   **M:**554
Ohm, Georg Simon (German physicist)   **E:**139–40
Ohms (units of measure of electric resistance)   **E:**139–40
Ohm's law (in electricity)   **E:**139–40
Ohno, Apolo Anton (American athlete)   **O:**118
Oil (Petroleum) *see* Petroleum and petroleum refining
Oil immersion lenses (of microscopes)   **M:**284
Oil lamps   **L:**231, 233
  picture(s)   **L:**232
Oil paints   **P:**30
Oil pump (of an automobile)   **A:**548
Oils   **O:**79–81 *see also* Fats
  body chemistry   **B:**296
  citrus peels   **O:**189
  coconut   **C:**392
  cosmetics made of   **C:**560
  cottonseed oil   **C:**568
  detergents and soaps   **D:**140
  Hanukkah celebrations   **H:**29
  hydrogenation   **G:**60
  important agricultural products   **A:**90
  lighting   **L:**231
  liquid fuels   **F:**487
  lubrication and lubricants   **L:**335
  materials from plants   **P:**298
  olive oil   **O:**101
  peanut oil   **P:**112
  perfumes   **P:**150–51
  poisonous plants   **P:**316–17
  soybeans   **S:**337
  whale oil   **W:**150, 154, 155
Oils, essential *see* Essential oils
Oil shale (slatelike rock)   **E:**221; **P:**175
Oil spills   **O:**29; **P:**175–76
  Alaska   **A:**158
  cleanup with genetically engineered bacteria   **G:**86
  water pollution   **W:**065–066
  picture(s)   **E:**302; **O:**29
    bird victim of oil spill   **B:**247
    Exxon Valdez   **P:**175
    onshore cleanup   **P:**176
Oil springs (places where petroleum seeps to Earth's surface)   **P:**168
Oil tankers *see* Tankers
Ojeda, Alonzo de (Spanish explorer)   **S:**292; **V:**295
Ojibwa (Indians of North America) *see* Chippewa
Ojos del Salado, Cerro (mountain, Chile–Argentina)   **C:**251
OK (American expression)   **W:**240–41
  picture(s)
    Van Buren cartoon   **V:**273
O.K. Corral, Shootout at the (1881)   **E:**7
Okalik, Paul (first premier of Nunavut)   **N:**412
Okanagan Valley (British Columbia)   **B:**405, 407
  picture(s)
    vineyard   **B:**404
Okanagon (Indians of North America)   **I:**188
Okanogan Highlands (Washington)   **W:**16–17, 21
Okapis (animals related to giraffes)   **H:**218
  picture(s)   **H:**217
Okavango River (in southwest Africa)   **B:**344
Okeechobee, Lake (Florida)   **F:**260, 262, 263; **L:**27, 33
  picture(s)   **L:**27
O'Keeffe, Georgia (American painter)   **O:**81; **U:**132
  picture(s)   **N:**193
    Black Iris (painting)   **U:**132
    Blue and Green Music (painting)   **D:**135
    Cow's Skull: Red, White and Blue (painting)   **O:**81
Okefenokee National Wildlife Refuge (Georgia)   **G:**140
Okefenokee Swamp (Florida–Georgia)   **F:**263; **G:**134, 136, 140
  picture(s)   **U:**79
Okeghem, Jean d' (Flemish composer and teacher) *see* Ockeghem, Jean d'
Okhotsk, Sea of   **O:**46
Okhotsk Current (in the Japan Sea)   **O:**46

Okinawa (Ryukyu Islands)   **P:**10
  karate, history of   **K:**195
  World War II   **W:**314–15, 316
Oklahoma   **O:**82–96
  Dust Bowl   **D:**355
  Oklahoma City   **O:**97
  Tulsa   **T:**330
  map(s)   **O:**93
  picture(s)
    Cherokee Heritage Center   **O:**90
    electronics industry   **O:**89
    Guthrie   **O:**90
    longhorn cattle   **O:**83
    National Cowboy Hall of Fame   **O:**87
    Native American festival   **O:**83
    Native American handicrafts   **O:**86
    Norman music festival   **O:**86
    oil derricks   **O:**88
    oil-industry worker   **O:**83
    Oklahoma City   **O:**92, 97
    Oklahoma State University   **O:**87
    Route 66 Museum   **O:**90
    stockyards   **O:**89
    Tulsa   **O:**91
    wheat field   **O:**84
    Wichita Mountains   **O:**84
Oklahoma! (musical by Rodgers and Hammerstein)   **M:**554
  picture(s)   **M:**554
Oklahoma, Territory of   **O:**82, 95, 96
  land rush   **P:**261
  picture(s)
    land rush   **P:**260
Oklahoma, University of   **O:**87, 88
Oklahoma City (capital of Oklahoma)   **O:**82, 87, 88, 89, 91, 97
  terrorist bombing (1995)   **F:**77; **O:**96; **T:**115; **U:**205
  picture(s)   **O:**97
    capitol building   **O:**92
    National Cowboy Hall of Fame   **O:**87
Oklahoma State University   **O:**87
  picture(s)   **O:**87
Okoume (tree)   **G:**3
Okra (Gumbo) (vegetable)   **V:**292
Oktoberfest (German festival)   **G:**152; **H:**163
Okuni (Japanese dancer credited with beginning Kabuki)   **D:**298
Olaf II (Saint Olaf, Olaf Haraldsson) (king of Norway)   **N:**348–49
Olaf V (king of Norway)   **N:**349
Olajuwon, Hakeem (American basketball player)
  picture(s)   **B:**95c
Öland (Sweden)   **S:**525
Old age   **O:**98–100 *see also* Aging
  Aztec society   **A:**576
  children's literature, treatment in   **C:**238
  deafness   **D:**49
  disabilities, people with   **D:**178
  drugs' side effects in the elderly   **D:**335
  family life cycle   **F:**40
  Glenn, John, and studies of older people in space   **G:**237
  homes designed for needs of   **H:**190
  medicines, dangers of confusing   **P:**355
  mental illness   **M:**223
  nutrition   **N:**427
  occupational therapy   **O:**15
  public-assistance programs   **W:**120
  social security   **S:**225–26
  picture(s)
    adult education   **E:**76
    man with Alzheimer's disease   **M:**222
Old age pensions *see* Social security
Old Bailey (Central Criminal Court in London, England)   **L:**89
Old Bear (painting by George Catlin)
  picture(s)   **U:**129
Old Church Slavonic (language)   **R:**380

Old Colony *see* Plymouth Colony
Old Comedy (period in Greek literature)   G:356
Old Constitution House (Windsor, Vermont)   V:314
Old Corner Bookstore (Boston, Massachusetts)   B:341–42
Old Dominion (nickname for Virginia)   V:346, 347
Oldenburg, Claes (American artist)   P:31; S:105; U:134
Old English language *see* Anglo-Saxon language
Old English literature *see* Anglo-Saxon literature
Old English sheepdogs
    picture(s)   E:379
Old Faithful (geyser, Yellowstone National Park, Wyoming)
        G:192; Y:355
    picture(s)   W:342
Old-fashioned (English) gardens   G:26, 46
"Old Folks at Home" ("Swanee River") (song by Stephen Foster)
        F:261, 262, 389
Old Fort Henry (Kingston, Ontario)   O:133
    picture(s)   O:132
Old French   F:433–34
Old Fuss and Feathers (nickname for General Winfield Scott)
        M:239b; S:89
Old Glory (nickname for the flag of the United States)
    picture(s)   F:243
"Old Gray Mare, The" (song)   H:235
Old Hickory (nickname given Andrew Jackson)   J:3
Old Hundredth (hymn)   H:323
Old Ironsides (American naval vessel) *see* Constitution
        (American naval vessel)
"Old Ironsides" (poem by Oliver Wendell Holmes)   H:172
Old Kingdom (2780–2250 B.C., ancient Egypt)   E:109,
        110–12
Old Line State (nickname for Maryland)   M:120, 121, 133
Old Maid (card game)   C:109
Old Man and the Sea, The (novel by Hemingway)   H:107
Old Man of the Mountain (New Hampshire rock formation)
        N:158
    picture(s)   N:151
Old Manse (Concord, Massachusetts, home of Emerson and
        Hawthorne)   E:202; H:65
Old Norse language   I:33; S:58f
Old North Church (Boston, Massachusetts)   B:342; R:193
    picture(s)   C:423
Old North State (nickname for North Carolina)   N:307, 318
Old Northwest *see* Northwest Territory
Old Plum, The (Japanese screen painting)
    picture(s)   J:51
Old Pretender (James Edward Stuart)   E:247, 248
Old Rough and Ready (nickname for Zachary Taylor)   M:239b;
        T:33
Olds, Ransom E. (American automobile manufacturer)
        A:542–43
Old South Meetinghouse (Boston, Massachusetts)   B:342
Old Spanish Fort (Pascagoula, Mississippi)   M:358
Old Spanish Trail (California)   C:26; O:275
    map(s)   O:273
Old Stone (Paleolithic) Age   A:428–29; S:380
Old Sturbridge Village (Massachusetts)   M:144, 524
Old Style calendar *see* Julian calendar
Old Testament (of the Bible)   B:156, 158–63; C:287
    Abraham   A:8–9
    Apocrypha   B:163–64
    brick making, record of   B:394
    Daniel in the Lion's Den (story)   B:172–73
    David   D:43
    David and Goliath (story)   B:169–70
    Dead Sea Scrolls   D:47
    Elijah   E:189
    Esther, Book of, contains the Purim story   P:549
    Ezra   E:432
    Hebrew literature   H:99
    Isaac   I:345
    Isaiah   I:345
    Jeremiah   J:79
    Jerome's translation   J:79

Jonah (story)   B:171–72
    Joseph   J:133
    Joshua (leader of Israelites)   J:134
    Judaism, Biblical origins of   J:101–3; R:147
    Moses   M:469
    Noah's Ark (story)   B:168–69
    poetry   P:354
    Septuagint is the translation of the Old Testament into
        Greek   B:157; J:103
    Solomon   S:251
    Ten Commandments   T:72–73
Old Testament Trinity (icon by Andrei Rublev)   R:375
Olduvai Gorge (Tanganyika)   A:351; L:96; P:440
"Old Woman in a Shoe, The" (nursery rhyme)   N:414
Old World (term used to refer to Europe or European
        civilization)
    continents of Europe, Asia, and Africa   C:537
    New World and Old World exchange foods   F:337
Old World monkeys   M:420, 421
    picture(s)   M:421
Olefin fibers   F:111, 112; N:437
Oleg (Viking chieftain)   R:368
Olfactory maps (of migrating animals)   H:202
Olga (Russian princess)
    picture(s)   R:371
Oligarchy (government by a few)   G:273
Oligocene epoch (in geology)   E:29
Oligochaetes *see* Earthworms
Oligopoly (in economics)   E:59
Olingos (animals related to raccoons)   R:29
    picture(s)   R:29
Oliphant, Patrick Bruce (editorial cartoonist)   C:127
"O, Little Town of Bethlehem" (carol)   C:118
Olive (fruit)   O:101
    ancient Olympic winners crowned with olive wreaths
        O:103, 104
    Spain is a leading producer   S:374
    picture(s)   O:101
        Andalusia (Spain)   S:373
        Greek olive grove   G:335
Olive oil   O:79, 81, 101
    Hanukkah celebrations   H:29
    Tunisia is one of the world's largest producers   T:335
    used in castile soap   D:140
Oliver, Joseph "King" (American jazz cornetist)   J:59
Oliver Twist (book by Charles Dickens)   D:151
    excerpt from   D:153–54
Olivier, Laurence (British actor and director)   T:160, 161
    profile
    picture(s)
        as Hamlet   D:297; T:161
Olivines (Peridots) (gems)   G:71, 72, 74
    August's birthstone   G:74
    some asteroids composed of   C:451
    picture(s)   G:73, 74
Olmecs (ancient people of Central America)   A:243; I:167;
        M:186
    pottery sculptures called "babies"   P:412
    pyramids   P:557
    picture(s)
        pottery sculptures called "babies"   P:412
        sculpture of stone head   A:243; I:167
Olmedo, José Joaquín (Ecuadorian poet)   L:68
Olmsted, Frederick Law (American landscape architect)
        C:318; P:77
Olvera Street (oldest street in Los Angeles)   L:307
Olympia (capital of Washington)   W:23, 26
    picture(s)   W:24
Olympia (in ancient Greece)   O:102, 103, 104
    statue of Zeus   W:218
Olympia (painting by Manet)   M:78
    picture(s)   M:78
Olympiad (four-year period)   O:102, 105
Olympians (Greek gods)   G:362–63, 364
Olympic creed   O:108

"On the Grasshopper and the Cricket" (poem by John Keats)
K:202

Ontology (branch of metaphysics)   P:192

On Your Toes (musical by Rodgers and Hart)   M:554

Onyx (quartz)   Q:8

O'odham (Pima; Papago) (Indians of North America)   A:392, 397, 400, 402; I:169, 183

Oolong tea   T:35

Oort, Jan Hendrik (Dutch astronomer)   A:471

Oort Cloud (orbiting the sun)   A:471; C:449; S:340d
space probes   S:353

Oozes (muds along the ocean floor)   O:21

Opacimeters (optical instruments)   O:185

Opals (gems)   G:70, 74
amulets   G:72
October's birthstone   G:74
picture(s)   G:70, 74

Op (Optical) art   P:32; U:134–35

Opatoshu, Joseph (Yiddish author)   Y:361

OPEC *see* Organization of Petroleum Exporting Countries

Opechancanough (Algonkin Indian chief)   I:202; V:358

Opelousas (Louisiana)   L:328

"Open, Sesame!" (famous magic words from *Arabian Nights* story)   A:340

Open admission (of universities)   U:225

Open adoptions   A:28

Open and closed shop   L:8

Open circulatory system (of invertebrates)   C:306

Open city   P:75

Open-Door Policy   M:193–94

Open enrollment (in public schools)   E:87

Open events (in tennis)   T:95, 98–99

Open fractures (broken bones)   F:160

Open-hearth furnace (for turning iron into steel)   I:333, 338

Open-pit bench mines   I:330; M:322
picture(s)   M:318; N:63

Open primary elections   E:129

Open Road (magazine)   M:17

Open shop (for labor in industry)   L:8

Open universe (in astronomy)   U:218

Opera   O:139–65 *see also* Ballet; Musical theater; Operetta
baroque period   B:69–70; M:539
Berg, Alban   B:145
Canada   C:68
classical age   C:351
Donizetti, Gaetano   D:285
festivals   M:555
France, music of   F:445, 446, 447
German   G:185–86, 188
Gluck, Christoph Willibald   G:241
Glyndebourne (England) festival   U:50
Handel, George Frederick   H:21
Italy, music of   I:387, 411–12
Metropolitan Opera and New York City Opera in Lincoln
Center for the Performing Arts   L:248
musical theater   M:552
Puccini, Giacomo   P:525
Renaissance music   R:161
romanticism in music   R:304
stories of famous operas   O:149–65
Strauss, Richard   S:466
Verdi, Giuseppe   V:304
voices required for   V:378
Wagner, Richard   W:2
picture(s)
Gershwin's *Porgy and Bess*   G:190

Opéra bouffe (Opera buffa)
development during classical period   C:351
development of comic opera   O:141
English comic opera of Gilbert and Sullivan   G:208–9
musical theater   M:553

Opéra comique   F:446, 447; O:144

Operating expenses (in economics)   B:472

Operating Forces (of the United States Navy)   U:111–12

Operating rooms (in hospitals)
picture(s)   M:208b

Operating systems (computer programs)   C:483

Operational amplifier (integrated circuit)   T:277

Operation Anaconda (in the war on terrorism)   T:117

Operation Bootstrap (in Puerto Rican history)   P:529

Operation Breadbasket (African American self-help program)
J:8

Operation Desert Shield (in the Middle East)   S:58e

Operation Desert Storm *see* Persian Gulf War

Operation Enduring Freedom (war on terrorism)   T:116–17

Operation Iraqi Freedom *see* Iraq War

Operation PUSH (People United to Save Humanity)   J:8

Operations, surgical *see* Surgery

Operation Sea Lion (Hitler's plan to invade England)
W:298–99

Operation Torch (plan for invasion of French North Africa in
World War II)   W:307

Operetta   O:166–68 *see also* Musical theater
Gilbert and Sullivan   G:208–9
musical theater   M:552–53
Offenbach, Jacques   O:54
plots of some well-known operettas   O:167–68
Strauss, Johann, Jr.   S:466

Ophthalmologists (doctors who specialize in diseases of the eye)
E:432; O:181

Ophthalmology (branch of medicine)   O:181

Ophthalmoscopes (optical instruments)   D:207; M:204; O:182

Opiates (type of drug)   N:15

Opinion polls   O:169–70
market research   S:20
psychological surveys   P:501
statistics   S:439–40, 441
television audience ratings   T:69

Opitz, Martin (German poet)   G:177

Opium (narcotic drug)   D:335; N:15

Opium poppies   P:297

Opium War (conflict between China and Britain)   C:270;
G:393; H:214
picture(s)   A:455

Oporto (Porto) (Portugal)   P:393, 394

Opossums (marsupials)   M:115; O:171
fur   F:502
marsupials   M:113, 114
picture(s)   M:69, 115; O:171

Oppenheimer, J. Robert (American physicist)   N:232–33
profile, 377; W:318

Opportunity (space probe)   M:107; O:10; P:279; S:358, 359

Opposable thumbs   M:421

Opposite arrangement (of leaves)   L:113, 114; P:306

Opposition (in astronomy)   S:246

Opposition of Lines: Red and Yellow (painting by Mondrian)
picture(s)   M:392

Opryland USA (theme park, Nashville, Tennessee)   N:16; T:80, 82

Ops (Roman goddess) *see* Rhea

Optical character recognition (OCR) devices
census questionnaires   C:167
computer input   O:55
mail sorting   A:533; P:396
phototypesetting   T:371

Optical compositing (in motion picture special effects)   M:484

Optical computers   C:494

Optical disks (for information storage)   C:482; O:55
sound recording   S:267

Optical fibers *see* Fiber optics

Optical glass   O:185

Optical illusions   O:172–77
color   C:428–29
Escher, M. C.   E:320
halftone illustrations   P:471
Magnetic Hill (New Brunswick)   N:138e–138f
mirage   M:341–42
motion pictures   M:478

Optical instruments O:178–85
  astronomers' tools A:475–76a
  contact lenses C:535
  lenses L:141–51
  microscopes M:281–86
  surveyor's level and transit S:519–20
  telescopes T:57–60
Optical lasers L:46d
Optical microscopes M:155, 281–85
Optical pickups (sound recording and playback devices) *see*
  Photodetectors
Optical telescopes A:475; O:7–8; T:57–59
Optician (maker of eyeglasses) O:181
Optic nerve (of the eye) E:429
Optics (study of light) L:212–26; P:229
  fiber optics F:106–7
  Newton, Isaac N:207
  optical instruments O:178–85
Optometrists (specialists who examine the eyes and fit glasses)
  E:432; O:181
Opus (in music) M:537
Oracles (in ancient religions)
  Delphi G:363
  extrasensory perception E:427
  prophecies were often riddles J:126
Oral contraceptives D:334
Oral literature (literature that is spoken and sung) L:258
  children's literature, history of C:228
  folktales F:307–8
  Greek poetry G:354
  legends, origins of L:129
  mythology M:568–77
Oral pathologist (in dentistry) D:115
Oral surgeon (in dentistry) D:115
Oral tradition (of folklore) F:304–12
  Africa, literature of A:76a–76c
  folk music F:322
Oran (Algeria) A:187
Orang Asli (indigenous people of Malaysia) M:54
Orange O:186–89
  resistant to spoiling F:339
  second most popular fruit A:91
  picture(s) F:267
    blossom F:261
    mold growing on F:339
    packing F:485
Orange Bowl (football game, Miami, Florida) F:361
Orangeburg (South Carolina) S:311
Orange Free State (province of South Africa) B:302; S:272
Orange-Nassau, House of (royal family of the Netherlands)
  N:120d, 121; W:173
Orange River (Africa) A:48; R:244; S:270
Orangutans A:325, 326, 327, 442
  feet and hands F:83
  infants M:70
  picture(s) A:285, 326, 443; P:457
    endangered species E:211
Oratorio (in music) M:539–40
  choral music C:283
  developed in baroque period B:70
  Handel's compositions E:292; G:184–85; H:21
  Haydn, Franz Joseph G:186
  Renaissance music R:161
  singing style for V:378
Oratory O:190–91 *see also* Public speaking
  Beecher, Henry Ward B:114
  Bryan, William Jennings B:416
  Cicero C:303
  Greek G:357, 359
  Henry, Patrick H:113
  Webster, Daniel W:98b–99
Orature (oral tradition in literature) *see* Oral tradition
Orbán, Viktor (prime minister of Hungary) H:299
Orbital resonance (of planets) P:343–44
Orbital velocity (speed of satellites) S:53, 340d, 340e

Orbiters (orbiting portions of *Viking* space probes) S:362
Orbiters (space shuttles) *see* Space shuttles
Orbiting vehicles *see* Satellites, artificial
Orbits
  asteroids C:450; S:340d
  comets C:452
  Earth's orbit E:9; P:277–78
  Earth's orbit and ice age theories G:117; I:15–16
  Gauss, Carl Friedrich G:64
  gravitation and planetary orbits G:320–21; S:242–44
  Jupiter P:279
  Mars M:105; P:278
  Mercury M:229–30; P:276
  moon's orbit M:446, 448, 449
  Neptune N:111; P:281–82
  Neptune's moons N:113
  planetary orbits P:275
  planetary orbits and spacecraft tracking S:340L
  Pluto and Charon P:282, 341–42
  satellites, artificial S:53–54
  Saturn P:280; S:55
  space shuttle A:467
  Uranus P:280; U:231
  Venus P:276; V:303
Orb-weaving spiders S:403–4, 405
Orcas *see* Killer whales
Orchards
  apple A:331, 332–33
  best locations for fruitgrowing F:482
  tractors F:53
  picture(s)
    apple A:331
Orchestra O:192–97
  baroque period in music B:70, 71
  classical age in music C:350
  conducting O:198–201
  harp for special effects H:36
  kettledrums, use of D:339
  musical instruments M:546–51
  music festivals M:555–56
  percussion instruments P:147–49
  romanticism in music R:304
  tuning up to avoid interferences of beats of sound S:262
  United States, music of the U:209–10
  Wagner's operas, role in G:188
  wind instruments W:184–85
  picture(s) O:192–93
    wind instruments W:184
Orchestra (first floor of a theater) T:157
Orchestra (performance space in ancient Greek theater)
  D:298
Orchestra conducting O:195, 197, **198–201**
  orchestra as an institution with a professional conductor
  O:197
  seating diagram of an orchestra O:196
  Toscanini, Arturo T:245
Orchestral music *see* Orchestra; Symphony
Orchestration (composing or arranging music for an orchestra)
  O:195
Orchids F:287; N:167–68; V:297
  picture(s) S:282
Ordeal, trial by J:163
Order of Lenin (Soviet award)
  picture(s) D:71
Orders (divisions of biological classification) A:264; L:207;
  T:27, 28
Orders (styles in Greek architecture) A:368; G:346
Orders, religious *see* Monks and monasticism; Nuns
Ordinance of 1785 O:67; P:516, 517
Ordinance of 1787 *see* Northwest Ordinance
Ordinary (early bicycle) B:177
Ordination of clergy C:287
Ordnance *see* Guns
Ordnance Corps (of the United States Army) U:102–3
Ordnung (Amish guidelines for living) A:220

Ordóñez, Antonio (Spanish bullfighter) **B:**451
Ordóñez, José Batlle y see Batlle y Ordóñez, José
Ordovician period (in geology) **E:**25, 27, 425
  table(s) **F:**384
Oregano (spice) **H:**121
Oregon **O:**202–16
  boundary settlements **P:**376; **T:**107, 108
  Crater Lake **L:**29
  Oregon Trail **O:**275–79
  pioneer life **P:**252
  Portland **P:**390
  map(s) **O:**213
  picture(s)
    Cannon Beach **O:**204
    Cape Kiwanda **O:**203
    Columbia River Gorge **O:**205
    Crater Lake **L:**26; **O:**210
    Eugene **O:**211
    Fort Clatsop National Memorial **O:**210
    Hells Canyon **O:**204
    John Day Fossil Beds National Monument **O:**210
    Mount Hood **O:**203
    Multnomah Falls **O:**210; **W:**059
    Portland **B:**460; **O:**206, 211; **P:**390
    Salem **O:**212
    ship at Portland's port **O:**209
    tulip crop **O:**209
    Willamette University **O:**207
    windsurfers in Columbia River Gorge **O:**203
Oregon Caves National Monument (Oregon) **O:**210
Oregon City (Oregon) **O:**207, 216
Oregon grape (evergreen shrub)
  picture(s) **O:**203
Oregon State University (Corvallis, Oregon)
  picture(s)
    botany student **O:**207
Oregon Territory **O:**216; **P:**375; **W:**26
Oregon Trail **O:**275–79
  Kansas **K:**183
  Nebraska **N:**89, 92
  Scotts Bluff National Monument (Nebraska) **N:**90
  territorial expansion **T:**108
  Wyoming **W:**344
  map(s) **O:**273
  picture(s) **O:**214, 275; **W:**140
    Nebraska **N:**94
Orellana, Francisco de (Spanish explorer) **A:**198; **E:**409
Ores **O:**217 see also the names of ores
  copper contained in more than 160 known ores **C:**554
  metals and metallurgy **M:**233–34
  mines and mining **M:**318–24
  Nevada **N:**127
  phlogiston, theory of **C:**208
  rocks **R:**265
Øresund (sound between Sweden and Denmark) **C:**551
Øresund Bridge (Denmark–Sweden) **S:**527
  picture(s) **D:**111
Orfeo (opera by Claudio Monteverdi) **B:**70
Orfeo ed Euridice (opera by Christoph Willibald Gluck) **G:**241;
  O:159
Orford, 1st Earl of see Walpole, Sir Robert
Organ **O:**218–19
  electronic organ **E:**155; **K:**239; **O:**218
  German compositions **G:**184
  keyboard instruments **K:**236–37
  Sweelinck, Jan Pieters **D:**373
  types of musical instruments **M:**551
  picture(s)
    pipe organ **K:**237
Organelles (cell structures) **B:**273–74; **L:**200
  brain cells **B:**362
  protozoans **P:**495
Organetto (medieval musical instrument) **M:**297
  picture(s) **M:**296
Organic chemistry see Chemistry, organic

Organic compounds see Chemistry, organic
Organic fertilizers **F:**96–97
Organic foods see Health foods
Organic gardening and farming
  fruitgrowing **F:**482
  health foods **H:**79
  vegetables **V:**288
Organic substances see Chemistry, organic
Organisms (living things) **L:**195
  evolution of **E:**372–73
  food chains **L:**205
Organization for Economic Cooperation and Development (OECD)
  O:220
Organization of African Unity (OAU) **A:**81; **O:**221
  Addis Ababa **E:**333
  dissolving of **A:**69
  Haile Selassie helped found **H:**4
Organization of Afro-American Unity (OAAU) **A:**79o; **M:**59
Organization of American States (OAS) **O:**221
  human rights **H:**287
  Latin America **L:**59
  Pan American Day **H:**167
Organization of Arab Petroleum Exporting Countries (OAPEC)
  O:222
Organization of Eastern Caribbean States (OECS) **S:**18
Organization of Petroleum Exporting Countries (OPEC) **I:**271;
  O:222; **P:**174
Organizations, national and international see also Clubs; the
  names of organizations
  Geneva has headquarters of many international
    organizations **G:**92
  parliamentary procedure **P:**81–82
Organized crime (large-scale activities by groups of criminals)
  C:585; **O:**223–25; **P:**485
Organized Trades and Labor Unions, Federation of (FOOTALU)
  L:14
Organ meats **M:**196
Organ music **G:**184
Organ of Corti (part of the inner ear) **E:**4, 6
Organ-pipe cactus **C:**5
Organ-pipe wasps (insects) **I:**247
  picture(s)
    nest **I:**246
Organs (functional parts of animals and plants)
  animal kingdom **K:**254–55
  body, human **B:**275
  controlled by autonomic nervous system **N:**117
  made up of various body tissues **L:**201
  What is the largest organ of your body? **B:**276
Organ transplants **M:**208d, 208g; **O:**226–27 see also Heart
  transplant
  animal to human **M:**209
  Barnard, Christiaan **B:**61
  cryogenic gases preserve donated organs **R:**134
  disease, treatment of **D:**209
  kidneys **K:**244
  liver **L:**270
  medicine, history of **M:**208h
  rejection, causes of **I:**97
  science, modern **S:**74
Organum (music) **F:**444; **M:**296, 538
Orient see Asia; East Asia
Oriental art and architecture see Asian art and architecture
Oriental dancing **D:**32; **T:**162
Oriental Exclusion Acts (in United States history) **O:**228
Orientalizing period (in Greek art) **G:**345
Oriental music see Asian music
Oriental rugs **R:**353, 355
  picture(s) **R:**354
Orientation (by the blind) **B:**257
Origami (art of paper folding) **O:**228–30
Original Dixieland Jazz Band **J:**59
Original sin (doctrine of the Roman Catholic Church) **R:**283
Origin of Species (book by Charles Darwin) **A:**359; **D:**41;
  E:375

Orimulsion (bitumen-based fuel oil)   P:175
Orinoco River (South America)   R:244; S:277, 280; V:296
Orioles (songbirds)
    picture(s)   M:121
Orion (constellation)   C:530–31; H:310; N:96; S:430
    picture(s)   P:232; S:428
Orion (in Greek mythology)   C:530–31; D:243
Orion's Belt   C:530
Orissa (state, India)   I:126
Orizaba, Mount (Pico de Orizaba) (Mexico)   M:243; N:285
Orkney Islands (northeast of Scotland)   I:366–67
Orlando (Florida)   F:268
Orlando, Vittorio Emanuele (Italian statesman)   W:290
    picture(s)   W:290
Orlando Furioso (poem by Ariosto)   I:407
Orléans, Maid of see Joan of Arc
Ormandy, Eugene (American orchestra conductor)   O:201
    profile
Ormerod, Jan (Australian author and illustrator)   C:237
    picture(s)
        illustration from Sunshine   C:241
Ormolu (gilded furniture mountings)   D:77
Ornithischia (group of dinosaurs)   D:174–76
Ornithology see Birds
Ornithopoda (group of dinosaurs)   D:174–75
Ornithopters (flapping-wing aircraft)   A:559
Ornithosis see Parrot fever
Oromos (a people of Ethiopia)   E:330
    picture(s)   E:330
Orontes River (Middle East)   L:120; S:550
OR operation (in Boolean logic)   C:487
Oroville Dam (California)   C:23
Orozco, José (Mexican painter)   M:247; O:231
    picture(s)   O:231
Orpen, William (English portrait painter)
    picture(s)
        portrait of William L. M. King   K:252
Orphanages   F:390
Orphan Girl at the Cemetery (painting by Delacroix)
    picture(s)   P:27
Orpheus (in Greek mythology)   G:367
Orr, Bobby (Canadian hockey player)   I:31 profile
Orrery (small model planetarium)   P:269
    picture(s)   P:269
Orsted, Hans Christian see Oersted, Hans Christian
Ortega, Aniceto (Mexican composer)   L:73
Ortega, Daniel (Nicaraguan political leader)   N:248; O:231
    picture(s)   N:247
Ortega y Gasset, José (Spanish philosopher and writer)   S:391
Ortelius, Abraham (Flemish publisher)   M:98
Orthodontics (field of dentistry)   D:115; O:232–33
Orthodox Churches see Eastern Orthodox Churches
Orthodox (Traditionalist) Judaism   J:143, 144–45, 146, 146b,
    147, 148–49
    Jerusalem   J:80–81
Orthography see Spelling
Orthopedist (doctor)
    picture(s)   D:235
Orthorhombic crystal system (in chemistry)
    picture(s)   C:603
Ortiz, Juan (Spanish adventurer)   D:138
Ortiz Rubio, Pascual (Mexican president)   M:251
Orvieto Cathedral (Italy)
    picture(s)   G:266
Orwell, George (English writer)   E:289, 322; O:234; S:82
Osage (Indians of North America)   I:179; K:186; M:378
Osage Plains (Kansas–Missouri)   K:178; M:368
Osaka (Japan)   O:235–36
    aquarium   A:337
    Expo '70   F:17
    World War II   W:317
    picture(s)   O:235, 236
Osama bin Laden (international terrorist) see Bin Laden, Osama
Osan (South Korea)   K:305
Osborne, John (English playwright)   D:305; E:290; O:237

Osceola (Native American warrior)   I:178 profile; O:237
    grave at Fort Moultrie   S:304
    Seminoles in Florida   F:275 profile
    picture(s)   F:275; I:178
Oscillators (in electronics)   E:155, 156; K:239
Oscilloscopes (medical instruments)   H:248; S:266
    picture(s)   P:229
Oseberg ship (Viking ship)   V:339
    picture(s)   V:340
Osen of Kasamori (woodcut by Suzuki Harunobu)   G:305
Osgood, Samuel (American soldier and political figure)   P:397
OSHA see Occupational Safety and Health Administration
Oshawa (Ontario)   O:129
Oshkosh (Wisconsin)   W:205
Oshkosh the Brave (Menominee Indian chief)   W:206 profile
Osiris (Egyptian god of the dead)   E:107, 108
    picture(s)   R:146
Osler, Sir William (Canadian doctor and teacher)   O:238
Oslo (capital of Norway)   I:2; N:345, 347; O:238–39; W:296
    picture(s)   N:347, 349; O:239
Osman I (Ottoman sultan)   O:259
Osmena, Sergio (Philippine statesman)   P:188
Osmium (element)   E:175; M:233
Osmosis (process in which liquids and gases pass through a
    membrane)   O:239–41; P:314–15
Ospedale degli Innocenti (Florence, Italy)   A:371
Osprey (bird)   B:220
    picture(s)   N:350; Z:388
Ossetia (region in Russia and Republic of Georgia)   G:148
Ostade, Adriaen van (Dutch painter)   D:365
Ostend Manifesto (document advocating U.S. acquisition of
    Cuba)   B:419; P:247
Osteoarthritis (type of arthritis)   D:189; S:184b
Osteoblasts (bone cells)   S:184a
Osteopathy (type of medical practice)   D:234
Osteoporosis (loss of minerals from the bones)   S:184a; V:371
Østlandet (region of Norway)   N:345
Ostracoderms (extinct fish)   F:184
Ostrava (Czech Republic)   C:621
Ostriches (birds)   O:242, 243
    eggs   B:230
    largest living bird   A:271
    Uruguay   U:239
    picture(s)   B:220, 235
        feet   B:220
        height compared with other ratites   O:244
Ostrogoths see Goths
Ostrovsky, Aleksandr (Russian playwright)   R:382
O'Sullivan, Maurice (Irish author)   I:328
Oswald, Lee Harvey (American accused assassin of John F.
    Kennedy)   K:210; O:246; W:12
    picture(s)   O:246
Otavalo (Ecuador)
    picture(s)
        market   S:288
Otavalo Indians
    picture(s)   E:58
OTC drugs see Over-the-counter drugs
OTEC see Ocean Thermal Energy Conversion
Otello (opera by Giuseppe Verdi)   O:160
Otero, Blas de (Spanish poet)   S:392
Otero Silva, Miguel (Venezuelan author)   V:298
Othello (tragedy by Shakespeare)   S:138
Oti River (Togo)   T:216
Otis, Elisha Graves (American inventor and manufacturer)
    E:185
Otis, James (American patriot and Revolutionary War leader)
    O:246; T:25
Otitis media (middle ear inflammation)   E:6
Oto (Indians of North America)   I:179
Otolaryngologist (doctor)
    picture(s)   D:235
Otoliths (part of the inner ear)   E:5
Otosclerosis (form of deafness)   E:6
Otoscope (instrument for examining the ear)   D:207; M:204

Ott, Mel (American baseball player) B:90 profile
  picture(s) B:90
Ottawa (capital of Canada) C:67; O:133–34, 247–50
  National Gallery of Canada N:39–40
  seat of the federal government C:50
  map(s) O:248
  picture(s)
    Library of Parliament L:179
    National Gallery of Canada O:250
    Parliament buildings and Rideau Canal O:247
    Parliament Hill C:50; O:134
    skating on Rideau Canal O:249
    Supreme Court building S:505
Ottawa (Indians of North America) I:179; M:269; P:382
Ottawa, University of (Canada) O:250
Ottawa Mint see Royal Canadian Mint
Ottawa River (Canada) O:124–25, 247, 249; Q:10; R:244
Otters M:72; O:251–52
  picture(s) O:251, 252
Otter trawlers (fishing boats) F:218
Otto, Nikolaus A. (German inventor) A:540; I:265, 281
Otto I (king of Greece) G:337; O:258
Otto I (Otto the Great) (Holy Roman emperor) H:176–77;
    O:258
  German states in the Middle Ages G:159; M:291
  Louis IV (king of France) L:309
  picture(s) O:258
    crown H:177
Otto II (Holy Roman emperor) H:177; O:258
Otto III (Holy Roman emperor) O:258
  picture(s)
    gospel book I:77
Otto IV (Holy Roman emperor) O:258
Ottoman Empire O:259–61; T:348–49
  conquest of Egypt E:104
  Crimean War C:587
  Greece G:337
  Hungary, history of H:298–99
  Islam I:351–52
  Istanbul I:377, 378
  Lepanto, Battle of (1571) S:157
  Macedonia M:4
  Middle East, early history of M:304
  Moldova, history of M:403
  Romania R:299
  sultans, list of O:261
  World War I W:283–85
  map(s) O:260
Otway, Thomas (English dramatist) E:277
Ouachita Mountains (Oklahoma–Arkansas) A:408; O:84, 85
Ouachita National Forest (Oklahoma) O:90
Ouagadougou (capital of Burkina Faso) B:453, 454
Oudenaarde, Battle of (1708) S:377
Oudney, Walter (British explorer of Sahara Desert) S:7
Oueddei, Goukouni (president of Chad) see Goukouni Oueddei
Ouémé River (Benin) B:144
Oughtred, William (English mathematician) M:165
Ouimet, Francis (American golfer) G:257
Ounce (measure of weight) W:114, 115
Ounces (cats) see Snow leopards
Ouray (Native American chief) C:443 profile
  picture(s) C:443
Our Cabaña (Mexico, center for World Association Girl Guides
    and Girl Scouts) G:219
Our Chalet (Switzerland, center for World Association Girl
    Guides and Girl Scouts) G:219
Our Father see Lord's Prayer
Ouricury wax W:78
Our Lady see Mary, Virgin
Our Lady of Guadalupe, Day of (religious holiday) R:155
Our Lady of Peace, Basilica of (Yamoussoukro, Ivory Coast)
    I:417
Our Lady of the Angels (shrine in Cartago, Costa Rica)
    C:564–65
Our Old Home (book by Hawthorne) H:65

Ouro Preto (Brazil) L:62
Our Young Folks (magazine) M:17
Ousmane, Mahamane (president of Niger) N:252
Outback (sparsely populated rural area of Australia) A:500,
    510
  picture(s) A:497
Outcault, Richard (American cartoonist) C:128
Outdoor advertising A:31–32
Outdoor cooking O:262
  camp cooking C:45–46, 47
  hiking and backpacking H:135
Outer Banks (North Carolina) N:306
Outerbridge, Mary (American tennis player) T:94
Outer City (Beijing, China) B:127b, 127c
Outer space see Space, outer
Outfielder (in baseball) B:80
Outlaws (criminals) O:263–64
  Billy the Kid N:192
  Cassidy, Butch U:254
  James, Jesse J:21
  Robin Hood R:251
Outlaws (performers of country rock music) C:573
Outlaw State (nickname for Missouri) M:380
Outlet glaciers G:223
Outlines O:265–67
  preparation of a speech P:519
  researching reports R:183
Outlying areas of the United States U:84–85, 88
Outpatient departments (of hospitals) H:248, 253; N:421
Outports (coastal villages of Newfoundland and Labrador)
    N:141, 146
  picture(s) N:142
Output devices see Input and output devices
Outrigger canoes C:101
Outside Over There (book by Maurice Sendak) S:116
Oúzo (Greek anise-flavored liquor) G:332
Oval projections (of maps) M:97
Oval window (of the middle ear) E:4
  picture(s) E:5
Ovambo (a people of southern Africa) N:8
Ovaries (of flowers) F:282, 286; P:307
Ovaries (of women) B:287; R:178
  menstruation M:219
  sex hormones G:228
Ovenbird U:239
Overbeck, Johann Friedrich (German painter) R:303
Overburden (material over rock) M:323
"Overcoat, The" (story by Nikolai Gogol) S:162
Overglaze (on pottery) P:408
Overgrazing (by animals)
  picture(s)
    effects on land G:319
Overhand knots
  macramé M:7b
  picture(s) K:286
    macramé M:7a
Øverland, Arnulf (Norwegian poet) S:58i
Overland trails O:268–82
  Mullan Trail (Montana) M:435
  Natchez Trace M:358
  Nebraska N:89, 92
  pioneer life P:252–53, 260
  westward movement W:144
  map(s) O:273
Overnutrition (getting too many nutrients) D:185
Overpopulation E:300–301; P:387–88
Overshot wheel (kind of waterwheel) W:069
Over-the-counter drugs D:333
"Over There" (song by George M. Cohan) N:23
Overtones (Harmonics) (of sound) S:263–64
Overture (musical work) M:542; R:304
Overweight, body D:194; F:338; N:428, 429; O:6
  diabetes D:145
Ovid (Roman poet) G:361; L:76; O:283; P:354
Ovimbundu (a people of Africa) A:259

PHOTO CREDITS

The following list credits the sources of photos used in THE NEW BOOK OF KNOWLEDGE. Credits are listed, by page, photo by photo—left to right, top to bottom. Wherever appropriate, the name of the photographer has been listed with the source, the two being separated by a dash. When two or more photos by different photographers appear on one page, their credits are separated by semicolons.

O

Cover © Vladimir Chaloupka, *Las Cruces Sun-News*/AP/Wide World Photos
2 Hulton/Archive by Getty Images
3 © Georg Gerster—Rapho Guillumette
4 © Bob Gibbons—Holt Studios International/Photo Researchers; © Norm Thomas—Photo Researchers.
5 © Martin Fenouillet—Fotogram
6 © Roger Ressmeyer—Starlight (all photos on page).
7 © Roger Ressmeyer—Starlight; © Peter French—California Association for Research in Astronomy.
8 © C. Allan Morgan—Peter Arnold, Inc.; © Keith Gunnar—Bruce Coleman Inc.
9 © Roger Ressmeyer—Starlight; JPL.
10 © Bruce Frisch—Photo Researchers
11 Space Science Institute/JPL/NASA; R. Sankrit and W. Blair (Johns Hopkins University)/ESA/NASA; CXC and S. Holt (F. W. Olin College of Engineering)/NASA; R. Sankrit and W. Blair (Johns Hopkins University)/NASA.
12 © Jack Fields—Photo Researchers
13 © A. Ramey—PhotoEdit
14 © A. Ramey—PhotoEdit; © Will Hart—PhotoEdit; © Barros & Barros—The Image Bank/Getty Images.
15 The American Occupational Therapy Association
16 © Richard Farrell—Photo Researchers
19 © Alec Duncan—Taurus Photos
20 © Stella Snead—Bruce Coleman Inc.
24 © Tom McHugh—Steinhart Aquarium—Photo Researchers; © M. I. Walker—Photo Researchers; Taurus Photos.
25 © Dave Woodward—Taurus Photos; © L. L. T. Rhodes—Taurus Photos; © Dave Woodward—Photo Researchers.
26 © Jack Donnelly—Woods Hole Oceanographic Institute
27 © Ronny Jacques—Photo Researchers; Courtesy of Texaco.
28 © Kaz Mori—Taurus Photos
29 © Bastide—Liaison Agency
30– Courtesy of Cunard Line
31
32 Princess Cruises
33 © Merie W. Wallace/AP/Wide World Photos/Paramount Pictures/20th Century Fox
34 © Institute for Exploration/AP/Wide World Photos
35 © Dave Fleetham—Tom Stack & Associates
36 Courtesy, NOAA Laboratory for Satellite Altimetry
37 Courtesy, NOAA (all photos on page).
38 © Woods Hole Oceanographic Institution
39 Courtesy, Ocean Drilling Program/Texas A & M University (all photos on page).
40 © Dave Tennenbaum—AP/Wide World Photos
41 The Granger Collection
43 Photodisc Blue/Getty Images
50 © Hal Beral—Photo Network/PictureQuest; © Jeff Rotman—Photo Researchers.
51 © Gerd Ludwig—Woodfin Camp & Associates; © Douglas Faulkner—Photo Researchers.
53 The Granger Collection
55 © Didier Ermakoff—The Image Works
56 © The Image Bank; © Jon Feingersh—The Stock Market.
57 The Granger Collection
58 © Frank Siteman—PhotoEdit
59 Bob Daemmrich—The Image Works
60 Charles Babbage Institute, University of Minnesota
63 © Richard A. Cooke III—Stone; © Jim Baron—The Image Finders; © Mark Segal—Panoramic Images.
64 © Jim Steinberg—Photo Researchers; © SuperStock.
65 © J. Quinn Photography

66 © J. Quinn Photography (all photos on page).
67 © Jim Schwabel—Photo Network; © David M. Dennis—Tom Stack & Associates.
68 © Jim Baron—The Image Finders
69 © Jim Baron—The Image Finders; © Jean Higgins—New England Stock Photo; © Jim Baron—The Image Finders.
70 © Michael Philip Manheim—The Image Finders; © J. Quinn Photography; © Jim Baron—The Image Finders.
71 © Jim Baron—The Image Finders; © Andre Jenny—Unicorn Stock Photos.
72 © SuperStock
74 © William Holmes—The Image Finders
75 The Granger Collection
76 The Granger Collection; Courtesy of Ohio Historical Society; AP/Wide World Photos.
77 UPI/Corbis-Bettmann
79 The Metropolitan Museum of Art, Alfred Stieglitz Collection, 1949
81 © The Georgia O'Keeffe Foundation/Artists Rights Society (ARS), New York/SuperStock
83 © Tom Edwards—Unicorn Stock Photos; © Jim Argo; © B. W. Hoffmann—Unicorn Stock Photos.
84 © François Gohier—Photo Researchers; © Jim Argo.
86 © Jay Foreman—Unicorn Stock Photos (all photos on page).
87 © Jim Argo; © Matt Bradley—Tom Stack & Associates.
88 © SuperStock
89 © Matt Bradley—Tom Stack & Associates; © Jim Argo.
90 © Jim Argo; © Fred Marvel—Oklahoma Tourism Photo; © Jim Argo.
91 © Jim Argo
92 © Tom Dietrich—Stone
93 © Paul E. Lefebvre
94 The Granger Collection
95 © James Schnepf—Liaison Agency; Brown Brothers.
96 Brown Brothers
97 © Jim Argo
98 Masterfile
99 © Bill Aron—PhotoEdit; Photodisc Blue/Getty Images; © David Young-Wolff—PhotoEdit.
100 © David Young-Wolff—PhotoEdit
101 © Ernest A. Weber—Photo Researchers
102 © Steve Holland—AP/Wide World Photos
104 © A. K. G., Berlin/SuperStock; Corbis.
105 © IOC/Olympic Museum Collection
106 © Bevilacqua/Corbis-Sygma; © Helen Gaillet—Liaison Agency; © IOC/Olympic Museum Collections.
107 © Pascal Rondeau—Allsport; © Shaun Botterill—Allsport.
108 © Rusty Kennedy—AP/Wide World Photos
109 © Laura Rauch—AP/Wide World Photos; © Mark Baker—Reuters/Archive Photos; © Shaun Botterill—Allsport; Sportschrome, Inc.; © Doug Pensinger—Allsport; © Susan Walsh—AP/Wide World Photos; Nancie Battaglia—*Sports Illustrated*/© Time Inc.
110 © Stephen Dunn—Allsport; Mexsport/Presslink.
111 Hulton Deutsch Library/Allsport; AP/Wide World Photos.
112 Allsport; © Hulton Getty—Liaison Agency; Corbis-Bettmann; © Kurt Strumpf—AP/Wide World Photos.
113 © Eric Schweikartt—*Sports Illustrated*/© Time Inc.; © Gerard Rancinan—Corbis-Sygma; © Lehtikuva Oy—Woodfin Camp & Associates; © Mike Powell—Allsport.
114 © Hulton Deutsch—Allsport; © IOC/Olympic Museum Collections.
115 © Walter Iooss—*Sports Illustrated*/© Time Inc.
116 © IOC/Olympic Museum Collections
117 © Paul Chiasson—AP/Wide World Photos; © Elise Amendola—AP/Wide World Photos.
118 © Susan Walsh—AP/Wide World Photos; © Doug Mills—AP/Wide World Photos.
119 © Yves Herman—Reuters/Corbis; © Rusty Kennedy—AP/Wide World Photos.

120 © Jeff Haynes—AFP/Getty Images; © Kevork Djansezian—AP/Wide World Photos.
122 Culver Pictures
125 © Malak
126 © Gary Gralle—The Image Bank; © Miller Comstock Inc.
127 © Malak; © Cameramann International Ltd.; © Malak.
128 © George Hunter—Miller Comstock Inc.; © Jim Merrithew—Miller Comstock Inc.
129 © George Hunter—Miller Comstock Inc.; © George Hunter—Miller Comstock Inc.; © E. Otto—Miller Comstock Inc.
130 © Kummels—Leo de Wys
131 © Malak; © E. Otto—Miller Comstock Inc.
132 © Miller Comstock Inc.; © Michael Yamashita—Woodfin Camp & Associates; © Malak.
133 © Guido Alberto Rossi—The Image Bank
134 © Porterfield-Chickering—Photo Researchers
139 © Ron Scherl—The Bettmann Archive
140 © Ron Scherl—The Bettmann Archive
141 © Ron Scherl—The Bettmann Archive (all photos on page).
142 © Serrailler—Rapho Guillumette
145 *Opera News*
146 *Opera News*
147 *Opera News*; Metropolitan Opera Archives; Metropolitan Opera Press Association, Inc., Metropolitan Opera Archives.
149 Bill Doll and Company
150 From *Opera Themes and Plots* by Rudolph Fellner, © 1958 Simon and Schuster, Inc.
151 Louis Melancon—Metropolitan Opera Production; National Broadcasting Co.
152 From *Opera Themes and Plots* by Rudolph Fellner, © 1958 Simon and Schuster, Inc.; Martha Swope—Metropolitan Opera National Company.
155 From *Opera Themes and Plots* by Rudolph Fellner, © 1958 Simon and Schuster, Inc.
157 Louis Melancon—Metropolitan Opera Production; Sedge LeBlang—Metropolitan Opera Production; Louis Melancon—Metropolitan Opera Production.
158 Louis Melancon—Metropolitan Opera Production; From *Opera Themes and Plots* by Rudolph Fellner, © 1958 Simon and Schuster, Inc.
166 © Sedge LeBlang
171 © Leonard Lee Rue III—Photo Researchers
172 © Diapofilm
174 © G. R. Higbee—Photo Researchers
175 © D. Mohardt—Photo Researchers
177 Copyright: M. C. Escher Heirs c/o Cordon Art-Baarn-Holland
178 The Granger Collection
179 © Rhoda Sidney—Leo de Wys; © Lester Sloan—Woodfin Camp & Associates.
180 David Dunlap Observatory, University of Toronto
182 Courtesy of Bausch & Lomb
183 © J. M. Mejuto—FPG International; © Bruno J. Zehnder—Peter Arnold, Inc.
185 Courtesy of Bausch & Lomb
186 © SuperStock; © Ray Doney.
192– © Koichi Kamoshida—Getty Images
193
194 © Audrey Dempsey; © Brad C. Bower—AP/Wide World Photos.
195 © Tony Freeman—PhotoEdit
197 © Lebrecht Music Collection
198 © Suzie Maeder—Lebrecht Music (all photos on page).
200 © Milton Feinberg—Stock, Boston/PictureQuest; AP/Wide World Photos.
201 Hulton/Archive by Getty Images (all photos on page).
203 © Eric Sanford—Tom Stack & Associates; © Kevin Sink—Midwestock; © William McKinney—Photo Researchers.
204 © Milton Rand—Tom Stack & Associates; © Pete Saloutos—The Stock Market.
205 © Jim Steinberg—Photo Researchers